D1477243

MEDIEVAL IRELAND

BARRYSCOURT LECTURES

Medieval Ireland
The Barryscourt Lectures I-X

MEDIEVAL IRELAND
The Barryscourt Lectures I-X

Published by the Barryscourt Trust
in association with Cork County Council
and Gandon Editions, Kinsale.

© The Barryscourt Trust and the
authors, 2004. All rights reserved.

ISBN 0946846 308

Series Editors   John Ludlow
                  Noel Jameson

THE BARRYSCOURT TRUST
Barryscourt Castle,
Carrigtwohill, Co Cork, Ireland
tel: +353 (0)21-4883864

Produced for the Barryscourt Trust
by Gandon Editions

Design   John O'Regan
                (© Gandon, 2004)
Production   Nicola Dearey
                Sheila Holland
                Gunther Berkus
Printing   Betaprint, Dublin
Distribution   Gandon Distribution

Gandon Editions is grant-aided by The
Arts Council / An Chomhairle Ealaíon

GANDON EDITIONS
Oysterhaven, Kinsale, Co Cork, Ireland
tel: +353 (0)21-4770830 / fax: 4770755
e-mail: gandon@eircom.net
web-site: gandon-editions.com

The Barryscourt Lectures and publication of the compilation volume were sponsored by:

CORK COUNTY COUNCIL
DUCHAS – THE HERITAGE SERVICE
THE IRELAND FUNDS

BARRY'S TEA LTD
THE DISCOVERY PROGRAMME
DEPT OF ARCHAEOLOGY, NUI GALWAY

Dúchas The Heritage Service

THE IRELAND FUNDS
PEACE CULTURE CHARITY

BARRY'S TEA

Contents

Lecture IV – *Irish Gardens and Gardening before Cromwell* by Terence Reeves-Smyth
illustration: Capt Doddington's house and garden at Dungiven, county Derry,
from Raven's Map, 1622 (courtesy Lambeth Palace Library, London)

Foreword

Barryscourt Castle is a fine 16th-century tower-house at Carrigtwohill, Co Cork. The Barryscourt Trust was established in 1987 with the aim of conserving, enhancing and developing the heritage potential of the castle.

In 1996, as the restoration of Barryscourt Castle neared completion and its presentation as a reinstated 16th-century domestic interior was initiated, it seemed appropriate that additional attention be paid to the historical and social background of the period. The Barryscourt Trust instituted a bi-annual series of lectures on Medieval Ireland at the castle. The lectures deal with aspects of medieval history, archaeology, art and architecture, and are delivered by scholars specialising in the period.

We are delighted to publish this first series of ten lectures in volume form, together with an introduction to Barryscourt Castle. A second series of ten lectures has already commenced, and a companion volume will be published in due course.

We would like to express our thanks to the first ten contributors in the lecture series: Tadhg O'Keeffe, AF O'Brien, Colin Rynne, Terence Reeves-Smyth, Dave Pollock, Victor Chinnery, Kieran O'Conor, David Sweetman, Brian Graham and Karena Morton.

We also wish to thank for moral and financial assistance: Cork County Council, Dúchas – The Heritage Service, The Discovery Programme, Peter Barry, The Ireland Funds, Dept of Archaeology, NUI Galway, and our publisher John O'Regan of Gandon Editions.

JOHN LUDLOW
Barryscourt Trust and Cork County Council

NOEL JAMESON
Barryscourt Castle

1 – 'Barryscourt Castle' by James Stark Flemming

opposite 2 – Conjectural reconstruction of Barryscourt in the 16th century (Dave Pollock)

An introduction to Barryscourt Castle

The seat of the Barry family, Barryscourt Castle, with its largely intact bawn wall and corner towers, is a fine example of an Irish tower-house. The Barrys, who became one of the principal Norman families in Ireland, came to this country in 1180 when Philip de Barri arrived from Manorbier in south Wales. Philip was the elder brother of Gerald of Wales (Giraldus Cambrensis), who was the chronicler of Norman Wales, and wrote of the Norman conquests in Ireland in his book *Expugnatio Hibernica*. The de Barris had been granted lands in Cork as Anglo-Norman control pushed west in the 12th century. By 1206, a charter of King John confirms the existence of a manor at Carrigtwohill, the nearby village, which was grant- ed a market in 1234. Barryscourt is strategically located between the important medieval ports of Cork and Youghal, and close to the early medieval route to the monastic settlement of Cloyne.

As a family, the Barrys were very prolific, and a large number of branches developed, the most powerful headed by the Barrymore, or 'Great Barry', in Barryscourt, and by the Barryroe, or 'Red Barry', in Timoleague. During the 14th and 15th centuries the Barrys intermarried with many of the principal native Irish families, acquiring descriptive Irish names. At the same time, however, the Barrys were either killing or being

below 3 – Barryscourt Castle, painted by A Whitelegge, 1895 (detail)
(courtesy A FitzGibbon)

4 – Barryscourt Castle from the west

killed by each other or by neighbours, both Gaelic and Norman. By the mid-16th century, therefore, the main Barryscourt line descended to an only daughter. In 1556 the lands passed to a distant cousin, James fitzRichard, head of the Barryroe branch of the family, producing an extensive and powerful combined lordship. James supported the Desmond rebellion, which resulted in his imprisonment in Dublin Castle. He died behind bars in 1581, and his son David destroyed the family castles to prevent them falling into English hands. The main seat, Barryscourt Castle, was 'defaced and despoiled', as Sir Walter Raleigh approached with an army. The following year Queen Elizabeth pardoned David Barry, and the year after he retook possession of his damaged castle. He married Ellen Roche, and remained loyal to the Crown in 1601 when the surrounding land was devastated by Hugh O'Neill's rebel army on his way to his abortive attempt to relieve the Spanish at Kinsale. The last head of the Barry family to occupy Barryscourt, David died in 1617 and was succeeded by his grandson, who moved to Castlelyons. During the Confederate war,

Barryscourt was attacked and taken in 1645. Cannon damage is still visible on the tower-house walls.

In the early 18th century, the Coppinger family took possession of Barryscourt, and built a new house close to the large tower. Little has survived of this house, but the older tower-house was remarkably intact when the Barryscourt Trust was established in 1987 with the aim of conserving, enhancing and developing the heritage potential of the castle. In the last decade of the 20th century, the shell of the massive tower-house was repaired and re-roofed by Dúchas, The Heritage Service. As work progressed, the tower-house, and the yard at its foot, have been investigated to provide a fuller picture of the original design.

The Early Castle

Even into the 19th century, the lands to the south and west of the castle were covered by high tides, and it is possible that the original approach to the castle was by boat. The present stream beside the castle used to meander through the ground under the bawn wall. Timbers from the the old stream suggest a watermill stood here in the first half of the 7th century, long before the arrival of the Barrys.

Fragments of a mortared stone building under the bawn may be the remains of a later mill, or possibly an early castle, apparently built by the Barrys around 1200AD. The building was still standing when the tower-house was constructed, but was taken down when the stream was diverted and the bawn wall was built.

The Tower-House

The large tower-house was built as one piece in either the 15th or 16th century. The stream was dammed and diverted into a series of ponds – which may have served as fish pens – around the building and its yard. The yard was later extended across the old stream and enclosed behind a high wall, probably in the 16th century [2]. Entry to the tower-house was at ground level. The present stone door frame is an early replacement, as the original appears to have been badly damaged in 1581. The door would either have shut tightly against the inside of the frame, wedged into position with a strong timber bar and protected by an iron grille, or shut against the outside of the frame with chains which passed through holes in the stonework. A second door, which is now blocked, can be seen almost over the main entrance. This was reached by ladder from the outside, and was the only access to a small first-floor room over a prison.

From a small lobby inside the main entrance, a door to the left opened onto a long flight of stairs climbing to the main chamber in the building – the Hall. In the roof of the lobby, a small trapdoor – a murder hole – allowed a guard to monitor waiting visitors until the door to the stairs or the door directly ahead into the large ground-floor room was unbolted and opened. This room was probably a store, and a very important defensive position. The narrow openings in the walls on three sides provided ground-level firing positions for archers and gunners.

A smaller ground-floor room was originally a dungeon or prison pit, entered via a trapdoor from above, rather than from ground level. The present entry was cut through when the building was repaired in the late 16th century. At that time the prison pit was converted to a water cistern, fed with rainwater from the roof, collected at the foot of the wall beside the main door, and channelled through the wall.

Today a wooden staircase leads to the large first-floor room [6]. The original entrance was from a door, still in use, halfway up the long stairs. This room has a fireplace and a flue, which opens through the tower-house wall rather than rising to a chimney. The room now contains a fitting collection of reproduction furniture and hardware of the 16th century. A door in one corner leads to a large garderobe, while a door in another corner leads to a firing position overlooking the bawn. A passage at the northern end leads past a small garderobe to a room with a fireplace, and down to a small room over the lobby. When the prison was converted into a cistern, a passage was cut from the small room to the original chamber over the prison. All the rooms at this level were vaulted. However, the main vault

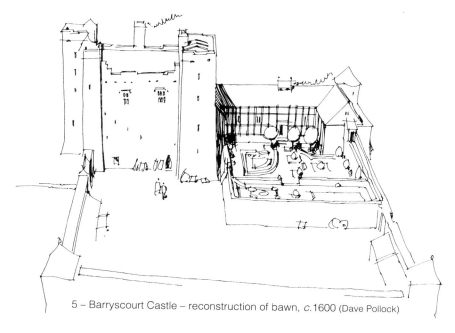

5 – Barryscourt Castle – reconstruction of bawn, c.1600 (Dave Pollock)

6 –The vaulted hall on the first floor

7 – The chapel off the Great Chamber on the second floor

8 –The oak-roofed Great Chamber on the second floor

9 – Second-floor fireplace mantle, with inscription dated 1588

was either taken down or fell down, and replaced. The pointed profile of the original can be seen at each end of the large first-floor room. The replacement vault has a sounder, rounder profile.

Above the vault was the main hall [8]. This room was refurbished more than any other in the years after 1581. Stone corbels were set into the walls to support a gallery or a garret storey, tucked into the roof space. A fine fireplace was inserted, blocking an earlier window, and the windows were replaced and the window seats beside them were cut away. The new features were inscribed and dated 1588 on the mantle over the fireplace, and 1586 on the window frame. The fireplace is inscribed 'DB ET ER ME FIERI FECERUT-ADO 1588' – 'D(avid) B(arry) and E(llen) R(oche) had me made AD 1588' [9].

From the main hall a tangle of passages lead up into the private chambers and down to defensive positions in the turrets and in the thickness of the walls. After the vault was replaced, some of these positions were no longer accessible. The door at the far end of the hall opens onto a passage leading to a chapel and a spiral stairs, which rises to the main bedchamber and gives access to the roof. A chapel [7] was a common feature in earlier Anglo-Norman keeps, but rare in tower-houses. A shelf under the eastern window formed the altar. Fragments of painted plaster have survived on the walls and the vaulted ceiling. The main bedchamber, over the chapel, was built with a garderobe in the corner, and had a large fireplace inserted or rebuilt. The mantle has the date 1596AD inscribed on one side, with space perhaps for a further inscription, which was never cut.

The Bawn

The bawn wall was probably built after 1581 to enclose the yard and a new range of buildings. Small towers were built on three corners, with the large tower-house occupying the fourth [5]. Windows built into the bawn wall provided light for a large hall, a lofty building constructed mostly of timber. The Hall overlooked a garden, walled off from the remainder of the bawn. This privy garden has now been redeveloped and the orchard has been restored north of the bawn.

DAVE POLLOCK
Dúchas – The Heritage Service

———

All illustrations in introductory section courtesy Dúchas – The Heritage Service, unless otherwise stated. Photographs by Con Brogan, Dúchas.

BARRYSCOURT LECTURES

BARRYSCOURT LECTURE SERIES

Barryscourt Castle is a fine 16th-century
tower-house at Carrigtwohill, Co Cork.
The Barryscourt Trust was established in
1987 with the aim of conserving,
enhancing and developing the heritage
potential of the castle.

In 1996, the Barryscourt Trust
instituted a bi-annual series of lectures on
Medieval Ireland. These will deal with
aspects of medieval history, archaeology,
art and architecture, and will be
delivered by scholars specialising in the
period. The lectures will be published
individually and in compilation form.

Barryscourt Lectures I
BARRYSCOURT CASTLE
AND THE IRISH TOWER-HOUSE
Tadhg O'Keeffe

Published by the Barryscourt Trust
in association with Cork County Council
and Gandon Editions, Kinsale.

© The Barryscourt Trust and the author,
1997. All rights reserved.

ISBN 0946641 82X

Publication of this inaugural
lecture was sponsored by
Cork County Council.

Series Editor   Noel Jameson
Design   John O'Regan
                   (© Gandon, 1997)
Production   Nicola Dearey, Gandon
Printing   Betaprint, Dublin
Distribution   Gandon, Kinsale

THE BARRYSCOURT TRUST
Barryscourt Castle
Carrigtwohill, Co Cork

BARRYSCOURT CASTLE
AND THE IRISH TOWER-HOUSE

Barryscourt Castle tower-house:
the north-east turret viewed from the Hall

THE BARRYSCOURT LECTURES I

Barryscourt Castle and the Irish Tower-House

Tadhg O'Keeffe

THE BARRYSCOURT TRUST
IN ASSOCIATION WITH CORK COUNTY COUNCIL AND GANDON EDITIONS

1 – View of Barryscourt Castle from the north-west
prior to restoration

THE TOWER-HOUSE IS THE LATE medieval Irish castle *par excellence*.[1] From the 1300s to the 1600s the great majority of Irish castles included, or were comprised solely of, tower-houses. What is perhaps most remarkable about the tower-house tradition is that by the end of the 15th century, all three populations in medieval Ireland – the Gaelic Irish, the English and the gaelicised English – had embraced it. This essay begins with an exploration of the beginnings of that tradition, before offering some reflections on Barryscourt Castle, and specifically on its main tower [1], which is one of the finest tower-houses in Ireland.[2]

The origins of the Irish tower-house: the topography of the medieval household, 1200-1500

The 14th-century flare-up of hostilities between the native and settler populations provides a historical context by which we might view the tower-house tradition, predominantly a feature of 15th and 16th-century Ireland, as detached from the Anglo-Norman castle-building tradition. Harold Leask offered an actual chronology: he argued that, following a whole century in which major building work had all but ceased, the tower-house phenomenon began with the early 15th-century offer of subsidies – generally £10 – to those in the Pale who were willing to build small towers to fortify their lands,[3] a scheme which reflects the failure of the earlier crown policy of ordering tenants to fortify lands or face confiscation.[4] The new orthodoxy in chronology, however, is that the tower-house first appeared not after 1420, but in the 14th century,[5] but no matter how narrow the chronological gap becomes, the tower-house still seems to be perceived in the literature as a phenomenon distinct from the Norman castle; the year 1300 forms an impenetrable *fin de siècle* barrier across which the Norman castle could not venture forward, nor the tower-house backwards. With little known about castle-building among the native Irish during the 13th century, the cross-cultural ubiquity of the tower-house seems to encourage the view that it would not have emerged without there first being a break in the earlier building tradition.

One can, however, see in the corpus of Norman castles sufficient architectural precedent, conceptual and physical, for the main elements of the later tower-house. Here we need to understand that castle architecture was, in general, driven less by the need to find the optimum military design, and more by the need to function efficiently as the residence of a lord and of his household (those who perform 'private tasks at his expense'[6]), and as an environment which expressed his power publicly and within which he could administer that power.

The spatial relationships between public and private spaces within castles are exceedingly complex, but are central to understanding the architecture of the buildings. One might make a distinction between halls which were essentially public buildings – places from which affairs of the territory under the protection of the castle were administered – and those which were essentially domestic but which had the capacity to take guests on certain occasions. It is likely, however, that few Irish castles – among them Dublin Castle[7] – had halls which served exclusively public functions. Most Irish halls, whether free-standing or contained within ranges of buildings, are probably best regarded as essentially domestic structures.

In the early 13th century at Adare Castle, county Limerick [2A], the keep or donjon was placed within an inner courtyard, with a hall in an outer courtyard beside the gateway; in the late middle ages, a second, larger hall, complete with external pilasters and an entrance porch, was added within the courtyard. The keep presumably contained private apartments, and its placement in the inner enclosure suggests that the deeper into the castle precinct one ventured, the more private the space. The contrast between the horizontal axis of the hall and the vertical axis of the private space was consciously executed. Schemes not unlike that at Adare can also be seen in the 13th-century castles of Trim, county Meath, and at Nenagh, county Tipperary; the description of the 'castle and hall' of Carlow being so decayed in 1307 that nobody would rent them suggests a similar configuration.[8]

At Carlingford, county Louth [2C], a long rectangular building of

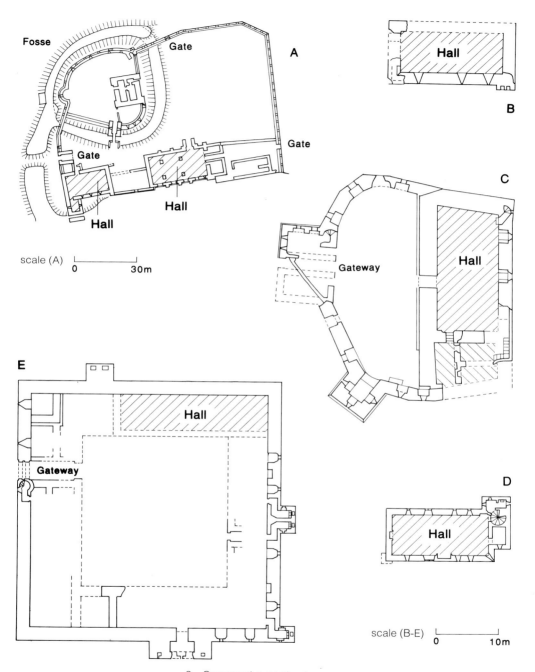

2 – Comparative castle plans:
Adare (A); Kindlestown (B); Carlingford (C); Coolhull (D); Ballymoon (E)

*c*1260, placed at the rear of a small courtyard of *c*1200, contained a first floor hall for most of its length, and the most private accommodation was placed not within a separate structure, but at one end of the hall. Ballymoon, county Carlow [2E], an enigmatic fortress dated by Leask to *c*1310, also has a long hall, and high-status residential space, marked by a projection containing a twinned garderobe, is attached to one end of it; unlike at Carlingford, the Ballymoon hall is fully integrated into a continuous range of buildings.

The domestic hall with the private residence attached to it, either above it or to one side, could be liberated from its setting alongside other buildings to stand freely within an enclosure. This is attested early in the 13th century;[9] it is apparently the case at the end of the 13th century at Rathumney, county Wexford and, in a slightly different configuration, at Kindlestown, county Wicklow [2B]. Coolhull, county Wexford [2D] is a 15th-century manifestation: here the private area is in tower form with a hall extending to one side of it.

Tower-houses such as Clara, county Kilkenny, and Roodstown, county Louth [3], one being a typical example of a southern and midland Irish tower-house and the other being typical of the Pale, differ from castles of Kindlestown or Coolhull type in shape: their axis is vertical rather than horizontal. A more fundamental difference is that in the tower-house, both the hall and the private rooms are made to conform to the shape of the building, so the difference in relative area between the hall and the private rooms lessens. In the case of Clara, the fourth-floor hall is still larger than other rooms within the tower, but is not as large as the hall in Coolhull. One can almost see the tower-house in embryo at Ballymoon: all of its rooms are of equal width, and even though they are arranged laterally rather than vertically, the castle's designer seems to be toying with the same concept of spatial regularity as informs the tower-houses.

If the strong vertical emphasis of the tower-house was inherited from the Norman keeps of the early 13th century, as seems likely, there are certain elements of tower-house architecture which are common to both keeps and free-standing halls of the 1200s. In the case of Clara, for example, the main stairs begins to the left of the main entrance, then rises uninterrupted to the fourth-floor hall, allowing one to move straight from the entrance to the hall without first entering a lesser room; the same arrangement is found in, for example, the early 13th-century cylindrical keep of Nenagh, county Tipperary (where the entrance is at first-floor level), and the early 13th-century hall of Grenan, county Kilkenny. Roodstown is considerably less complex than Clara, but here too the stairs is arranged so that one can ascend within the tower without first entering lower status rooms.

———

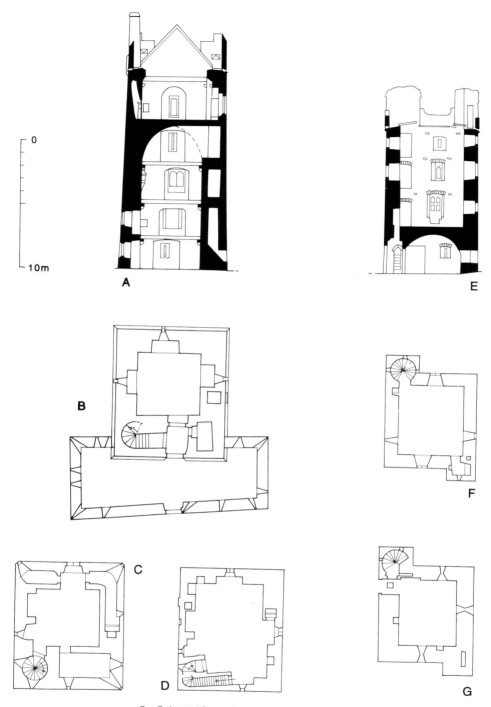

3 – Selected floor plans and cross-sections
Clara (A – Cross-section looking west; B – Ground-floor plan; C – Second-floor; D – Fourth-floor)
Roodstown (E – Cross-section looking east; F – First-floor plan; G – Ground-floor plan)

The continuity of architectural thinking between the 13th and 15th centuries is not surprising, but does it represent continuity in the social-historical contexts of the castles? Even within the colonial area, comparatively few tower-house builders of the 14th and 15th centuries were descended from the castle-owning population of pre-1300; instead, many of the tower-houses may have belonged to those who had previously resided in moated sites, monuments about which scholarship in Ireland was largely ignorant until recent decades.[10] The moated site is the principal relic feature of Anglo-Norman rural settlement in midland and southern Ireland. These sites were not castles in the sense in which that word was used by contemporary society; rather, they were protected farmsteads, presumably of manorial free tenants, and are generally unrecorded in historical sources. Moated sites may have been built for the best part of a century, beginning early in the 13th century, and most seem to have contained a single house or hall, along with ancillary buildings. In central and north Leinster, and in Ulster, moated sites are quite rare, and free tenants seem to have perpetuated into the 13th century the tradition of building mottes. Density maps of moated sites and tower-houses, based on the distributions of rectangular earthwork enclosures and castles as marked on Ordnance Survey maps,[11] show a general geographical correspondence [4], and one might reasonably suggest that the tower-house, having become established in the area where the moats indicate a strong Norman presence, spread north-westwards into the Gaelic lands of Clare.[12] This is not to suggest

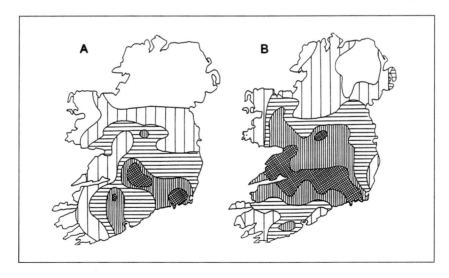

4 – Density maps of moated sites (A) and tower-houses (B)
the gradations are 2-10, 10-20, 20-30 and 30+ sites per 2500km²

that the tower-houses first appeared within moats, nor that they are architecturally related to the halls or houses within the moats, but it might safely be anticipated that future research on moat interiors will show the latter of these at least to be the case.

The Irish adoption of the tower-house is a most interesting phenomenon. Between the 12th and 14th centuries, their preferred forms of settlement and domestic architecture are largely unknown to us,[13] which is curious given the havoc the Gaelic Irish wreaked on the colony, both by territorial expansion and by cultural assimilation. The late middle ages would not have been first time that the medieval Gaelic Irish imported into their society a type of fortification which had originated elsewhere. One might think back to the pre-Norman 12th century. A consensus view of modern scholarship is that Ireland had already embraced feudalism by the time the Anglo-Norman conquest and settlement began in 1169.[14] Among the manifestations of this mode of social organisation in the early 1100s is the appearance in native sources of *caistél* or *caislén*.[15] Even more than the great cathedrals of Europe, whose construction in the high middle ages – 12th to 14th centuries – was made possible by the feudal organisation of contemporary society, it was the castle which embodied the concept of feudalism, and the use of this word in an Irish environment signposts a society conscious of the symbolism of language. The monuments themselves are unknown to us since none survives, but evidence which is largely circumstantial strongly indicates that for these castles, Irish kings, whom we know to have been embracing the pan-European Romanesque style for churches under their patronage, adapted the elevated settlement earthwork or motte, a monument then current in England and Continental Europe.[16]

The adoption of the tower-house by the Irish does not, however, represent an anglicisation of Gaelic society, even though the tower-houses which inspired imitation were environments designed and equipped for the domestic rituals of colonial society. Henry Chrysted tells us that Ó Néill, Mac Murchada, Ó Briain and Ó Conchobhair adopted only temporarily the manners and styles of the English court following their acceptance of knighthoods from Richard II.[17] Raymond, viscount of Perelhos and of Roda in Roussillon, encountered Ó Néill whilst journeying to St Patrick's Purgatory in 1397. Despite having an inquiring interest in overseas customs, Ó Néill informed Raymond that he regarded Gaelic Irish customs as 'the best and most perfect in the world'. Raymond observed a warrior society, living in poverty close to the cattle on which they depended; he noted that kings, bishops and others in the nobility went barelegged and barefoot, and that neither women nor men were unwilling to expose their private parts.[18]

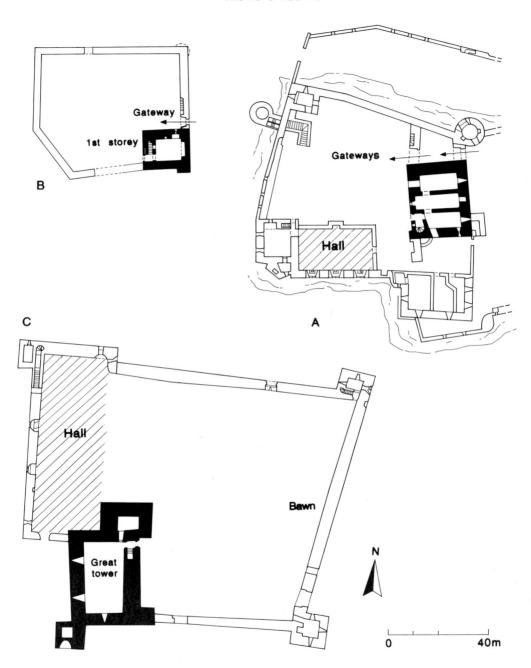

5 – Outline ground plans of Cahir Castle (A), Rathmacknee Castle (B),
Barryscourt Castle (C)

The tower-house of Barryscourt Castle: artefact, environment, symbol

Barryscourt Castle, or at least its tower-house, can certainly be considered from an architectural perspective to belong in the top rank of Irish late-medieval buildings.[19] Its layout adheres to a simple conception: the tower-house and adjacent structure, which can reasonably be identified as a hall, occupy one entire side of a quadrangular enclosure, with a curtain or bawn wall embracing a courtyard which extends eastwards of the two buildings. Both the tower-house and hall have turrets at their outermost corners, and these are mirrored in the small towers which protect, or at least define, the corners of the enclosure. The main entrance gateway into the courtyard – there is a second entrance in the north wall of the bawn – is overlooked by the tower-house [5C]. The plan type is not unusual: it is a variation on a theme which can be found at Cahir, county Tipperary, and Rathmacknee, county Wexford [5A, B].

A published survey of 1991 offers a detailed description of the buildings and a suggestion for the constructional sequence by which the castle arrived at its present configuration.[20] More recent survey work by the National Monuments and Properties Service of the Office of Public Works (now the Department of Arts, Culture and the Gaeltacht) has yielded a more accurate and comprehensive record of the remains, fulfiling

6 – View of Barryscourt Castle tower-house from the west
prior to restoration

the clear expectation of the compilers of the original report that the castle would continue to reveal its complexity.[21]

The tower-house, dating to c1550 on stylistic grounds, visually dominates both the castle and the landscape in which the castle is set [6]. It is our principal concern here, and a brief description of it, highlighting some of the evidence for substantial structural alterations to its original form, is necessary. Like many of the largest Irish tower-houses, its ground plan is comprised of a central block, at the corners of which are projecting turrets. The scheme is deployed here in a curiously asymmetrical manner: there are only three projecting turrets, leaving one of the corners (the north-west) unprotected. All three turrets are of different sizes, even the two which are diagonally opposite each other at the north-east and south-west corners, while the turret to the south-east is exceptional among the three in having one of its faces flush with the side wall of the main block.[22] The indifference to symmetry which is apparent in the ground plan, and indeed in the elevations, separates this castle from the likes of Bunratty, county Clare, where one can sense a progression towards the fully domestic house in which symmetry is part of the aesthetic. The Barryscourt tower-house is also rather squat in appearance, since its large central block, which rises to three storeys, has a lower parapet level than the turrets, each of which has five habitable storeys.

Entry into the tower is by a doorway – clearly inserted in the 16th century – at the north end of the east wall of the central block. Upon entering, a stairs rises to the left (the south side) while a doorway leads forward into the large apartment which is the lowest of the three floors. Narrow rectangular windows provided security for this large room, but at the cost of natural lighting. Only the large north-east turret has an accessible chamber at this lower-floor level, and this was reached from the main apartment through a door passage which was clearly mined out of the wall, whereas its original entry seems to have been through the floor of the chamber above. The main stairs rises southwards along the north side of the main block, terminating in a small lobby which opens into the main private hall at second-floor level. Halfway along the ascending stairs is a doorway, apparently an insertion, leading into the large first-floor apartment. This is roofed by a round barrel vault, which in turn provides the stone floor to the hall above, while a wooden floor separates it from the apartment below. The present vault is clearly a replacement of an earlier, pointed barrel vault, rough masonry traces of which still survive at the short ends of the hall [7]. The main first-floor apartment is no more effectively lit than that below, but it has a fireplace in its west wall which was inserted after the original vault had been replaced; a large circular patch of in-filled masonry located at the south end of the underside of the replacement vault may represent a cavity to allow smoke rise from a floor hearth,

7 – View of first floor room from the north showing traces of original vault

8 – The private hall: view from north prior to restoration

in which case the insertion of the fireplace is even later that the replacement of the vault. Narrow passages lead from the main apartment here into all three turrets. The south-west turret contains a long garderobe passage, but the south-east turret has a simple chamber which, in being L-shaped, exploits the thick wall of the central block. The north-eastern turret, however, has two floors at this level, both reached by ascending or descending flights of steps, which are in turn reached by a mural passageway between the turret and the main block. The upper floor has a small private chamber with a latrine outside its door at a slightly lower level. The lower-floor room has a musket loop overlooking the main entrance; it is set within an embrasure which was created by the blocking of a doorway. Also at the level of the lower of the two floors is a small mural chamber with a murder hole; this is contained within the thickness of the wall of the main block and directly above the entrance lobby.

The upper hall, a private hall, merits closer attention [8, 9]. Entered from the main stairs at the south end of the west wall, it was an elaborately appointed room, with five substantial, mullioned windows, one on the south wall and two on each of the side walls, providing abundant lighting. The northern window on the west wall bears the inscription DB ET ER ME FIERI FECER ADO 1586. A fireplace was inserted in front of, and thus blocking, the east-wall window, and is inscribed A D'O 1588 IHS DB ET ER ME FIERE FECERUT;[23] prior to this, heating was probably provided by a central hearth.[24] The hall originally had an open-timber roof supported principally on corbels along the side walls, and some medieval plaster survives on the walls beneath the line of corbels.

No less than six doorways open off the hall to provide access by corridors or by stairs to other rooms. Three doorways lead to stairs which ascend to give access to the upper chambers of the turrets and to parapet level. The stairs at the north end of the hall was reached by a long corridor, which also gave access to the castle's private chapel. The same stairs gives access to a passageway higher up, which leads towards the most important private chamber in the castle, located directly above the chapel and possessing a latrine (inserted), elaborate windows, all externally rebated and chamfered), and a fireplace inscribed with the legend A.D.O. 1596. Opposite the entrance to this chamber is a doorway-like opening in the end wall of the hall. An insertion of the late-16th century, it may have opened onto a landing or gallery over the hall, but is more likely to have provided the lord with a vantage point from which to view events in the hall below.

Three doorways lead from the hall to descending stairs, with two of these stairs giving access to chambers in the south-west and south-east turrets. The third – a broken doorway in front of the south window on the east wall – leads into a vaulted mural chamber which runs north-south

9 – The private hall: plan
SE   South-east turret
SW   South-west turret
NE   North-east turret
MC   Mural chamber
       (numbers refer to storey
       levels [see Fig.10])
Plan after R. Stapleton, Dept of Arts,
Culture and the Gaeltacht

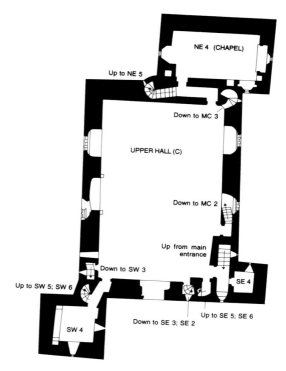

10 – A planning diagram of
Barryscourt tower-house.

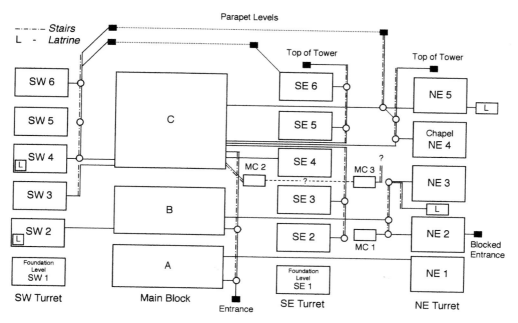

immediately above the main stairs. A wall seals this chamber at its north-ern end. Another stairs, now concealed in the north-east corner of the hall, descended into a similar mural passage at the same horizontal level further to the north along this side of the castle. These mural chambers are partly in-filled with rough masonry from the haunches of the present vault over the first floor, which suggests that they belong in the primary phase of the tower-house and were abandoned when the new vault was built.

There was no continuous access around the tower at parapet level. The ascending stairs in the south-west corner led to doorways opening onto the south and west parapets, but the former, wedged behind the bat-tlements and in front of the gable of the hall below, terminated at the south-east turret, while movement along the latter was encumbered by the chimney of the fireplace inserted in the hall below.

Lines of communication within the tower-house are complex, and routes between parts of the building were far more circuitous than might be expected in a tower-house. This is ostensibly a consequence of differ-ences between the heights of the main apartments and of the chambers within the turrets, and also of variations in the number and sizes of habit-able spaces within the tower-house. But the complexity of the pattern of access reflects more specifically the stratification within the household: not all rooms were of equal status, and the corridors and stairs expressed this by facilitating certain movements within the building, while making difficult or inconvenient the movements between other rooms by effec-tively increasing the distance between them. Some impression of this complexity can be given by translating the design of the Barryscourt tower-house into a planning diagram[25] [10] in which the main spaces with-in the tower are indicated by rectangular boxes of approximate propor-tions; horizontal bars represent corridors (lines of lateral movement within the tower), and vertical bars represent stairs (lines of vertical movement). Junctions – points at which the traveller through the building faces a choice between entering a space or continuing along a horizontal or verti-cal line – are represented by small circles. Other lines cross each other in the diagram, but no spatial or access relationships between them can be inferred; rather, such lines are a natural by-product of attempting to depict complex movement patterns within a building of Barryscourt's ground plan.

The planning diagram represents the tower-house in its final, pre-sent form. It is clear how much of the accommodation within the tower-house was accessible only through the hall (C): rooms SW 3-6, SE 2-6, and NE 4-5, MC2 and presumably also MC3, and the parapets, could only be reached by first entering this hall. Thus it acts as a form of courtyard around which other rooms are positioned, taking into its embrace not only those rooms which rise higher in the castle than it, but also rooms which are below it in the south-east and south-west turrets. The main stairs in

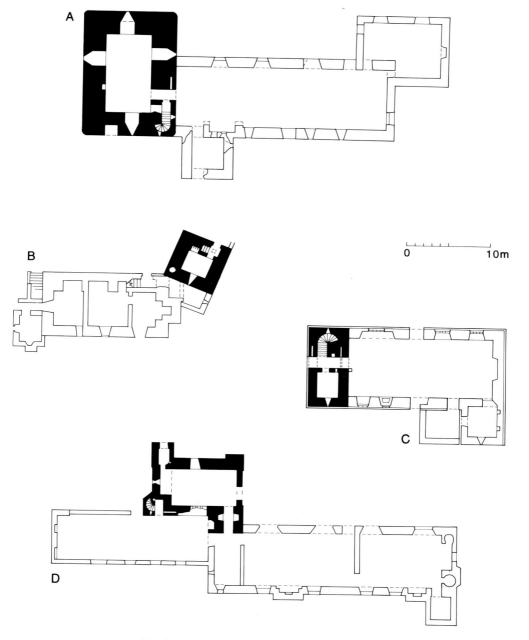

11 – Comparative tower and hall / house plans
Loughmoe, county Tipperary (A); Slade, county Wexford (B);
Lemanagh, county Clare (C); Athlumney, county Meath (D)

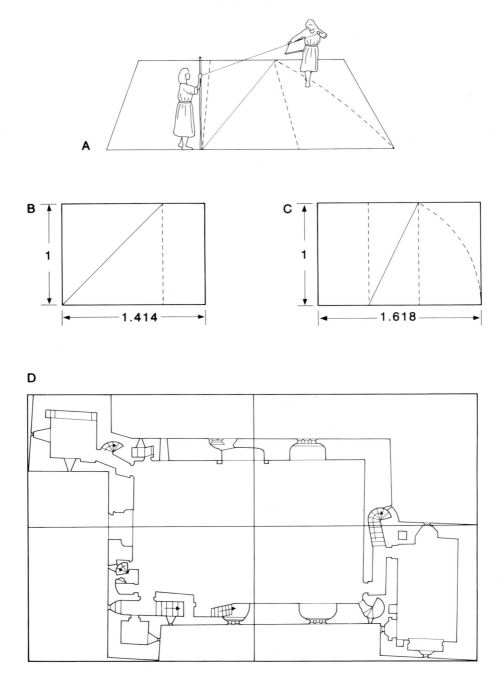

12 – The laying-out of proportional rectangles (A-C);
the Golden Section applied to Barryscourt tower-house (D)

the west wall of the castle ensured that one could enter the tower-house and ascend to the hall without having first to pass through any other room, but most of the other rooms in the tower-house were inaccessible without first entering the hall.

Given the evidence of alteration already been outlined above – evidence which has been forged into a comprehensive sequencing[26] – one might ask how the tower-house functioned originally. Before addressing this question, it is appropriate to consider the spatial and chronological relationship between the tower-house and the adjacent external hall to its north [5C].

———

In the majority of Irish instances where one has the tower and adjacent hall in the manner seen at Barryscourt, usually the latter is a later addition, often of the early post-medieval period [11]. The suggestion has been made that at Barryscourt, the hall is earlier, and that it has an even earlier foundation beneath it.[27] The fabric evidence for the present hall being early is far from unequivocal; certainly it follows a plan scheme which was used in the 13th century, with its projecting latrine at one end, and the external rebating and chamfering on its partially rebuilt windows is an embellishment which enjoyed particular vogue in the 13th century. But evidence which most firmly places the hall's construction *after* that of the tower relates to the method by which the tower itself was laid out.

The process of building in the middle ages was not based on *ad hoc* judgements of the relative proportions appropriate to the structure in question, but on tried and trusted proportional schemata of considerable antiquity, principal among them being those expressed by the ratios 1:1.4142 (or 1:√2) and 1:1.618 (the Golden Section).[28] These are mathematical expressions of long-used practical processes of laying out rectangles. Both involved the laying out of a square on the ground, marking the diagonal of the whole square or of half of it with a length of rope, then swinging the rope until it lined up with the side of the square [12A-C]. Medieval masons did not necessarily need to know the mathematics of their creation – that they were, in other words, expressing geometrically irrational numerical proportions – but the evidence of large buildings suggests they were knowledgeable about the whole number ratios approximating to 1:√2, the Golden Section and other ratios.[29] Acknowledging that masons possessed a knowledge of mathematics frees us to undertake metrical analysis; but it also contains the potential to create rather than recover schemata: plans may be analysed to reveal depths of mathematical consistency which were unknown to the masons but which were by-products of the simpler schemata.

The external hall at Barryscourt follows a simple ratio of 1:3, but the tower was apparently laid out within a Golden Section rectangle: the entire structure can be inscribed within a rectangle whose length is 1.618 times the width, with the width (east-west) of the north-east turret taking up half the width of the rectangle [12D] . The revelation is significant. Firstly, it helps clarify the relationship between hall and tower: given that this system was probably laid out on the ground rather than calculated, it is improbable that the latter could have been laid out to this proportional scheme so effectively had a hall already been standing to the north-west. Secondly, it suggests that tower-houses, like earlier Norman castles,[30] were laid out using sophisticated systems, and were not incidentally planned.

––––––

Returning to the tower-house itself, there are many indications that, notwithstanding the proportional system used in it, the tower-house is not the product of a single campaign of building, no matter how prolonged. Some observations regarding sequence might be offered here, but with the concession that on-going examination of the fabric may necessitate a revision in the suggested sequence. First of all, the evidence of an original pointed vault above the first-floor apartment is incontrovertible. Its collapse, probably very early in the tower-house's history, meant a new vault was needed, and the builders appear to have decided that a round barrel was more secure. Were substantial alterations made to the lay-out of the castle's interior at this point?

Two principal observations throw light on this issue. The first concerns mural chambers MC2 and MC3 [10]. The pointed vault had haunches wide enough to facilitate these chambers, but both of these were partially in-filled with the rubble haunches of the round vault when it was built, and the stairs connected to MC3 was abandoned. Where did this stairs lead? There is no evidence that it opened onto the hall, at least not directly. It may have opened onto the corridor which now leads to the chapel. Did it descend any lower than the mural chamber? There is no clear evidence that it did, and as the stairs leading to MC2 did not, so the same may be true here also. The second point relates to the main, mural stairs of the tower which runs directly beneath these mural chambers. That stairs begins its ascent at ground level in the entrance lobby, which is associated with the present ground floor doorway. That doorway is an insertion [13]. The tower may well have been entered originally at this point, but through an earlier doorway.

In favour of this suggestion is the stairs itself. It is not unknown for stairs to run along the entire length of a wall before turning into a spiral or exiting into a room.[31] Below the level of the entrance into first-floor level, the steps do seem to rise at a slightly different angle from those higher up, but this may not reflect a structural change but an error of judgement in the construction. There is certainly no reason to associate it with the inserted entrance doorway below: if the stairs had needed resetting because of a new doorway, one might find greater evidence of extensive rebuilding.

Alternatively, as has been suggested on the basis of an in-filled opening in the external wall of the tower,[32] the original entrance was half-way along the stairs as it ascended from ground level to the hall, with the entrance lobby here possibly extended northwards to what is now the murder hole chamber, MC1. Attractive though this suggestion is, it demands too many structural changes. It requires, first of all, that no steps descended to ground-floor level: the steps would have to have stopped at the level of the mural entrance lobby. Secondly, that entrance lobby, as the vestibule serving the entire tower, would have needed to have been much wider than the stairs passage itself. It seems more likely that the infilled ope was a large window embrasure, and this would explain why it is not apparent on the exterior of the castle [13]. Also, it would be unusual to enter the tower at the level of the first-floor room but not be able to get direct access to it; the doorway which gives access to it from the main stairs is an insertion, albeit one which may pre-date the collapse of the vault.[33]

One might then hypothesise that the tower was indeed entered at

13 – View of lower exterior east wall of the tower-house
prior to restoration

ground level from the north end of its east wall, that the entrance lobby led directly into the ground floor, and that the stairs ascended to the hall *by-passing* the next floor level until, early in the tower's history, a doorway was broken into that first-floor room. How then did one enter that room originally? One possibility is that one descended into it from the hall via the stairs known to have been attached to MC2, but it is more likely perhaps that the blocked entrance at first-floor level in the north-east turret provided the direct access. The position of the castle's chapel may be pertinent here.

———

The layout of the tower-house reflected the social geography of the Barryscourt Castle community by creating linkages between some living spaces and by denying linkages between others. The elevations and details of the tower were no less expressive of the social order: the treatment of the tower's wall openings – windows and doors – varied according to the status of the room, or more particularly the status of the room's expected occupants. Those rooms given the most elaborate visual appearance will invariably be those with latrines or fireplaces. Thus the hierarchy or stratification within a household was encoded in a manner clearly legible to us.

The castle chapel, located within the north-east turret, was incorporated as was any other room in the access system within the tower-house, and like other rooms, its function was apparent from its furnishings: the sill of the east window, an elaborate double-cusped light set in a narrow vaulted embrasure, projected as an altar mensa, while a similar window in the south wall originally had a quatrefoil piscina in its sill.[34] A row of small holes about one metre above ground level runs along the plain north wall of the chapel, possibly marking the position of fixed stalls.

It may seem that this room could be placed anywhere within the tower provided the access was in keeping with the geography of the castle. But there were two pre-requisites for equipping the castle with a chapel. One was that the space be oriented east-west. The other was that it be located over an entrance.

Whether it was a feature of secular buildings prior to the Anglo-Norman arrival is unknown, but it is inherently likely that pre-Norman Irish kings had chapels within their fortresses, and that international architectural tradition – with which they were doubtless familiar – dictated that above the entrance was the proper place. The Normans certainly chose that position more often than not.[35] Trim Castle, county Meath, for example, has a chapel at second-floor level in the east turret of its keep, directly over the original entrance. Here the lord reached it from his private chamber above by descending one floor via a stair, a scheme similar to that at Barryscourt. The simpler scheme at Grenan also recalls Barryscourt: here a mural chapel is placed at one end of the upper hall, directly above the main entrance, and that hall, like at Barryscourt, was reached by a stairs ascending the length of the tower from a small entrance lobby.

If one accepts that the second floor of the north-east turret (NE2) was an entrance floor, then the chapel is indeed positioned above it, albeit separated by a domestic chamber (NE3). The south window with its piscina overlooked both this entrance and the present ground-floor entrance.

———

The widespread use in the middle ages of proportional schemata originally used in Antiquity may well have been intended to give buildings a classical imprimatur. It is difficult to imagine that the builders of Barryscourt were aware of, not to mention concerned with, the classical antiquity of their scheme, and to suggest otherwise might merit from the castle's builders a criticism rather like Turner's of Ruskin: 'he knows a great deal more about my paintings than I do, he puts things into my head and points out meanings I never intended.'[36] One could alternatively hold Schnaase's view that 'the retrospective view of the historian ... is fuller and richer than that which the contemporaries of past artists could have had.'[37] The Barryscourt builders certainly did conform to an iconographic motif of some antiquity in placing their chapel above the entrance to the tower-house, whether they were conscious or not of the iconographic meaning.

Epilogue

'We are come to the castle already. The castles are built very strong, and wth. narrow stayres, for security. The hall is the uppermost room, lett us go up, you shall not come downe agayne till tomorrow. The lady of the house meets you wth. her trayne. Salutations paste, you shall be presented wth. all the drinkes in the house, first the ordinary beare, then aqua vitae, then sacke, then olde-ale, the lady tastes it, you must not refuse it. The fyre is prepared in the middle of the hall, where you may sollace yor. selfe till supper time, you shall not want sacke and tobacco. By this time the table is spread and plentifully furnished wth. variety of meates, but ill-cooked and wthout sauce. When you come to yor. chamber, do not expect canopy and curtaines.'[38]

One can only guess that the reception which greeted Luke Gernon, a travelling Englishman in Ireland, when he called at a castle seeking hospitality in 1620 was typical of the age. Gernon's account of poorly cooked meat, straw-strewn floors, and a lady retiring early to her bed chamber, brings to life the reality of an evening in a well-to-do household at the end of the middle ages; it also suggests that the castles were less forbidding than the stark ruins might today suggest, and were instead places of rudimentary comfort at which strangers were sometimes made welcome.

By the time that Gernon was touring the country, the Irish castle was in the throes of its third and final morphological, functional and conceptual transformation. In the mid-17th century, the castle's incarnation as fundamentally a military establishment, or at least as part of the administrative apparatus of a militarised society, was several centuries in the past. Two centuries, perhaps three, before Gernon's visit, the greater number of castles were private fortresses, most of them possessing as a main element a tower-house. If these tower-houses contributed to a strategy of local or regional defence, that contribution was incidental to their primary roles as barriers against personal violence and theft. Within a century of Gernon, the domestic, entirely non-fortified house, was already in sight. If its emergence reflects a consciousness of contemporary English domestic architecture, or at least of such Irish manifestations of it as Carrick-on-Suir, county Tipperary, its actual realisation c1600 was facilitated largely by a social environment in which landed gentry perceived Ireland to be entering into a quiet phase of history. No less significant in effecting this radical change in architecture was the need to rethink defensive systems in an age in which gunpowder was commonplace. It is a curious irony of Gernon's account that by 1620, a castle like that into which he had welcomed – a type we know as a tower-house – would have been considered rather passé as a formal building type. The line of architectural evolution of the castle had, by that time, bifurcated: the private fortress was now a house furnished with timber floors throughout, well-lit windows, and exposed chimneys, and defended with narrow musket apertures, while star-shaped forts containing barracks buildings were entirely military in conception. Thus the concern of castle-builders, real or imagined by us, to reconcile the conflicting needs of defense and domesticity within a single building was finally resolved by a clear structural-functional polarisation.

———

The author

Tadhg O'Keeffe is a lecturer at the Department of Archaeology, University College Dublin. He is author of numerous articles on medieval Irish settlement and architecture, and his forthcoming book on Bridgetown Priory, county Cork – a study of the architecture of Augustinian Canons Regular in medieval Ireland – will be published by Cork County Council and Gandon Editions in June 1997.

Acknowledgements

It is a pleasure to acknowledge the Barryscourt Trust for inviting me to offer this contribution to the understanding of the castle. My thanks also to Noel Jamieson, Judith Monk and Red Tobin for sharing their views on the castle with me; to Richard Stapleton and Aighleann O'Shaughnessy for permission to make use of new survey material in figs. 9 and 12; to Margaret Coughlan for advice on the chapel and its context; and to Niamh Ó Broin for all the line drawings (except fig. 4). Finally, special acknowledgement is due to John Ludlow, whose initiative and energy have been central to the success of work at Barryscourt Castle.

Photographs – courtesy of the Department of Arts, Culture and the Gaeltacht

Drawings – by Niamh Ó Broin

Notes and References

1 HG Leask, *Irish Castles and Castellated Houses* (Revised ed., Dundalk, 1946), pp75-112; M Salter, *Castles and Stronghouses of Ireland* (Malvern, 1993) contains descriptions, plans and photographs. The outline plans of castles other than Barryscourt which have been used here are based on drawings in Leask and Salter; the Roodstown drawings are based on C Casey and A Rowan, *North Leinster* (Harmondsworth, 1993).

2 Barryscourt Castle is described and analysed in J Monk and R Tobin, *Barryscourt Castle: An Architectural Survey* (The Barryscourt Trust, 1991). More recent survey work has been carried out at the castle by Richard Stapleton, Department of Arts, Culture and the Gaeltacht, in the context of a programme of conservation and restoration.

3 Leask, *Irish Castles*, pp76-9

4 *Calendar of documents relating to Ireland…, 1171-[1307]*. Ed. HS Sweetman and GF Handcock. 5 vols. (PRO, London, 1875-86), 1171-1251, no.1576; *Cal Doc Irel 1252-1284*, no.411

5 TB Barry, 'The archaeology of the tower-house in late medieval Ireland' in H Anderson and J Wienberg (eds.), *The Study of Medieval Archaeology* (Stockholm, 1993), pp211-17; TE McNeill, 'The origins of tower-houses', *Archaeology Ireland*, 6, 1 (1992), pp13-14

6 G Duby (ed.), *A History of Private Life. II Revelations of the Medieval World* (Cambridge, Mass, 1988), p63; for a discussion of the medieval household see TE McNeill, *Castles* (London, 1992), pp47-72, K Mertres, *The English Noble Household, 1250-1600: Good Governance and Politic Rule* (Oxford, 1988), and M Thompson, *The Medieval Hall. The Basis of Secular Domestic Life, 600-1600 AD* (Aldershot, 1995), pp110-117.

7 In 1243 a hall here was built by order of Henry III. It was to be 120 feet long and 80 feet wide with glazed windows and a rose window, 30 feet in diameter, behind the dais. The king and queen were to be depicted on the same gable wall, and a great portal was to provide entrance to the hall. *Close rolls of the reign of Henry III, 1227-[1272]*. 14 vols. (PRO, London, 1892-1963) 1242-7, p23; see JB Maguire, 'Seventeenth century plans of Dublin Castle', *RSAI Jn.*, 104 (1974), 5-14

8 *Cal Doc Irel 1302-7*, no.617

9 Grenan, county Kilkenny, and Moylough, county Galway: McNeill, 'Origins of tower-houses', p14

10 G Hadden, 'Some earthworks in Co. Wexford,' *Cork Hist. Soc. Jn.*, lxix (1964), pp118-22; RE Glasscock, 'Moated sites and deserted boroughs and villages: two neglected aspects of Anglo-Norman settlement in Ireland', in N Stephens and R Glasscock (eds.), *Ir. Geog. Studies* (Belfast, 1970), pp162-8; TB Barry, *Moated Sites in south-east Ireland* (Oxford, 1977)

11 Glasscock, 'Moated Sites'; C. Ó Danachair, 'Irish tower houses and their regional distribution,', *Béaloideas* xlv-xlvii (1977-9), pp158-63

12 T O'Keeffe, 'Rural Settlement and Cultural Identity in Gaelic Ireland 1000-1500,' *Ruralia 1996, Památky archeologické – Supplementum 5* (Prague, 1996), pp142-53

13 Discussed in ibid.

14 D Ó Corráin, *Ireland before the Normans* (Dublin, 1972), is still the most valuable account

15 MT Flanagan, 'Irish and Anglo-Norman warfare in twelfth century Ireland' in T Bartlett and K Jeffrey (eds.), *A Military History of Ireland* (Cambridge, 1996), p61

16 R Higham and P Barker, *Timber Castles* (London, 1992), pp78-113; O'Keeffe, 'Gaelic Ireland 1000-1500'

17 J Watt, 'Gaelic polity and cultural identity' in A Cosgrove (ed), *A New History of Ireland. II Medieval Ireland 1169-1534* (Dublin, 1987), p350

18 JP Mahaffy, 'Two early tours in Ireland', *Hermathena* xviii, 40 (1914), pp3-9

[19] The castle's history has summarised in Monk and Tobin, *Barryscourt Castle*, pp4-7. The history of the Barry family is discussed by KW Nicholls, 'The development of lordship in county Cork, 1300-1600' in P O'Flanagan and CG Buttimer (eds.), *Cork History and Society* (Cork, 1993), pp178-81

[20] Monk and Tobin, *Barryscourt Castle*, pp51-64

[21] Monk and Tobin, *Barryscourt Castle*, 2

[22] Tower-houses with three corner towers or turrets are uncommon; parallels for the general conception of Barryscourt's ground plan can be found in the English Pale.

[23] DB and ER refer to David Barry and Ellen Roach respectively. David Barry died at Barryscourt in 1617 (Monk and Tobin, *Barryscourt Castle*, pp6-7)

[24] The south wall may have had a fireplace before the great window was inserted.

[25] The seminal work is PJ Falkiner, 'Castle planning in the 14th century', *Archaeol. Jn.* 120 (1963), pp215-35; G Fairclough, 'Meaningful constructions – spatial and functional analysis of medieval buildings', *Antiquity* 66 (1992), pp348-66

[26] Monk and Tobin, *Barryscourt Castle*

[27] Monk and Tobin, *Barryscourt Castle*, Fig. 4

[28] A useful summary is provided by N Coldstream, *Masons and Sculptors* (London, 1991), pp37-8; P Kidson, 'A metrological investigation', *Courtauld Warburg Inst. Jn.* 53 (1990), pp71-97

[29] For example, Salisbury Cathedral: P Kidson, 'The historical circumstances and the principles of the design' in T Cocke and P Kidson, *Salisbury Cathedral: Perspectives on the Architectural History* (London, 1993), pp35-91

[30] For example, TA Heslop, 'Orford castle, nostalgia and sophisticated living', *Architectural History* 34 (1991), pp36-58, and RA Stalley, 'The Anglo-Norman keep at Trim: its architectural implications', *Archaeology Ireland* 6, 4 (1992), 16-19

[31] This is the case in the early 13th-century hall at Grenan, county Kilkenny; the tower house of Carrigaphooca, county Cork, is not dissimilar; coincidentally perhaps it too was designed without wall fireplaces.

[32] Monk and Tobin, *Barryscourt Castle*, 30

[33] One cannot physically associate the re-vaulting of the first floor with the insertion of the doorway which gives access to it from the main stairs. Indeed, it is likely that the doorway is earlier than the new vault given that the room's fireplace may have been inserted before the vault collapsed.

[34] R Day, 'Notes from the Croker and Caulfield Manuscripts, etc, in Smith's History of Cork, with notes, *Cork Hist. Soc. Jn.*, 1A (1892), p144

[35] NJG Pounds, 'The chapel in the castle', *Fortress* 9 (1991), pp12-20

[36] B Cassidy (ed.), *Iconography at the Crossroads* (Princeton, 1993), p7

[37] M Podro, *The Critical Historians of Art* (New Haven, 1982), p33

[38] Leask, *Irish Castles*, pp91-2

BARRYSCOURT LECTURES

BARRYSCOURT LECTURE SERIES

Barryscourt Castle is a fine 16th-century
tower-house at Carrigtwohill, Co Cork.
The Barryscourt Trust was established in
1987 with the aim of conserving,
enhancing and developing the heritage
potential of the castle.

In 1996, the Barryscourt Trust
instituted a bi-annual series of lectures on
Medieval Ireland. These will deal with
aspects of medieval history, archaeology,
art and architecture, and will be
delivered by scholars specialising in the
period. The lectures will be published
individually and in compilation form.

Barryscourt Lectures II
THE IMPACT OF THE ANGLO-
NORMANS ON MUNSTER
AF O'Brien

Published by the Barryscourt Trust
in association with Cork County Council
and Gandon Editions, Kinsale.

ISBN 0946641 838

Publication sponsored by:

• Dept of Arts, Heritage,
  Gaeltacht and the Islands
• Cork County Council

Series Editor   Noel Jameson
Design   John O'Regan
                  (© Gandon, 1997)
Production   Nicola Dearey, Gandon
Printing   Betaprint, Dublin
Distribution   Gandon, Kinsale

THE BARRYSCOURT TRUST
Barryscourt Castle
Carrigtwohill, Co Cork

THE IMPACT OF THE
ANGLO-NORMANS ON MUNSTER

Inchiquin Castle
near Youghal, Co Cork

The Impact
of the Anglo-Normans
on Munster

AF O'Brien

THE BARRYSCOURT TRUST
IN ASSOCIATION WITH CORK COUNTY COUNCIL AND GANDON EDITIONS

Prelude to Invasion

The Anglo-Norman invasion of Ireland in the late 12th century must be seen as part of a wider movement of western European colonial expansion. The invasion, conquest and settlement of much of Ireland in the late 12th and early 13th centuries, therefore, was part of a general movement of expansion and colonisation extending from the core areas of western Europe to the European periphery, which, by that time, included Ireland. A vibrant feudal socio-economic system was at the heart of this development. Accordingly, the western European feudal aristocracy, which inspired the movement, imposed the stamp of their own political and socio-economic organisation on the conquered lands. Thus, this movement of expansion and colonisation had the effect of integrating the newly conquered lands with the old, the core areas of western Europe.[1]

Moreover, the Anglo-Norman (or English) invasion and colonisation of much of Ireland from the late 12th century onwards was in many respects similar to, for example, the contemporary German penetration of the Slav regions of central and eastern Europe.[2] Both processes of colonisation were prompted by similar expansionary impulses and were underpinned by similar notions of cultural and racial superiority. Furthermore, both reflected the contemporary spirit of militant Christianity which produced, by the late 11th century, the crusading ideal. That ideal, it must be remembered, was by no means confined to the waging of war against Islam, whether in the middle east or Islamic Spain. It could be, and in fact was, directed against all perceived enemies of western or Latin Christianity. In this connection, it should be said that the term 'enemy' could be interpreted widely so as to include Christians whose practices and mores were at variance with those prescribed by the norms of contemporary Latin or western Christianity.

By the 12th century, Christianity as practised in Ireland was archaic by the standards of contemporary western Europe. Indeed, in important respects its norms were utterly aberrant from the new western European orthodoxy. This was particularly so in the matter of ecclesiastical organisation and in regard to marital and sexual mores. Although the differences between church organisation and structure in Ireland and that which obtained in the western European core had been narrowed to some degree by a series of church councils held in Ireland in the course of the 12th century, important structural differences remained, notably in the matter of the role of the episcopate. Moreover, from the contemporary papal point of view and that of ecclesiastical reformers within and without Ireland the church in Ireland continued to be subject to control by the secular power to an unacceptable degree. Likewise, Irish marriage law was attacked by church reformers. As the western church came to control and regulate marriage in the course of the 12th century, 'Celtic marriage law was regarded as thoroughly disreputable ... Thus, it is not surprising that it should be in the matter of sex and marriage and within the circle of ecclesiastical reformers that we can detect the earliest signs of the approach of a new and hostile attitude to Celtic peoples.'[3] Accordingly, Irish sexual mores and marriage laws increasingly came to be regarded as 'scandalous'. Thus, the aberrant situation in Ireland was not only criticised by native reformers but was used as a pretext for invasion by the Anglo-Normans.[4] Accordingly, the crusading ideal was invoked as a pretext for the invasion. Indeed, in 1154-55, Henry II had been granted a papal bull, *Laudabiliter* authorising him to invade Ireland in order to reform the church. At that time, Henry II did not proceed further in the matter, but, on coming to Ireland in the aftermath of the invasion, he convened the Synod of Cashel (1172) 'to undertake the reformation of the Irish church along English lines and in compliance with the papal mandate *Laudabiliter*, which had called upon Henry and his lieges to extirpate the "filthy abominations" and "enormous vices" of the Irish'.[5] Thus, from the outset, the principle of the crusade had been invoked by the invader. While pointing to the aberrant ecclesiastical and moral situation in Ireland, and in justifying invasion by invoking the principle of holy war and crusade, however, the invader, clerical or lay,

'...made a neat elision. For, while twelfth-century Anglo-Norman incursions into Ireland were motivated, in the words of a contemporary source, by the desire for "land or pence, horses, armour or chargers, gold and silver ... soil or sod", the invaders were able to claim "some show of religion" by portraying the Irish, in the words of St Bernard, as "Christians only in name, pagans in fact".'[6]

The consequences for the Irish were dire. Thus,

'...although Christianity was ancient in Ireland, the history of the country in the twelfth and thirteenth centuries seems to be marked by processes very similar to those that were taking place in the areas of northern and eastern Europe being incorporated into Latin Christendom at that same time. The incursion of a feudal cavalry elite, the immigration of peasant settlers, the formation of chartered towns, the introduction of a more widely diffused documentary literacy and coinage – all those aspects of Irish history can be paralleled in other areas experiencing the expansionary wave of the High Middle Ages. A colonial settlement in Munster would have a strong resemblance to one in Brandenburg. Ireland ... [was] subject to many of the same processes of conquest, colonisation and cultural and institutional transformation as eastern Europe or Spain.'[7]

Clearly, this passage raises several points which require amplification and explication, and this will be done, directly or indirectly, in the course of the present lecture. There is, however, one further matter which should be addressed immediately, because it throws further light not only on some of the issues raised so far, but also on the crucial question of the making of an English colonial attitude, an attitude which was central to the whole thrust of invasion, conquest and domination.

In England, by the 12th century, Ireland and the other Celtic countries 'were perceived as poor and primitive societies – primitive in that they had failed to climb the ladder of evolution of human societies which twelfth-century intellectuals like Gerald [de Barri or Gerald of Wales] took for granted. By contrast the English saw themselves as prosperous, peaceful, law-abiding, urbanised and enterprising.'[8] These attitudes reflected the thinking of another 12th-century commentator, William of Malmesbury, whose system of classification of peoples 'divided men and women into the civilised and the barbarians' on the basis of the level of their socio-economic development. What this amounted to was nothing less than 'the creation of an imperialist culture'.[9] By the time of the Anglo-Norman or English[10] invasion of Ireland, ideas such as these were well established and current. Accordingly, Irish society was condemned as 'economically underdeveloped and indeed culpably backward. [Its] agriculture was primitive and pastoral; town life, trade and money were more or less absent; forms of economic exploitation and exchange were primitive.' Moreover, 'defects of character were the obvious explanation for economic backwardness.' Furthermore, Irish society, since, unlike contemporary England, it lacked a centralised political authority, was 'politically immature'. Finally, 'the social customs and moral, sexual and marital habits' of Irish society showed that at best it was at 'an early stage of social evolution ... at worst that "this barbarous nation" was "Christian only in name" and was ... in fact pagan.'[11]

Such ideas could be deployed to advantage in the process of conquest and colonisation. Thus, the characterisation of the invasion and conquest of Ireland 'as the struggle of "civilization" with "barbarism" ... was immensely satisfying to advocates of the dominant life-style, who thereby assured themselves of their own superiority and of the desirability of the conquest or conversion of their rivals'.[12]

These ideas are strongly reflected in the writings of Gerald of Wales. His commentaries on the condition of Ireland at the time of the invasion and on the early course of that invasion are particularly important, not least because of the fact that he was 'a member of one of the leading families involved in the venture [and] could draw on the memories of his uncles and cousins who had been battling in Ireland for twenty years'.[13] His uncle, Robert fitz Stephen, had led the first party of invaders who landed at Bannow Strand, county Wexford, on 1st May 1169, and, as we shall see, together with Miles de Cogan, was enfeoffed by Henry II of the whole demesne of Desmond, essentially the Mac Carthy kingdom of Cork, while Gerald's brother, Robert de Barri, who also had landed at Bannow, was the first of the Barry family in Ireland.

Gerald joined the entourage of Henry II in 1184, and came to

Ireland with Henry's son, the future King John, in 1185, and he made a third visit in 1199. 'The result of his literary work during 1185 and the following two or three years was his first account of Ireland and its early history, his *History* or *Topography of Ireland*.' Again, 'within twenty years of the coming of the Anglo-Normans to Ireland in 1169 Gerald of Wales had composed his Conquest of Ireland (*Expugnatio Hibernica*).'

Gerald's writings reflect both the militaristic, entrepreneurial attitudes of the class to which he belonged – the feudal military aristocracy – and the disparaging, dismissive, even racist attitude to the Irish to be found in contemporary England.

'Gerald saw the native Irish as typical barbarians, whose life, lived so close to nature, promoted vigour, hardiness and courage but denied them the "arts" of civilization. Drawing upon classical ideas about the progress of civilization, he speculated as to the causes of their poverty and backwardness. Unlike most peoples who progressed from pastoralism to agriculture to urban life, the Irish had remained wedded to the pastoral pursuits of their ancestors. This accounted for their sloth and poverty... The seclusion of Ireland from the benevolent influence of more advanced societies left them hopelessly and helplessly wrapped in the cocoon of their antiquated and limited way of life.'[14]

These attitudes served to engender a sense of mission on the part of English colonists in later medieval Ireland. Moreover, it is not without significance that these same arguments were made by the English conquerors and colonisers of Ireland in the later 16th and early 17th centuries and that, in that context, the works of Gerald of Wales were consulted and his arguments and assertions reiterated.[15]

Irish society, a traditional kindred based society, was politically and economically inferior to feudal society, with its intensive arable farming based on manorial organisation, which English society had become long before the invasion of Ireland. Moreover, Irish economic inferiority had important military consequences also and English superiority in arms was clearly demonstrated as the invasion and conquest of Ireland progressed. Thus, 'the use of mailed soldiers was itself an indication of socio-economic development... We have here an unequal struggle between an industrially advanced power and a pastoral economy.'[16]

———

The Anglo-Norman Invasion:
The Domination of Munster

As is well known, the proximate cause of invasion was the conflict which developed in the mid-12th century between Diarmait Mac Murchada, king of Leinster, and Tigernán Ua Ruairc, king of Bréifne, primarily for supremacy over the declining kingdom of Meath. In fact, given the robust, vibrant and expansionist nature of Anglo-Norman society with a ruling aristocracy whose ethic was military, people totally committed to warfare, an invasion of Ireland was quite likely at some stage. Indeed, as we have seen, Henry II himself had considered undertaking such a venture in 1154-5 and to that end had sought and obtained papal blessing thereby raising his projected invasion to the status of crusade or holy war. In the event, the invasion when it came was remarkably successful from the outset because of both massive Anglo-Norman military superiority, as far as technology and tactics were concerned, and competing interests and rivalries between Irish kings.

With regard to the Anglo-Norman conquest of almost all of Munster in the space of thirty years or so, therefore, three elements are particularly striking. First, there is the matter of the contribution made by political rivalries between Irish kings and contention within ruling Irish dynasties to Anglo-Norman success. In many cases these rivalries antedate the invasion. A striking example of this was the continuing struggle between the Mac Carthys and the O'Briens for domination of Munster, a struggle which often involved the high king, Ruaidrí Ua Conchobair especially, who had his own political objectives. Second, the sheer military prowess and superiority of the Anglo-Normans, made a major contribution to their success, although, as we shall see, that did not always guarantee victory. Finally, a major element in the situation was the way in which, certainly within two or three decades of the first invasion, many of the original invaders or their descendants were marginalised by the English crown in favour of other interests, often courtiers or persons close to the English king who were in receipt of a flow of patronage.

The story of the conquest itself is rather complicated, and for that reason, for present purposes, as far as possible should be reduced to essentials. My starting point in Munster is the city of Waterford itself and the western part of the present county Waterford. On his arrival in Ireland in October 1171, Henry II, for several reasons, not the least of which was his desire to curb Strongbow's power, detached from his lordship of Leinster the town of Wexford and the cities of Dublin and Waterford (in the autumn of 1170, Waterford was captured by Richard fitz Gilbert de Clare, Strongbow, and Raymond le Gros) and retained them for himself.[17] In 1173 Strongbow embarked on an attack on Munster. 'The Normans plundered Lismore, and defeating both an Ostmen fleet from Cork and [Diarmait Mac Carthaig, king of Desmond] brought back a considerable prey to Waterford.'[18] Early in 1174, under Hervey de Montmorency, 'the attack on Munster was resumed, only to meet with complete defeat near Thurles. Strongbow retreated to Waterford, and, according to Giraldus [Gerald de Barri] "all the people of Ireland with one consent rose against the English".'[19] Further territorial arrangements affecting Waterford were made by Henry II at the council of Oxford in 1177. 'Ossory was separated from [Strongbow's lordship of] Leinster and attached to the royal demesne lands of Waterford, now defined as extending to the Blackwater beyond Lismore and given into the custody of Robert le Poer.'[20] In the course of the Anglo-Norman settlement, 'a large part of the [present] county [Waterford] was reserved to the royal demesne in the form of the honor of Dungarvan (comprising six of the eight cantreds and corresponding roughly to the modern baronies of Decies).'[21] By the so-called treaty of Windsor between Henry II and the high king of Ireland, Ruaidrí Ua Conchobair, in 1175 this region was included in the lands reserved to the English.[22] In the period 1177 to 1182 – the years immediately following the council of Oxford – the Anglo-Normans, under William fitz Audelm, appear to have consolidated 'the occupation of [county] Waterford though we hear nothing of the process'.[23] By the 1180s, not only were the city of Waterford and the territories immediately adjacent to it firmly under Anglo-Norman control, but also the colony was in process of expansion in that region. These developments were further promoted by King John on his arrival in Ireland in 1185. Thus, 'in the march between Leinster, the heartland of the lordship, and the Irish kingdom of Desmond lay what is nowadays Co Waterford; and one of John's first actions was to build castles in the area to protect this vital march.'[24] By the closing decade or so of the 12th century, there is clear evidence of a continuing penetration by the Anglo-Normans of the territories comprising the western part of the present county Waterford. Thus,

'...in 1204, the province of Dungarvan, as it was called, amounting in all to one cantred[25] was granted to King John, by Domhnall Ó Faoláin, apparently as part of the continuing political settlement of the region. This grant was followed immediately by consequential grants of land in the area, including one of five burgages at Dungarvan, made in September 1205, to the priory of Conall (near Newbridge, County Kildare) and the Augustinian canons of Llanthony. This grant is particularly revealing for the reference to burgage tenements would suggest that the borough or town of Dungarvan had been founded some time about 1205 at latest; it is a reasonable surmise that it was founded shortly after the transfer of the territory of Dungarvan to the [English] crown, that is to say about 1204-5. Once founded, however, the English crown seems to have made determined attempts to promote the fortunes of its new borough. This included, notably, the grant, made by King John on 3 July 1215 to his burgesses of Dungarvan, of all the liberties and free customs of Breteuil,[26] the small Norman town whose liberties and customs became the model for so many of the smaller boroughs in England ... and in Ireland in the thirteenth century.'[27]

The developing colony in county Waterford was further secured by John's programme of castle building, to which reference has already been made, and by other action taken by him. Thus,

'...north of Waterford lay what is now co. Tipperary and again to provide security here for the borders of Leinster and to reduce Leinster's vulnerability to attack from Munster, he granted vast estates in the area to his trusted vassals, among them William de Burgh, ancestor of the famous Burke family, and Theobald Walter, ancestor of the Butlers ... what [John] was doing here was providing a buffer-zone between the English settlers in Leinster and the native kings of Munster.'[28]

The situation regarding both the O'Brien kingdom of Thomond, corresponding broadly to the present counties Clare, Limerick, and Tipperary and the Mac Carthy kingdom of Desmond, roughly the present county Cork, must now be examined.

Our starting point here is the submission made by both Diarmait Mac Carthaig, king of Desmond, and Domnal Ua Briain, king of Thomond, to Henry II shortly after his arrival in Ireland in October 1171. Mac Carthaig, we are told by Gerald de Barri, came to King Henry at Waterford and

'...was drawn forthwith into a firm alliance with Henry by the bond of homage, the oath of fealty, and the giving of hostages; an annual tribute was assessed on his kingdom and he voluntarily submitted to the authority of the king of England. The king moved his army from there [Waterford] and went first of all to Lismore, where he stayed for two days, and from there continued to Cashel. There, on the next day, Domnall king of Limerick met him by the river Suir. He obtained the privilege of the king's peace, tribute was assessed on his kingdom in the same way as on Diarmait's, and he too displayed his loyalty to the king by entering into the very strongest bonds of submission.'[29]

After Henry II's departure from Ireland in 1172, 'the submissions of the Irish [kings] still had to be translated into fact, though the agreement of the kings of Desmond and Thomond had enabled Henry to put garrisons in Cork and Limerick.'[30]

The political situation in Ireland in the 1170s and 1180s was chronically unstable. Thus, 'several of the Irish province-kings had willingly submitted to Henry II when he came to Ireland in 1171. They did so for a variety of reasons, but partly at least because they believed that he would act as their protector against the aggression of the English barons. In the interval between 1171 and 1185 the Irish had become all the more aware of the need to find themselves a protector, because the expansion of the colony was proceeding apace and their status was being rapidly undermined.'[31]

Anglo-Norman pressure on Desmond intensified in 1176,[32] despite the provisions of the treaty of Windsor of 1175. 'It is fairly clear what Henry II wanted out of the treaty with [Ruaidrí] Ua Conchobair. He sought to safeguard whatever gains had already been made in Ireland.' By the terms of the treaty, Ua Conchobair was obliged 'not [to] meddle with those lands which the lord king has retained in his lordship and in the lordship of his barons'. 'Those lands were Meath, Dublin, Wexford and all Leinster, and that part of Munster from Waterford to Dungarvan.' The rest of Ireland would be subject to Ua Conchobair as high king of Ireland.[33] Nonetheless, notwithstanding the provisions of the treaty, Anglo-Norman expansion continued beyond the designated English colonial area, the invasion of Ua Briain's kingdom of Thomond was but one example of this, indicating that, however acceptable to Henry II the treaty with Ua Conchobair may have been, it made no appeal to Anglo-Norman military adventurers intent on carving out lordships for themselves. Indeed, as events were to show, the significance of the treaty, as a key element in English royal policy towards Irish rulers, quite quickly diminished. Accordingly, at the council of Oxford in 1177, Henry II made speculative grants of the kingdoms of Cork and Limerick.[34] Thus,

'...Cork from the Blackwater to Brandon Head in Kerry [was granted] to Robert fitz Stephen and Miles de Cogan, who were to hold it between them by the service of sixty knights,[35] and Limerick to three courtiers, none of whom had any previous connection with Ireland, and who surrendered the grant later in the year on the grounds that the land had still to be conquered[36] when it was granted to Philip de Braose ... The grant of Limerick led to no immediate occupation, for when de Braose, accompanied by fitz Stephen and de Cogan, advanced on the town the [Ostmen] citizens set fire to it, and de Braose decided to abandon all attempt at conquest...

But though Limerick was left for the time being, Cork was successfully occupied, the Normans being assisted by [Muirchertach Ua Briain, son of Domnall Mór Ua Briain, king of Thomond]. The city itself was already held by a Norman governor, Richard of London (it had been expressly reserved to the king at Oxford, but there seems to be no evidence as to how or when it had been occupied), and the Normans thus had a secure base from which to operate. They seem to have come to an agreement with [Diarmait Mac Carthaig] after a conflict of which we have no details, and obtained seven cantreds, which they divided by lot, while ... the remaining twenty-four cantreds of the kingdom [of Desmond], evidently left in [Mac Carthaig's] possession, were to pay a tribute which was to be divided between them, while they acted jointly as the king's representatives in his city of Cork and its cantred; Fitz Stephen took the area east of the city, where consider-able progress seems to have been made with Norman settlement in the next few years; de Cogan had the cantreds west of it, but we have little evidence as to the occupation of this area. The twenty-four cantreds [which had been left to Mac Carthaig] of course included south Kerry ... De Cogan himself was assassinated in 1182, and a general rising of the Irish under [Diarmait Mac Carthaig] followed, but fitz Stephen, who was besieged in Cork, was relieved by Raymond le Gros, and the position was restored.'

Thus, in the period immediately following Henry II's council of Oxford in 1177 when Henry dropped 'all pretence of abiding by the Treaty of

Windsor' and 'took the cities of Cork and Limerick into his own hands',[37] the Anglo-Normans made massive incursions into Munster occupying not only much of the Mac Carthy kingdom of Desmond, but also significantly penetrating the O'Brien kingdom of Thomond and establishing control over much of the present county Tipperary. Plainly, conquest on this scale in such a short period of time testifies strongly to the superior military organisation of the Anglo-Normans, and to the outstanding military technology and tactics which they deployed. That military supremacy, however, was reinforced by other factors, notably the political tensions existing between rival Irish kings. Thus, the policies and attitudes of Irish kings, pursuing their own competing interests, also made a marked contribution to Anglo-Norman success. Irish kings were quite capable of enlisting Anglo-Norman support.[38] Some examples of this, particularly germane to our consideration of the political situation in Munster in the 1170s and 1180s, will illustrate this point.

In 1170, in resisting Ruaidrí Ua Conchobair's disposition of the province of Munster whereby it had been divided into two kingdoms, the O'Brien kingdom of Thomond and the Mac Carthy kingdom of Desmond, Domnall Ua Briain, who was Diarmait Mac Murchada's son-in-law, seized upon Ruaidrí's failure to recapture Dublin from the Anglo-Normans and 'sought and readily obtained the assistance of some of his father-in-law's foreign allies'. In the event, 'the temporary assistance of the foreigners was of little avail to Domnall, but the foreigners themselves had learned the way to Limerick, and had learned, moreover, that they could go with a small expeditionary force across Ireland and return in safety.'[39] Again, it has been argued that after the Treaty of Windsor, Ruaidrí Ua Conchobair's attitude to the Anglo-Normans changed, 'for he invited the Normans to join him in an expedition against Donnell O'Brien of Thomond: Limerick was taken about the time the treaty was being drawn up and a Norman garrison placed in the town.'[40]

The city of Limerick was subsequently lost by the Anglo-Normans, but by 1195[41] 'the Normans were in occupation in the city of Limerick, apparently with the consent of the O'Briens, and, probably in 1197, John gave the city a charter granting it all the liberties of Dublin. At the same time he granted Hamo de Valognes [land in Co Limerick]. The sons of Maurice fitz Gerald all had grants in the county, as had William de Burgo... By the end of the [12th] century, the Norman occupation of Munster was well on the way to consolidation, for in north Tipperary (the medieval county of Tipperary represents the eastern half of the former kingdom of Limerick[42]) we find Theobald Walter active around Nenagh.' Any significant advance into Thomond had been frustrated by Domnall Mór Ua Briain. 'His death in 1194 and the return of Philip of Worcester in the following year added impetus to the efforts of William de Burgo to colonise south Tipperary. The effective and widespread colonisation in those parts by the closing years of the century gave Theobald [Walter] a solid Norman backing to his frontier lands in Ely [O'Carroll] and Ormond.'[43] The late 12th century, therefore, saw significant Anglo-Norman advances in Thomond. Thus,

'...the dominant figure in the early part of [this renewed] movement [of expansion] was William de Burgh, to whom John granted lands in south Tipperary and the east of modern County Limerick at the time of his 1185 expedition. Other magnates, notably Theobald Walter, Philip of Worcester, and Hamo de Valognes ... were also active in the area. For Anglo-Norman expansion, Donal's death in 1194 was crucial. He left three sons who ... often competed with one another for control of Thomond; they were also involved in constant disputes and alliances with the O'Connors of Connacht to the north and the Mac Carthys of Desmond to the south. William de Burgh in particular benefited from these conditions. He had married one of Donal's daughters, thus insinuating himself into Thomond politics, and was in an excellent position to lend support – at a price – to one or other, or all, of his brothers-in-law. His power was also increased by a period spent in charge of the city of Limerick. By the turn of the century much of County Limerick had been granted by John to William de Burgh, Hamo de Valognes and other lords; and the O'Briens had little alternative but to acquiesce in the endowment of men on whom they were frequently dependent.'[44]

By the late 12th century, therefore, 'the newcomers had ... absorbed much of O'Brien's kingdom of Thomond, and had removed eastern Cork from Mac Carthy's control.'[45] Having forced Diarmait Mac Carthaig to surrender to them seven cantreds of his kingdom of Desmond, it now fell to Robert fitz Stephen and Miles de Cogan to parcel them out among their military followers, their vassals, by a process called sub-infeudation. 'It is not possible to give a full account of the early sub-infeudation of the "kingdom of Cork", or even to be sure how far it was carried in the lifetime of the original grantees.'[46] We know that fitz Stephen

'...besides making large grants out of the three cantreds to the east of Cork [city] originally ... allotted to him ... made what we may call "speculative grants" of lands far removed from the cantreds. Thus, by his charter to Philip de Barry he granted not only Olethan [Uí Liatháin], but also two other cantreds, to be determined by lot. What these two cantreds were ultimately decided to be, we know from John's confirmatory charter to William de Barry, Philip's son, made in 1207. They were "Muscherie Dunegan" [Muscraige Donnagain] and [Killeedy], of which the former is roughly represented by the barony of Orrery and Kilmore [including small adjacent parts of the baronies of Duhallow and Fermoy], County Cork, and the latter was comprised in the barony of Glenquin, County Limerick.'[47]

Elsewhere in east Cork Anglo-Norman settlement continued.

Thus, 'to Alexander, son of Maurice Fitz Gerald, Fitz Stephen seems to have made a grant of Imokilly, which was the origin of the Fitz Gerald property there.'[48] The name Imokilly is an anglicisation of Uí Meic Caille. 'The territory of Imokilly, sometimes referred to as Oglassyn, consisted of the southern portion of the Uí Liatháin territory. The lands which it comprised included Inchiquin, Clonpriest, Killeagh and Kilcredan. At the time of the Anglo-Norman invasion of Munster, the territory was ruled by the family of Ó Mic Thíre, described in the annals as kings of Uí Meic Caille or of Uí Glaisín. These two were not entirely synonymous, and the former name of the territory was derived from an earlier ruling family – the Uí Meic Caille – whom the Uí Meic Thíre had superseded as kings.'[49] In fitz Stephen's time, other landholders in Imokilly were Raymund Mangunel, who held Cahirultan in the parish of Ballyoughtera, and Robert and Thomas des Auters or de Altaribus while Alexander and Raymond fitz Hugh were established in Fermoy.[50] It is possible that fitz Stephen's castle 'was at, or was proposed to be built at, Castlemartyr'. He seems to have given Castlemartyr to the des Autirs (de Altaribus later Sawters) brothers, but he may have retained the site of the castle. 'Early in the 13th century, Castlemartyr was acquired from the des Autirs brothers by Richard de Carew, apparently the first of the Carews who were heirs to Fitz Stephen's seigniory of half of the kingdom of Cork.'[51]

We know rather less about de Cogan's lands. 'As to the four cantreds assigned to Miles de Cogan on the western side of Cork we have no direct information, but they perhaps included the barony of Muskerry and a broad strip along the coast between the harbours of Cork and Glandore. In 1207 King John made large grants within these districts to Richard de Cogan, Philip de Prendergast and Robert Fitz Martin, to hold of the king in fee. Also a grant [was made] to David de Rupe [Roche] of the cantred of Rosselither (Rosscarbery).'[52] The lands given to Philip de Prendergast were 'in the district between Cork and Innishannon, where the important manor of "Beuver" (Beauvoir) or Carrigaline was afterwards formed', while Richard de Cogan received lands in Muskerry 'where his descendants long held the manors of Dundrinan and Carrigrohane More'.[53] Other names in this region which can be mentioned are Philip de Barry, who held the borough of Innishannon, where both a market and fair existed certainly by 1256 but probably earlier,[54] and the de Courcys who appear to have begun the settlement at Kinsale. Here, in the early thirteenth century, they built 'strongholds at Ringrone opposite Kinsale, and at Oldernass or the Old Head of Kinsale'.[55] The growth and development of the town 'occurred in the course of the thirteenth century'.[56]

Subsequently, 'a number of castles were placed along the south coast of County Cork at important natural harbours or inlets,' notably between Bantry Bay and Dunmanus Bay, at Baltimore, or Ringarogy Island, in the neighbourhood of Glandore, and at Timoleague and Dundeady (or Galley Head).[57] Further advances in Desmond were made by the English in the period 1206 to 1215.[58] The death of Domnall Mac Carthaig in 1206 gave rise to a struggle between his sons for the succession. In these circumstances, 'an attempt was now made by the English to gain control over the whole of Desmond.' The conditions which now obtained favoured the English. 'As usual the invaders supported one Irish claimant against the other.' With Irish support, the English succeeded in penetrating further into Desmond. By 1215 we have record of at least the beginning of a programme of castle-building in Desmond. 'A string of castles was built along the valley of the river Maine in Kerry ... and the line was completed to the sea by a castle at Killorglin near the mouth of the river Laune. This was the line which for centuries separated Kerry proper from Desmond, and the castles were evidently intended to protect the settlement in Kerry ... from attacks of the Irish of Desmond. These castles seem to have been erected by John and Maurice ... grandsons of the first Maurice Fitz Gerald, whom we soon find as the principal landowners in Kerry.' About 1215 they also built another castle 'at Dunlo to the west of the lower lake of Killarney'. In addition, 'another group ... was erected by [Robert de] Carew about the head of the estuary of Kenmare, and he also erected another castle at Dunnamark near Bantry.' Dunnamark, however, was burned by the Irish in 1260 in the course of their recovery of lost territories.[59]

Conquest and settlement on this scale, of course, precipitated large-scale movements of people and resettlement of population. Not only was there an inward movement of people, immigration by new Anglo-Norman rulers and settlers, but also a significant displacement of the existing Irish population. This latter movement, however, could be quite complex because it could be brought about as much by rivalry and contention between different Irish kindred groups as by Anglo-Norman conquest. Pressure by the Anglo-Normans, however, complicated and exacerbated relations between different Irish kindred groups. Some instances of this kind of induced population movement have been noticed by Orpen.[60] Thus,

'...the O'Mahonys would ... appear to have been supreme in Kinalea and Kinalmeaky until extruded by the Prendergasts and Cogans, but even before the coming of the Normans the clan is said to have extended westward up the Bandon River to West Carbery, where they wrested some lands from the O'Driscolls, O'Cowhigs, and others ... the O'Mahonys were eventually subjected to a branch of the Mac Carthys, and confined by them to the district between Bantry Bay and ... Roaring Water [Bay].

In 1178 and subsequently the O'Briens expelled the O'Donovans from Croom and Bruree in the valley of the Maigue, and other Eoghanacht septs from different parts of County Limerick, and their expulsion paved the way for the Geraldine settlement there. The O'Donovans fled southward across Mangerton and settled in the northern parts of Carbery, where Castledonovan preserves their name and marks their principal centre. The O'Driscolls and their kinsmen, thus pressed by the O'Donovans and the O'Mahonys on the north-west, and afterwards by the Normans on the east, were eventually confined to the district between Ivahagh and Castlehaven, only a comparatively small portion of their ancient tribe-land, which is said to have been at one time coterminous with the diocese of Ross.

To the forward movement of the Anglo-Normans through southern Tipperary in 1192 may presumably be ascribed the expulsion of the O'Sullivans from the valley of the Suir about Clonmel and Caher. They subdued the earlier occupants [O'Sheas, O'Moriartys, O'Connells, and others] of two of the great peninsulas in Kerry and Cork, and became divided into two main branches. O'Sullivan Mór held sway over a large district between Dingle Bay and Kenmare River, and O'Sullivan Bere eventually occupied most of the peninsula between Kenmare River and Bantry Bay. Similarly the O'Keefes of Fermoy, who settled in Duhallow, were presumably driven out of their former seat by the Roches, who seem to have been settled in Fermoy before the close of the twelfth century.'

Thus, by the early 13th century, within fifty years of their invasion of Ireland, the Anglo-Normans controlled much of the province of Munster and, indeed, large parts of Leinster and virtually all of eastern Ulster. Only Connacht remained outside their grasp and quite soon that was to be threatened also. These conquests were followed by substantial settlement, both urban and agrarian, by the invader. Thus, 'the late twelfth and earlier thirteenth centuries saw the formal distribution and practical occupation of the Irish land that was being won by the military energies and political skills of the Anglo-Norman invaders.'[61] At this juncture, the broad pattern of settlement and change, as far as the province of Munster is concerned, should be examined.

Town walls, Youghal, Co Cork

The First Munster Plantation:
Settlement and Socio-Economic Change and Development

While the conquered areas came under new political management (and that in itself was sufficiently important to make the Anglo-Norman conquest and settlement one of the formative developments in Irish history, indeed the formative development in the modern era), the impact of the invasion was far greater than that. The conquest and settlement struck very deep roots indeed, for it brought about marked socio-economic change also. That observation, of course, is intended to set the conquest and settlement in context; it is not intended to diminish in any way its political significance. It would be hard to exaggerate the political consequences, in the context of Irish history as a whole, of the events of the late 12th and early 13th centuries. As Empey has pointed out, 'in spite of everything – the Gaelic recovery, economic decline, the virtual collapse of royal authority – the fact remains that Ireland would never again be Gaelic in the sense that it had been before 1169.'[62]

Plainly, therefore, the Anglo-Norman conquest of much of Ireland was a development of the greatest magnitude. The invasion, moreover, profoundly affected not only the politics and racial composition but also the economy of medieval Ireland.[63] While some of the changes which occurred in the 12th and 13th centuries were due to causes other than the invasion, not the least of which was the demographic revolution and burgeoning economic growth which Europe as a whole witnessed in this period, there is no doubt that the invasion and settlement, quite apart from its political consequences, brought pronounced social and economic innovation. This included the introduction into Ireland of the feudal socio-economic system. Part of this process was the establishment of the manorial economy in the conquered areas. Thus, an inflow of settlers increased the population of Ireland way beyond any level which could have occurred by way of natural increase, undermined finally in the conquered and planted areas the traditional bonds of kindred society, and contributed greatly to the considerable growth which 13th-century Ireland witnessed. An increased population also made available to lords the labour services necessary to sustain the labour-intensive, arable farming, manorial economy. These were the conditions which underpinned the vast economic growth of the 13th century. Canon Empey's description of the social composition of later medieval Knocktopher, county Kilkenny,[64] is particularly informative in this regard, since that situation, in all essentials, was replicated in other parts of the English lordship of Ireland where colonisation and settlement were most intense, giving, in his memorable phrase, 'demographic depth to the colony'. Thus,

'...that the knights played a vital military role, supplied leadership, constructed mottes, is not open to question, but to the extent that they formed a numerically small aristocracy they can hardly be regarded as typical of the large number of immigrants who manned the manors, villages, and towns that sprang up in the wake of the conquest. In the cantred of Knocktopher not more than eight men would have ranked among the knights, including the lord of the manor himself. Far more representative of the colonial population would be the small free tenant holding a few acres at most, or the poor burgess holding on average about six acres of land. Naturally the arrival of such humble folk remained unsung. All we know for certain is that numerous manorial extents from about 1275 onwards testify to the presence of a frequently dense settlement of these poorer settlers. Let us look at the evidence of the Knocktopher extent. In 1312 ... the proportion of small free tenants to tenants holding 60 acres and upwards is about 3:1. In fact there was almost certainly a sizeable number of cottiers and gavelers occupying the lowest rung of the immigrant population, but they are not mentioned in this particular extent... The cottiers seem to have occupied the lowest rung of the social ladder: they inhabited hovels ... standing on a plot of less than an acre. They owed labour services on the manor, and they must have depended upon seasonal employment on the demesnes to supplement whatever they could wring from their wretched plots. Such people can only have been recruited from a surplus, landless proletariate in England and Wales. Starvation drove them from England; near starvation attracted them to marginally better conditions on the Irish frontier. Yet, together with the burgesses [the inhabitants of the newly founded or promoted boroughs], small immigrants of this type were vital to the long-term stability and endurance of the settlement, and vital to the survival of its distinctive culture. It gave demographic depth to the colony. Alone the knights would have been submerged by Gaelic culture like the Norse before them.'

Immigration, therefore, was essential for the maintenance of the later medieval English lordship of Ireland which rested on conquest, settlement and colonisation. From his examination of the sources relating to Knocktopher, Empey has concluded that, while there was a certain French or Fleming presence, the majority of the newcomers, or planters, were either English or Welsh. Thus, as he points out,

'...a number of surnames that frequently recur in our sources indicate that the burgess and small tenant population was predominantly English, with a strong Welsh element: Prout, Datoun, Shortal, Harper, Thundyr, White, Grant, Den, Dobyne, Porter, Bath, Long, Ellis, Salter, Robok; and Howel, Howling ... Griffin, Walsh, Rys (Rice). Others, like Power (le Poer), de la Barre, Barret, Roch, Fleming, suggest French or Flemish origins. The strength of the Welsh element in the population is reflected in the dedication of the parish church (St. David's) in Knocktopher. The ethnic structure of the manor population consisted of three classes: a predominantly 'French'[65] knighthood forming a landowning aristocracy; a numerically significant immigrant population composed mainly of poor English and Welsh elements, constituting perhaps 90% of the free population; and the indigenous Irish population, forming perhaps 90% of the unfree population.'[66]

This basic structure appears to have been widespread throughout the colony as can be seen from other studies.

Thus, studies[67] of the manor of Inchiquin in east county Cork, of which the seaport town of Youghal was a major component, likewise indicate heavy migration and settlement, particularly in the late 12th and

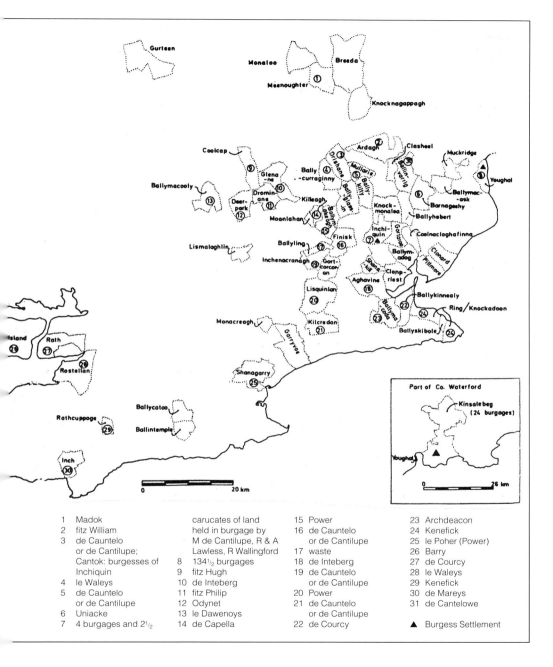

1	Madok		carucates of land	15	Power	23	Archdeacon
2	fitz William		held in burgage by	16	de Cauntelo	24	Kenefick
3	de Cauntelo		M de Cantilupe, R & A		or de Cantilupe	25	le Poher (Power)
	or de Cantilupe;		Lawless, R Wallingford	17	waste	26	Barry
	Cantok: burgesses of	8	134½ burgages	18	de Inteberg	27	de Courcy
	Inchiquin	9	fitz Hugh	19	de Cauntelo	28	le Waleys
4	le Waleys	10	de Inteberg		or de Cantilupe	29	Kenefick
5	de Cauntelo	11	fitz Philip	20	Power	30	de Mareys
	or de Cantilupe	12	Odynet	21	de Cauntelo	31	de Cantelowe
6	Uniacke	13	le Dawenoys		or de Cantilupe		
7	4 burgages and 2½	14	de Capella	22	de Courcy	▲	Burgess Settlement

Manor of Inchiquin
(with key to townlands and their principal free tenants)

early 13th centuries. Among the names of burgesses of Youghal in the 13th and early 14th centuries we find the following: Unak, Madoks, Frend, Mey, White, fitz Robert, Magnoll, Bryt, Lang, Lawles, Gunstall, Taillour, Cotiller, Lydeford, Wace, Adlard, Flemyng, Don, Hore, Masoun, Beaufo, Lerstowe, Porpeys, Everard, Brown, Samson, Fulbourn, Baker, Lyndesay, Olyver, Faunt, Wallen or Wallens and Walsh (plainly relating to Wales), Cosyn, Gent, Deget, Pollard, Paynton, Wynchecombe, Astole, Hanedon, Gannow, Byng, Crok, Wyppell, Gannow, Davy, Enyas, Blak, Keyr, Stakepoll, More, Smyth, Harnes, Kerd (described as a carpenter), Helyer, Yong, des Autirs (or Sawters), Ley, Boys, Ryng, Fernok, Crokker, Morwagh (or Morrogh), Parys, England, Danyel, Wanibo, Barred (or Barret), Russell, Rossilly, Newport, Roche, Cordew, Lilly, Smoyll, Haket, and Cristofre.

 With regard to Waterford, in 1304 we find reference to one Jordan of Bristol, citizen of that city.[68] Jordan served as provost of Waterford in 1305.[69] Other mayors of Waterford in the 13th and early 14th centuries were John le Tyler (1294-6), Ralph de Hampton (1296-1300), and Eymar de Godar (1304-5 and 1311). Examples of Waterford burgesses in the same period are Richard de Barry, Adam Botingdon, Servasius Copale, Roger Goldsmith, Robert le Paumer, Gilbert Nest, and Nicholas of Portsmouth.[70] It has been pointed out that in the city of Waterford (as, indeed, in the other major towns of the colony)

'...in practice the city government was oligarchical in nature. In the thirty years between 1280 and 1310 eleven men dominated the main positions within the city government. The same names crop up in a variety of sources as mayor, bailiff, collector of the fifteenth, purveyor, custos of the prisage of wine, and collector of the custom of wool and hides.

 Many of the officeholders were immigrant traders and merchants who rose to high office within a few years. Eymar de Godar referred to in 1295 as a merchant of Gascony is mayor of Waterford by 1305. He was a man of great wealth for in 1306 he acted as pledge for the sheriff of the county who owed a large sum of money to the exchequer. de Godar was again elected mayor in 1311 and previously he held the post of bailiff, custos of the prisage of wine and collector of the custom of wool and hides. Jordan of Bristol, who bought the franchise of the city, was elected bailiff on a number of occasions, collector of the custom of wool and hides, collector of the small custom and purveyor for the king's army. Ralph de Hampton held the office of mayor for four years, between 1296-1300, and was bailiff in 1288. de Hampton was involved with the Ricardi of Lucca the Italian bankers and was also a purveyor. He held lands in the county and was a man of some wealth when he died in 1301.'[71]

A similar immigrant merchant elite governed the city of Cork and manned the offices of local government there under the English crown.

 Some examples of 13th and early 14th-century Cork burgesses and merchants, whose names clearly indicate their immigrant status, are Walter of Gloucester (1217),[72] Bernard de Montibus (1285),[73] William le Ware (1286),[74] Alexander of London (1295),[75] Peter de Parys (1295),[76]

Richard de Hereford (1330),[77] and John Donati (1338).[78]

Later medieval Cork, too, had its urban patriciate, which came into being in the aftermath of the Anglo-Norman conquest. The basic composition of that oligarchy remained unchanged certainly from the 14th century until the revolutionary changes of the late 1640s and early 1650s. Thus, as KW Nicholls has pointed out,

'...a list of the "ancient natives and inhabitants of the citty of Cork", drawn up in 1652, after they had been finally expelled from the city by the New English, contains 253 names; they include 36 Goolds,[79] 28 Roches, 19 Tirrys,[80] 18 Gallweys,[81] 18 Coppingers [82] and 18 Meades or Miaghs (two forms of the same name). The Sarsfields,[83] Morroghs [84] and Mortells [85] each numbered ten.

More than half the freemen of the city at the end of the old order, therefore, belonged to six surnames, an illustration of the degree to which control of the city, its trade and administration at this period was exercised by a "patriciate" of great merchant families.' [86]

All of these had migrated to Cork, directly or indirectly, and most appear to have established their commercial ascendancy there in the course of the 14th or 15th centuries, many if not all of them, presumably, rising from the second rank by means of successful trading ventures to displace merchants and burgesses who had entrenched themselves in the mercantile, social and political life of Cork in the first phase of the colony's development in the late 12th and 13th centuries. Indeed, many of them had migrated to Ireland in the company of many others too numerous to mention here,[87] although reference at least should be made to names such as Bordeaux (Burdeux), Creagh, Droup (Drop), Gayner, Heyne (Heine), Llewellyn (Leboulyn, Lawelen, Lewelyn), Lombard, Mangnel, Pollard, de la Pulle, Reith (Reyth, Reche, Reyht), Skiddy (Skide, Skydy), Stakpoll (Stakepol), Staunton (Stawnton), Tanner (Tannour), Taverner, Taylor (le Taillour, Tailliour), Vincent, Walsh (Walshe, Walsch, le Waleys, Walens),[88] Water or Waters, White, Whitty(Whittey, Wythie, Wythy), and de Wynchedon.[89]

This list, of course, excludes such an important Cork merchant family as the Ronayne (O'Ronayne or Ronan) family for the simple reason that the Ronaynes, while they migrated to Cork and to Youghal and Kinsale, were not immigrants to Ireland. On the contrary, this family was Gaelic Irish in origin, which, by means of a grant of denization secured for them by the earl of Desmond in the late 15th century, 'enjoyed the benefits of English law which permitted them to engage in trade in the king's dominions and to secure their interests in English law'. The Ronaynes went on to acquire 'considerable property in Cork, Kinsale, and Youghal', as a consequence of which activities they 'ranked among the urban patriciate there from the later fifteenth century onwards'.[90]

Thus, although people who were ethnically Irish were to be found within and without later medieval Cork – some like the Ronaynes being in the first rank of Cork merchants and members of the ruling urban oligarchy, while others like Rore Honethan,[91] mariner and merchant, being active in trade on a more modest scale – most merchants and burgesses and almost all the urban patriciate in Cork, Youghal, and Kinsale in the late Middle Ages were in origin immigrants.

As Empey has pointed out,[92]

'...that this immigration occurred was due only indirectly to the conquest, which did no more than create an opportunity for potential settlers. Such people had to exist and exist in considerable numbers. The fact they did exist was due to the quite exceptional economic and demographic factors which prevailed over most of feudal Europe at the particular moment when the Normans launched their assault on Ireland. The timing was coincidental, but it was a coincidence which transformed the whole character of the conquest, and ultimately the composition of the population of this island.'

Individual case studies confirm this assessment. Thus, McEneaney has shown that 'the development of Waterford was further enhanced by population growth in Europe which ensured that enough merchants, traders and craftsmen of continental and English origin could be encouraged to settle in the city. As early as 1212, Waterford had to be enlarged from its original nineteen acres by a further thirty-three. The city paid the second highest farm at the exchequer, and as the farm was originally calculated on house totals, it implies that Waterford had, after Dublin, the greatest density of settlement and probably population in the colony.'[93]

In response to these buoyant economic conditions which brought about a remarkable growth in trade, there was considerable expansion of settlement, both agrarian and urban, in 13th-century Ireland. Particularly important in this connection was a striking urban growth and expansion. Existing towns flourished and expanded, and many new ones were founded. This is particularly so in the case of the seaport towns of Viking origin, but growth was by no means confined to them. Urban growth was accompanied by the development of an extensive network of weekly markets and yearly fairs, which, apart from their local trading significance, acted as points for the distribution and marketing of imported goods and the collection for export of goods produced in their localities. Thus, together with boroughs, markets (some but not all of which were associated with boroughs) and fairs constituted an impressive commercial infrastructure. This, of course, was the situation throughout the English lordship of Ireland, and not just Munster, but some examples from Munster, largely but not exclusively from county Cork, will illustrate these developments.

Most of the markets and fairs were established in the course of the 13th century, very many of them in the first half of that century. Thus, in 1234, markets were established at Youghal, Buttevant and Carrigtwohill, county Cork, and Buttevant also acquired a yearly fair. In 1242, Dungarvan, county Waterford, was given the right to hold a yearly fair, while, by mid-century, Innishannon, county Cork, had both a market and a fair. Examples of yearly fairs established before 1230 are the cities of Limerick and Waterford; Tipperary (1226), Athassel (1224), Clonmel (1225) and Cashel (1228), county Tipperary; and Adare and Knockainy (1226), county Limerick. By 1230, also, weekly markets existed, for example, at Emly (1215), county Tipperary, and Mungret (1225), county Limerick.

By the end of the 13th century, in county Cork alone, at least thirty-seven market towns were known to the English government in Ireland. At that time, they were well within the English lordship of Ireland. These market towns were the city of Cork and the towns of Timoleague, Carrigtwohill, Buttevant, Ballyhay, Midleton, Castlemartyr, Cloyne, Mogeely, Tallow, Corkbeg, Glanworth, Castlelyons, Shandon, Mallow, Bridgetown, Ballynamona, Carrig, Kilworth, Mitchelstown, Ballynoe, Carrigrohane, Ballinacurra, Doneraile, Dunbulloge, Innishannon, Grenagh, Ballyhooly, Kinsale, Ringrone, Ringcurran, Ovens, Castlemore, Ballinaboy, Carrigaline, Douglas, and 'del Fayth', which was located in the bishop's town in the present Barrack Street/Dean Street area of Cork city.

It will be noted that all these markets and fairs were located in the areas most densely settled and heavily manorialised by the Anglo-Normans in the late 12th and 13th centuries. In the case of county Cork, that consisted, for the most part, of the north and east, where the soil was particularly fertile. This was replicated elsewhere. In counties Limerick and Tipperary, for example, 'the manors that emerged should be regarded as sizeable lordships, dependent on the centres such as Nenagh, Dunkerrin, Thurles, Knockgraffon, Castleconnell or Grean, from which they came to take their names.'[94] Manors and boroughs such as these constituted the heartland of the lordship, places where the colony had taken deepest root. Political security and the productivity of the soil had encouraged large-scale settlement based on inward migration by settlers from England and Wales, and, not infrequently, even further afield. This was to be particularly significant for the long-term survival of the colony in the face of the very serious adverse political and economic conditions which set in in the course of the 14th century.[95] In Munster, as indeed in other areas of the colony, the Irish recovery, which was certainly under way early in the second half of the 13th century, 'loosened the colonial hold in the marginal areas that had not been heavily settled'.[96] Where the colony was strongly entrenched, however, it managed to survive, and in this it was aided by objective, political realities. Thus, for example,

'Gaelic Ireland, because of its own weaknesses and rivalries, was never able completely to overrun the colony even when the latter was at its weakest and subject to greatest threat. The position of the colony was further strengthened by the fact that it continued to dispose of certain resources and to enjoy certain advantages. The development of urban life had been one of the great achievements of the colony in the epoch of its foundation in the thirteenth century. However damaged the towns were by the catastrophic events of the fourteenth century [as the colony encountered Irish recovery and the loss of territory and massive economic and political contraction and decline], much of the life they had generated survived. This is particularly true of the major port towns of the region [Munster], Cork, Youghal, Kinsale, [and Waterford and Limerick]. By surviving they were particularly well placed to form bridges between Gaelic and English Ireland, not least by way of trade, and, as the economy in Ireland and in western Europe generally recovered in the later fifteenth century, these towns, as the major maritime trading centres of the region, grew increasingly wealthy and their urban patriciates stronger.'[97]

If the Irish could not overturn the colony, even had they in fact wished to do so, the colonists, the 'English of Ireland', as they called themselves, could not complete the conquest of Ireland or even adequately defend themselves by military means, since they no longer had the requisite financial resources or manpower.[98] In these circumstances, a *modus vivendi* between both ethnic groups evolved, and a symbiotic relationship between the two developed. This served to diminish, if not altogether dissipate, the racial antipathy to the Irish which was endemic in the English colony from the outset.

Henceforward, 'the political interests of both could be accommodated as circumstances warranted and trading relations of all kinds entered into to the mutual advantage of both.'[99] These were the conditions which existed in late-medieval Ireland as a whole, and they were strongly pronounced in the province of Munster. The complete English conquest of Ireland in the late 16th and early 17th centuries brought to completion a programme of conquest begun in the late 12th century, and 'marked in Munster, as indeed in Ireland as a whole, the passing not only of the mixed polity which was so striking a feature of later medieval Ireland, but even of the Gaelic order itself'.[100]

———

The author

AF O'Brien is Statutory Lecturer in History at the National University of Ireland, Cork, and a member of the History Department there. He has lectured widely in Ireland, England, France and Germany, and has published extensively in the field of later medieval Irish history, particularly in regard to the key questions of conquest, settlement, colonisation, and internal and external trade. He is at present working on a number of studies concerning economic activity and Irish overseas trade in the later middle ages. In 1996, he was elected Fellow of the Royal Historical Society, London.

Acknowledgements

I would like to thank the Barryscourt Trust for inviting me to offer this contribution to an understanding of the socio-political context in which the Barrys settled in Ireland and in which Barryscourt came into being. Thanks are due also to Sheila Lane, Director, Archaeological Survey of Co Cork, and her staff, in particular Ursula Egan.

Illustrations

Photographs courtesy of the Archaeological Survey of Co Cork
Map by the author

––––––

Notes and References

[1] For a discussion of these developments, see R Bartlett, *The Making of Europe: Conquest, Colonisation and Cultural Change 950-1350* (London, 1993)

[2] For what follows, see AF O'Brien, 'Ireland: conquest, settlement and colonisation c.1169 to c.1641' in D Ó Ceallaigh (ed.), *New Perspectives on Ireland: Colonisation and Identity* (forthcoming)

[3] J Gillingham, 'The beginnings of English imperialism', *Journal of Historical Sociology*, v (1992), pp392-409: 403-5

[4] *ibid.*

[5] WR Jones, 'England against the Celtic fringe: a study in cultural stereotypes', *Journal of World History*, xiii (1971), pp155-171: 166-7

[6] Bartlett, *The Making of Europe*, pp22-3

[7] *ibid.*, p21

[8] Gillingham, 'English imperialism', p401

[9] *ibid.*, pp 405-6; idem 'The English invasion of Ireland', in B Bradshaw et al (eds.), *Representing Ireland: Literature and the Origins of Conflict 1534-1660* (Cambridge, 1993), pp24-42

[10] For the argument that the term 'English', rather than Norman, Anglo-Norman or Norman-French, is the appropriate one for the invaders of Ireland in the late 12th and 13th centuries, see Gillingham, 'English invasion'.

[11] RR Davies, *Domination and Conquest: the Experience of Ireland, Scotland and Wales 1100-1300* (Cambridge, 1990), pp20-23

[12] Jones, 'England against the Celtic fringe', pp155-6

[13] JJ O'Meara (ed.), *Gerald of Wales: the History and Topography of Ireland* (Harmondsworth, 1982) pp12, 14; Bartlett, *The Making of Europe*, p97

[14] Jones, 'England against the Celtic fringe', p160

[15] For a fuller discussion of these points, see O'Brien, 'Ireland: conquest, settlement and colonisation'

[16] Gillingham, 'English imperialism', pp402-3; see also Bartlett, *The Making of Europe*, pp76-7

[17] S Duffy, *Ireland in the Middle Ages* (Dublin, 1997) p86

[18] AJ Otway-Ruthven, *A History of Medieval Ireland*, (2nd ed., London, 1980) pp54-5

[19] *ibid.*

[20] *ibid.*, p61

[21] CA Empey, 'County Waterford in the thirteenth century', *Decies*, 13 (Jan 1980), pp7-16: 8; see also his 'Anglo-Norman county Waterford, 1200-1300' in W Nolan and TP Power (eds.), *Waterford: History and Society – Interdisciplinary Essays on the History of an Irish County* (Dublin, 1992) pp131-46

[22] Duffy, *Ireland in the Middle Ages*, pp90-91

[23] Otway-Ruthven, *Medieval Ireland*, pp61-3

[24] Duffy, *Ireland in the Middle Ages*, pp99-100

[25] A cantred is described as 'the name applied by the Anglo-Normans (usually when making grants of land) to pre-existing territorial units', the term being later applied to the 'administrative divisions of certain counties' (R Frame, *Colonial Ireland, 1169-1369* (Dublin, 1981) p144). Unlike contemporary German expansion in central and eastern Europe, which in many other respects was similar to Anglo-Norman expansion in Ireland, the Anglo-Normans, since they 'came into a settled country and inherited pre-existing land divisions', having conquered territory 'made as much use as possible of the pre-existing land divisions' (A Simms, 'Core and periphery in medieval Europe: the Irish experience in a wider context' in WJ Smyth and K Whelan (eds.), *Common Ground: Essays on the Historical Geography of Ireland Presented to T Jones Hughes* (Cork, 1988) pp22-40, 26, 33-4).

[26] In that same year, 1215, the city of Waterford was given a charter of liberties by King John (Otway-Ruthven, *Medieval Ireland*, p123). For a discussion of the grant of liberties, privileges and immunities made, by way of charters of one kind or another, to Irish boroughs in this period, see AF O'Brien, 'The development of the privileges, liberties and immunities of medieval Cork and the growth of an urban autonomy c.1189 to 1500' in *Journal of the Cork Historical and Archaeological Society*, xc (1985) pp 46-64. For the laws of Breteuil, see M Bateson, 'The laws of Breteuil', in *English Historical Review*, xv (1900) pp73-8, 302-18, 496-523, 754-7; xvi (1901), 92-110, 332-45.

[27] AF O'Brien, 'The development and evolution of the medieval borough and port of Dungarvan, county Waterford, c.1200 to c.1530' in *Journal of the Cork Historical and Archaeological Society*, xcii (1987) pp85-94

[28] Duffy, *Ireland in the Middle Ages*, pp99-100. The Butlers, later earls of Ormond, were to play a major role in the politics of later medieval Ireland, not least because of their conflict with successive earls of Desmond until the total collapse of the Desmond earldom in 1583.

[29] AB Scott and FX Martin (eds.), *Expugnatio Hibernica: the Conquest of Ireland by Giraldus Cambrensis* (Royal Irish Academy, Dublin, 1978) pp93-5

[30] Otway-Ruthven, *Medieval Ireland*, p49

[31] Duffy, *Ireland in the Middle Ages*, p101

[32] Otway-Ruthven, *Medieval Ireland*, pp61-3

[33] Duffy, *Ireland in the Middle Ages*, pp89-90

[34] For what follows, see Otway-Ruthven, *Medieval Ireland*, pp.61-3

[35] This can be compared with the service of one hundred knights by which Strongbow had held Leinster, and the service of fifty knights due from Hugh de Lacy's lordship of Meath which consisted of the modern counties of Meath and Westmeath.

[36] This is a striking illustration of a process whereby Anglo-Norman lords and their followers in the vanguard of conquest in Ireland could be marginalised as a consequence of grants of lands in Ireland made by the English crown to the king's intimates or persons in his entourage or service who played no part whatever in the conquest of Ireland.

[37] Duffy, *Ireland in the Middle Ages*, pp90-91; see also Frame, *Colonial Ireland*, p18

[38] Essentially, Anglo-Norman lords were opportunists (in the nature of things they simply had to be), and, accordingly, they too could ally themselves with ruling Irish dynasties or rival Irish dynastic segments (Irish polity was particularly prone to segmental rivalries), but the difference was that it was Irish kingdoms which were under attack and in jeopardy. Cross-racial alliances of this kind, of course, further complicated Irish politics.

[39] GH Orpen, *Ireland under the Normans 1169-1333* (4 vols, London, 1911-20), i, pp177-8

[40] Otway-Ruthven, *Medieval Ireland*, pp56-7

[41] *ibid.*, p73

[42] CA Empey, 'The Norman period, 1185-1500' in W Nolan and TG McGrath (eds.), *Tipperary: History and Society – Interdisciplinary Essays on the History of an Irish County* (Dublin, 1985) pp71-91: 71. Thomond (the kingdom of Limerick) 'meant the present counties of Limerick, Clare, Tipperary and North Kerry, "as Domnall Mór [Ua Briain] then enjoyed them", or ... the territory defined by the dioceses of Killaloe, Kilfenora, Limerick, Emly and Cashel' (G Cunningham, *The Anglo-Norman Advance in the South-West Midlands of Ireland 1185-1221* (Roscrea, 1987) pp54-5).

[43] Cunningham, *Anglo-Norman Advance*, pp55-7

[44] Frame, *Colonial Ireland*, pp32-5

[45] *ibid.*

[46] Orpen, *Normans*, ii, p43

[47] *ibid.*, pp43-4. Olethan corresponds to the modern baronies of Barrymore and Kinnatalloon and the north liberties of Cork city (L Ó Buachalla, 'An early 14th-century place-name list for Anglo-Norman Cork', in *Dinnseanchas*, ii, 3 (1967), pp61-5). Philip de Barry, to whom his uncle Robert fitz Stephen granted the cantred of Olethan, 'arrived in Cork in February, 1183, to undertake the governance of the cantred' (L St John Brooks, 'Unpublished charters relating to Ireland, 1177-82', *Proceedings of the Royal Irish Academy*, xliii C (1936) p333).

[48] Orpen, *Normans*, ii, pp43-5

[49] D Ó Murchadha, 'The Uí Meic Thíre of Imokilly' in *Journal of the Cork Historical and Archaeological Society*, lxxxii (1977) pp93-101. For the descent of the manor of Imokilly in the later middle ages which involved an extension of the fitz Gerald interest in east Cork and west Waterford, see AF O'Brien, 'The settlement of Imokilly and the formation and descent of the manor of Inchiquin, Co. Cork' in *Journal of the Cork Historical and Archaeological Society*, lxxxvii (1982) pp21-6, and idem 'The territorial ambitions of Maurice fitz Thomas, first earl of Desmond, with particular reference to the barony and manor of Inchiquin, Co. Cork' in *Proceedings of the Royal Irish Academy*, lxxxii C (1982) pp59-88.

[50] Orpen, *Normans*, ii, pp44-5

[51] Brooks, 'Unpublished charters', pp348-9. Carew's right to succession was challenged by the English crown early in the 14th century on the grounds that fitz Stephen 'was a bastard and died without heir of his body' (O'Brien, 'Territorial ambitions', pp61-5).

[52] Orpen, *Normans*, ii, pp45-6

[53] Orpen, *Normans*, iii, p118

[54] AF O'Brien, 'Politics, economy and society: the development of Cork and the Irish south-coast region c.1170 to c.1583' in P O'Flanagan and CG Buttimer (eds.), *Cork: History and Society – Interdisciplinary Essays on the History of an Irish County* (Dublin,

1993) pp83-154: 93

[55] Orpen, *Normans*, iii, p129

[56] O'Brien, 'Politics, economy and society', pp89-90, 93

[57] Orpen, *Normans*, iii, pp128-9

[58] For what follows, see *ibid.*, pp125-9.

[59] Carew succeeded to the lands of Robert fitz Stephen. At his death, fitz Stephen held in demesne of the king-in-chief, in his moiety of the lordship of Desmond, the manor of Dunnamark (the castle appears to have been built later) in Kilmocomoge, near Bantry, with demesne lands there. An inquisition into fitz Stephen's lands and their descent, made in 1331, found that 'the castle, manor and lands [of Dunnamark] were by then worth nothing yearly because of war and destruction by the Irish' (O'Brien, 'Territorial ambitions', pp61-2, 61 n.10).

[60] Orpen, *Normans*, iii, pp120-22

[61] Frame, *Colonial Ireland*, p69

[62] CA Empey, 'Conquest and settlement: patterns of Anglo-Norman settlement in north Munster and south Leinster' in *Irish Economic and Social History*, xiii (1986) pp5-31

[63] For what follows, see O'Brien, 'Politics, economy and society'; idem 'Economy, growth and settlement in medieval Ireland' in *Group for the Study of Irish Historic Settlement Newsletter*, no.3 (Autumn 1994) pp3-7; idem 'Medieval Youghal: the development of an Irish seaport trading town, c.1200 to c.1500', in *Peritia*, 5 (1986) pp346-78; idem 'Medieval Dungarvan'; idem 'The royal boroughs, the seaport towns and royal revenue in medieval Ireland', *Journal of the Royal Society of Antiquaries of Ireland*, 118 (1988) pp13-26; idem 'Commercial relations between Ireland and France c.1000 to c.1550' in J-M Picard (ed.), *Aquitaine and Ireland in the Middle Ages* (Dublin, 1995)

[64] CA Empey, 'Medieval Knocktopher: a study in manorial settlement', part I, *Old Kilkenny Review*, ii (1982), pp329-42: 337-9

[65] With regard to the meaning of French in this context, Empey points out that 'by "French" I mean a feudal aristocracy whose outlook, values, and social attitudes were fashioned by French chivalry. Whether French was still widely used by members of this class in Ireland is less important than the wider cultural tradition to which I am referring. Language and cultural tradition are not synonymous' (*ibid.*, p338n. 25).

[66] *ibid.*, p338

[67] For what follows see AF O'Brien, 'Medieval Youghal: the development of an Irish seaport trading town, c.1200 to c.1500', *Peritia*, v (1986), pp346-78: 352-5

[68] E McEneaney, 'Mayors and merchants in medieval Waterford city, 1169-1495', in Nolan and Power (eds.), *Waterford: History and Society*, pp147-76: 151

[69] *ibid.*, 174

[70] *ibid.*, Appendix I, pp173-5

[71] *ibid.*, pp152-3

[72] *Calendar of Documents Relating to Ireland, 1171-1251*, no.806; *Calendar of Patent Rolls, 1216-25*, p105

[73] *CDI 1285-92*, no.169

[74] Public Record Office, London, Exchequer Accounts Various, E101/231/6; *CDI, 1285-92*, no.251; *1293-1302*, no.520; *Calendar of Close Rolls, 1296-1302*, pp157-8

[75] PRO, Exchequer Accounts Various, E101/232/16; *CDI, 1293-1301*, no.226

[76] *CDI, 1293-1301*, no.226

[77] *CCR, 1330-33*, p138

[78] John Donati, son of Thaddeus Donati, an Italian banker operating in Ireland at the end of the 13th century, was a Lombard born in Ireland. In 1338 he was in dispute with the mayor, bailiffs and commonalty of Cork because, to his legal disadvantage, they refused to accept him as a denizen (PRO, Chancery Miscellanea, C47/10/19).

[79] Gowelys, Gowildis

[80] Tyrry, Tirry

[81] Galway

[82] Copyner, Copener

[83] Sareffield, Saresfild

[84] Morragh, Morbagh, Morogh

[85] Martell

[86] KW Nicholls, 'Two islands, one street' in *Cork Examiner*, 13 March 1985

[87] I hope to develop this in future studies of later medieval Irish society and economy.

[88] With regard to Walsh or its variant forms, Empey has pointed out that 'the name Walsh, or Welsh ... appears in our sources in its latin form 'Walensis', which may mean either 'the Welshman' or 'from Wales', so that he could as well be a Norman or a Fleming from Wales as a native Welshman' (Empey, 'Knocktopher', pp337-8).

[89] The de Wynchedon family was one of the leading merchant families of Cork in the later Middle Ages. They flourished, particularly, in the 13th and 14th centuries, but as late as the end of the 15th century 'a William de Wynchedon was active in Cork's trade with Bristol'. It is possible that the family had declined by the time of the Cromwellian expulsion, perhaps in the course of the 16th century. For the de Wynchedon family, see O'Brien, 'Politics, economy and society', pp103-6.

[90] *ibid.*, pp134-5

[91] Rore Honethan (the name has all the appearances of an Anglicisation of the Gaelic) was master of the *Jamez of Cork*, which was trading in the port of Bristol in 1479-80. Among the Cork merchants whose goods were shipped on that vessel by Honethan were Edmund Staunton, William Wynchedon, John Galway, Patrick Creagh, Thomas Goolde, Thomas Skiddy, Geoffrey White, Morris Seisena, Thomas Sarsfield, William Water, Edmund Roche, Denis Morgan, and Nicholas Walshe (EM Carus-Wilson, *The Overseas Trade of Bristol in the Later Middle Ages* (2nd ed., London, 1967), pp218-89).

[92] Empey, 'Knocktopher' p339

[93] McEneaney, 'Waterford mayors and merchants', p153. For the growth of the city of Cork in this period, see O'Brien, 'Politics, economy and society'.

[94] Frame, *Colonial Ireland*, p71

[95] These conditions are discussed in some detail in O'Brien 'Politics, economy and society'.

[96] Frame, *Colonial Ireland*, p122

[97] O'Brien, 'Politics, economy and society', pp129-30

[98] *ibid.*, pp114-29

[99] *ibid.*, p133

[100] *ibid.*, pp142-3

———

BARRYSCOURT LECTURES

BARRYSCOURT LECTURE SERIES

Barryscourt Castle is a fine 16th-century
tower-house at Carrigtwohill, Co Cork.
The Barryscourt Trust was established in
1987 with the aim of conserving,
enhancing and developing the heritage
potential of the castle.

In 1996, the Barryscourt Trust
instituted a bi-annual series of lectures on
Medieval Ireland. These will deal with
aspects of medieval history, archaeology,
art and architecture, and will be
delivered by scholars specialising in the
period. The lectures will be published
individually and in compilation form.

Barryscourt Lectures III
TECHNOLOGICAL CHANGE
IN ANGLO-NORMAN MUNSTER
Colin Rynne

Published by the Barryscourt Trust
in association with Cork County Council
and Gandon Editions, Kinsale.

ISBN 0946641 846

Series Editor	Noel Jameson
Design	John O'Regan
	(© Gandon, 1998)
Production	Nicola Dearey, Gandon
Printing	Betaprint, Dublin
Distribution	Gandon, Kinsale

THE BARRYSCOURT TRUST
Barryscourt Castle
Carrigtwohill, Co Cork

TECHNOLOGICAL CHANGE
IN ANGLO-NORMAN MUNSTER

Vertical overshot mill from Agostino Ramelli, *Le diverse et artificiose machine*
(Paris, 1588), pl.119

Technological Change in Anglo-Norman Munster

Colin Rynne

THE BARRYSCOURT TRUST
IN ASSOCIATION WITH CORK COUNTY COUNCIL AND GANDON EDITIONS

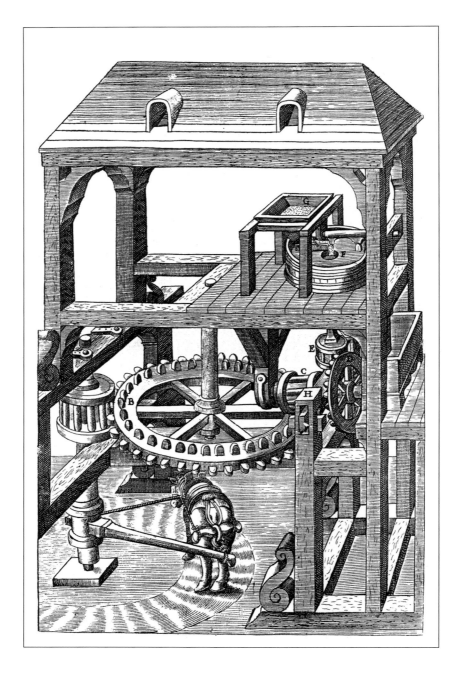

1 – Horsemill from Agostino Ramelli, *Le diverse et artificiose machine* (Paris, 1588), pl.122

INTRODUCTION

The uses of industrial energy in the Anglo-Norman period in Ireland have scarcely been considered. For the most part this is because archaeological evidence, in direct contrast to that of the preceding early medieval period, has proved to be elusive. Nonetheless, the documentary evidence for the use of water power within the Anglo-Norman lordship is quite extensive, whilst that for some mills, such as the King's Mills at Ardee in county Louth, has proved to be amongst the most comprehensive in medieval Europe (see below). The watermill, it is clear, was an important part of the economic infrastructure of Anglo-Norman Ireland. Yet there were other industrial prime movers. Animal-powered mills had been introduced into Ireland in the early medieval period, while the Anglo-Normans built the first Irish windmills on the east coast. On present evidence it would appear that wind-powered mills were rare in the greater part of Anglo-Norman Ireland, and it seems likely that these, as in the case of windmills in more recent times, were a supplement rather an alternative to water-powered mills.

The Anglo-Norman period in Munster can be characterised as one of remarkable economic growth.[1] But we should not forget that the agrarian economy which it effectively replaced was by no means a backward one. Agricultural development was advanced enough to enable the widespread use of water-powered grain mills amongst all levels of early Irish society. Nor, for that matter, on the basis of the archaeological evidence for the use of water power before the Anglo-Norman settlement, can Ireland be considered a technological backwater in the early medieval period. Yet, while Anglo-Norman settlers would have found that the native Irish were accomplished millwrights, they had their own distinctive contribution to make, laying, as they did, the seeds of future industrial development in Ireland. In this short essay, I will attempt to outline the extent of their contribution to the development of industrial energy in Ireland, with special reference to the Munster area. A glossary of technical terms is provided in an appendix.

———

1 – Animal Power

The likely use of animal-powered machinery in medieval Ireland has received little attention. There is, however, some documentary evidence for their use in the same period in the term *marcmuilenn* ('horsemill'), which occurs in two medieval glossaries. Lest there be any doubt as to the type of mill involved, it is glossed as *muilenn im-sai ech*, 'a mill which is turned by a horse'.[2] The clear implication here is that this is a horse-powered grain mill, in which the animal turns a wheel in a horizontal plane, where the animal moves in a circle to turn a wheel set on a central pivot. The likelihood is that the motion of the wheel turned by the horse was transferred to the upper millstone by means of an intermediate gear wheel [1]. Donkey-powered, direct-drive grain mills (i.e. without gearing) are known from Roman Britain from at least the 1st century AD, but there is currently no evidence which would suggest that they continued to be used after the Roman withdrawal.[3] In the post-Roman period in Britain, the earliest documentary evidence for the use of horsemills comes from Oxen-le-Flatts in county Durham, in existence in 1193, but there is at least one possible 10th-century site at the Anglo-Saxon palace at Cheddar in Somerset, yet horsemills are not mentioned in the Domesday Survey of 1086.[4] Nonetheless, it is conceivable that horsemills were introduced into Ireland from Britain in the early medieval period, where the Irish would, in any case, have already been familiar with geared watermills (see below). The circumstances in which such mills were used in Ireland, however, are by no means clear. Elsewhere in Europe, animal-powered mills were generally used in areas where water power could not be relied upon, or in fortified settlements. Similar considerations may well have applied in medieval Ireland. However, in the Anglo-Norman period, all of the major Irish towns were well serviced by water-powered mills in their immediate environs or, as in the case of Droop's Mill in medieval Cork, within the walled citadel itself. In the present state of our knowledge there is little to suggest that horsemills were commonly used on either Anglo-Norman manors or in towns.

2 – Water Power

Ireland shows a remarkable precocity with regard to the development of water-powered mills in the early medieval period. Indeed, the earliest examples of certain varieties of watermill, which are documented throughout Asia and Europe, have been found in Ireland. Furthermore, the earliest vernacular terms for the principal components of the horizontal-wheeled mill, in any European language, are in Old Irish. In the 6th/7th-century law tract *De Ceithri Slichtaib Athgabála* ('on the the four sections of distraint'), we find the earliest vernacular terms for horizontal-wheeled mill components in any European language. *De Ceithri Slichtaib Athgabála* lists what are termed the 'eight parts of the mill' along with a number of everyday items upon which, in cases of distraint (i.e. the seizure of goods or chattels in lieu of payment), there was a stay of execution. The implication is of course that if the component parts of a horizontal-wheeled mill could feature in such cases by the turn of the 7th century AD, then these mills must have been extremely common in early Irish society. This latter circumstance is fully confirmed by the Irish archaeological record, but the evidence is much more wide-ranging than one might reasonably expect. For not only had a specialised craft of millwrighting grown to prominence in early medieval Ireland, but there are also clear indications that in the same period regional millwrighting styles had already evolved.

In Ireland double-flume mills are, on present evidence, at least as early as the 7th century AD. The earliest known Irish horizontal-wheeled

2 – Conjectural reconstruction of double-flume horizontal watermill at Little Island, county Cork, c.630 AD

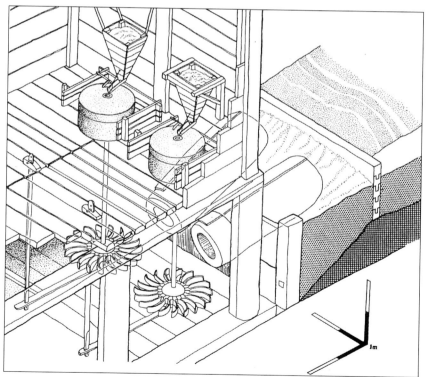

mill site at Little Island in county Cork [2], is of this type, and the Irish examples in general have close analogues in the eastern Mediterranean region, particularly in Romania. They are also referred to in 14th-century Tuscan documents, and more recent examples have been recorded in Bulgaria, Yugoslavia and Greece.[5] Horizontal-wheeled mills utilising up to three flumes have been recorded in the Austrian Tyrol and the Caucasus. Indeed, mills with anything up to six penstocks have been recorded in Romania. On present evidence, the Romanian multi-penstock *ciutura* mills, in which the individual penstocks are angled into each other, provide the closest parallels for the early Irish examples.[6]

Thus far Ireland has produced the earliest evidence for the use of tide mills. The 7th-century double penstock mill, discovered on Little Island in the estuary of the River Lee in county Cork, along with its vertical undershot counterpart (which had been built alongside it), are the earliest known examples of tide mills in either Europe or Asia. The Little Island mills effectively predate the earliest known documentary reference to tide mills by almost four centuries. The present-day distribution of horizontal-wheeled tide-mills (all of which have dished paddles) includes Portugal, Brittany and northern Spain.[7]

The landscape of Munster would have contained a large number of watermills on the eve of the Anglo-Norman conquest. Watermills and related features such as dams, millponds and millraces, were clearly common features of the early historic Irish landscape, so much so that early Irish jurists went to great lengths to provide a legal framework for the water rights pertaining to them, as is evidenced by the law tract *Coibnes Uisci Thairidne* ('Kinship of conducted water'). From the early Irish law tract on distraint *De Ceithri Slichtaib Athgabála*, it is clear that term *lind* or *tir linde* was in use in 6th-century Ireland to denote millponds, the earliest-known non-Latin term for this feature in post-Roman Europe. Occurrences of related terms in other vernacular languages are somewhat later. The earliest known use of the Old English compound *mylepul* ('millpond'), for example, occurs in an Anglo-Saxon charter of AD 833.[8] There can be little doubt that by the later medieval period, millponds were common features of the landscape, the maintenance of which along with related features such as a millraces and sluices often proved to be a heavy financial burden on both monastic and manorial estates.

That a specialised craft of millwrighting existed in early medieval Ireland is made explicit in the early Irish documentary sources. In the law tracts, ample recognition is given to the *saer mulinn*, or millwright, who is accorded the status of an *Aire Désa* , the lowest grade of nobility. In a story of the mythical *ard rí*, Cormac MacAirt, related by the poet Cuán ua Lothcáin (d.1024), Cormac was said to have brought a millwright (*saer muilinn*) over from England to construct a watermill, to relieve his mistress, Ciarnait, from the labour of the hand mill.[9] Indeed, according to *Uraicecht Becc* ('small primer'), millwrights were also accorded the same status as other master carpenters such as wood carvers, shipwrights and those capable of making an oratory (*durthech* or 'oak house'). Furthermore, in Triad 106 the construction of a watermill is included in 'three payments' (*dulchinni*), in which assistance to a craftsman is apportioned a share as the craftsman cannot complete the work by himself and is obliged to employ another worker (*gniae*).[10]

However, while millwrighting may have been at an advanced stage in Munster – before the conquest – relative to other European regions, Ireland's larger monasteries do not seem to have developed their water resources for either industrial or domestic purposes to the same extent as their early medieval European counterparts. Why pre-Norman Irish monasteries should be under-developed in this regard is by no means clear. The growth of the larger monastic centres in early medieval Ireland is generally quite similar to that of the large Benedictine establishments of the Carolingian period. Armagh and Clonmacnoise, for example, had brought large areas of land under their control from which they derived substantial profits, in much the same way as Benedictine monasteries such as St Germain des Pres and Lorsh had carved out sizeable territories in central Europe.[11] Furthermore, during the 8th and 9th centuries, many Irish church estates were organised on similar lines to St Gall.[12] But despite these similarities it is not until the 1140s, when the larger European monastic orders such as the Cistercians and the Augustinians became established in Ireland, that the hydrotechnology associated with these orders was introduced into Ireland.

The vertical-wheeled watermill in Ireland is at least as old as the horizontal-wheeled variety. Three early medieval sites at Little Island, county Cork (c.AD 630) [3], Morett, county Laois (c.AD 770), and Ardcloyne, county Cork (c.AD 787), employed vertical waterwheels, but while the Little Island example was contemporary with the twin-flume horizontal-wheeled mill on the same site, the overall relationships between both varieties of mill in early medieval Ireland are still not clearly understood.[13] An annalistic entry for AD 651 (see above), which refers to the murder of two boys in a mill at Maelodran, most likely refers to a vertical-wheeled mill. The argument to the effect that the incident took place in a horizontal-wheeled mill is based largely on the assumption that vertical-wheeled mills did not exist in Ireland at this period.[14] However, this assumption is now known to be baseless, whilst in any case the injuries inflicted on Dúnchad and Conall could only have been inflicted by a vertical waterwheel.

As in many parts of Europe, the horizontal-wheeled mill in Ireland was gradually replaced by vertical-wheeled mills. In the aftermath of the

Anglo-Norman conquest and settlement of Ireland in the late 12th century, new customs and technology were introduced. Indeed, the vertical waterwheel, and other industrial processes and power transmission systems associated with it, are likely to have been used on Anglo-Norman manors and on the monastic estates of the Cistercian and Augustinian houses established in Ireland. Nonetheless, the horizontal-wheeled mill survived in Ireland throughout the medieval period, and in certain parts of Ireland (particularly on the western seaboard) it was still relatively common in the middle of the 19th century. Until quite recently, the cluster of early medieval dates for Irish horizontal-wheeled sites, and the apparent absence of high-medieval sites from the archaeological record, led to the suggestion that a shortage of timber for building purposes seriously curtailed mill-building activity. However, there are unambiguous references to

3 – Conjectural reconstruction of vertical watermill
at Little Island, county Cork, c.630 AD

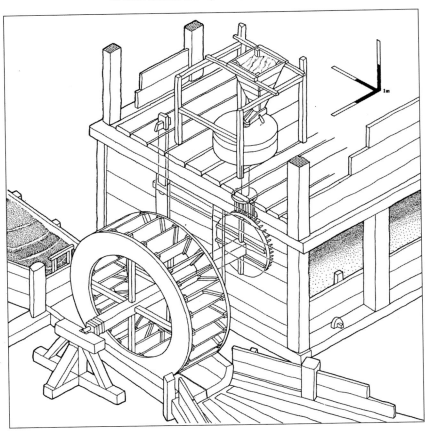

horizontal-wheeled mills in Irish documentary sources dating to the period after the 1st millennium AD. In the 11th-century text of *Togail Bruidne Da Derga*, there is a clear-cut reference to a *sciatha* or horizontal waterwheel paddle (see above). Furthermore, the use of the O.Ir term *oircel* (which forms part of the 'eight parts of the mill' in *De Ceithri Slichtaib Athgábala*, see above) also occurs in *Fled Bricenn*. That this term should survive into the 12th century is a fair indication that the audience of the copyist would have been familiar with its meaning, and there can be little doubt that such mills were in existence at this point in time. The archaeological record also confirms this. It is now clear that there are at least one 12th-century horizontal-wheeled mill site at Clonlonan, county Westmeath (c.AD 1145), and a 13th-century example from Corcannon, county Wexford (c.AD 1228).[15] Doubtless, further sites of similar date will eventually come to light. Thus far it is clear that of the twenty-eight watermill sites dated to the period AD 630 to 1228, just over half (56%) were built with timbers felled in the period AD 770 to 850.[16] But it is also important to note that for every dated site, there is at least a further medieval mill site recorded in the 19th or early 20th century which has not been scientifically dated. Both the documentary and archaeological evidence, therefore, clearly confirm the co-existence of both horizontal and vertical-wheeled watermills in Ireland during the high medieval period.[17]

The use of water-powered corn mills in Ireland from the Anglo-Norman period onwards is reasonably well-documented in contemporary sources.[18] However, until quite recently, the archaeological evidence was somewhat limited, particularly for mills in urban environments. Many of Ireland's principal coastal towns such as Dublin, Cork and Waterford developed from Viking trading ports, and for the most part the beginnings of urban development in Ireland date to the latter part of the 1st millennium AD. The development of urban centres in Ireland led to the establishment of watermills within their immediate environs, and the consequent adaptation of the water supply of these mills to different hydrological conditions. In both medieval Dublin and Cork, for example, which were both established on tidal rivers, water-powered mills tended to avoid their tidal reaches. For the most part, watermills were constructed on tributaries which traversed the higher ground, overlooking the towns, before discharging into the tidal stretches of the main river. This basic locational pattern continued well into the 19th century, and was only really modified when the introduction of steam-powered prime movers enabled industries to become established directly on the quaysides of Ireland's main ports. In Dublin and Cork, these non-tidal tributary streams tended to become extensively regularised from the Anglo-Norman period onwards. The River Poddle in Dublin, for example, had become effectively canalised for industrial and domestic water-supply purposes by the 13th century.

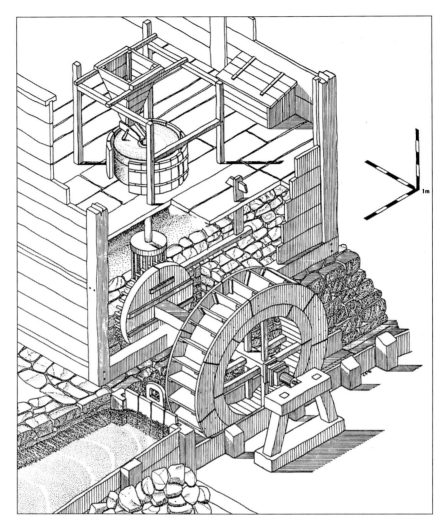

4 – Conjectural reconstruction of Anglo-Norman watermill
at Patrick's Street, Dublin, in early 13th century

The vast majority of the watermills erected during the Anglo-Norman period in Munster and, indeed, throughout Ireland, were involved in the processing of cereal crops. In 1990 the remains of a Anglo-Norman vertical undershot grain mill were excavated at Patrick Street in Dublin [4]. The mill had been built early in the 13th century, and almost entirely rebuilt in the 14th. Its waterwheel was positioned directly over a canalised section of the River Poddle, a tributary of the Liffey.[19] Similar mills would have been quite common throughout the Anglo-Norman

Lordship, particularly on rivers in low-lying areas. In many of its essentials there is little difference between the Patrick Street mill and the undershot watermills known from early medieval Ireland, in terms of both likely power and output. However, there is currently no evidence for the use of either breastshot or overshot waterwheels in early medieval Ireland, although if they were never used in this period, they would almost certainly have been introduced in the Anglo-Norman period (see below).

Water supply was, of course, an important locational consideration for Europe's larger monastic orders, and no less so when they established houses in Ireland during the 12th century. No less than fifty-one of the fifty-six Augustinian houses, and eighteen of the twenty-five Cistercian houses in Ireland were sited on the banks of rivers. Water was needed for the domestic offices of the abbey as well as for powering the abbey's mill, and in many cases, great effort was expended in procuring an adequate supply. At the Augustinian abbey of Athassel, county Tipperary, a millrace was cut across a meander loop on the River Suir over a mile wide in amplitude. This was no mean feat when one considers that the completed channel was over 2000ft (c.609m) long, and required a bridge over 40ft (12.19m) wide to span it. At Holy Cross Abbey, county Tipperary, a series of islands in the River Suir, which effectively created a narrow water channel, enabled the monks to cut a short millrace from it for the abbey mill. However, sites at which a small tributary flowing down a steep slope in a river valley, thus providing a low-volume, fast-flowing water source, were prized. Good examples of such sites were exploited by Cistercian abbeys, such as Monasternenagh, county Limerick, and Augustinian sites such as Bridgetown, county Cork, Rathkeale, county Limerick, and Cahir, county Tipperary.[20]

3 – Wind power

The introduction of the wind-powered mill into Ireland is unquestionably an Anglo-Norman development, although the first recorded instance of such a mill occurs almost one hundred years after the first recorded English windmill of 1185. The earliest documented windmill in Ireland was at work at Kilscanlan, near Old Ross, county Wexford, in AD 1281.[21] This is most likely to have been a post mill, in which the actual mill building is rotated about a central wooden pivot in order that the wind sails can face into the prevailing wind [5]. The entire structure could be rotated through 360 degrees by means of a *tail pole*, which enabled the miller to adjust the position of his sails to accommodate changes in wind direction, by the simple expedient of rotating the entire mill building. The mill machinery was contained within a wooden framework, and the entire structure was

5 – Post mill from Agostino Ramelli, *Le diverse et artificiose machine*, pl.133
opposite 6 – *Pacata Hibernia* map of Youghal, c.1590

usually erected on high ground, often on a specially prepared mound, adjacent to a township. A number of possible medieval windmill mounds have been identified at Diamor, Bartramstown, Derrypatrick, Hurdlestown and Agher in county Meath,[22] but there are no other published examples from the rest of Ireland. A small number of windmills are likely to have been used in medieval Munster, especially on the west coast. Indeed, the number of documented windmill sites in the Munster area in more recent times is extremely small. The late 16th-century *Pacata Hibernia* map of Youghal, county Cork, shows a post-mill outside the town walls [6]. On present evidence it would appear that postmills were no longer built in Ireland after the 17th century, and there are no surviving examples. In the main, the distribution of windmills in Ireland is confined to the east coast, with notable concentrations in counties Wexford and Down. There are two principal reasons for this. To begin with, both counties were important cereal producers thanks to favourable climatic conditions and proximity to large centres of population. However, as the catchment areas of many of the rivers on the east coast were somewhat restricted, both regions experienced difficulty in expanding their milling capacity based on water-power alone.[23] From the Anglo-Norman period onwards, therefore, the introduction of the windmill was an important technological innovation on the east coast of Ireland. In the greater part of Munster, however, it was a supplementary source of industrial energy, water-powered sites, for the most part, not being in short supply.

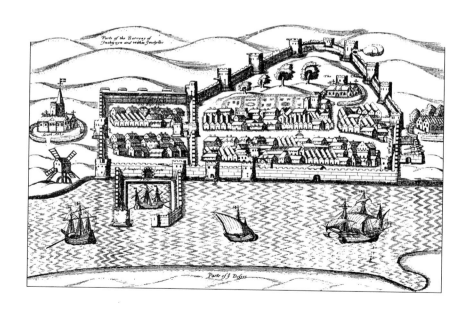

INDUSTRY AND MECHANISATION
IN ANGLO-NORMAN MUNSTER

Grain Milling

The rapid expansion of tillage in Ireland during the Anglo-Norman period meant that by the late 13th century the island was a net exporter of cereals, with many religious orders, principally in Britain, but also a number in France, obtaining supplies from Ireland.[24] The development of more complex distributive networks for cereals in the Munster area can be gleaned from archaeo-botanical evidence from the medieval town of Waterford. With the exception of oats, all of the cereals brought into the town for consumption were fully processed in the countryside (whereas oats were brought in in sheaves),[25] prior to being milled within the town or in water-powered mills within its immediate environs. Anglo-Norman corn-drying kilns, in which the grain was dried to facilitate milling, have been recorded in Waterford and Cork, which clearly indicates that this essential pre-milling process was also conducted within walled towns.[26]

The archaeological evidence for water-powered grain mills in Anglo-Norman Munster is extremely limited. Indeed, there is only one excavated example in Ireland, from Patrick's Street in Dublin, which can be firmly dated to this period, although a second site at Ballyine, county Limerick, is likely to date to the high-medieval period. At Ballyine, the remains of a stone-built mill house and wheelrace for a vertical breastshot waterwheel were investigated, along with a millpond about 940m^2 in extent.[27] However, while no date for the site other than pre-1857 (i.e before the first edition of the Ordnance Survey of the area) was advanced for the site, the remains of the machinery associated with it clearly indicate that it is medieval. The fragmentary remains of some ten 'pivot stones', which would have formed the lower part of a footstep bearing upon which the pinion gear would have rotated, were found in the tail race of the mill, into which they had been discarded when they had worn out. Very similar stones were recovered from an 8th-century undershot watermill at Morett, county Laois, and while these can be associated with more recent horizontal-wheeled mills in Ireland and elsewhere, where vertical waterwheels are concerned they are generally associated with Roman and medieval contexts.[28] Further evidence for the medieval date of this mill can be adduced from the wooden mill components recovered from the site. No less than eight gear pegs or teeth similar in size and general morphology to those recovered from English medieval sites at Chingley forge, Kent, period I (c.1300-50) and Bordesley Abbey (late 12th to early 14th centuries) were found, along with a small section of the waterwheel's shroud (i.e. a curved wooden plate forming the outer walls of the buckets, set on the periphery of the waterwheel).[29] By comparison with similar English mill components, therefore, this must surely be a medieval water-mill. However, while the Chingley and Bordesley Abbey sites were associated with iron-working, the recovery of millstone fragments from the Ballyine site indicate that it was a grain mill. If this is a medieval site, as now seem likely, then it is the earliest known example of a breastshot mill in Ireland.

The scarcity of excavated Anglo-Norman water-powered grain mills, given their frequency in existing documentary sources, is somewhat puzzling. In certain cases, these sites are likely to have been reused by later industrial mills, but a large number of sites remain to be discovered. Indeed, there are no published examples of Anglo-Norman water-powered millstones, nor, for that matter, have any examples of imported millstones from the Anglesey quarries, or France, been identified thus far.[30] Millstones would have had to be replaced every few years, and so we might expect to find fragments of discarded millstones near mill sites, or reused as building stone at other sites.

In the Anglo-Norman period, the expense to the lord of maintaining a mill was unrelenting. Frequent repairs necessitated by flooding to mill channels and ponds and the replacement of worn machinery would have been a heavy financial burden on the manor: grain mills, it is clear, were expensive to build and maintain. By the 14th century, larger more elaborate watermills than those investigated at Ballyine and Patrick's Street were in operation, such as the King's Mills at Ardee in county Louth and in Dublin. These mills were larger and may perhaps be unrepresentative of those elsewhere in the lordship, although at Ardmayle, county Tipperary, in 1305, two mills were valued at twenty-four marks per annum.[31] By the turn of the 14th century, both iron and steel is used for the mill's bearings and nails are used extensively in the mill buildings, as evidenced at Ballyine and in contemporary accounts. At the Kings Mills in Dublin in 1314, for example, 53s 2d was spent on timber boards and nails for the mill building, while 25s $6^1/_2$d – almost half that amount – was expended on iron and steel for the journals and bearings. By way of comparison, the mill iron of Leymille and the Maltmille at Ardee in 1305, owned by Edward I, were respectively valued at 5s and 4s. In this latter case, however, the lower values would appear to be associated with their poor condition. Nonetheless, the millstones of the 'old and broken' Cornmille at Ardee appear to have been originally bound with iron hoops valued at 18s.[32] The use of iron bands as reinforcement for the millstones is a refinement absent in the early medieval examples, and is a clear indication that larger millstones were being employed from at the least the 14th century onwards. Furthermore, it is unlikely that steel – an expensive commodity – was used in pre-Norman Irish watermills, or indeed in Gaelic areas during the Anglo-Norman period.

The expense involved was necessary to fully exploit the feudal obligation of 'suit to the mill', whereby the lord's tenants were legally bound to bring all of their cereals to the lord's mill to be ground. The miller was empowered to charge a toll (*multura*) for this service (usually $1/16$ or $1/20$ of the meal or flour ground in the mill), and effectively the private ownership of watermills or rotary querns was outlawed, the lord's reeve being empowered to seize and destroy them. None of the tenants of Coole and Britway in county Cork in 1365 was 'to have a hand mill (*molam manualem*) without the lord's permission, and if they have [a hand mill] they will be fined'.[33] As late as 1637, for example, the tenants of Dr John Richardson in the Barony of Tyrhugh, county Donegal, were still required to 'grind their corn at the mill built upon the college land [i.e. Trinity College, Dublin] by Francis Bressy late deceased and pay the accustomed toll...', whilst both the seneschal and the millers were empowered to search the tenant's houses for quernstones.[34] Manorial tenants were also under obligation to assist in repairs to ponds and watercourses, as at Coole and Britway in 1365, where an ordinance states 'they are obliged to clean the millpond (*millepolle*)'.[35]

In the inventory of the King's Mills at Ardee, we find a rare mention of a copper *enee*, a vessel used to measure the toll.[36] The manner in which the grain was poured in to the measures was strictly regulated, the grain being mounded over the top of the vessel and then struck off with a strike or strickle. What remained was then pressed into the measure, whereupon the entire process was repeated until the vessel was tightly packed. Deliberate anomalies in this process were a continuous source of grievance for medieval tenants, with millers often being accused of dishonesty. The medieval stereotype of the dishonest miller is best illustrated by Chaucer in *The Canterbury Tales*, and in *The Laws and Usages of the City of Dublin*, of 1309, an extremely short shrift was afforded to dishonest millers: 'If a miller take corn to grind, he shall take it by the strike measure, and shall take it to the [customer's] house full and well pressed two or three times. And if the miller be guilty of larceny of corn or flour to the value of four pence, he shall be hanged in the mill on a beam.'[37]

In Gaelic areas, however, feudal practices were ignored and it seems likely that both privately owned horizontal- and vertical-wheeled mills, along with rotary querns, continued to be used. This is not, however, an index of technological regression nor of the relative underdeveloped state of Gaelic agrarian economy. As has been seen, the native Irish had long been familiar with both direct-drive and geared mills, both horse and water powered. The Anglo-Normans chose to exploit their estates using the technology of the vertical-wheeled mill, but in other areas of Europe feudal lords used horizontal-wheeled mills. In the *Contado* of Florence, for example, a region demonstrably more developed in the high middle ages than any region of the Anglo-Norman lordship in Ireland, a considerable number of horizontal-wheeled mills operated under feudal custom.[38] Indeed, apart from iron millstone hoops, there is little difference between the horizontal-wheeled mills of northern Italy in the high-medieval period and contemporary examples in Ireland.[39] Needless to say, medieval Florence could hardly be characterised as a technologically backward area.

Textiles – The Woollen Industry

One of the main Anglo-Norman contributions to the expansion of the agrarian economy in areas under their control, was the creation of large flocks of sheep, which were to become a particularly important sector of the agricultural regime of the Cistercian order in Ireland.[40] The increase in the numbers of sheep in Ireland during this period is partially confirmed by the amount of sheep bones recovered from the excavations in medieval Waterford.[41] In the early part of the Anglo-Norman lordship, raw wool was exported to Flanders, where it was spun and woven into cloth. By the beginning of the 13th century, however, the manufacture of woollen cloth was expanding within the medieval lordship, and by the 13th century, as will be seen below, one of the key finishing processes for woollen cloth had become mechanised. This is one of the most important Anglo-Norman technological developments in the Munster area.

Spinning, as in earlier periods, was undertaken with a distaff and spindle: the spinning wheel was not introduced until the 14th century in Britain and Ireland.[42] Long fibre or staple wool was wound on to a distaff, which was mounted on a stand, or, if the spinner desired some mobility, it could be attached to her belt. A wooden stick, with a whorl (a stone or bone weight) attached to one extremity, was used as a spindle for drawing out the fibres and imparting a twist to the yarn. The whorl or weight also acted as flywheel by partially regulating the rotation of the spindle. In Waterford city, distaffs have been recovered from 12th and 13th-century contexts, and these, along with weighted spindles, would have been used in almost every peasant household.[43]

In the early medieval period, handlooms were of the vertical warp-weighted design, on which the warp or vertical threads were hung on a simple vertical frame, which could be stood up independently or leaned up against a wall. The warp threads were weighted down by stones (generally referred to as loom weights), and the weft or horizontal threads were threaded through from side to side. The weaver would periodically beat up the weft with a long wooden sword beater. However, in the 13th century, a more sophisticated two-beam horizontal loom, the forerunner of the handlooms used in Ireland until recent times, was introduced. The horizontal loom enabled longer pieces of cloth to be woven, and could be operated much faster, and thus more productively, than the warp-weighted loom. A boat-shaped shuttle was now used to carry the weft smoothly across the warp. A shuttle from a horizontal loom was recovered during recent excavations in Waterford, from a 12th or early 13th-century context, and is similar to a 13th-century example from Cork city.[44] Other artefacts from medieval Waterford related to weaving include a number of items likely to be weaver's swords from mid to late 12th-century contexts.[45] A probable weavers' comb (used for beating in the weft threads in a piece of cloth) dating to the mid to late 12th century, and a number of pin beaters, which were used to press the weft threads up against the section of cloth already woven, were also found.[46] Similar beaters were also recovered during the excavations at Grand Parade, Cork.[47]

Spinning and weaving were carried out manually throughout the medieval period, but as the volume of production increased, an important mechanical aid was introduced to revolutionise an important finishing process for woollen cloth. Fulling, in which newly woven cloth was pounded in an alkaline liquor consisting of stale urine or a special kind of clay called fullers earth, was a process in which the cloth was divested of any dirt or grease absorbed by it during the spinning of the yarn and its subsequent weaving on the loom. The cloth is at once thickened and compacted, whilst the fibres shrink and matt together in such a way that the weave is no longer distinguishable. Traditionally this process was carried out by men trampling the cloth in wooden troughs ('walking'), but by the second half of the 10th century in Italy, this became the first ever textile process to be mechanised.

In the fulling mill, which is generally associated with the introduction of the horizontal loom, the stamping action of human feet is replaced by the beating action of swinging wooden hammers [7]. Its rapid diffusion in the 13th century can be linked to the development and expansion of new cloth-producing regions in Europe, which included Ireland.[48] The existence of fulling mills is recorded at Clones, county Monaghan in 1211-12, only a few decades after the earliest known English fulling mill at Newsham in Yorkshire of 1185.[49] By the late 1270s (and probably earlier), fulling mills were at work in the vicinity of Youghal, county Cork. Fragments of fulled cloth have even been recovered from medieval excavations in Dublin, Cork and Waterford.[50]

From the 13th century onwards, the Munster area, and the county of Cork in particular, became the principal producer of woollen cloth in Ireland, with the largest concentration of fulling mills in Ireland. Manufactured woollen goods such as Irish friezes and mantles were exported through the ports of Cork.

7 – Fulling mill from Vittorio Zonca, *Novo teatro di machine et edificii per varie et sicure operation* (Padua, 1607), p68

8 – Water-powered bellows (B) and water-powered trip hammer (D),
from Georgius Agricola, *De Re Metallica* (Basel, 1558), book ix

Mining and Metalworking

Very little is known about mining in early medieval Ireland. There is extensive evidence for ironworking throughout Munster on habitation sites of the period, although there is no evidence for the use of anything other than bowl furnaces.[51] At one early medieval ringfort, at Lisleagh, county Cork, over 800kg of slag from smelting operations was recovered from the ditch where it had been dumped.[52] Clearly this was the result of smelting operations over a considerable period of time. From the earliest times up until the late 16th century, wrought iron in Ireland was produced in one step in a *bloomery*, by smelting the iron directly from its ores. This is generally referred to as the *direct process*, to distinguish it from the *indirect process* whereby cast iron is produced in a blast furnace and later refined to make wrought iron. In primitive bowl furnaces, where temperatures reached about 800°C, a spongy mixture of metal and slag was formed, which was then hammered on an anvil to both consolidate the iron and remove as much slag as possible. The bloom, after being worked at the forge, was then ready for immediate use. However, while this process was easy on fuel, it was profligate of the ore, where as much as 70% of the metal was discarded with the slag. During the later medieval period, it became possible to increase the amounts of semi-molten slag by raising the temperature in the furnace to around 1,150°C. A large proportion of the slag could now be tapped off in the furnace during the smelting process, and the amount of slag which had to be hammered out from the bloom greatly reduced. The introduction of water-powered bellows and hammers (see below) greatly assisted these processes and led to an increase in iron production.

Our knowledge of ironworking in Gaelic areas during the Anglo-Norman period is virtually non-existent, although it seems likely that iron continued to be smelted on a small scale in bloomery furnaces.[53] At the present showing, however, there is no evidence for the use of water-powered bloomeries in medieval Ireland. Bar iron ('peyces of iron') processed in continental bloomeries appears to have been imported with bulk salt from Spain and Brittany.[54] Iron and steel were expensive commodities, although both would have been in demand for a wide variety of purposes. Imported iron, we may assume, was extensively traded within the hinterland of Munster's ports. The manner in which it was reforged was, until quite recently, a further matter of conjecture. In 1994 the remains of a late 13th-century water-powered forge, where lengths of bar-iron were worked under a trip hammer, activated by a waterwheel, to form tools and other implements, were excavated near the North Gate Bridge in the city of Cork. At this remarkable site, the remains of the mill race and the forge building (including the forge's wooden anvil) were examined in situ [8 and

9]. The mill had been built on the banks of the River Lee within the precincts of the medieval walled town, immediately adjacent to the quayside, where bulky cargoes of perhaps charcoal and bar iron could be discharged.[55] This is the first example of a water-powered forge built within a walled town to be investigated in Europe, and shows the lengths that the Anglo-Norman inhabitants of Cork were prepared to go to ensure regular supplies of iron implements.

9 – A 15th-century hammer forge, from Hugo Spechtshart, *Flores Musicae* (Strasbourg, 1488)

Attempts to source and exploit non-ferrous metals such as silver, lead and copper during the reign of Edward I in Munster do not seem to have been very successful. And for the most part, during the high medieval period, nearly all of the metals needed within the Lordship were imported. Lead, for example, was imported from Wales: some ten stones of it were purchased in 1286-7 to roof a castle at Great Island near Dunbrody Abbey in Waterford harbour.[56] Nonetheless, most Irish lead ores are argentiferous or silver-bearing, and the basic demand for lead ore would have been for specie, where the silver would have been separated from the lead after smelting. Silver was the only desirable impurity of the smelting process, and this was refined from the lead in a process called *cupellation*, during which the lead was reheated in a shallow hearth (the *cupel*) to 1000-1100°C. An air blast was used to oxidise the lead to litharge (PbO) or lead oxide, in which the base metals were absorbed: the silver was not oxidised and could be collected at the bottom of the cupel. The earliest lead smelters used in Ireland were probably *bole hearths*, in which a primitive hearth was built within a stone-walled enclosure, on an exposed site open to the prevailing winds. Large pieces of lead ore were simply layered with brushwood and timber which were ignited. As lead has a low melting point of 327°C, smelting readily took place, the molten lead running off into a stone mould constructed at the side of the hearth. In 1264, indeed, there is a record of four miners and smelting specialist working at a site called 'Oulys' (Oola on the Limerick-Tipperary border?).[57] Silver is also likely to have been mined from 1289 to 1303 at Knockaunderrig (Silvermines), county Tipperary, where Italians appear to have been involved in its extraction.[58]

SOME CONCLUSIONS

The origins for the exploitation of Munster's hydro-power resources clearly lie in the early medieval period. These were significantly expanded in the Anglo-Norman period, with the expansion of water-powered grain mills and the introduction of mechanised processes for fulling woollen cloth and forging iron. The native Irish had, in any case, already become accomplished in the craft of millwrighting, with their basic repertoire extending to both horizontal and vertical-wheeled mills. We can safely assume that both types operated in Gaelic areas throughout the medieval period, where they remained in private ownership and impervious to feudal custom. On the basis of the Ballyine and Patrick Street vertical-wheeled watermills, it is clear that these are no great technological advance on the excavated Irish examples of the 7th and 8th centuries AD. It is interesting, nonetheless, that the Ballyine mill is breastshot, although we cannot as yet rule out the possibility that these existed in early medieval Ireland. There are, in any case, few grounds for supposing that the Patrick Street undershot mill was in any way more efficient than, say, the early medieval example at Morett, county Laois. If the Anglo-Norman contribution to the development of grain milling in Munster was in increased production, then it is likely to have been by increasing the number of mills rather than in improving the productive capacity of individual mills. Only in the early 14th century do we find evidence for larger, more productive mills and these, on present evidence, were uncommon.

By the middle of the 12th century, newly established monastic orders in Ireland such as the Cistercians were already introducing new systems of water management, for both domestic and industrial needs. Larger, more elaborate millraces were now engineered near larger rivers such as the Suir, the Blackwater and the Liffey, to take full advantage of more constant water supplies. The Anglo-Norman contribution lies thus in the further exploitation of existing water sources, and the introduction of mechanised processes for the finishing of woollen cloth and iron processing. It also seems likely that the number of grain-processing mills was increased to meet the demand from the expanding rural and urban populations. And herein lie the origins of Irish water-powered industries. Water power was the backbone of Irish industry for the greater part of the 18th and 19th centuries. It alone provided some respite from the near crippling restraint the island's lack of suitable mineral fuels for industrial use placed on its ability to industrialise. The Anglo-Normans were the first to exploit the hydro-power of Ireland's larger rivers, and in doing so they established a pattern of use which was continued by later industrial concerns.

———

The author

Dr Colin Rynne is curator of the Cork Butter Museum at Shandon. He is an archaeologist, and has published extensively on the development of water-power in early medieval Ireland, but in recent times has tended to specialise in industrial archaeology. His books include *The Archaeology of Cork City and Harbour* (1993), *The Industrial Archaeology of Cork City and its Environs* (1998), and *The Cork Butter Market, 1720-1924* (1998).

Acknowledgements

My thanks to Noel Jameson of Barryscourt Castle, and John Ludlow of Cork County Council, for comments on earlier drafts of the text, to Judith Monk for an important reference from the Pipe Roll of Cloyne, and to John O'Regan of Gandon Editions for his patience.

———

Notes and References

1   The economic development of Anglo-Norman Munster has been ably and comprehensively dealt with in a series of papers by AF O'Brien, most notably in 'Politics, economy and society: the development of Cork and the Irish south-east region c.1170 to c.1583' in P O'Flanagan and CG Buttimer (eds.), *Cork History and Society – Interdisciplinary essays on the history of an Irish county* (Dublin, 1993), pp83-154. The best up-to-date summary of these developments is AF O'Brien, *The Impact of the Anglo-Normans on Munster*, Barryscourt Lectures II (Cork, 1997).

2   G MacEoin, 'The early Irish vocabulary of mills and milling', in BG Scott (ed.), *Studies on Early Ireland: Essays in Honour of M.V. Duignan* (Belfast, 1982), pp13-19: 18

3   O Williams-Thorpe and RS Thorpe, 'The provenance of donkey mills from Roman Britain', *Archaeometry*, 30, 2 (1988), pp275-89

4   See R Holt, *The Mills of Medieval England* (Oxford, 1988), pp17-20, who argues convincingly that the original interpretation of the excavator of certain structures such as a horse mill is probably the correct one; see PA Rahtz, 'The Saxon and medieval palaces at Cheddar', *Medieval Archaeology*, 6-7 (1962-3), pp53-66, and J Langdon, *Horses, oxen and technological innovation: the use of draught animals in English farming from 1066 to 1500* (Cambridge, 1986), pp117-18

5   J Muendel, 'The horizontal mills of medieval Pistoia', *Technology and Culture*, 15 (1974), pp194-25: 218, no.4; H Inalcik, *The Ottoman Empire: The Classical Age 1300-1608*, trans. by Norman Itzhnowitz and Colin Imber (London, 1973), pl, 43; LC Hunter, 'The living past in the Appalachias of Europe: watermills in Southern Europe', *Technology and Culture*, 8 (1967), pp446-66

6   P Kozmin, *Flour Milling*, trans. by M Falkner and T Fjelstrup (London, 1917); F Strauss, 'Mills without wheels in the 16th-century Alps', *Technology and Culture*, 12 (1971), pp23-42; Rusdea, 'Die Löffelradmühlen aus dem Tismanatal', pp199-219

7   F Castel Branco, 'A Plea for the Study of Tide Mills In Portugal', *Trans. International Molinological Soc.*, 2 (1971), pp81-3; C Rivals, 'Tide mills in France', *Trans. International Molinological Soc.*, 3 (1973), pp159-65; JP O'Reilly, 'Some further notes on ancient horizontal mills, native and foreign', *Proc. Royal Irish Academy*, section C, XXIV (1902-4), pp58-84

8   P Rahtz, P and D Bullough, 'The parts of the Anglo Saxon Mill', *Anglo-Saxon England*, 6 (1977), pp15-39: 20

[9] W Stokes, *Lives of the Saints from the Book of Lismore* (Oxford, 1890), p861; E Gwynn, *The Metrical Dindsenchas* (Dublin, 1903), pp22-3

[10] F Kelly, *Early Irish Law* (Dublin, 1988), 61

[11] W Horn, 'Waterpower and the plan of St. Gall', *Jn. Medieval History*, 1 (1975), pp219-58: 248; HN Nitz, 'The Church as Colonist: the Benedictine Abbey of Lorsch and planned Walldkufen colonisation in the Odenwald', *Jn. Historical Geography*, 9, 2 (1983), pp105-126

[12] C Doherty, 'Hagiography as a source for economic history', *Peritia*, I (1982), pp300-28

[13] C Rynne 'The Introduction of the Vertical Waterwheel into Ireland: Some Recent Archaeological Evidence', *Medieval Archaeology*, 33 (1989), pp21-31; information on the Ardcloyne site was kindly supplied by Rose Cleary, Field Officer, Department of Archaeology, University College Cork.

[14] G Mac Eoin, 'The Death of the Boys in the Mill', *Celtica*, X (1983), pp60-64

[15] I am indebted to Victor Buckley, Senior Archaeologist, Dept of Arts, Heritage, Gaeltacht and the Islands, and John Sheehan, Department of Archaeology, University College Cork, for information on the Clonlonan mill. For the date of the Corcannon site, see M Moore, *An Archaeological Inventory of County Wexford* (Dublin, 1996), p45.

[16] MGL Baillie, *A Slice Through Time – dendrochronology and precision dating* (London, 1995), p126

[17] C Rynne, 'The craft of the millwright in early medieval Munster', forthcoming in M Monk and J Sheehan (eds.), *Early medieval Munster* (Cork, 1998)

[18] See J Lydon, 'The mills at Ardee in 1304', *Jn. County Louth Archaeological and Historical Society*, 4 for 1980 (1981), pp259-63

[19] C Rynne, 'The Patrick Street Watermills – Their technological context and a note on the reconstruction' in C Walsh, *Archaeological Excavations at Patrick, Nicholas and Winetavern Streets, Dublin* (Dingle, 1997), pp81-9

[20] G Carville, *The Occupation of Celtic Sites in Ireland by the Canons Regular of St. Augustine and the Cistercians* (Kalamazoo, Michigan, 1982), pp29-47

[21] F Hamond, 'Power Generation', in FHA Aalen, K Whelan and M Stout (eds.), *Atlas of the Irish Rural Landscape* (Cork, 1997), p225

[22] M Moore, *Archaeological Inventory of County Meath.* (Dublin, 1987)

[23] As note 21, p226

[24] AF O'Brien, 'Politics, economy and society: the development of Cork and the Irish south-coast region c.1170 to c.1583' in P O'Flanagan and CG Buttimer (eds.), *Cork, History and Society – Interdisciplinary essays on the history of an Irish county* (Cork, 1993), pp83-154, infra. 99-101

[25] J Tierney and M Hannon, 'Plant remains' in MF Hurley, OMB Scully and SWJ McCutcheon, *Late Viking Age and Medieval Waterford – Excavations 1986-1992* (Dublin, 1997), pp854-93: 892

[26] MF Hurley and CM Sheehan, 'Ovens and kilns' in MF Hurley, OMB Scully and SWJ McCutcheon, *Late Viking Age and Medieval Waterford – Excavations 1986-1992* (Dublin, 1997)

[27] M Walsh, 'A watermill at Ballyine, Co. Limerick', *Jn. Cork Historical and Archaeological Soc.*, lxx (1965), pp14-25

[28] HT Knox, 'Notes on gig-mills and drying kilns near Ballyhaunis, County Mayo', *Proc. of the Royal Irish Academy*, 26C (1906-7), pp263-73; S Maxwell, 'Paddles from horizontal mills', *Proc. of the Society of Antiquaries of Scotland*, lxxxviii (1954-56), pp231-2; LS Garrad, 'Items in the collection of the Manx Museum likely to be from horizontal mills', *Proc. of the Isle of Man Natural History and Archaeological Society*, 9 (1982-84), pp218-22; F Galhano, *Moinhos e Azenhas de Portugal* (Lisbon, 1978), desenho 18; A Jespersen, 'Portuguese Mills', *Trans. International Molinological Soc.*, 2 (1971), pp69-87;

C Irimie and C Bucur, 'Typology, distribution and frequency of watermills in Romania in the first half of the twentieth century', *Trans. International Molinological Soc.*, 2 (1971), pp421-36. Stone footstep bearings for vertical-wheeled mills are also known from Romano-British watermills; see RJ Spain, 'Romano-British watermills', *Archaeologia Cantiana*, 100, pp101-28, fig.12.

[29] DW Crossley, *The Bewl Valley ironworks, Kent, c.1300-1730*, Royal Archaeological Institute Monographs (Leeds, 1975), fig. 9c; GG Astill, *A medieval industrial complex and its landscape: the metalworking watermills and workshops of Bordesley Abbey* CBA research report 92 (York, 1993), pp214-16

[30] For the importation of millstones into Ireland in high medieval period, see T O'Neill, *Merchants and Mariners in Medieval Ireland* (Dublin, 1987), p92

[31] J Lydon, 'The mills at Ardee in 1304', p259

[32] *ibid.*, p262

[33] P MacCotter and K Nicholls (eds.), *The Pipe Roll of Cloyne* (Rotulis Pipae Clonensis) (Cloyne Literary and Historical Society, Cork 1996), p73.

[34] RJ Hunter, 'A seventeenth-century mill in Tyrhugh', *Donegal Annual*, IX, no.2 (1970), pp238-40

[35] *The Pipe Roll of Cloyne* (Rotulis Pipae Clonensis), p73

[36] J Lydon, 'The mills at Ardee in 1304', p262

[37] R Bennett and J Elton, *A History of Cornmilling*, vol. III (London, 1900), p199

[38] J Muendel, 'The distribution of mills in the Florentine countryside during the late middle ages' in JA Raftis (ed.) *Pathways to medieval peasants* (Toronto, 1981), pp83-115

[39] J Muendel, 'The horizontal mills of medieval Pistoia', *Technology and Culture*, 15 (1974), pp194-225

[40] T O'Neill, *Merchants and mariners*, 58; K Down, 'Colonial society and economy in the high Middle Ages' in A Cosgrove (ed.), *A New History of Ireland. II Medieval Ireland 1169-1534* (Oxford, 1987), pp439-91

[41] F McCormick, 'The animal bones' in MF Hurley, OMB Scully and SWJ McCutcheon, *Late Viking Age and Medieval Waterford – Excavations 1986-1992* (Dublin, 1997), pp819-53: 823

[42] MF Hurley and SWJ McCutcheon, 'Wooden Artefacts' in MF Hurley, OMB Scully and SWJ McCutcheon, *Late Viking Age and Medieval Waterford – Excavations 1986-1992*, p588

[43] *ibid.* For spinning techniques in the medieval period, see P Walton, 'Textiles' in J Blair and N Ramsay (eds.) *English medieval industries – Craftsmen, techniques, products* (London, 1991), pp319-54: 324-5

[44] MF Hurley and SWJ McCutcheon, 'Wooden Artefacts' in MF Hurley, OMB Scully and SWJ McCutcheon, *Late Viking Age and Medieval Waterford – Excavations 1986-1992*, p583

[45] *ibid.*, p595

[46] *ibid.*, p598, p670

[47] MF Hurley, 'Excavations at Grand Parade II and Grand Parade I 1984', *Jn. Cork Hist. and Arch. Soc.*, vol. xcv, no. 354 (1990), p73

[48] P Malanima, 'The first European textile machine', *Textile History*, 17 (2) (1986), pp115-28

[49] AT Lucas, 'Cloth finishing in Ireland', *Folklife*, vol. 6 (1968), pp18-67: 20; EM Carus Wilson, 'An industrial revolution of the thirteenth century', *Economic History Review* II (1941), repr. in EM Carus Wilson (ed.) *Essays in Economic History* (London, 1954), pp41-60: 45

[50] E Wincott Heckett, 'Report on textiles, Grand Parade II and Grand Parade I 1984' in MF Hurley, 'Excavations at Grand Parade, Cork II', *Jn. Cork Hist. and Arch. Soc.*, vol.

xcv, no.254 (1990) pp64-87: 81-5; E Wincott Heckett, 'Textiles, cordage, basketry and raw fibre', MF Hurley, OMB. Scully and SWJ McCutcheon, *Late Viking Age and Medieval Waterford – Excavations 1986-1992*, pp743-60: 749

[51] BG Scott, *Early Irish ironworking* (Belfast, 1991), pp154-9

[52] M Monk, 'Excavations at Lisleagh ringforts, north Cork', *Archaeology Ireland*, 2 (2) (1988), pp57-60

[53] K Nicholls, Gaelic society and economy in the high middle ages, in A Cosgrave (ed.), *A New History of Ireland.II Medieval Ireland 1169-1534* (Oxford, 1987), p418

[54] T O'Neill, *Merchants and mariners*, pp90-1

[55] MF Hurley, *Excavations at the North Gate Cork* (Cork, 1997), pp45-9

[56] T O'Neill, *Merchants and mariners*, p93

[57] D Cowman, 'The metal mines of Tipperary', *Tipperary Historical Jn.* (1992), pp105-115: 105

[58] A Gleeson, 'The silver mines of Ormond', *Jn. Royal Society of Antiquaries of Ireland*, vol. 75 (1) (1937), pp101-16; D Cowman, 'The Silvermines – Sporadic Working, 1289-1874', *Tipperary Historical Jn.* (1988), pp96-115

Glossary of Technical Terms

BREASTSHOT WATERWHEEL – a VERTICAL WATERWHEEL which receives incoming water about half way up its circumference.

CORN DRYING KILN – in Ireland, during the Anglo-Norman period or later, a device for drying cereal grains prior to milling.

DOUBLE FLUME MILL – a variety of HORIZONTAL-WHEELED MILL which uses two flumes or water delivery chutes to develop and direct a jet of water onto the vanes of separate horizontal waterwheels.

HORIZONTAL MILL – a watermill with a waterwheel inclined in the horizontal plane, whose power is transmitted to the upper, rotating millstone, via a vertical shaft.

MILLPOND – an artificial reservoir in which water is stored for use by a watermill.

MILLRACE – a man-made water channel used to lead water to a watermill.

OVERSHOT WATERWHEEL – a variety of VERTICAL WATERWHEEL which receives incoming water on the upper part of its circumference.

PIVOT STONES – in horizontal and vertical-wheeled watermills a stone which supports the gudgeon of an upright driveshaft.

ROTARY QUERN/HANDMILL – a rotary grindstone which consists of a stationary lower millstone and an upper, rotating millstone turned by a wooden handle.

UNDERSHOT WATERWHEEL – a variety of VERTICAL WATERWHEEL in which the incoming water is directed onto floats or paddles at the lowest part of its circumference.

VERTICAL WATERMILL – a watermill whose waterwheel turns in a vertical plane on a horizontal axle, whose motion is transmitted to the millstones through gear wheels set at right angles to each other.

WROUGHT IRON – this is almost pure iron, containing only a small amount of carbon (not more than 0.15%). It is a soft, ductile material (i.e could be drawn into wire), which could be reworked by a smith if reheated, but could not be hardened or tempered like steel.

BARRYSCOURT LECTURES

BARRYSCOURT LECTURE SERIES

Barryscourt Castle is a fine 16th-century
tower-house at Carrigtwohill, Co Cork.
The Barryscourt Trust was established in
1987 with the aim of conserving,
enhancing and developing the heritage
potential of the castle.
     In 1996, the Barryscourt Trust
instituted a bi-annual series of lectures on
Medieval Ireland. These will deal with
aspects of medieval history, archaeology,
art and architecture, and will be
delivered by scholars specialising in the
period. The lectures will be published
individually and in compilation form.

Barryscourt Lectures IV
IRISH GARDENS AND GARDENING
BEFORE CROMWELL
Terence Reeves-Smyth

Published by the Barryscourt Trust
in association with Cork County Council
and Gandon Editions, Kinsale.

© The Barryscourt Trust and the author,
1999. All rights reserved.

ISBN 0946641 96X

Publication of this lecture
was sponsored by
Cork County Council.

Series Editor   Noel Jameson
Design   John O'Regan
                 (© Gandon, 1999)
Production   Nicola Dearey, Gandon
Printing   Betaprint, Dublin
Distribution   Gandon, Kinsale

THE BARRYSCOURT TRUST
Barryscourt Castle
Carrigtwohill, Co Cork

IRISH GARDENS AND GARDENING
BEFORE CROMWELL

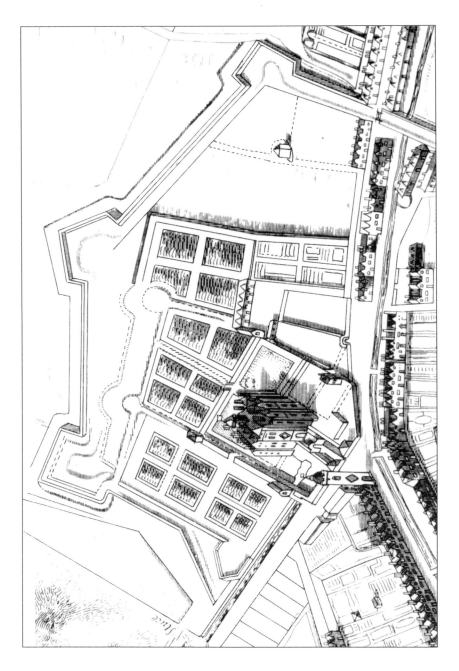

1 – Detail from a bird's-eye view of Belfast, dated 1685,
showing Sir Arthur Chichester's house at Belfast with surrounding gardens and courts

Irish Gardens and Gardening before Cromwell

Terence Reeves-Smyth

THE BARRYSCOURT TRUST
IN ASSOCIATION WITH CORK COUNTY COUNCIL AND GANDON EDITIONS

2 – Tully Castle: view of the early 17th-century-style garden
created in the castle's bawn

INTRODUCTION

Considerable variation existed in the form and function of Irish gardens during the centuries prior to the 1600s, and although the range of plants was largely restricted to European varieties, gardens were far from colourless or uninteresting.[1] Culinary and medicinal plants predominated, but from medieval times, and perhaps even before, gardens were perceived not just in purely utilitarian terms, but also as places of leisure. Thus, physic gardens, orchards and even kitchen gardens were often designed for recreation as well as utility. The idea of the pleasure garden as an art form came fully to prominence in late Tudor and Jacobean Ireland, when plants were increasingly appreciated for their own sake and gardens were designed for ornament, amusement and as a means to indicate status or social achievement. Continental Renaissance ideas, exemplified in the use of terracing, statuary and other architectural features within coherent and symmetrical garden layouts, were well established by 1641 when Ireland was plunged into war. In the years that followed, there was little opportunity for gardening, and further developments ceased until after the Restoration of 1660.

Throughout their development from early times to the mid-17th century, Irish gardens were confined within enclosures. Like a picture in a frame, physical boundaries were considered an integral part of a garden's layout; walls, banks, hedges and fences were all employed, and these served to keep livestock and people out and to provide much needed shelter for the plants within. Garden enclosures were not unique to Ireland, but the frequently unsettled conditions of the country no doubt contributed to their prevalence; indeed, at times they also functioned as part of the defensive network relating to a manor or castle.

Enclosure boundaries are a feature of early gardens that may be expected to leave some sort of imprint in the archaeological record, while path layouts, flower beds, basins and other features can also leave traces in various forms. The value of analytical field survey and excavation in investigating such relict features has been fully demonstrated in recent decades, and garden archaeology is now an established discipline in Britain and elsewhere.[2] Undoubtedly, the most obvious and identifiable relict gardens date from the 1660 to 1740 era, when very structured, extensive and geometrical layouts predominated, but there are some good survivals from the pre-Cromwellian period. An example is the early 17th-century garden at Dunluce Castle, county Antrim, where flights of terraces and raised flower beds are preserved as upstanding earthworks in permanent pasture.[3] The quality of survival in this case owed much to the castle being deserted within decades of the garden's creation, although this is unusual as most of Ireland's great houses of this era either survived or were later rebuilt on or near the same site.[4] Consequently, the associated gardens were invariably altered or swept away by later activities – often a succession of garden layouts, each reflecting the changing fashions of its period. Such multi-period sites can be archaeologically rewarding in themselves, but ultimately our best source of information must derive from the minority of gardens abandoned at early stage.

In the long term, much of our knowledge of pre-17th-century gardens will inevitably derive from programmes of fieldwork and excavation, but to date the potential of garden archaeology in Ireland has yet to be fully realised.[5] Meanwhile, heavy reliance must be placed upon the historical record. Unfortunately, although documentary sources contain plenty of references to gardens and orchards, this by itself is of limited value beyond indicating that garden-making was widely practised in Ireland from earlier medieval times. More exact information on layout, content and size is scarce, due to a paucity of surviving records and to illiteracy among gardeners prior to the 1700s. Instructions were given verbally, garden catalogues were rarely compiled, plant acquisitions were often by exchange, and those purchased were seldom specified individually on bills. The difficulties are exacerbated by the backwardness of social history research in Irish medieval studies and by the fact that a great deal of manuscript material remains unpublished.[6] Nonetheless, much can be inferred from the available records, while comparative English material can be used in the generalities of the field.

3 – Aerial view of Dunluce castle gardens
showing terraces and raised beds

PREHISTORIC GARDENING

Horticulture is rarely if ever mentioned, let alone discussed, in the context of Irish or British prehistory, but the probability is high that some form of gardening existed at this time. Unfortunately, despite the wealth of evidence for cultivation from pollen studies, field systems and ard marks, we still know surprisingly little of the range and relative importance of the plants grown in prehistory.[7] Part of the problem derives from a lack of waterlogged deposits – the most valuable class of evidence – and our consequent dependence upon carbonised remains, supplemented by seed impressions on pottery. From these sources we know that naked and hulled barley, rye and primitive wheats, such as emmer and einkorn, were grown in the Irish Neolithic, but the range cultivated may have been more numerous than presently known as relatively few sites have been extensively sampled for charred remains. Furthermore, the food plants likely to be preserved in carbonised form are inherently biased towards those crops which needed to be parched over or in the domestic fire as part of the processing before consumption.[8] Most edible greens, notably root vegetables and brassicas, are unlikely to leave any identifiable trace, and although legumes (peas and beans) sometimes have to be kiln-dried or parched before storage, this may have been unnecessary in the Neolithic or Bronze Age if summer temperatures were appreciably higher than today.

It could be argued that many of the plants cultivated in continental Europe during prehistory were probably also grown in Ireland, provided the environmental conditions were favourable. Trade and cultural links extended over wide areas, and besides, it is unlikely that new colonisers would have abandoned their basic complement of seed stocks. As legumes accompanied cereals in the early advance of agriculture,[9] their early arrival in Ireland is likely.[10] The vine may likewise have had an early appearance, as grape pips, most probably *Vitis sylvestris*, have been discovered in early Neolithic levels as far north as Sweden, as well as in England.[11]

Alexanders (*Olusatrum, Petroselinum alexandrinum*), beet (*Beta*) and coriander (*Coriandrum*) go back to the Iron Age or earlier, and there is also continental evidence for use of the common goosefoot or fat hen (*Chenopodium album*) as a vegetable, and for the deliberate cultivation of other arable weeds, notably Pale Persicaria (*Polygonum lapathifolium*) and Gold of Pleasure (*Candina satina*).[12] Leeks, celery and carrots may also have been grown in Ireland during prehistory, but unfortunately, being so highly perishable, they will always be difficult to detect. However, the wild leek (*Allium babingtonii*), which grows today in the west of Ireland and is related to species found in south-west Europe, might be descended from such early imports.[13]

The value of plants to make and dye cloths was widely appreciated in prehistory. Flax (*Linum usitatissum*), which was harvested for its oil-rich seeds (linseed) and its bast fibres to make linen, was cultivated in Ireland from at least the early Bronze Age, and appears to have been widespread by early Christian times.[14] We have no direct evidence for dyes on Irish prehistoric levels as yet, but the sophistication of jewellery and personal ornaments in both the Bronze Age and Iron Age indicates a wealthy and fashion-conscious society which probably used clothing colours to denote the wearer's rank, as was done in early historic times.[15] In the English Iron Age, woad (*Isatis tinctoria*) was used as a blue and possibly pink dye,[16] while other dye plants known to have been cultivated from European prehistoric contexts include weld (*Reseda luteola*) and Aaron's rod (*Verbascum thapsus*) for yellow, field madder (*Sherardia arvensis*) for pink, and safflower (*Carthamus tinctoria*) for orange.[17] Such plants would probably have been grown in special gardens rather than alongside the arable.

———

4 – Woad (*Isatis tinctoria*)

THE EARLY CHRISTIAN PERIOD

It is clear that the Romans, during their four centuries of domination of Britain, were responsible for introducing a wide range of fruit, vegetables and flowers, as well as new methods of horticulture.[18] Some seeds and plants no doubt arrived in Ireland during the period of empire, but it was not until the 5th century, with the arrival of Christian missionaries, that any real semblance of Roman gardening techniques and plants were adopted here.[19] The church brought Ireland into direct contact with the Romanised world, introducing, among other things, literacy and a knowledge of continental lifestyles and values. In the monasteries, which multiplied in number during the 6th and 7th centuries, classical literature was avidly read, including texts on botany, agriculture and horticulture, notably Pliny's *Naturalis Historia* and the specialist works of the *De re Rustica*.[20] Horticultural expertise was undoubtedly also brought by some of the scholars who flocked from the continent to the Irish monastic schools and by monks returning from their European travels as missionaries or 'pilgrims of grace'. The gardening interest of some of these monks is illustrated by the story of Saint Fiachra, a Donegal nobleman, who travelled to France in the 7th century and founded a monastery deep in the forests of Breuil near Meaux. Here he created a garden so fine that he has since been regarded as the patron saint of gardeners.[21]

The early Irish monasteries took horticulture seriously in order to meet the demands of their self-sufficient lifestyles and to satisfy their communal or penitential dietary emphasis on vegetable rather than meat products. The size of their gardens has yet to be established, but they were almost certainly located within the termons or boundaries of the *monasteria*. Typically, these enclosures took the form of a curvilinear outer vallum or embankment, with an inner, eccentrically placed smaller one.[22] The church and graveyard occupied the inner precinct, while the outer zone would have contained the fenced gardens and orchards, with industrial activity areas near the perimeter, all interspersed with the monks' cells.

Modern excavation of these ecclesiastical enclosures in Ireland is very limited, but extensive work has been undertaken on a number of sites in south-west Scotland (Dalriada), where early Irish monasticism also flourished. At Whithorn in Galloway, one such *monasterium* produced clear botanical evidence for the cultivation of both medicinal and culinary herbs from the 6th century. Among the medicinal assemblages here, one contained elder (*Sambucus nigra*), hemlock (*Conium maculatum*) and woundwort (*Stachys arvensis*), while another included species with properties that were particularly appropriate to digestive problems, such as chickweed (*Stellaria media*), dog rose (*Rosa cania*), mustard (*Brassica nigra*), coriander (*Coriandrum sativum*) and dill (*Anethum grave lens*).[23]

While archaeological evidence remains sparse, the early written tracts are quite unambiguous about the existence of gardening both in the monasteries and among the population at large. These sources derive principally from the law-texts, annals, saints' lives, poetry and sagas, and mostly date from the 7th to the 9th centuries.[24] They make it clear that a prosperous farm often had an enclosed garden (**lubgort**) situated outside the **les**.[25] A whole range of garden plants are mentioned, and indication is given that their cultivation sometimes required specialist skills; for example, we are told that one of the seven officers of the church was a gardener (**lubgortóir**) and that on Iona, and presumably other monasteries, there was an officer whose duties was that of gardener (*hortulanus*).[26]

Vegetables, fruit and herbs were cultivated, and particular attention was apparently given to those with medicinal properties. The law tract 'Bretha Crólige', which seems to have formed part of the *Senchas Már*, states that 'no person on sick maintenance is entitled in Irish law to any condiment except garden herbs (**lus lubgort**) for it is for this purpose that gardens (**lubgort**) have been made.'[27] One plant often mentioned as a condiment for invalids, and apparently much cultivated, was leafy celery (**imus** / *Apium graveolens secalinum*), believed to prevent sickness 'and does not stir it up, prevents thirst and not infect wounds'.[28]

Identification of plant varieties from the early sources can cause confusion in some instances, but it is evident that the most frequently mentioned vegetable in the texts, **cainnenn**, was a bunching or shallot type of onion.[29] The leek (**borrlus**) was also commonly grown, possibly as a substitute for garlic, and can probably be identified with the variety *Allium babingtonii* found in western Ireland today.[30] Cabbage (**braisech**) featured in monastic diets, sorrel (**samhadh** / *Rumex acetosa*) was used in salads,[31] while skirrets (**cerrbacán** / *Sium sisarum*),[32] chives (**foltchép** / *Allium sechoenoprasum*) and kale (**meacain murrathaig**) were also cultivated, as were peas and beans. Other food plants not apparently mentioned, but likely to have been grown, include parsnip, beet, lettuce, radish and vervain, while in addition to dill and coriander mentioned above, monastic herb gardens probably also included such umbellifers as fennel, alexanders, parsley and lovage.

An important horticultural development of the period was the appearance of orchards (**aballgort**) containing apples, plums and possibly other fruit. Apples do not breed true from seed and most cannot be reproduced from suckers or cuttings, so in common with many other fruit trees, their cultivation demands the vegetative propagation of clones by grafting.[33] The technique appears to have had its origin in the far east, possibly western China, and to have arrived in the Mediterranean around 1000 BC or earlier.[34] The Romans, who employed a wide range of grafting methods, notably cleft grafting, root grafting and budding, are usually credited with introducing the art to northern Europe.[35] Earlier claims have been made on the basis of apple finds in prehistoric contexts, but these have proved to be the result of confusion between the small native European wild 'crab apple' (*Malus sylvestris*) and larger domesticated varieties.[36] As the evidence stands at present, it would appear that the technique of grafting, and with it cultivated apples, plums and possibly pears, were most likely carried to Ireland by the monks in the 5th or 6th centuries.

The early written sources make a clear distinction between native sour wild apples (**fiaduball**) and sweet cultivated apples (**ubla cumrae**). Indeed, one text apparently recognises the existence of different varieties of cultivated apples, and heavy fines were imposed for stealing them.[37] Many of the monasteries probably had orchards; at Tallaght, the Culdees were allowed to eat apples on festival days with their bread so long as 'each man's share of apples was three or four, if they be big ones; if they chanced to be small, each man's share was not to exceed the number of five or six.'[38] The garden plum (*Prunus domestica*), which like the apple was propagated by grafting, was also cultivated at the time (**áirne cumra**),[39] but neither the pear nor the damson seem to be mentioned in early texts, though they were widely grown in contemporary Europe.[40]

The much-quoted statement that Ireland had 'no lack of vines', written by the Venerable Bede (673-735) towards the end of his life, may not be such an exaggeration as some would believe.[41] Wine was indispensable for celebrating the sacrament, and the monks consequently needed a regular supply. Some importation was likely, particularly once the Norse towns were established in the 9th and 10th centuries, but transporting wine can be difficult and many monasteries were in remote locations. Considering the degree of self-sufficiency practised by the monasteries, and the probable mildness of the climate at the time, it is more than likely that the grapevine (*Vitis vinifera*) was often cultivated by the monks themselves.[42]

Some of the garden plants of the Early Christian period were grown for industrial purposes. Flax or **lin** (*Linium usitatissimum*) was widely cultivated,[43] particularly for linen tunics (**léine**), which were worn under the cloak.[44] Teasal (*Dipsacaceae sativus*) was possibly grown for fulling, and hemp (*Cannabis sativa*) for making rope fibre. The latter is an Asiatic plant, which was introduced to northern Europe by the Romans and was known to the Vikings.[45] Many dye stuffs are derived from plants, most notably woad (*Isatis tinctoria*), which is often mentioned in the early Irish sources (**glaisen**) and was clearly widely grown.[46] In one tale, the Queen of Tara is represented as having her own woad garden (**glaisengort**), while an 8th-century law-text gives details of some of the processes employed to obtain the blue dye.[47] There are also references to the cultivation of roid, which Professor Kelly has convincingly shown was the dye-plant true mad-der (*Rubia tinctorum*), a native of south-west Asia.[48] The roots of madder were used to obtain alizarin (Turkey red), and was widely available from Roman times.[49] The onion (*Allium cepa*) was probably used for yellow dye, as was possibly fairy flax (*Linum catharticum*) and dyer's rocket or weld (*Reseda luteola*). Aside from cloths, a wide selection of dyes were needed for the illuminated manuscripts, some of which were undoubtably of veg-etable origin, though research has shown that many mineral-based dyes were also imported for the purpose, such as red lead, verdigris, orpiment and ox-gall.[50]

It seems likely that some garden plants were introduced with the establishment of permanent Norse settlements from the 10th-century. Excavations in Dublin and Waterford have produced considerable archaeobotanical assemblages, bringing evidence of town diets and of plants grown in and around urban areas.[51] Fruit and nuts were eaten, while some of the herbs and vegetables found include leafy celery (*Apium grave-olens*), carrot (*Daucus carota*), fennel (*Foeniculum vulgare*), radish (*Raphanus raphanistrum*), mustard (*Brassica nigra*) and other members of the brassica (cabbage) family. The evidence also suggests that fat hen (*Chenopodium album*) and some members of the *Polygonum* genus (persi-caria and knotweeds) were deliberately cultivated for food. Some of the 'weeds' found may have been grown for medicine, including chickweed, mallow, hemlock, henbane and woundwort. As one might expect, the assemblages are very similar to those found at York, though at York the examination of vegetable tissue in addition to just the analysis of seeds allowed such plants as leek (*Allium porrum*), woadwaxen (*Genista tincto-ria*), Scandinavian clubmoss (*Diphasium complanatum*) and true madder to be identified – plants which were probably also present in Dublin at this time.[52] Most of these urban gardens, which appear to have been fairly rudi-mentary, were located behind the street houses in small plots where they jostled for space with sheds or byres and cesspits.

———

5 – Anemones
from Parkinson's *Paradisus*, 1629

THE MEDIEVAL PERIOD

Our knowledge of medieval gardens and gardening has been revolutionised in recent decades, thanks in large measure to the brilliant scholarship of the late John Harvey, whose classic work on the subject was published in 1981.[53] By piecing together a mosaic of information from many different sources, Harvey has enabled us to visualise gardens of the period in a way that had not been previously possible. He also established that medieval gardens shared similar characteristics across northern Europe, with a similar range of plants, so despite the fragmentary nature of the Irish evidence, we do have a very clear picture of the kind of gardens that the continental monasteries and the Norman settlers brought to Ireland in the 12th century.

Harvey and subsequent researchers have emphasised the central role of the monasteries in developing and disseminating horticultural expertise across Europe in the Middle Ages.[54] In Ireland, where the continental houses spread far beyond the limits of Norman expansion, their role was enormously important, and remained so until the Dissolution in the 16th century. With their emphasis on self-sufficiency and on a disciplined, corporate lifestyle, the monasteries practised a highly efficient system of agricultural, water and woodland management, and appreciated the importance of land drainage, soil enrichment, coppicing and crop rotation.[55] A knowledge of trees and plants was encouraged through well-stocked monastic libraries, often containing laboriously hand-copied herbals, and an exchange network of seeds and cuttings flourished among the monasteries, notably in the Cistercian order.[56] Herbs were grown for medicinal and culinary purposes, flowers for church decoration and religious festivals, and fruit and vegetables for guests and the community itself, which, at times, ate virtually no meat. For the medieval monks, gardening also had an important spiritual dimension: they believed that Adam and Eve's disobedience in the Garden of Eden – the Doctrine of the Fall of Humanity – meant that one avenue of seeking association with God was through gardening.

It is clear from the *Monastic Extents* of 1540 to 1541 and other documents that monastic gardening in Ireland tended to be focused within the area of the precincts.[57] These enclosures have been somewhat neglected in Irish archaeological research, though all the continental houses in Ireland adopted them, including the friaries.[58] The concept stemmed from the Rule of St Benedict, where clearly defined, self-contained precincts were advocated to ensure that the monks could be spared the temptation to roam abroad and encouraged to perform their necessary tasks within the spiritual sanctuary:

'The monastery should, if possible, be so arranged that all necessary things, such as water, mill, garden and various crafts, may be within the enclosure, so that monks may not be compelled to wander outside it, for that is not at all expedient for their souls.'[59]

A small minority of Irish precincts were delimited by walls, notably Kells (county Kilkenny) and Athassel (county Tipperary), but the majority were enclosed by earthen banks and ditches.[60] In their heyday, these enclosures, particularly those of the Benedictine and related establishments, were busy and crowded places, far removed from the quiet and tranquil places they are today. Some idea of their appearance can be gauged from the early 9th-century monastic plan of St Gall and from the 16th-century plan of St Vedast's Abbey, both depicting a whole series of gardens of all shapes, functions and sizes, jostling for space in the precincts amidst domestic and industrial buildings.[61] Analogous images are found in monastic accounts, for example, Norwich Cathedral Priory and Beaulieu Abbey in Hampshire.[62] In Ireland, the mid-14th-century Register of the Hospitaller's Priory at Kilmainham similarly shows a proliferation of vegetable gardens, herb gardens, pleasure gardens and orchards scattered within the outer and inner precincts.[63] These were wedged in amidst a motley array of structures, such as the brewhouse, dairies, forges, carpenters' shops, stables, granaries, barns, storage and food-processing buildings. There were kitchen gardens, hostiliars' gardens, obedientiary gardens and numerous garden

6 – Borage (*Borago officinalis*) in the medieval-style physic garden
created in the grounds of Grey Abbey, county Down

plots attached to the many *camerae* for permanent guests and others with-in the Kilmainham enclosure.[63] Many other monasteries also had infirmary gardens and some had almoners' gardens. All of these would have been enclosed in some way, either with paling or wattle fences and in some cases with stone walling.[65] Thorn hedges were probably not a feature of the precinct, but were commonly used to enclose manorial gardens of the peri-od, such as those on the Earl of Norfolk's Leinster estates.[66]

In some cases, the size of the monastic precinct was not big enough to accommodate all the gardens and orchards, and some had to be located outside.[67] Precinct areas mostly varied from one to twelve acres, though some of monastic enclosures in the Dublin suburbs, notably St Mary's Abbey, were much larger.[68] Areas under productive garden obviously var-ied according to the size and demands of each monastery, but it is worth noting that the great country houses of the 19th century, whose require-ments had much in common with medieval monasteries, needed between three and five acres of intensively managed kitchen gardens. The Cistercian abbey of Beaulieu had about ten acres of garden to support a community of 120 brethren and 250 hired workers,[69] so on this basis we could estimate that an abbey such as Graiguenamanagh, with fifty monks and sixty laybrothers, would have needed at least three acres of gardens and orchards – more than half the precinct area.[70] With the decline in the size of monastic communities in the 14th century, it is likely that garden acreages also fell.

As the location of the various precinct gardens was probably deter-mined by the layout of the monastic buildings, the kitchen gardens would be expected to lie close to the cook house. Practicality meant that grid-like plans were usually followed, as depicted in the St Gall plan, with raised beds, supported by boards or low wattle edgings, flanked by paths, which often doubled as irrigation channels. Most of the vegetables culti-vated in the monasteries, and by the population at large, were pottagers, so-called because they were cooked in a large metal pot to make pottage soup – the basic hot dish of the Middle Ages, which was usually eaten alongside the staples of bread and ale.[71] The main ingredients included leeks, onions, chibols, shallots, porrets, peas, broad beans, leafy beets and colewort leaves, flavoured with parsley, garlic and hyssop, and often including some meat or fish.[72] Many other herbs and seasonings were also grown for use in pottage or eaten raw as salad, but root vegetables did not come into general use until the late Middle Ages, when carrots, parsnips, skirrets, rapes and turnips were all commonly added to pottage.

A good idea of the range of vegetables and herbs available in Ireland during the Norman era can be obtained from a poem written in doggerel verse called the 'Feate of Gardening', dating to about 1300 and attributed to Master Jon Gardener. This treatise, which is the first coherent account of horticultural techniques in English, was probably composed in England rather than Ireland, but both surviving manuscripts have Irish origins and include references to 'all the herbs of Ireland'.[73] It contains sections on trees, grafting, viticulture, the onion family, coleworts, parsley and herbs generally, including a long list with seasonal advise and a concluding section on saffron. There are plants for medicinal and ornamental use, but the main basis of the list are potherbs, salads and sweet herbs, mainly for use in pottage or as flavouring. Some of these included alexanders, borage, cress, water cress, fennel, grounsel, lettuce, smallage, nepp (*Nepeta cataria*), orach (*Atriplex* and related genera of *Chenopodiaaceae*), radish, spinach and tansy. Principal sweet herbs and condiments include calamint, coriander, dill, dittander (*Lepidium*), hyssop, lavender, mints, sage, savory, thyme and wood sorrel. In all, one hundred herbs and vegetables are listed, excluding the probable varieties involved in many entries – a considerable number if compared with what was probably available in Ireland a few centuries earlier.[74]

A large number of the plants listed by Jon Gardener had medicinal properties, and many of these would have been grown in the monastery's infirmary garden, where they could be used by the resident *phisicus* or *medicus*.[75] Poisons such as mandrake, hemlock, henbane and opium poppy were normally included in the physic garden,[76] so a grid layout with raised beds was invariably used to ensure their segregation from plants which may have been used in cooking. Diet and health were, in fact, closely linked in medieval medicine, and fruit and vegetables were thus commonly included in the infirmary garden. Herbs and flowers such as lilies, roses, wormwood, polypody, dill, camomile, flag irises and saffron might be distilled or dried to make compound medicines, salves or tonics that could be used for general ailments, to treat blood letting or to protect against plague or disease.[77] These gardens also served as recreational areas for the convalescent monks, and often assumed an ornamental aspect with tunnel arbours, trellises and perhaps a small pond for growing aquatic plants such as waterlilies, which were used medically. Considering the important role some Irish monasteries played in caring for the sick, it is likely that a number of infirmary gardens covered large areas.[78] The one at Westminster Abbey occupied two acres,[79] so we should be careful not to assume that the physic garden was a tiny plot tucked away behind the infirmary.[80]

Physic gardens were often the location of beehives – a standard feature of monasteries and manors alike. Bees have been 'cultivated' in Ireland from pre-Christian times and have had a long association with gardening. They pollinated herbs and flowers, produced honey – used for sweetening, for mead and medication – and also beeswax for candles, writing tablets, seals and adhesives. Loghives appear to have been used by the Early Christian monks who were noted beekeepers, while wickerwork skeps were in general use by the Norman period; skeps of coiled straw seem not to have become widely employed in Ireland until the Tudor period.[81] There are references to 'bee-towers' or 'honey-towers' for keeping hives in medieval Ireland,[82] but it seems likely that most hives were kept in open-fronted shelters – a practice that continued until the early 19th century.

Beehives were sometimes located in the orchard, as were dovecotes, which are often mentioned in medieval accounts.[83] Most orchards were probably regularly laid out in a grid pattern,[84] and could be extensive in size; in 1303 the manor of Santry, county Dublin, had two hundred apple trees and one hundred pear trees, implying an area of at least three acres,[85] while the manor of Old Ross in Wexford was producing nine bushels of apples for sale in the 1280s.[86] Many of the monasteries could boast several orchards: at St Thomas's Abbey (Dublin) there were eight, Greatconnell (Kildare) had six, and Inistioge (Kilkenny) had five.[87] Some of these may have been 'cemetery orchards' – an age-old association that is depicted on the St Gall plan as rows of trees flanking the monks' graves.[88] Undoubtably, apples predominated in Irish orchards, most likely including varieties of Costards, Pearmains and Bitter-sweets, the latter being for cider.[89] The most widely appreciated pears of the period included Wardens, Sorells, Caleols and Gold Knopes, all of which were usually cooked and put into preserves, puddings and pies. Dessert pears may have been comparatively rare, though there is one apparent reference to a *Bon Chrétien* in the prior's garden of St John's Priory, Kilkenny.[90] Plums and cherries were also grown, and other fruits might have included filberts, walnuts, medlars and perhaps even figs in some sheltered places.[91] The favourable climatic conditions that existed prior to the 14th century would certainly have suited figs, and, indeed, grave-vines,[92] for which there is some evidence in the form of both vineyards and winepresses, despite the fact that Ireland was known to be importing a great deal of wine from France during this period.[93]

Orchards were greatly valued in the Middle Ages for their blossom, and many were utilised as recreation grounds, complete with paths, flowers and arbours. Conversely, pleasure gardens often included flowering fruit trees as part of their design. Ornamental gardening was an important feature of the period, particularly in the monasteries, where gardens were frequently created for prayer and mediation, known as 'paradises', or for entertainment purposes. Pleasure gardens also existed in the secular world, many, no doubt, being located within the bawn of the castle or manor. The Continental and English evidence demonstrates such gardens followed a fairly basic formula, being usually small, enclosed, square or rectangular plots with raised beds and much 'carpenter's work' in the form of trellises, fences and arbours. The area was often quartered with sanded or gravelled paths, leading to a central feature such as a pool or perhaps a bay tree (*Laurus nobilis*) – a symbol of constancy and a popular evergreen. Turfed seats, sometimes enriched with small flowers such as camomile and thyme, frequently edged the garden perimeter or occupied suitable corners, perhaps in association with potted plants, which were widely used in monasteries and elsewhere at this time.[94] Another striking characteristic was the large amount of woodwork employed in the form of garden furniture, fences, railings, trellises or tunnel arbours, the latter sometimes enclosing the area like a cloister.[95] These would have been wreathed with trained apple trees or climbers, such as vines or eglantine (*Rosa rubiginosa*), while the garden beds would have contained shrubs, flowers and herbs, the most popular being highly scented plants like roses and lilies.[96] Both white roses (*R.alba*) and red roses (*R.gallica* and *R.gallica* 'Officinalis') were grown in Ireland during this period, and, together with lilies and irises, were particularly in demand in the monasteries to decorate the church. Chaplets and garlands of roses were also regularly worn by the clergy on festival days until the Reformation. Indeed, the church often stipulated the payment of one or more roses, sometimes specified as red roses, as the annual rental for small holdings.[97]

Depending on their size, gardens of the period often included lawns. Invariably these were studded with flowers, such as sweet violets, periwinkles, primroses, daisies, cowslips and wild strawberries – the so-called 'flowery medes'. For Albertus Magnus, writing in 1260, 'nothing refreshes the sight so much as fine short grass', and it was for precisely this reason that the monastic cloister garths contained lawns. Indeed, except for a few very occasional references to roses, lilies, pines and junipers, all of which had symbolic values, there is no evidence for the growing of anything other than turf in the cloister.[98] The colour green was considered to have a tranquillising effect, as Hugh de Fouilly remarked:

'The green turf in the middle of the cloister refreshes encloistered eyes and their desire for study returns. It is truly the nature of the colour green that it nourishes the eyes and preserves their vision.'[99]

Isolated trees may have occasionally been planted in Irish monastic cloisters, though the famous yew at Muckross grows in the accumulation of debris which fills the court, and was therefore planted after the friars had departed.[100] There is some evidence for tree-planting in the medieval period, but the subject has yet to be fully explored and lies outside the scope of this paper. However, it must be said that the orthodox view that woodland planting did not take place until the 17th century is difficult to support in the light of our current understanding of underwood and timber management in Anglo-Norman Ireland.[101]

———

7 – Artichoke
(*Cynara scolymus*)

8 – Lismore Castle Gardens, county Waterford:
the raised walk above the upper terrace showing walls and corner tower

THE ELIZABETHAN AND EARLY STUART PERIOD

The gardens that evolved in Britain, France and the Low Countries during the 16th century remained fundamentally medieval in character. Features such as quartered enclosures, raised beds, tunnel arbours and trellises all continued, while the late-medieval vogue for knots or geometric patterns defined by perennial plants was developed into a major garden component, particularly in England.[102] From the time of the dissolution of the monasteries however, an undercurrent of change was slowly revolutionising garden design. The emergence of a new wealthy elite promoted the creation of larger and more magnificent gardens, while Italian Renaissance ideas, which flooded into Britain following the accession of James I, encouraged houses and gardens to be designed as single units.[103] In addition, exotic plants began arriving back in increasingly large quantities from newly discovered parts of the world, and gardening skills were improving, notably in the breeding of new flower strains with bigger double blooms. Above all, printed books started to make their mark on horticulture, such as Hill's *Proffitable Arte of Gardening* (1568), *The Gardeners Labyrinth* (1577) and Gerald's *The Herbal* (1595).[104] These and other publications made information on the form of gardens and their contents available to an increasingly wider audience, leading to greater standardisation in taste and design.

Ireland must have had many gardens during the Elizabethan and early Stuart periods; at least 3,500 are noted in the *Patent Rolls of James I*, despite the fact that only a small minority of the compilers considered them worthy of inclusion. Most were undoubtably plots for vegetables, but the great magnates had fine pleasure gardens and some of these were of considerable size. The tenth Earl of Ormonde's Tudor house at Carrick-on-Suir, built from 1565, had extensive courts on the north and west sides, no doubt filled with fashionable gardens, while the Desmond Roll of 1583 recorded that Newcastle West, county Limerick, had a garden with two fish ponds in the main enclosure and another three-acre garden and orchard outside the curtain walls.[105] Nearby, at Askeaton Castle, the Earls of Desmond also had a half-acre garden, 'triangular in plan, in which a fishpond lies to the south, all of which is enclosed with a stone wall'.[106] A bird's-eye view of Askeaton in *Pacata Hibernia* depicts this garden as being laid out in regular square plots, and while we have no further information, it is probable that each of these plots contained knots with delimiting wooden rails incorporating images of Geraldine heraldry.

The only visual representation of a garden during this period in Ireland is a bird's-eye view of the Master's garden at Trinity College, Dublin, in the 1590s. This depicts a large plot divided into compartments of different designs – a closed knot of diamonds and rectangles containing flowers, another with some form of emblematic design, one incorporating roses, and an open knot, presumably with coloured sands. There are no planting details, but in 1605 Harry Holland signed a deed allowing him 'the use and possession of the College's five gardens and the great orchard', being permitted to take half of 'all the herbs, lavender, roses and fruit of the trees'. He was required to grow turnips, cabbages. parsnips, carrots, artichokes, onions, leeks 'and other things as they shall need for 30 persons or 8 messes as the cook shall think good'.[107] Little mention is made of the garden flora, but a wide range was commonly available by this time, such as wallflowers, jasmine, lilac, syringa, species of iris and lily, hyacinth, tulip and double carnations. Edmund Spencer refers to many of these in his poetry, and no doubt grew them in his garden at Kilcolman, county Cork.[108] His contemporary and friend, Sir Walter Raleigh, introduced a number of his own plants, including the sweet-smelling yellow wallflower from the Azores and the Assane cherry from the Canaries, both of which he established first at Assane and later at Dromona. In his garden at Myrtle Grove in Youghal, Raleigh also grew the American tobacco plant, but is perhaps best remembered for his role in introducing the potato, which had such rapid and remarkable success in Ireland.[109]

Raleigh was a beneficiary of the land settlements resulting from the expansion of government control in Ireland at this time – a policy that brought waves of colonists, undertakers and administrators in ever-increasing numbers during the first four decades of the 17th century. It was land owners such as these, the so-called 'new English', who were the most eager to adopt the Italian Renaissance fashion for designing gardens in strict symmetrical relationship with the house, often with terraces, stairways, waterworks and sculpture. An early example was Sir Nicholas Malby's great garden from the 1580s, laid out in front of his new mansion at Roscommon Castle.[110] For Malby and other members of his class, gardens were a very visible means of proclaiming newly found status and wealth. Many of the 'old English' also saw themselves as upholders of civilised (i.e. anglicised) standards in Ireland and were willing to create gardens in the new style, but most appear to have done so with rather less ostentation than the new English. The more traditionally minded Gaelic landowners however, appear to have largely rejected Renaissance ideas, and while we know comparatively little of their gardening, it is likely many continued to create late-medieval style gardens until the 1640s.[111] As always there were exceptions, and much may have depended upon a family's wealth, geographical location and intermarriage with other socio-political groups.

The richest and most successful of the new settlers in Ireland during this period was Richard Boyle, the Great Earl of Cork, whose garden creations at Youghal and Lismore are documented in his diaries.[112] His house within the town walls of Youghal, 'The College', which lay beside Raleigh's

9 – Youghal, county Cork: view of Boyle's lower garden terrace looking towards the Sacred Heart Convent, formerly Richard Boyle's residence in the town

old home at Myrtle Grove, was flanked by two massive terraces, 160 yards long, cut into the hillside overlooking the town c.1612-14. The grounds occupied an area of about six acres, all typically enclosed behind stone walls with circular bastions. The terraces are depicted on a map of Youghal in *Pacata Hibernia*,[113] where they appear to be shown as a series of knot gardens, no doubt incorporating stairways, balustrading and statues, while some of the plants included a consignment of roses from Bristol in 1613.[114] The garden walls and terracing at Youghal are still present, as are those at Lismore Castle, which must count as the most impressive garden remains from this period in Ireland. The Lismore garden comprises a three-acre rectangular enclosure with enclosing high stone walls and turrets built in 1626, and contains a raised walk at one end and a series of terraces, stairways and a central path aligned on the town's medieval cathedral.[115] The planting details are unknown, but we can assume it contained topiary, globes, standard bays, pots of carnations and some statuary, all incorporated into elaborate knots, and perhaps even a fashionable *parterre de broderie* of clipped box which could be admired from the terraces above.

As at Lismore, pleasure gardens of the early Stuart period frequently functioned as part of the outer defences of the manor, often symmetrically flanking both the front forecourt, or bawn, and the house itself, thus allowing the gardens to be enjoyed from the main reception room win-

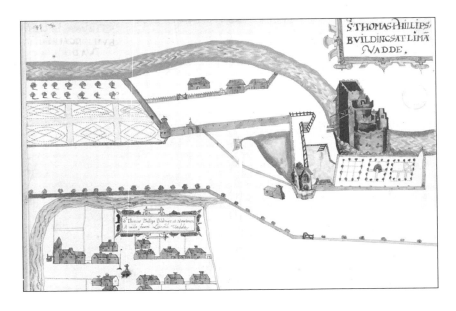

10 – Limavady
Raven's map for Sir Thomas Phillips, 1620

dows. Many of these enclosures had round turrets in the corners, which, in addition to their defensive role, probably served as viewing stations for the gardens. Indeed those at Galgorm, county Antrim (c.1620), and at Ballygalley Castle, county Antrim (c.1625),[116] were converted into summer houses during the 19th century. At Rathcline, county Longford, a network of rectangular towers protected the garden, and at Rosemount, county Down (c.1634), gun bastions were used.[117] There was also a bastion in the corner of Sir Thomas Phillip's pleasure garden at Limavady, as shown on Thomas Raven's 1622 drawing. Covering about a third of an acre to the north of the castle, this garden is depicted as having been subdivided into three large plots, each apparently delimited by topiary, with an arbour in the centre. The drawing also shows an enclosed kitchen garden and orchard located further away to the east, overlooked by a circular dovecote but outside the main castle defences.[118]

Some of the fortified gardens covered considerable areas. At Mallow Castle, the two gardens and orchard flanking the bawn covered four acres, and at Newtownards, the network of walled courts with flankers built by the Montgomery family in the 1630s occupied seven acres.[119] At Lemnagh, county Clare, the great house of the O'Briens, there were walled enclosures covering eleven acres, described in 1639 as comprising 'walled gardens, fish ponds, a pair of summer houses and a brick tower'.[120] Much still survives, notably an eight-acre enclosure which contains a brick-built summer house with classical niches, traces of fish ponds, a turret and a remarkable raised walk flanking the northern side of the enclosure. Walking was then a popular pastime and a number of gardens of the period were equipped with raised walks. Chichester House in College Green, Dublin, had a long, twenty-foot-wide terrace overlooking the gardens,[121] and at Jigginstown, county Kildare, there were impressive raised walks around a large rectangular garden fronting the south side of this palatial house built by Thomas Wentworth's from 1635.[122] As it was intended as a residence for both the Lord Deputy and the King, the garden undoubtably contained a suitably grand *parterre de broderie*, possibly with a central fountain. The raised walks here, from which the gardens could be admired, also had a defensive function, with their outside faces being lined with walling and brick-built turrets placed in the corners.

Earthen banks and palisades were also commonly used to protect gardens. Even William Bulkeley's fine house at Old Bawn near Dublin (c.1635), with its network of flanking courts, including a one-acre pleasure garden, was enclosed by a massive ditch.[123] A spectacular example of gardens being fortified with earthen banks was at Birr, where Sir Laurence Parsons enclosed about two acres north-east of the bawn in 1620-29. These gardens, defended with banks, bastions and a large stone-built 'garden tower', are depicted on a 1691 map of the town, and shown then to have contained three regimented rows of rectangular beds. Planting details are lacking, but each probably contained a knot or parterre.[124]

North of the gardens at Birr lay an extensive orchard enclosed by hedges. In the Birr papers there are records for the purchase of cherry trees from Croghan in 1622 and for cherry trees and plum trees from Thurles in 1625.[125] Orchards were now a very important component of Irish gardens, and the number of named varieties being planted was increasing rapidly. Many were being imported from England, but Ireland was already developing its own centres for fruit cultivation, notably in Kilkenny,[126] while the best published work on fruit for the period was written by an Irishman.[127] The Earl of Cork had apples, pears, peaches, nectarines, apricots and cherries at Lismore, and acquired Irish stock whenever possible; for example, Daniel Sullivan of Berehaven sent him Harvey apples and *Bon Chrétien* and *Bergamotte* pears, in addition to *arbutus* or cane apples for his garden

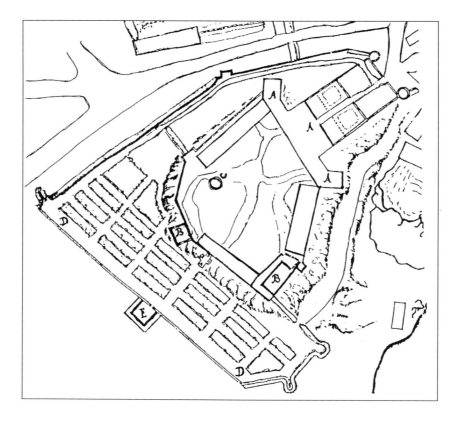

11 – Detail from Michael Richard's 'Plan of the town and castle at Birr' showing the castle bawn and gardens in 1691

in England.[128] Quinces, bullaces, mulberries, medlars, filberts and damsons were also available at this time, and the various fruit trees, either full or half standards, were normally planted in a quincunx,[129] often with an underplanting of grass enriched with sweet violets, spring bulbs, strawberries and perhaps the occasional rose bush. As in medieval times, the orchard was frequently treated as a pleasure ground, with straight paths, perhaps bordered with gooseberries or common berberis, aligned upon statuary, bowers or a summer house.

There were, of course, many palisaded or walled gardens of the period, which were not defensive in the military sense. At Dungiven, county Derry, the formal garden attached to the rear of Captain Doddington's gabled house and bawn was enclosed by a plain wall without turrets. The garden here, as depicted on Raven's 1622 plan, shows a quartered layout, with each of the four plots containing a diagonal arrangement of knots focused upon a central feature.[130] No doubt many other such houses had similar gardens; at Monea, county Fermanagh, for example, there is clear archaeological evidence for such an enclosure, presumably originally palisaded, flanking one side of the house and bawn. The gardens at Dunluce, county Antrim, which contained terraces, raised beds and a bowling green among its features, were also apparently enclosed on the landward side by a palisade.[131]

Whereas most gardens and orchards flanked the bawn or main fortified enclosure of Irish early 17th-century houses, some bawns were themselves large enough to accommodate gardens. Thomas Raven's plan of Macosquin, county Derry, shows the house in the centre of a large rectangular bawn, flanked by garden courts down one side,[132] while Sir Toby Caulfield's fine Renaissance house within the star-shaped fort of Charlemont, county Armagh (c.1622-24), was similarly surrounded by symmetrical courts, some of which almost certainly contained gardens.[133] A plan of the fort at Monaghan, built by Sir Edward Blaney in 1614, depicts a layout of six square compartments, each with complex knots, and three rectangular fishponds, all axially aligned on the rear of the house.[134] No doubt Blaney's main house at Castleblaney had a similarly grand garden, but the plan of this fort, like so many other surveys of the period, unfortunately did not include the gardens.[135]

Some of the smaller plantation bawns of this period might have contained gardens. At Tully, county Fermanagh, excavations in the 1970s revealed a series of cobbled paths, which were subsequently used as the base for a garden reconstruction.[136] However, most such bawns probably served as forecourts, and, as such, would have been treated in a manner typical of entrance courts in England throughout the 17th century. Normally this involved a wide path down the centre, a cross path and perimeter paths, the latter often running close to the walls. The square or rectangular areas created by this arrangement were occupied, not with knots or parterres, but with grass *plats*, and at the more pretentious houses these *plats* would have been delimited with topiary, with perhaps a statue or urn in the centre of each. Few, if any, flowers would have been included in what was a very masculine affair intended to project a sense of dignity to the house.[137] The front court at Portumna (c.1620), undoubtably the most dramatic bawn-court in Ireland,[138] was almost certainly treated in this way, as were, in all probability, other bawns of the period, such as Burntcourt (county Tipperary) and Coppinger's Court (county Cork).

The use of grass to make hand-cut designs in gardens, known as *Parterres à l'anglaise* or *gazon coupé*, was apparently starting to become popular at this time.[139] An amusing reference to something like this form of gardening comes from Sir William Brereton's visit to the Lord Primate of Ireland's palace in Drogheda in 1635, where he found a:

'pretty neat garden and over against the window in the gallery end, upon a bank, these words in fair letters are written: 'O MAN, REMEMBER THE LAST GREAT DAY. The bank is bare, the proportion of the letters is framed out in grass.'[140]

In the same year, Brereton also visited other houses and gardens, such as Lord Conway's manor at Lisburn, but it was Joymount in Carrickfergus and Belfast Castle which impressed him most. Both houses belonged to Sir Arthur Chichester, the Lord Deputy of Ireland from 1605 to 1616, and both reflected his considerable wealth, status and power.

Joymount, named in honour of Chichester's patron Lord Mountjoy, was built between 1610 and 1618. It is depicted on Phillip's map of Carrickfergus of 1685 (with inset view) as a fine three-storey 'stately house' with mullioned windows and projecting bays, approached from the south over a drawbridge and through a gatetower with domed corner turrets leading axially into a walled forecourt.[141] East of the house Brereton found:

'a graceful terrace and a walk before the house as at Denton, my Lord Fairfax's house. A fine garden and mightly spacious orchards and as they say have a goodly store of fruit. I observed on either side of this garden and twixt the garden and orchard a dove house placed one opposite the other, a most convenient place for apricockes.'[142]

From contemporary maps it can be established that this 'fine garden' was a rectangular half-acre plot bordering the east side of the house. It was divided by paths into four sections, with a circle, perhaps a basin and fountain, in the centre. A pair of dovecotes symmetrically flanked each side of this garden, with an orchard to the north and more gardens to the south. Just east of the garden and outside the town walls lay a large five-acre 'bordure d'arbre', probably an orchard, crossed and recrossed by vistas of trees in a cruciform plan.[143] In 1683 Richard Dobbs noted that he had seen

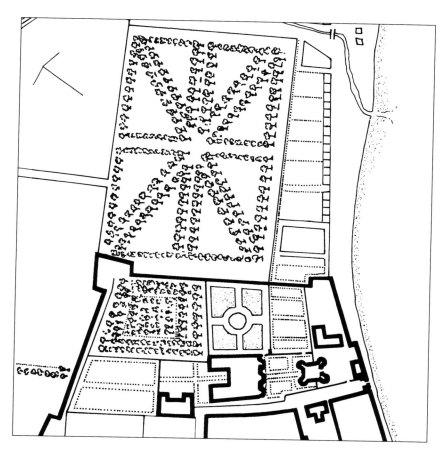

12 – A plan and inset view (c.1685) of Sir Arthur Chichester's house and gardens at Joymount, Carrickfergus, built between 1610 and 1618

'cherries ripe (at Joymount) in May', and likewise had seen 'very good musk-melons here about 1658 and '59'.[144]

Brereton also admired Chichester's 'dainty stately house' at Belfast and his 'dainty orchards and gardens and walks planted out'. This was a tall, multi-gabled brick building begun about 1611, and, like Joymount, enjoyed the protection of the town defences – a factor which helped it to fully develop an extensive network of surrounding walled courts. These are depicted in a remarkable bird's-eye view of Belfast in 1685, where the house is shown to occupy the centre of a large walled court, flanked by walled gardens and orchards on the east, south and south west sides.[145] They contained among other things a 'cherry garden', an 'apple garden', a bowling green and arbours. There are also references to the growing of strawberries, currants and gooseberries, and to the payment of wages for rolling, cleaning, weeding and wheeling in ashes and cinders for the paths.[146] Further details are sadly lacking, but a garden of this quality would undoubtably have contained grass *plats*, knots and embroidered parterres, as well as statuary, topiary and waterworks – in short, all the trappings that epitomise Renaissance gardening in the period before the outbreak of war in 1641.

———

EPILOGUE

In October 1641 Lord Barrymore was hosting a dinner at Castle Lyons, his great house in county Cork, itself noted for its fine gardens and orchards, when it was announced to the disbelieving guests that rebellion had broken out in Ulster.[147] Within a year, those at the table, including the Great Earl of Cork and Lord Muskerry, would be fighting on different sides in what proved to be the most destructive and bloodiest war in Ireland's history. Over the next ten years, numerous great houses built across the country during the early Stuart period would be destroyed and their gardens abandoned, many of which would remain in ruins, never to be rebuilt. Ornamental gardening came to a halt, though vegetable gardens undoubtedly continued; the population still had to eat and gardens were probably a more reliable source of food than the more distantly located and less defendable fields of arable and livestock.

In the years following Cromwell's campaign, enough stability returned to the country for ornamental gardening to begin again. At Monkstown, county Dublin, the stern regicide, General Ludlow, laid out a fine garden 'famous for thy apples and thy pears, for turnips, carrots, lettuce, beans and peas'.[148] Also at this time, William Petty, who arrived in Ireland on leave from the University of Oxford, attempted in 1653 to set up a physic (botanic) garden in Dublin in co-operation with another army physician, Benjamin Worsley.[149] However, while new plants, especially fruit trees, began arriving into Ireland, it was not until the Restoration of 1660 that gardening was once again energetically embarked upon. In this new dawn, gardens were ultimately divested of their old enclosures and the symmetry of the house and garden was extended into the landscape through long perspectives. The concept of the 'designed landscape' had arrived, and with it a new age in garden history.

———

The author

Terence Reeves-Smyth is a Dublin-born archaeologist and architectural historian working in the Environment and Heritage Service (DOE, Northern Ireland). He has lectured widely and published books and articles on garden history, archaeology and architecture.

Acknowledgements

The author would like to thank the Barryscourt Trust for their invitation to contribute this piece on early garden history, and to Noel Jameson for his patience in awaiting its arrival. Thanks also to my colleagues in the Environment and Heritage Service for many long and productive discussions on this topic.

List of Illustrations

1　Detail from a bird's-eye view of Belfast, dated 1685, showing Sir Arthur Chichester's house at Belfast with surrounding gardens and courts (source: Map of Belfast, 1685 [NLI, Ms 3127-41])

2　Tully Castle: view of the early 17th-century-style garden created in the castle's bawn (source: Monuments & Buildings Record, Belfast [© HMSO - Dept of the Environment, NI])

3　Aerial view of Dunluce castle gardens showing terraces and raised beds (source: Monuments & Buildings Record, Belfast [© HMSO - Dept of the Environment, NI])

4　Woad (*Isatis tinctoria*) (source: Fuchs, *De Historia Stirpium*, 1542)

5　Anemones from Parkinson's *Paradisus*, 1629 (source: J Parkinson)

6　Borage (*Borago officinalis*) in the medieval-style physic garden created in the grounds of Grey Abbey, county Down (source: Monuments & Buildings Record, Belfast [© HMSO - Dept of the Environment, NI])

7　Artichoke (*Cynara scolymus*) (source: Besler, *Hortus Eystettensis*, 1613)

8　Lismore Castle Gardens, county Waterford: the raised walk above the upper terrace showing walls and corner tower (source: the author)

9　Youghal, county Cork: view of Boyle's lower garden terrace looking towards the Sacred Heart Convent, formerly the College of Our Lady of Youghal, Richard Boyles's residence in the town (source: the author)

10　Limavady: Raven's map for Sir Thomas Phillips, 1620 (source: PRONI, T/1576)

11　Detail from Michael Richard's 'Plan of the town and castle at Birr' showing the castle bawn and gardens in 1691 (source: T McErlean and B Jupp, Historic Landscape Survey of Birr Castle Demesne, 1996)

12　A plan and inset view (c.1685) of Sir Arthur Chichester's house and gardens at Joymount, Carrickfergus, built between 1610 and 1618 (source: Philip's town plan of c.1685 [BL: K Top 51-42 & 44])

―――

Notes and References

[1] In historical perspective, gardening is understood to mean the culture of plants of any kind, while the term 'garden' denotes a plot where plants are grown. See J Harvey, *Mediaeval Gardens* (Batsford, London, 1981), pp1-2

[2] C Taylor, *The Archaeology of Gardens* (Shire Books, Risborough, 1988); AE Brown (ed.), *Garden Archaeology*, Council of British Archaeology Research Report No. 78 (London, 1991); D Jacques (ed.), *The Techniques and Uses of Garden Archaeology*, Jn. of Garden History, vol. 17, 1, special issue (1997). See also Royal Commission inventories and numerous papers in *Garden History*, the Journal of the Garden History Society

[3] No plan of the earthworks are published; see M Meek, *Dunluce Castle* (Environment and Heritage Service, Belfast, 1995)

[4] T Reeves-Smyth, 'The Natural History of Demesnes', in JW Foster and H Chesney (eds), *Nature in Ireland: A Scientific and Cultural History* (Lilliput, Dublin, 1997), pp549-72

[5] This is changing. In recent years many garden archaeological surveys (all unpublished) have been undertaken as part of the Great Gardens of Ireland Restoration Programme. In Northern Ireland progress has been made with the creation of a comprehensive Parks and Gardens Inventory and Register within the NI Monuments and Buildings Record (Environment and Heritage Service, Belfast). Garden excavations have taken place at Antrim Castle and Kylemore, but garden traces have incidentally been recognised on other excavated sites, viz. Barryscourt.

[6] The all too common failure to publish translations of manuscripts is also detrimental to research – most of us have better ways to occupy our time than grappling with Latin dictionaries.

[7] MA Monk, 'Evidence from Macroscopic Plant Remains for Crop Husbandry in Prehistoric and Early Historic Ireland: A Review', *Jn. of Ir. Archaeology*, iii (1985-6), pp31-6. K Jessen and H Helbaek, 'Cereals in Great Britain and Ireland in Prehistoric Times and Early Historic Times', *Biologiske Skrifter*, iii, 2, pp1-68; G Hillman, 'Crop Husbandry: Evidence from Macroscopic Remains' in I Simmons and M Tooley (eds), *The Environment in British Prehistory* (Duckworth, London, 1978), pp183-91; JM Renfrew, *Palaeoethnobotany: Prehistoric Food Plants of the Near East and Europe* (Methuen, London, 1973)

[8] A Fenton, 'Net-drying, pot drying and graddening: small scale drying and processing techniques', *Sage och sed*, yearbook of the Royal Gustav Adolfs Academy (1982), pp86-106

[9] D Zohery and M Hopf, *Domestication of Plants – The Old World* (Clarendon, Oxford, 1988; 2nd ed. 1993)

[10] No pulses have yet been found in Irish prehistoric contexts, Monk 'Macroscopic remains', p34. However, in England, the Celtic bean (*Vicia fabia celtica*) has been identified in late Neolithic levels, and the pea (*Pisum sativum*) has been recovered in Bronze Age contexts.

[11] G Jones and A Legge, 'The grape in the Neolithic of Britain', *Antiquity*, 61 (1987), pp452-55; G Rausing, 'The wheeled cauldrons and the wine', *Antiquity*, 71 (1997), pp994-99

[12] M Hanf, *The Arable Weeds of Europe with their Seedlings and Seeds* (BASF, Hadleigh, 1983); L Bouby, 'Two early finds of gold-of-pleasure (*Camelina sp.*) in middle Neolithic and Chalcolithic sites', *Antiquity*, 72 (1998), pp391-98

[13] WT Stearn, 'European species of allium and allied genera of Alliaceae: A synonymic enumeration' in *Ann. Musei Goulandris*, 4 (1978), pp83-198; EC Nelson, '*Allium babingtonii*' in WF Walsh and EC Nelson, *An Irish Florilegium II* (Thames and Hudson,

London, 1988), pp50-51

14 Monk, 'Macroscopic remains' p34; V Hall, 'The historical and palynological evidence for flax cultivation in mid-Down', *Ulster Jn. of Archaeology*, 52 (1989), pp5-9

15 M Dunlevy, *Dress in Ireland* (Batsford, London, 1989)

16 JB Hurry, *The Woad Plant and its Dye*, ed. AR Horwood (Oxford, 1930); JH Betty, 'Cultivation of woad', *Textile History*, 9 (1978), pp112-17. Unlike many dyes, woad requires no mordant, but an alkali such as potash is necessary to make it soluble.

17 F Brunello, *The Art of Dying in the History of Mankind* (Vicenza, 1973); H Godwin, *History of the British Flora* (Cambridge, 1975, 2nd ed.)

18 Except for some excellent work at Pompeii, research into Roman horticulture is limited, particularly in relation to Britain. See S Applebaum, 'Roman Britain' in HPR Finberg (ed.), *The Agrarian History of England and Wales*, vol. i, ii (CUP, Cambridge, 1972); P Grimal, *Les Jardins Romains* (Paris, 1943; revised ed. 1969); E MacDougall and WF Jashemski (eds), *Ancient Roman Gardens* (Dumbarton Oaks, Washington, 1981).

19 From the macrofossil evidence, we can be sure that the Romans in Britain had field bean (*Vicia faba*); leek (*Allium porrum*); pea (*Pisum sativum*); alexanders (*Smyrnium olusatrum*); coriander (*Coriandrum sativum*); dill (*Anethum graveolens*); fennel (*Foeniculum vulgare*); white mustard (*Sinapis alba*); parsley (*Papaver somniferum*); rue (*Ruta graveolens*) and savory (*Satureja sp.*). Fruits included sour cherry (*Prunus cerasus*); medlar (*Mespilus germanica*); black bulberry (*Morus nigra*) and plum (*Prunus domestica*). The cultivation of walnut (*Juglans regia*) is doubtful. The pernicious goutweed or ground elder, better known to Irish gardeners today as bishop's weed (*Aegopodium podagraria*), was introduced to Britain by the Romans as a vegetable, and probably also arrived in Ireland during Early Christian times. By 1380 it was known as 'the devil of the garden'; see JH Harvey, 'Botanical Incunabula', *Historic Gardens Review*, summer (1998), pp21-5.

20 In chronological order, the four works of the *De re Rustica* are those of Cato (234-149 BC), Varro (116-27 BC), Columella (mid-1st century AD) and Palladius (writing AD c.380-95). Except for Cato, these authorities were widely read in monasteries throughout the Middle Ages.

21 Originally just the patron saint of French gardeners, he also founded the monastery of Ullard in Kilkenny, and died in AD 670; see ES Rohde, *The Story of the Garden* (London, 1932), p60.

22 K Hughes, *The Church in Early Irish Society* (Methuen, London, 1966); K Hughes and A Hamlin, *Celtic Monasticism: The Modern Traveller to the Early Irish Church* (Seabury, New York, 1981; 1997 ed. Four Courts Press, Dublin)

23 P Hill, *Whithorn and St Ninian, The Excavation of a Monastic Town 1984-91* (Sutton, Stroud, 1997) with contribution from JP Huntley, pp252-95.

24 F Kelly, *Early Irish Farming: A Study based mainly on the Law-texts of the 7th and 8th centuries AD* (Institute of Advanced Studies, Dublin, 1997); DA Binchy (ed.), *Corpus Iuris Hibernici*, 6 vols (Dublin, 1978)

25 Kelly, *Early Irish Farming*, p368

26 Kelly, *Early Irish Farming*, p250

27 DA Binchy, 'Bretha Crólige', *Ériu*, 12 (1938), pp1-77: 22-3

28 DA Binchy, 'Sick maintenance in Irish law', *Ériu*, 12(1938) pp78-134: 108; DA Binchy, 'Bretha Crólige', p36

29 Kelly, *Early Irish Farming*, p251-53

30 Stearn, 'European species of allium...', p83

31 AT Lucas, 'Irish food before the potato', *Gwerin*, 2 (1960-2), pp8-43; AT Lucas, 'Nettles and charlock as famine food', *Breifne*, 1 (1959), pp137-46

[32] Professor Kelly gives the translation of the old Irish **Corrbacán** as skirret. However, some garden historians would argue that skirrets were not introduced until medieval times. Other than bulbs, the skirret is the first recorded root crop in England, being grown by the abbot of Westminster in 1273. It originally hailed from China. However, the water parsnip (*Sium latifolium*) is native to these islands.

[33] Cultivated fruit trees that usually demand grafting include apples, pears, plums and cherries. Those that can be cultivated without grafting include sycamore figs, olives, date palms, vines and pomegranates. The latter group appear much earlier in the European archaeological record.

[34] WC Cooper and H Chapot, 'Fruit production with special emphasis on fruit for processing', in S Nagi, PE Shur and MK Valdhuis, *Citrus Science and Technology*, vol. 2 (Aui, Westport, 1977), pp1-127; Zohery and Hopf, *Domestication of Plants*, pp129-62

[35] KD White, *Agricultural Implements of the Roman World* (Cambridge, 1967); KD White, *Roman Farming* (Cornell University, Ithaca, 1970)

[36] An apple recently discovered in a late Bronze Age context in Haughey's Fort, county Armagh, is due to be sent to Oxford for DNA testing (Dr Jim Mallery pers. comm.). It is most probably a native wild apple (usually 1.5-3.0 cm diameter), many of which have been found in European prehistoric contexts, such as the Swiss lake villages.

[37] Kelly, *Early Irish Farming*, pp259-62

[38] JGD Lamb, 'The apple in Ireland; its history and varieties', *Econ. Proc. of the Roy. Dublin Soc.*, 4 (1951), pp1-61; EJ Gwynn, 'The rule of Tallaght', *Harmarthena*, 42 (1927) 2nd supplement

[39] Kelly, *Early Irish Farming*, pp261-62

[40] Pliny noted twenty-two varieties of apples and thirty-six of pears. These numbers declined with the collapse of the Roman Empire, but it is clear from Charlemagne's list of plants that a considerable number of apple and pear varieties were being cultivated by AD 800; see R.von Fischer-Benzon, *Altdeutsche Gartenflora* (Leipzig, 1894); Harvey, *Mediaeval Gardens*, pp28-32

[41] B Colgrave and RAB Mynors (eds), *Bede's Ecclesiastical History of the English People* (Oxford, 1969; reprinted 1979), book 1, chapter 1

[42] There is a medieval reference to a vineyard on Iona; see J De Suse (ed.), *Ionae Vitae Sanctorum Columbani*, vol. 2, 25 (Leipzig, 1905), p292. It may be significant that realistic depictions of bunches of grapes are occasionally included on High Cross panels, as at Duleek and Old Kilcullen; see W Crawford, 'Carved panels representing the symbolic vine', *Jn. Roy. Soc. Antiq. Ir.*, 46 (1916), 181-2. The only reference to wine being imported into early monasteries comes from the Life of St Ciaran of Clonmacnoise, where a mention is made of wine arriving from Gaul coming up the Shannon, T O'Neill, *Merchants and Mariners* (Irish Academic Press, Dublin, 1987), p44.

[43] Monk, *Macroscopic remains*, p34

[44] Kelly, *Early Irish Farming*, p269

[45] H Godwin, 'The ancient cultivation of hemp', *Antiquity*, 41 (1967), pp42-9

[46] Kelly, *Early Irish Farming*, p264-67. Woad capsules have been found at the raised rath site at Deer Park Farms, county Antrim; E Allison, A Hall and H Kenward, 'Living conditions and resource exploitation at the Early Christian rath site at Deer Park Farms, Co. Antrim: evidence from plants and invertebrates', Technical Report 35, (Environmental Archaeology Unit, University of York, 1997).

[47] Kelly, *Early Irish Farming*, p265

[48] Kelly, *Early Irish Farming*, p267-269

[49] G Schaeffer, 'The cultivation of madder', *CIBA Review*, 39 (1941) 398-406. It should be noted that madder seeds have been found at Boho rath in Fermanagh and in association with E-ware pots at Tesshan crannog, county Antrim. Madder traces have also

been found at Deer Park Farms in county Antrim (Dr Chris Lynn pers. comm.). In medieval times, true madder was by far the most common dye for textiles, but there is no record of its import into these islands until the 14th century; see P Walton. 'Dyes on medieval textiles' in *Dyes on Historical and Archaeological Textiles*, 3 (1984), pp30-4.

[50] R Fuchs and D Oltrogge, 'Colour material and painting techniques in the Book of Kells' in F O'Mahony (ed.), *The Book of Kells: Proc. of a Conference at Trinity College Library* (Scolar Press, Dublin, 1994)

[51] GF Mitchell, 'Archaeology and Environment in Early Dublin, Medieval Dublin Excavations 1962-81', *Roy. Ir. Acad. Proc.*, series C, 1 (1987); S Geraghty, 'Viking Dublin: botanical evidence from Fishamble Street, Medieval Dublin excavations 1962-81', *Roy. Ir. Acad. Proc.*, series C, 2 (1996); B Collins, 'Plant remains' in C Walsh, *Archaeological Excavations at Patrick, Nicholas and Winetavern Streets, Dublin* (Brandon, Dublin, 1997), pp228-36; J Tierney and M Hannon, 'Plant remains' in M Hurley, O Scully and SWJ McCutcheon, *Late Viking Age and Medieval Waterford, Excavations 1986-1992* (Waterford Corporation, 1997), pp854-983

[52] AR Hall, HK Williams and JRA Greig, 'Environment and living conditions at two Anglo-Scandinavian sites', *The Archaeology of York: Past and Present*, 14 (CBA, London, 1983); AR Hall, PR Tomlinson, RA Hall and GW Taylor, 'Dyeplants from Viking York', *Antiquity*, 58 (1984), 58-60

[53] J Harvey, *Mediaeval Gardens* (Batsford, London, 1981);subsequent contributions include E MacDougall (ed.), *Mediaeval Gardens* (Dumbarton Oaks, Washington DC, 1986); S Landsberg, *The Medieval Garden* (Thames and Hudson, London, 1997); M Stokstad and J Stannard, *Gardens of the Middle Ages: An exhibition catalogue* (Spencer Museum of Art, Kansas, 1983)

[54] E and R Peplow, *In a Monastery Garden* (David and Charles, London, 1988); P Meyvaert, 'The medieval monastic garden' in EB MacDoughall (ed.), *Mediaeval Gardens*, pp23-53; T McLean, *Medieval English Gardens* (Collins, London, 1981; 2nd ed. 1994), pp13-58; CS Briggs, 'Garden Archaeology in Wales' in AE Brown (ed.), *Garden Archaeology*, pp138-40; G Coppack, *Abbeys and Priories* (Batsford, London, 1990), pp78-80

[55] Harvey, *Mediaeval Gardens*, pp57-58. Nurseries for grafts and seedlings were also established in monasteries across Europe; one existed at Kilmainham in the early 14th century: JC Walker, 'Essay on the rise and progress of gardening in Ireland', *Trans. Roy. Ir. Acad.*, 4(*Antiquities*, 1799), pp3-19; D'Alton, *The History of County Dublin* (Tower Books, Cork, 1987; facsimile of 1838 ed.), p313.

[56] The most comprehensive analysis of medieval Irish monasticism is R Stalley, *The Cistercian Monasteries of Ireland* (Yale University Press, London, 1987)

[57] NB White (ed.), *Extents of Irish Monastic Possessions 1540-1541* (Stationery Office, Dublin, 1943); see also, Irish Record Commission, *Irish Patent Rolls of James I* (Stationery Office, Dublin, 1966)

[58] See Stalley, *Cistercian Monasteries*, pp176-78, for a brief discussion of the precinct in an Irish context. Excavations in Ireland have been very focused upon limited areas, mostly within the claustral ranges. For a useful summary, see TB Barry, *The Archaeology of Medieval Ireland* (Methuen, London, 1987). Recently it has been accepted that the precinct needs to be the focus of future study; KD O'Conor, *The Archaeology of Medieval Rural Settlement in Ireland*, Discovery Programme monograph (Stationery Office, Dublin, 1998), pp142-44.

[59] J McCann (trans.), *The Rule of St. Benedict* (London, 1976), p74

[60] In some cases the medieval precinct incorporated Early Christian termon boundaries; see A Hamlin, 'A recently discovered enclosure at Inch Abbey, County Down', *Ulster Jn. of Arch.*, 40 (1977), pp85-8. Security became increasingly important by the 14th

century, and many of the walled precincts belong to this period. The largest and most impressive walled precinct in Ireland was St Mary's Abbey in Dublin (c.27 acres or 11ha).

[61] W Horn and E Born, *The Plan of St. Gall* (University of California Press, Berkeley, 1979); I Brou (ed.), *The Monastic Ordinale of St. Vedast's Abbey, Arras*, 2 vols (Henry Bradshaw Society 86, 1955)

[62] C Noble, 'Norwich Cathedral Priory Gardeners' Accounts, 1329-1530' in *Farming and Gardening in Late Medieval Norfolk*, (Norfolk Record Society, 1997), no. 61, pp1-92; SF Hockey (ed.), *The account book of Beaulieu Abbey* (Roy. Hist. Soc., Camden) 4th series, xvi; AB Bartlett, *Beaulieu Monks at Work; Production and Labour in the Account Book of Beaulieu Abbey, 1269-70* (London, 1979)

[63] C McNeill (ed.), *Registrum de Kilmainham: Register of Chapter Acts of the Hospital of Saint John of Jerusalem in Ireland, 1326-1339 under the Grand Prior, Sir Roger Outlaw* (Stationery Office, Dublin, 1932); C McNeill, 'The Hospitallers at Kilmainham and their guests', *Jn. Roy. Soc. Antiq. Ir.*, 54 (1924), pp15-64.

[64] Obedientiary gardens probably became more common in the later Middle Ages. Abbots and priors often had their own gardens, as at St Mary's and at Newgate (Hospital of John Baptist) in Dublin, *Pat. Rolls James I*, Pat. 8-2-lxvii, and *Monastic Extents*, p55. At Graiguenamanagh, the Abbot's garden was damaged by flooding in 1475; G Carville, *Norman Splendour: Duiske Abbey* (Belfast, 1979), p91

[65] For example, stone walls were noted at Armagh (Peter and Paul) priory, *Pat. Rolls James I*, Pat. 16-iii-530-vii; at Duleek some garden walls were plastered, E St John Brooks, 'Fourteenth century monastic estates in Meath', *Jn. Roy. Soc. Antiq. Ir.*, 83 (1952), pp140-49

[66] PH Hore, *A History of the Town and County of Wexford*, I (London, 1900), pp10-41; J Mills, 'Accounts of the Earl of Norfolk's Estates in Ireland 1279-1294', *Jn. Roy. Soc. Antiq. Ir.*, 22(1892), pp50-62. Garden boundaries at Old Ross, county Wexford, were sheltered by thorn hedging, palisades and ditching.

[67] As at Fermoy, county Cork, Hoggs, county Dublin, and Fethard, county Tipperary; see *Pat. Rolls James I*, Pat. 9 (4) xxviii; Pat. 13 (3) iii; Pat. 15 (3) viii. Urban monasteries often had garden plots scattered within and outside the town, as at Wexford; see *Pat. Rolls James I*, Pat. 4 (1) xxxii.

[68] Precinct areas are given in *Monastic Extents* and *Pat. Rolls James I*. It is important to recognise that these areas are mostly medieval acres or 'great measure' (gm), equivalent to about $2\frac{1}{2}$ statute acres. 'Small measure' is also occasionally employed; this is the same as the Irish Plantation acre of 1.6 statute acres. The English or statute acre was only occasionally used in Ireland until the 19th century; see J Mills, 'Notices on the Manor of St. Sepulchre, Dublin in the fourteenth century', *Jn. Roy. Soc. Antiq. Ir.*, 19 (1889), p35, n2.

[69] Beaulieu accounts of 1269, see Hockey (1975)

[70] A Gwynn and RN Hadcock, *Medieval Religious Houses* (Longman, London, 1970), p133

[71] JH Harvey, 'Vegetables in the Middle Ages', *Garden History*, 12 (1984), pp89-99

[72] Peas and beans from gardens were eaten green, those from the fields were used dry. Ireland was a major producer and exporter of field peas and broad beans in the Norman period.

[73] A Zettersten, 'The virtues of herbs in the Loscombe manuscript', *Acts Universitatis Lundensis*, sectio 1, 5 (1967), pp8-33; JH Harvey, 'The first English garden book: Mayster Jon Gardener's treatise and its background', *Garden History*, 13 (1985), pp83-101; EC Nelson, ' "This garden to adorne with all varieties": The garden plants of Ireland in the centuries before 1700', *Moorea*, 9 (1990), pp37-54.

74 The following plants are included in Jon Gardener's lists: 'Adderstongue' (cuckoo-pint); agrimony; alexanders; avens; betony; 'bigold' (corn marigold); borage; brook-lime; bugle; calamint; camomile; campion; caraway; centaury (lesser); clary; colewort; comfrey; coriander; cowslip; cress; water cresses; daffodil; bruisewort (daisy); dill; 'dittany' (dittander); horseheal (elecampane); felwort (gentian); fennel; feverfew; fox-glove; garlic; glaswin (flag iris); gromwell; 'groudsel'; 'half wood' (?bittersweet); hartstongue; henbane; herb Robert; 'herb Walter'; hollyhock; 'honeysuckle' (?Meliotus); horehound (white); hyssop; langdebeef; lavender; leek; lettuce; lily; 'liver-wort'; marsh (smallage); mints; motherwort (mugwort); mouse-war; nepp; Oculus Christii (wild clary); onion; orach; orpine; parsley; pellitory; peony; periwinkle; pim-pernel; ribwort (plaintain); waybread (plantain); polypody; primrose; radish; 'red may-weed'; roses (red and white); rue; saffron; sage; St John's Wort; sanicle; savory (winter and summer); 'scabious'; senevy (mustard); southernwood; 'spearwort'; 'smearwort'; 'spinach'; stitchwort; strawberry; tansy; teasel (wild); thistle ('Wolf's'); thyme; tutsan; valerian; vervain; violet; wallwort; waterlily; woodruff; hindheal (wood sage); wood sorrel; wormwood; yarrow. See Harvey, *The first English garden book*, pp93-100. The absence of rosemary (introduced into Britain c.1340) helps to date the list; see JA Harvey, 'Medieval plantmanship in England: the culture of rosemary', *Garden History*, 1 (1972), pp14-21.

75 Some monasteries had a series of separate infirmaries; Lexington in 1228 mentions some Cistercian houses having one for the monks, one for the laybrothers and another for the poor; Stalley, *Cistercian Monasteries*, p173.

76 Dr Nelson has tentatively identified deadly nightshade (*Atropa belladonna*), and the opium poppy (*Papaver somniferus*) on decorated floral motifs at Corcomroe Abbey. Lily of the valley (*Convallaria majalis*) was also identified; Stalley, *Cistercian Monasteries*, p274, n40.

77 NG Siraisi, *Medieval and Early Renaissance Medicine* (University of Chicago Press, Chicago, 1990)

78 The 12th-century papal prohibitions against monastic involvement in lay medicine appears to have had little effect in Ireland, where some monasteries treated lay patients as well as their own brethren until the dissolution. Medieval lay medicine in Ireland tended to be a hereditary practice, at least in rural areas. For background on monk-physicians, see EA Hammond, 'Physicians in medieval English religious houses', *Bull. Hist. of Medicine*, 32 (1958), pp105-20; DA Amundsen, 'Medieval canon law on medical and surgical practice by the clergy', *Bull. Hist. of Medicine*, 52 (1978), pp23-43.

79 JH Harvey, 'Westminster Abbey: The infirmarer's garden', *Garden History*, 20 (1992), pp97-115

80 A monastic 'physic garden' has recently been recreated at Grey Abbey in county Down by the Environment and Heritage Service. It contains many plants that one might expect to find in such a garden, but in size must be regarded only as a miniature version of the real thing.

81 Kelly, *Early Irish Farming*, p108-13; E Crane, *The Archaeology of Beekeeping* (London, 1983); E Crane, 'Bee bop a loo bole', *Arch. Ir.*, 6, no. 21 (1992), pp15-17

82 There was a 40 ft. high bee-tower at Mellifont, and another at Clonmore, county Louth, 50 ft. high, built c.1230. The latter had a series of floors, each with louvred windows to allow bees to come and go. JK Watson, *Bee-keeping in Ireland: A History* (Glendale, Dublin, 1976).

83 Some monasteries had several dovecotes or culvert houses. Mellifont had four within its precincts; *Pat. Rolls James I*, Pat. 3 (1) xvii. Most Irish medieval dovecotes were probably wooden structures with thatched roofs, but a handful of stone-built beehive-

type examples survive, notably Kilcooley and Shanagolden (both in county Tipperary) and Ballybeg (county Cork).

[84] Archaeology has the potential to verify this, as it has done at Dunstable Priory; see S Moorhouse, 'Ceramics in the medieval garden' in Brown (ed.), *Garden Archaeology*, p115.

[85] HS Sweetman (ed.), *Calender of Documents relating to Ireland 1302-1307* (London, 1887; reprinted 1974 by Kraus, Leichtenstein), p86, item 255

[86] Hore, *A History of the Town and County of Wexford*, p25

[87] *Monastic Extents*, pp2, 170, 185

[88] Landsberg, *The Medieval Garden*, pp36-8

[89] The various sorts of pippin didn't become popular until the 15th century. Cider may never have been the popular drink in Ireland that it was in England at this time, but cider presses are occasionally mentioned in Irish medieval documents; for example, there was one at Kilsaran Manor in Louth; see D MacIvor, 'The Knight's Templar's in County Louth', *Seanchas Ardmhacha*, 4 (1960-62), pp72-91.

[90] K Lamb and P Bowe, *A History of Gardening in Ireland* (National Botanic Gardens, Dublin, 1995), p12, n31 (from an early 19th-century source)

[91] Figs feature in Irish documents of the period, notably in kitchen accounts, viz. Kells Priory in 1382 and the Priory of the Holy Trinity, Dublin, in 1338; NB White (ed.), *Irish Monastic and Episcopal deeds* AD *1200-1600* (Stationery Office, Dublin, 1936), p76; J Mills (ed.), *Account Rolls of the Priory of the Holy Trinity, Dublin, 1337-1346* (Dublin, 1891). Both figs and walnuts have been found in medieval archaeological contexts in Dublin; see Mitchell, *Archaeology and Environment*, p25.

[92] HH Lamb, *Climate: Present, Past and Future*, vol. 2 (Methuen, London, 1977), pp435-37; HH Lamb, *Climate, History and the Modern World* (Methuen, London, 1982)

[93] A vineyard is mentioned as part of the manor of Old Ross (see Hore, *A History of the Town and County of Wexford*), while in 1228 a winepress was noted by Lexington, probably at Jerpoint; Stalley, *Cistercian Monasteries*, pp45, 173. For a useful summary of the Irish wine trade, see O'Neill, *Merchants and Mariners*, pp44-57.

[94] Moorhouse, 'Ceramics in the medieval garden' in Brown (ed.), *Garden Archaeology*, pp102-6, figs. 9 (2, 3, 4). For turf-topped seats, see Landsberg, *The Medieval Garden*, pp51-3; Noble, *Farming and Gardening*, p10, n66

[95] This can hardly be understated, for most illustrations of medieval gardens depict wood-work, often a great deal, while documents speak the same story. Irish medieval gardens are unlikely to have been any different, especially as there was no shortage of either timber or joiners.

[96] For garden flowers of the period, see T McLean, *English Medieval Flowers* (Barrie & Jenkins, London, 1989); M Innes and C Perry, *Medieval Flowers* (Kyle Cathie, London, 1997)

[97] Usually to be paid on the feast of the Nativity of St John the Baptist (in June). For example, see E Curtis (ed.), *The Calender of Ormond Deeds (1172-1350)*, pp155, 163, 164, 186, 192, 225, 235, 237, 266, 277, 289, 298, 300, 301, 305, 313, 324, 339, 340, 345, 349, 356, 367, 382, 408, 450, 464, 588, 612, 629; Sweetman (ed.), *Calender of Documents relating to Ireland 1302-1307*, p81; White (ed.), *Irish Monastic and Episcopal Deeds* AD *1200-1600*, pp75-6 (A57/99)

[98] Landsberg, *The Medieval Garden*, pp35-6; Noble, *Farming and Gardening*, p14, n96, 97, 98

[99] U Eco, *Art and Beauty in the Middle Ages* (Yale, London, 1986)

[100] H Leask, 'Muckross', *Jn. Cork Hist. Arch. Soc*, 45(1940), pp85-96. The yew here was probably planted in the late 17th century, when the friary was linked to the gardens at Muckross house by an avenue of elms. Young noted it had a diameter of two feet in

1776.

[101] H Jager, 'Land use in medieval Ireland: A review of the documentary evidence', *Ir. Econ. Soc. Hist.*, 10 (1983), pp51-65; A O'Sullivan, 'Woodmanship and the supply of underwood and timber to Anglo-Norman Dublin' in C Manning (ed.), *Dublin and Beyond the pale: Studies in Honour of Patrick Healy* (Wordwell, Dublin, 1998), pp59-68. Many of the monastic 'ash groves' or 'ash parks' mentioned in accounts could be plantations. Usually these were 'reserved for the repairs of the house'; see *Pat. Rolls James I*, Pat. 15 (3) iv. One of these groves lay within the precinct of St Mary's Dublin; *Pat. Rolls James I*, Pat. 8 (2) lxvi. See Pat. 3 (1) xxvii; Pat. 9 (4) xxvi; Pat. 10 (2) i; Pat. 17 (iii) lxxxii (Duleek).

[102] Knot-making first emerged during the 15th century and remained fashionable until the end of the 16th century. The spaces were either filled with coloured earth or gravels (open knots) or with flowers (closed knots). Designs were commonly adopted from textiles, tapestries or pattern books.

[103] R Strong, *The Renaissance Garden in England* (Thames and Hudson, London, 1979); J Antony, *The Renaissance Garden in Britain* (Shire, Princes Risborough, 1991). Both of these books concentrate upon the art historical and design aspects of gardens of this period, but without any good discussion of the plants used.

[104] D Mountain (Thomas Hill) *The Gardeners Labyrinth* (facsimile of 1577 ed., Garland, New York, 1982); J Gerard, *The Herball* (London, 1597; facsimile, Senate, London, 1998)

[105] TJ Westropp, 'The Desmond's castle at Newcastle Oconyll, Co. Limerick', *Jn. Roy. Soc. Antiq. Ir.*, 39 (1909), pp42-55, 350-68. It may be noted that Peyton's 1586 survey noted the 'great orchard' as four acres and the large garden as three acres. It lay on the west side of the bawn, occupying the site of the 18th-century walled garden.

[106] TJ Westropp, 'Notes on Askeaton, Co. Limerick', *Jn. Roy. Soc. Antiq. Ir.*, 34 (1904), pp111-32: 119; S O'Grady (ed.), *Pacata Hibernia*, vol. 1 (Downey, London, 1896), p63 (facing)

[107] EC Nelson, ' "Reserved for the Fellow", Four centuries of gardens at Trinity College, Dublin' in CH Holland (ed.), *Trinity College Dublin and the Idea of a University* (Dublin, 1991), pp185-222; see also Nelson, *The garden plants of Ireland*, p41; P Bowe, 'The Renaissance garden in Ireland', *Irish Arts Review*, 11 (1995), pp74-81

[108] Bowe, 'The Renaissance garden', p76; JP Collier (ed.), *The Poetical Works of Edmund Spencer* (London, 1891), p187

[109] JP Hennessy, *Sir Walter Raleigh in Ireland* (Kegan Paul, London, 1883); RH Salaman, *History and Social Influence of the Potato* (CUP, Cambridge, 1949; rev. ed. by JG Hawkes, 1985). The potato was recorded as growing at Grey Abbey, county Down, as early as 1606; see GH Hill (ed.), *The Montogomery Manuscripts 1603-1706* (Archer, Belfast, 1869)

[110] D Murphy, 'The castle of Roscommon', *Jn. Roy. Soc. Antiq. Ir.*, 21 (1890-91), pp546-86. The Essex estate papers have a drawing showing a grand avenue leading from the town to the castle. Avenues were perhaps unusual at the time, but apparently featured at a number of early Stuart gardens, as at Termon McGrath, county Donegal, Old Bawn, county Dublin, Loughmoe, county Tipperary, and Lemnagh, county Clare. The straight tree-lined avenue became a hallmark of demesne layouts in the late 17th and early 18th centuries; see T Reeves-Smyth, 'Demesnes' in FHA Aalen, K Whelan and M Stout (eds), *Atlas of the Irish Rural Landscape* (Cork University Press, 1997), pp197-205.

[111] Some idea of the plants grown by the Gaelic Irish during the early Stuart period may possibly be gauged from the lists of plants prepared by Philip O'Sullivan Beare, c.1620. It includes parsley, camomile, fennel, mint, tamarisk, hyssop, wormwood, rue, mustard,

rosemary, sage, cabbage, pumpkin, radish, lettuce, parsnip, sunflower and lily. Fruit listed included apples, pears, arbutus, walnut, chestnut, pine and mulberry; see TJ O'Donnell (ed.), *Selections from the Zoilomastix of Philip O'Sullivan Beare* (Stationery Office, Dublin, 1960) appendix A.

[112] AB Grosart (ed.), *The Lismore Papers*, 10 vols (London, 1868-8); D Townshend, *The Life and Letters of the Great Earl of Cork* (Duckworth, London, 1904)

[113] S O'Grady (ed.), *Pacata Hibernia*, vol. 1 (Downey, London, 1896), p27 (facing). This map dates to about 1620. For an earlier map of Youghal c.1580, see *Jn. Roy. Soc. Antiq. Ir.*, 19 (1868-69), p469.

[114] Grosart, i, p243. One hundred apples trees, prunes and quinces were imported from England in 1616 for the orchard, probably located outside the main garden walls to the south-west. In the 1640s, during the siege of Youghal, the garden leadwork was melted down for shot. The lower terrace is presently the convent garden, while the upper terrace is now a field, which fortunately has survived bungalow development because of its inaccessible location beneath the town walls.

[115] Grosart, iv, pp185, 206-219; Bowe, 'The Renaissance garden' pp75-8. The enclosure and adjacent orchards to the west are depicted on a map of Lismore c.1640; see M Girouard, 'Lismore Castle', *Country Life* (1964) August 6, 13. Defended garden enclosures were not unique to Ireland. There were good examples at Ware Park, Audley End and Hazelbury; see M Girouard, *Robert Smythson and the Elizabethan County House* (Yale, Lodnon, 1983,), p315, n28

[116] One of the turrets at Ballygalley (on the road side) is an Edwardian folly; the other surviving turret is original. It overlooks a raised terrace in the garden south of the bawn. For a useful outline history of Ballygalley Castle and Galgorm Castle, see CEB Brett, *Buildings of County Antrim* (Ulster Architectural Heritage Society, Belfast, 1996), pp23; 72-3.

[117] Rathcline plan, see NLI, Ms 8646 (6); W Harris, *The Ancient and Present State of County Down* (Dublin, 1744), p268

[118] Sir T Phillips, *The view of the Survey of the Plantation of the City and County of Londonderry* (PRONI, T.1576). Traces of the garden enclosures are still visible today.

[119] R Dunlop, 'An unpublished survey of the plantation of Munster in 1622', *Jn. Roy. Soc. Antiq. Ir.*, 54 (1924), pp128-45: 143; HG Leask 'Mallow Castle', *Jn Cork Hist. Arch. Soc.*, 49 (1944), pp19-24. During the 1640s a garrison was stationed in the gardens. The present house (built by Blore in 1837) stands within the old gardens, but the long terrace in front may be original to the early Stuart period. For Newtownards, see EM Jope (ed.), *An Archaeological Survey of County Down* (HMSO, Belfast, 1966), p260; Map of Newtownards 1720 (PRONI, T.2491/1).

[120] TJ Westropp, 'Excursions – Lemaneagh Castle', *Jn. Roy. Soc. Antiq. Ir*, 30 (1900), pp403-7.

[121] CP Curran, 'The architecture of the Bank of Ireland', *Bull. Ir. Georgian Soc.*, 20 (1977)

[122] HG Leask, 'New light on Jigginstown' in EM Jope (ed.), *Studies in Building History* (London, 1961), pp244-46; M Craig, 'New light on Jigginstown', *Ulster Jn. Arch*, 33 (1970), pp107-10. The house is 127 yards long with two front doors. Maurice Craig has suggested to the author that it may have been built to accommodate both the King and his Viceroy simultaneously in separate residences.

[123] HG Leask, 'House at Oldbawn, Co. Dublin', *Jn. Roy. Soc. Antiq. Ir.*, 43 (1913), pp314-25. Probably with an interanl bank or palisade. Unfortunately this site has now been demolished.

[124] 'Plan of the town and castle of Birr by Michael Richards, 1691' (Worcester College, Ms. YC 20 ccvi); T McErlean and B Jupp, *Historic Landscape Survey of Birr Castle Demesne*, vol. 1, report for the Earl of Rosse (Belfast, 1996), pp29-30

[125] The Birr papers have a payment (1625) for 'hedging 192 perches of the hedge of the orchard' and 'for rootinge the old apple trees and plum trees and throwinge downe of those bankes and raisinge the ground at the south corner of the orchard', the latter reference implying the existence of an orchard at Birr in the O'Carroll days. In 1643 the orchard featured in the Birr siege when Preston dug trenches across it. These trenches are still visible in the park; McErlean and Jupp, *Birr Castle Demesne*, p30.

[126] Fynes Moryson writing in 1598 described Kilkenny as memorable for its pleasant orchards, and says 'of the apple we have some fine old Irish varieties not excelled by any modern introduction'; F Moryson, *Itinerary* (London, 1617). Many well-known Irish varieties probably have their origin in the Tudor or early Stuart periods, such as the Scarlet Crofton, Irish Peach and Kerry Pippin. For a description of varieties, see Lamb, *The Apple in Ireland*, pp23-58.

[127] *The Fruiterers Secrets* (1604), later reissued as *The Husbandmans Fruitfull Orchard* (1608, 1609) by the mysterious Irishman, NF, of whom nothing else is known.

[128] Townsend, *The Great Earl of Cork*, p296. The strawberry tree (*Arbutus unedo*), Ireland's first horticultural export, was 'discovered' in Kerry and sent to England in the 1580s. It was much prized by gardeners during the 17th century for its scarlet fruits (uneatable) and white flowers; see Lamb and Bowe, *A History of Gardening in Ireland*, p15; EC Nelson and WF Walsh, *Trees of Ireland, Native and Naturalized* (Lilliput, Dublin, 1993), pp86-94. The Earl of Cork's house in England was Stalbridge Park, Dorset, long since demolished. The garden here was laid out by the famous designer Isaac de Caus; see Grosart, *Lismore Papers* (1886), p64; HM Colvin, 'The south front of Wilton House', *Arch. Jn.*, cxi (1954), pp181-90.

[129] The quincunx took two basic forms: the simplest had trees planted at the notional corners of a square, while the other more popular form had a fifth tree in the centre of the square, making a more complex pattern. Tree-spacing varied from fifteen to twenty-five feet.

[130] Sir T Phillips, *The view of the Survey of the Plantation of the City and County of Londonderry* (PRONI, T.1576). A substantial portion of Dungiven bawn has been excavated, see NF Brannon and BS Blades, 'Dungiven bawn re-edified', *Ulster Arch. Jn.*, 43 (1980), pp91-6; N Brannon, 'Archaeological excavations at Dungiven priory and bawn', *Benbradagh*, 15(1985), pp15-18. A small trench was put into the garden site during the 1982 excavations, but nothing was recovered. Sadly, the area was subsequently planted with trees, so the potential for good garden archaeology here is very limited (N Brannon pers. comm.).

[131] Earthworks are visible on aerial photographs in the Monuments and Buildings Record (EHS, Hill Street, Belfast)

[132] Proposed 'plot' for the Merchant Taylor's house and bawn. Probably not completed in form depicted on this plan; TW Moody, *The Londonderry Plantation 1609-41* (Belfast, 1939), p261, fig. 2

[133] Bird's-eye view of Charlemont c.1630 (British Library, Add. Ms. 24200, f.39)

[134] These fish ponds were for holding fish rather than breeding them. Similar ponds were a feature of other gardens of the period and may have been more common than we can appreciate on the basis of the present evidence. Examples included Old Bawn, county Dublin, Loughmoe Castle, county Tipperary, and Lemnagh, county Clare. The fish ponds within the walled enclosures at Newtownards, county Down, and Dalway's Bawn, county Antrim, may also be early 17th century. Fish ponds may also have been a regular features of medieval monastic precincts, examples being known at Cork Friary (*Pat. Rolls James I*, Pat. 13 (1) xxxviii) and Fethard, county Tipperary (*Pat. Rolls James I*, Pat. 14 (3) iii). For an assessment of fish ponds, see CK Currie, 'Fishponds as garden features, c.1550-1750', *Garden History*, 18 (1990), pp22-46; CK Currie,

Medieval Fish, Fisheries and Fishponds (BAR, Oxford, 1988), series 182.

[135] Monaghan and Castleblaney (Baile Loergan), plans c.1614 (TCD, Ms. 1209-32)

[136] M Meek, Tully Castle Guide Card (DOE (NI), Belfast, 1984). The garden work, created with plants known from this period, was supervised by Philip Wood of Enniskillen on behalf of the Environment and Heritage Service.

[137] It is relevant to note that such forecourts served as an outdoor extension to the hall, traditionally a male preserve, where tenants and others would be received by the master of the house. The earliest Irish depiction of such a court is a print c.1670 of Ballintober, county Cork, see R Ffolliott, *The Pooles of Mayfield and other Irish Families* (Hodges Figgis, Dublin, 1958), p150

[138] The present garden 'restoration' in the front court of Portumna Castle owes more to a vivid imagination than to historical or archaeological accuracy. The orchards and gardens at Portumna in the 1630s flanked the east and south sides of the house and bawn, while the west side overlooked the deer park, as at Mallow. No detailed study of the Portumna layout has been published, but for some background on the house, see M Craig, 'Portumna Castle, Co. Galway' in *The Country Seat: Studies in the History of the British Country House* (London, 1970), pp36-41; M Craig, 'Portumna Castle', *Gatherum*, 7 (1976), pp1-8.

[139] The *gazon coupé* was especially associated with gardens of the late 17th and early 18th centuries.

[140] W Brereton, *Travels in Holland, the United Provinces, England, Scotland and Ireland, 1634-1635* (Chetham Society, Manchester, 1844), p127; Walker, 'The rise and progress of gardening in Ireland', pp3-18. From 1625 to 1656, the post of Primate was held by Archbishop James Usher, so presumably he was responsible for this 'pretty neat garden'. The use of the term 'framed' might imply that the letters, which one might suppose were cut out of the grass, were all enclosed by a large surround of topiary.

[141] Phillip's town plan (NLI, Ms 3137-42)

[142] Brereton, *Travels*, p127-8. The reference is to Thomas, first Baron Fairfax (1560-1640) of Denton and Nunappleton, North Yorks.

[143] Town plans c.1685 (BL, K Top 51-46; 51-44; 51-45); Goubet's town plan of 1690-95 (NLI, Ms 2742-4)

[144] PRONI T.707/1; J Irvine, 'Richard Dobbs – notes from his description of County Antrim in 1683', *Glynns*, 7 (1979), pp35-49

[145] Map of Belfast 1685 (NLI, Ms 3137-41); reprinted by the Linen Hall Library

[146] Great Roll of Belfast 1666, see Belfast G Benn, *A History of the Town of Belfast from earliest Times to the Close of the Eighteenth Century* (Ward, Belfast, 1877), p242

[147] Townsend, *The Great Earl of Cork*, p196

[148] GT Stokes, 'The antiquities from Kingstown to Dublin', *Jn. Roy. Soc. Antiq. Ir.*, 23 (1893), pp343-56

[148] KT Hoppen, 'Sir William Petty: polymath 1623-1687', *History Today*, 15 (1965), pp126-34; Nelson, 'The garden plants of Ireland', p44

THE BARRYSCOURT LECTURES

———

The Barryscourt Trust
presents a series of bi-annual lectures on Medieval Ireland
at Barryscourt Castle, Carrigtwohill, Co Cork

———

I
BARRYSCOURT CASTLE AND THE IRISH TOWER-HOUSE
Tadhg O'Keeffe
October 1996 (published: May 1997)   ISBN 0946641 82X

II
THE IMPACT OF THE ANGLO-NORMANS ON MUNSTER
AF O'Brien
May 1997 (published: October 1997)   ISBN 0946641 838

III
TECHNOLOGICAL CHANGE IN ANGLO-NORMAN MUNSTER
Colin Rynne
October 1997 (published: April 1998)   ISBN 0946641 846

IV
IRISH GARDENS AND GARDENING BEFORE CROMWELL
Terence Reeves-Smyth
May 1998 (for publication: February 1999)   ISBN 0946641 96X

V
OUTSIDE THE TOWER – RECENT EXCAVATIONS AT BARRYSCOURT
Dave Pollock
October 1998 (for publication: March 1999)   ISBN 0946641 978

VI
BARRYSCOURT CASTLE REFURBISHED
Victor Chinnery
May 1999 (for publication: July 1999)   ISBN 0946846 197

VII
LANDSCAPE AND SETTLEMENT IN EAST CORK, 1100-1700
Kieran O'Conor
October 1999 (for publication: December 1999)   ISBN 0946846 197

———

For further details on the lecture series, contact:
The Barryscourt Trust, Barryscourt Castle, Carrigtwohill, Co Cork (tel 021-883864).

The Barryscourt lectures will be published individually,
and a clothbound compilation will be published at three-yearly intervals.
For further details on the publications, or to order copies, contact: Gandon Distribution
Oysterhaven, Kinsale, Co Cork (tel 021-770830 / fax 021-770755).

BARRYSCOURT LECTURES

BARRYSCOURT LECTURE SERIES

Barryscourt Castle is a fine 16th-century tower-house at Carrigtwohill, Co Cork. The Barryscourt Trust was established in 1987 with the aim of conserving, enhancing and developing the heritage potential of the castle.

In 1996, the Barryscourt Trust instituted a biannual series of lectures on Medieval Ireland. These deal with aspects of medieval history, archaeology, art and architecture, and are delivered by scholars specialising in the period. The lectures are being published individually, and a clothbound compilation will be published at four-yearly intervals .

Barryscourt Lectures V
THE BAWN EXPOSED: RECENT EXCAVATIONS AT BARRYSCOURT
Dave Pollock

Published by the Barryscourt Trust in association with Cork County Council and Gandon Editions, Kinsale.

© The Barryscourt Trust and the author, 1999. All rights reserved.

ISBN 0946641 978

Publication of this lecture is sponsored by

Dúchas The Heritage Service

Series Editor   Noel Jameson
Design   John O'Regan
                 (© Gandon, 1999)
Production   Nicola Dearey, Gandon
Printing   Betaprint, Dublin
Distribution   Gandon, Kinsale

THE BARRYSCOURT TRUST
Barryscourt Castle
Carrigtwohill, Co Cork

THE BAWN EXPOSED:
RECENT EXCAVATIONS AT BARRYSCOURT

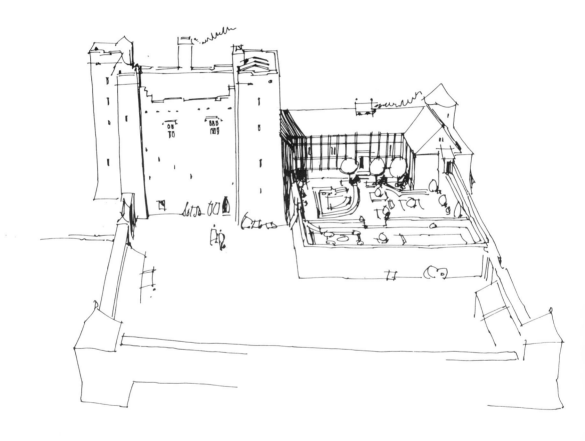

1 – Barryscourt Castle
Suggested reconstruction of bawn, c.1600

The Bawn Exposed: Recent Excavations at Barryscourt

Dave Pollock

THE BARRYSCOURT TRUST
IN ASSOCIATION WITH CORK COUNTY COUNCIL AND GANDON EDITIONS

2 – Barryscourt Castle
The tower-house and bawn wall from the south

INTRODUCTION

Barryscourt Castle is a tower-house with a bawn (an enclosed yard). The tower-house is particularly large, and the bawn is well protected by corner towers [2]. Both the tower-house and the bawn wall survive in remarkably good condition, but the castle is not intact. Windows in the bawn wall show that at least one building in the bawn has disappeared [4].

The current restoration programme at Barryscourt has called for a series of archaeological excavations. Floors in the tower-house were investigated by Olga Finch (1992) and Colin Rynne (1994). The cut for a drain in the bawn was investigated by Ann Marie Lennon (1988 and 1992), and the site for a soakaway pit outside the bawn was excavated by Colin Rynne (1994). In 1996 I excavated the site for a new soakaway inside the bawn, and returned in 1997 to investigate areas

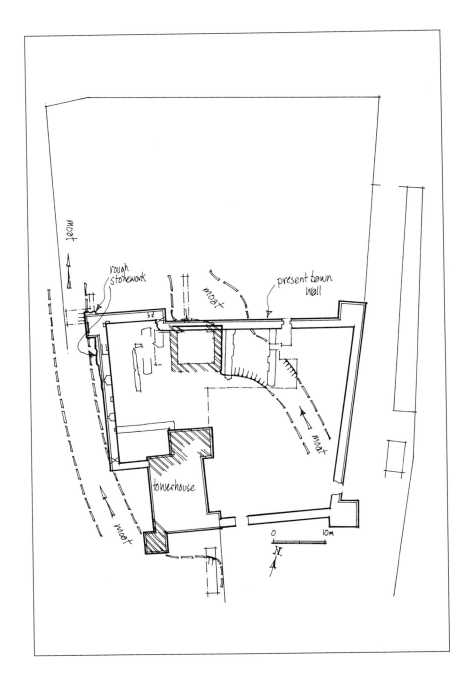

3 – Barryscourt Castle
General plan of moat and later bawn wall

for restoration as garden and yard outside and inside the bawn. This year a large part of the bawn was opened, ahead of garden and yard restoration, to investigate the site of the missing building and to throw light on a few other problem areas.

Two versions of a bawn have emerged at Barryscourt [3]. The earlier was irregular in shape and enclosed by a moat; the later is the bawn we see today, almost square and enclosed by a stone wall with a tower at each corner. The remains of buildings and open spaces in the earlier bawn are fragmentary, damaged by the rearrangement and by the later use of the walled enclosure as a vegetable garden and farmyard, but the remains in the walled bawn have fared better.

———

4 – Barryscourt Castle
East wall of bawn, window and entry to wall passage

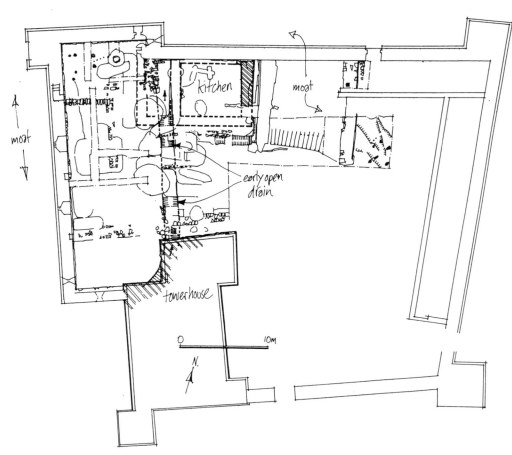

Barryscourt Castle

5 – Plan of early buildings, and earlier open drain
6a – Section into the moat south of the bawn
opposite 6b – Section into the moat north of the bawn

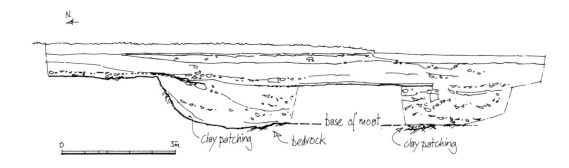

THE MOATED CASTLE

The earliest feature on site has nothing to do with the castle, but is nonetheless extremely important. It was an open drain, a linear ditch with an upcast bank on the east side, probably crowned with a hedge. It is associated with a fallow soil over much of the site, part of an enclosed field system (literally a green-field site) onto which a castle was imposed [5].

The original castle comprised a number of mortared stone buildings and an enclosing bank and ditch. The ditch was quite unlike anything around the fields, with steep sides and a wide, flat base [6]. Generally, it was cut into clay subsoil, but where it was cut into permeable bedrock, the rock was patched with clay.[1] A fine silt in the bottom of the ditch suggests standing water; the ditch appears to have been a wet moat, fed from springs. (A forceful spring pours water into a stream just to the east of the site today. Other springs were encountered whilst excavating the moat in 1997.)

At Barryscourt, the moat appears to respect the tower-house. Unfortunately, the point where the ditch and the building collide has not been excavated; there is no direct evidence that the two were constructed together. But there is a direct link between the moat and another mortared building, probably a kitchen, and there is a strong suggestion that the kitchen and tower-house were constructed together.

The kitchen was built directly on a platform of clean material (no domestic refuse), upcast from digging the moat, and both the kitchen and the tower-house were built over the field drain (the earliest feature on site) when the drain was half filled with clean silt.

The silt in the ditch is a natural accumulation of soil, blown and washed from the fields in the years before the construction of the castle. The half-filled ditch was fully infilled below the tower-house, but was left open where it passed the end of the kitchen. Because the gable wall of the kitchen slightly invaded the ditch, a row of vertical stakes was driven into the hollow to retain a platform under the new wall.

Although the tower-house and kitchen are well separated on site,

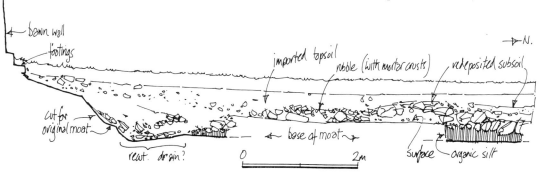

their interference with the old field drain at the same time (after clean silt had been accumulating and immediately before domestic refuse appeared) suggests construction at the same time.

The moated enclosure – the original bawn – has been pieced together into an unlikely shape [7]. The moat runs around the north-east corner of the kitchen, along its east gable, but then turns sharply east and starts to swing towards the south. Its position below the later east wall of the bawn is betrayed by a string of relieving arches spreading the weight of the wall over the softer ground of the infilled ditch. On the south side of the tower-house, the ditch appeared in a test trench in 1997 (cut into bedrock and 'patched' with clay), and on the west side a similar ditch was encountered by Colin Rynne a few years earlier.[2] The ditch appeared again in a small test trench at the north-west corner of the site, at the foot of the later corner tower.

We can be fairly confident that the ditch ran continuously from Colin Rynne's test trench to the north-west corner and beyond. The position of a complementary upcast bank to the east is shown in rough stonework at the foot of the later bawn wall [8a, 8b]. This stonework attracted the attention of the architectural survey, and was originally attributed to an early phase of mortared stone buildings at Barryscourt. However, the masonry now appears to be part of the later bawn wall, the

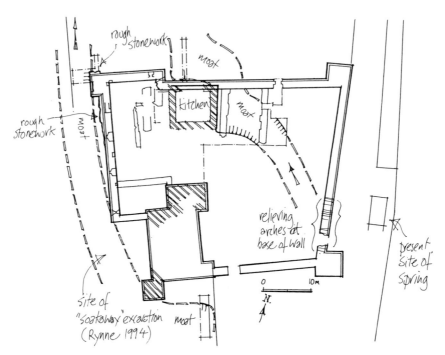

Barryscourt Castle

8a, 8b – Rough
stonework at the foot
of the bawn wall, at
the north-west corner

opposite
7 – Plan of moat

ragged, unfaced foot of a wall built in a trench. Clearly the trench was cut into a bank that has since disappeared – the upcast bank on the east side of the moat.

When the evidence for a moat is assembled, we have an incomplete picture of something approximating to an 'L' shape in plan. This is not the normal plan for a moated site. Indeed, the possession of a moat does not qualify Barryscourt for membership of the group of monuments known as moated sites. This term is reserved for a type of medieval monument appearing in England and Ireland, normally a civilian settlement, a manor house or farmstead with an enclosing ditch, rather than a stone or timber castle with a ditch amongst its defences. Whilst the moated Barryscourt does not present the traditional image of a castle at this stage (it has no defensive wall), it has a tower-house at its centre, a very incongruous element.

Generally, moated sites are thought to have been fashionable in Ireland from the early 13th century to the 14th century. The earliest tower-houses are unlikely to have appeared before the end of that period. Of the thousand or so moated sites thought to be scattered over the Irish countryside,[3] only a handful have been excavated. Kilmagoura, county Cork, produced a carbon-14 date of AD 1163-1393 (calibrated), and Rigsdale, county Cork, produced two pennies of Edward I and a few sherds of Saintonge polychrome ware (suggesting occupation around AD 1300). Two of the other sites (Kilferagh, county Kilkenny, and Ballyveelish, county Tipperary) were dated from pottery to the late 13th century/14th century.[4] The dating appears to be fairly consistent.

Moated sites have been associated with English colonisation in the 13th century,[5] and their demise has been linked to the troubles of the 14th century, amongst them the Black Death and the Bruce Invasion.[6]

In the first Barryscourt lecture, Tadhg O'Keeffe chose a construction date of c.1550 for the tower-house at Barryscourt 'on stylistic grounds'.[7] Others have favoured a 15th-century date.[8] The lack of original openings for handguns suggests an early date, but suggestions of original double-splayed loops for artillery on the ground floor (restored as single-splays) are in keeping with a date in the first half of the 16th century.[9] The date remains ambiguous and nowhere near acceptable for a moated site.

If we look at the finds recovered from the excavations, however, a different picture emerges. Colin Rynne recovered pottery from his segment of the moat. He gave it a preliminary date of the late 14th century.[10] The excavation in the bawn in 1996 produced sixty sherds of pottery. All have been dated to the 13th/14th century, none to the 15th century, and none to the 16th century.[11] (The sherds recovered in 1997 and 1998 have not yet been studied.) The pottery is apparently in order for a moated site, but challenges the evidence of the standing buildings. We have a problem.

A specialist in the field has claimed that 'the late medieval period from the Black Death to the accession of the Tudor kings is a notoriously difficult period for pottery studies.'[12] I hoped that the date of manufacturing the pottery could be pushed later, to embrace the recorded use of Barryscourt up to and through the 16th century. But it could not.

The pottery at Barryscourt falls into three distinct types. The majority is Irish, produced somewhere in the area around Cork. (No kiln site has been identified, but the clay used has weathered from the Old Red Sandstone of this part of the country.) Some is French, from the wine-producing Saintonge region, and some is English, from kilns at Redcliffe in Bristol. The Redcliffe pottery was popular at Bristol Castle through the 14th century, but continued into the 15th century.[13] Conceivably, a few vessels from the first half of the 15th century may have found their way to Barryscourt, but these would have been antiques by the mid-16th century. The Saintonge ware would also have survived well beyond its expected life by the mid-16th century, and Clare McCutcheon has suggested that the local ware was only produced during the lifespan of the foreign types, 'as evidenced by the lack of variety both of fabrics and of vessel forms'.[14]

We cannot explain away the anachronistic pottery by claiming that it belongs to an earlier occupation of the site; the cleanly silted land drain below the tower-house indicates that there was no earlier site. If we put to one side the information from the land drain, we are still confronted with the fact that the historically recorded occupation of the site, in the second half of the 16th century, is completely unrepresented by the pottery. Either the occupants were extremely careful with their pottery, or they had none, apart from a number of heirlooms. The first option is unlikely, leaving us with the aceramic theory, that one of the most prestigious families in the country found it fashionable to have no new pottery in the 16th century.

The decline in popularity of pottery in the 14th century and 15th century has been recognised by specialists working in Ireland and England. In England the decline has been linked to economic distress, and particularly the reduction of markets in towns, but a resurgence has been seen in the later 16th century.[15] At Barryscourt there is little indication of a late 16th-century revival of interest in pottery.

The implications of having little contemporary pottery in the late medieval period are fairly serious, but compounded by the survival of older vessels in circulation. Moated sites cannot be dated by pottery alone; it appears possible that at least two from the handful of excavated sites in Ireland (Kilferagh and Ballyveelish)[16] were occupied, even built, in the 16th century.

In Scotland the small tower-house at Craigcaffie, Galloway, was built with a surrounding moat of normal, trapezoidal plan in the 16th century [9, 10],[17] and a good deal nearer to Barryscourt a moat was found whilst erecting new farm buildings beside the tower-house with walled

9 – Craigcaffie Tower, Galloway, Scotland
The trench in the foreground cuts into the infilled moat

10 – Craigcaffie Tower,
Galloway, Scotland
Sketch plan

11 – Clonamicklon Castle,
county Tipperary
Sketch plan (after Moran)

12 – Clonamicklon Castle
Section through moat
(after Moran)

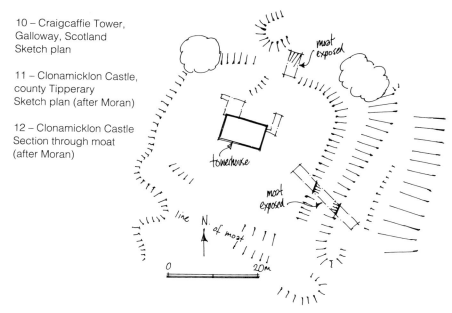

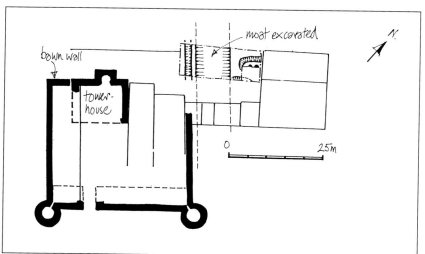

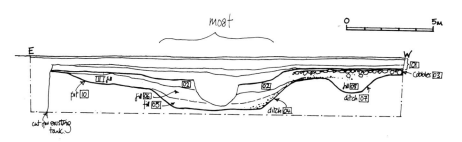

bawn at Clonamicklon, county Tipperary [11, 12].[18] Two sites in county
Wexford have both curtain walls and moats, and two sites in county
Kilkenny had ruined mortared stone buildings in 1840.[19] The large moated
site at Richfield, county Wexford, encloses gardens, several yards and a
tower-house.[20] For some or all of these Irish sites, the construction of the
tower-houses and curtain walls may postdate digging the moats, but the
moats were still sufficiently fashionable to be left open rather than infilled
when the masonry appeared.

The tallest building at Barryscourt, the tower-house, occupied the
heel position in the irregular 'L' shape of the moated enclosure. A second
stone building, the likely kitchen, stood in the limb to the north; a third
may have stood in the limb to the east. (Mortared stonework was observed
underground when cutting for a drain to the east of the tower-house.)[21]

The second mortared building is very badly preserved, but was large
and well built [13, 14]. The walls are almost completely robbed, but the
battered foot of the east gable has survived in the edge of the moat, and
the west gable has been so neatly robbed that we can make out the wall
thickness. Scorched limestone slabs and baked clay flooring against the
west gable suggest the position of a fireplace and chimney; other patches
of scorching on the floor and a few holes are thought to be from the use
rather than destruction of the building. The presence of water is implied

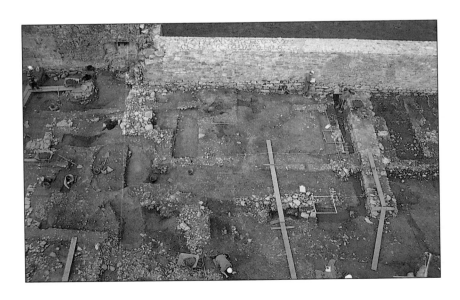

13 – Barryscourt Castle
Scant remains of the kitchen, etc, from the south

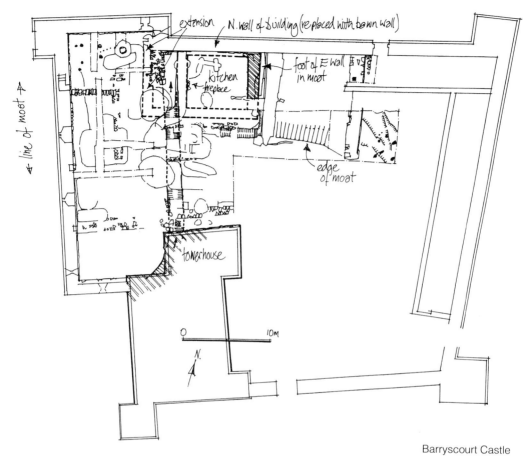

extension   N. wall of building (replaced with bawn wall)

foot of E wall
in moat

kitchen
fireplace

line of moat

edge
of moat

towerhouse

0   10M

N.

Barryscourt Castle

14 – Plan of kitchen, etc
15 – Tentative reconstruction of
the moated bawn, c.1580

by a drain in the north wall (in the bawn wall – the rebuilt north wall of the building). In area, the building is large enough to have been a tower-house itself, but the side walls were probably too thin to have taken the weight of a vault overhead, and the building is more likely to have been a two-storey kitchen or brewhouse. A small extension was added to the west end of the building, but was damaged and not repaired.

The kitchen was built on a platform of upcast material thrown from the moat to the north and east. Upcast from the moat to the west was thrown into a bank along its edge (represented by the rough stonework at the foot of the later bawn wall [8a]). The bank was probably crowned with a fence or a hedge. It is unclear (due to later damage) whether or not a narrow row of timber buildings was constructed against the bank, looking into the bawn [15].

————

1581

The kitchen was damaged shortly before the moated bawn was replaced with a stone wall. This damage – the work of David Barry – probably represents one of the few historically dated events at Barryscourt. In 1581, Barry had his own properties 'broken and burnt' and his main seat at Barryscourt 'defaced and despoiled' rather than deliver them intact to Walter Raleigh. Clearly he did not have the tower-house razed to the ground, but he may have broken off the battlements and may have seriously damaged other buildings in the bawn. When the site was restored and walled shortly afterwards, the kitchen was largely rebuilt and a new range was constructed against the new wall. The walled bawn was never seriously 'defaced and despoiled'. Much of the new range was built in timber, and never burned down.

————

opposite 16 – Barryscourt Castle
plan of bawn wall, new buildings, etc

THE WALLED CASTLE

The surviving fabric of the north wall of the kitchen was taken down and rebuilt as part of the new bawn wall. The kitchen extension was abandoned, but the original building appears to have been restored. The moat to the east, inside the new bawn, was infilled with its own bank and with rubble, a good deal of it with mortar crusts (rubble from the old kitchen or the third stone building?).

Two elegant seated window embrasures and a large garderobe were built into the west side of the bawn wall, and a range of new buildings was attached [16]. A two-storey building, apparently with mortared stone walls (only the foundations survived), fitted the corner beside the tower-house. The remainder of the range had a timber wall on narrow stone footings, overlooking the bawn [17]. A box drain carried water from the open bawn,

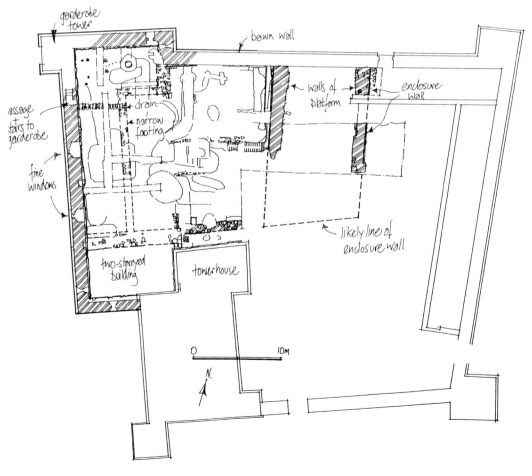

17 – Barryscourt Castle
Remains of the timbered range, from the south

under the building, and through the bawn wall, and a large rectangular sump in the middle of the building may have helped drainage.

The main chamber in the range was long but narrow, only five metres wide internally. Its floor would have been wooden, at the level of the windows (with a storage space below), and its ceiling would have been flat at the top of the standing wall or rising into the timberwork of the roofspace. The fireplace was either central or against the south gable wall (which was shared with the two-storey building). The chamber was either a hall or a gallery; its shape and position are similar to the Elizabethan gallery built with a new range at Ormond Castle, Carrick-on-Suir.

The position of the main entry to the chamber is suggested by the arrangement of garden features in the bawn.

THE GARDEN IN THE BAWN

A number of unusual features were found in 1996 – shallow trenches cut into the bawn and filled with soil in the heyday of the castle. They were interpreted as garden beds, part of a decorative arrangement. There was no sign of the beds in the piece of bawn opened in 1997, but they reappeared in 1998, confined to the ground in front of the new range.

The beds are generally linear or rectangular, surviving as shallow, flat-bottomed hollows containing a layer of stones with soil (and midden) between. The soil filtered down from above, from the raised bed, and the stones were deliberately laid, probably for drainage. A number of later planting holes can be found in some beds, small bowl-shaped cuts with a similar fill. A few large bowl-shaped cuts, with a great deal of stone towards the base, were probably planting holes for trees.

Generally, the ground level in the garden did not survive, but two small pieces of garden path subsided into settling drainage ditches. The path was made of small pieces of sandstone, debris from a nearby *fulacht fiadh*, which was also used to surface the yard inside the north gate.[22] The cast of a wooden board, used to box in the raised bed, was found beside one fragment of path. This particular bed had at least one chamfered corner [18, 19].

There was no indication of vertical stakes to hold the boards in position; the lengths of board were probably pegged together. (Excavations at the early 17th-century Great Garden at Kirby Hall, Northants, similarly found no stakeholes but a number of nails for joining the boards.)[23]

The archaeological excavation of gardens has been pursued seriously in Britain since the 1980s, but the size of the areas involved has frequently

Barryscourt Castle
18 – Remains of bed with chamfered corner, from the south-east
19 – Plan of bed with chamfered corner, and other features

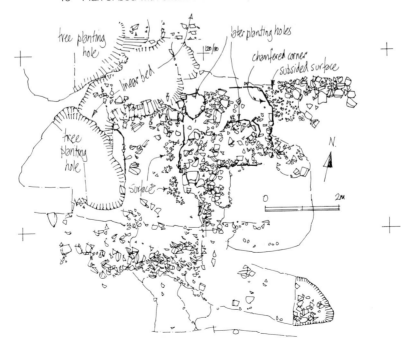

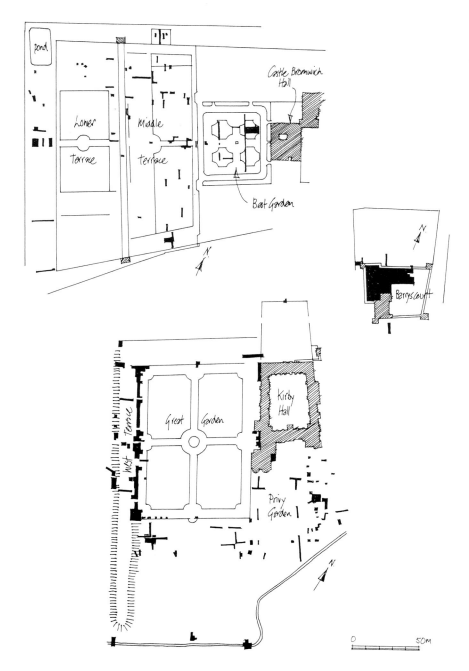

20 – Garden areas excavated (in black) at Kirby Hall (after Dix *et al*),
Castle Bromwich Hall (after Currie and Locock), and Barryscourt (to scale)

forced a sampling approach rather than area excavation [20]. The fear of destroying the entire garden and thus depriving future generations of the chance to reinterpret has tended to bolster this approach. As a result, the sequence of change has been well recorded, but the pattern of planted beds at any period has not emerged.[24] At Barryscourt, the area excavation of the bawn has exposed all surviving remains of the enclosed garden, and the interpretation of the garden has only been possible because it has been fully exposed.

The suite of stone and timber buildings set into the north-west corner appears to be part of the original design of the walled bawn. The design may have envisaged the bawn as a single, large, open yard, but at an early stage a substantial mortared dividing wall was built, with a battered foot towards the remainder of the bawn. Only a few courses of this wall have survived, but it probably stood to the height of the main bawn wall and could have accommodated a wall walk. The wall may have crossed the bawn in a straight line, but more likely turned towards the north-east corner of the tower-house, isolating the corner of the bawn with the suite of timbered buildings. The garden was arranged in this enclosed corner, but not immediately.

The restored kitchen was probably dismantled before the garden was planted. The far end – the east end – of the small walled enclosure appears to have been raised to an unknown height (it was taken down again much later) with soil and midden and building rubble, and revetted with a second battered, mortared wall before two beds were set in the remaining enclosure, potentially to take hedging [21]. The beds, represented by stone rubble in linear trenches, are narrower than the 1.1m wide (by 0.45m deep) hedging trenches defining the parterres at the early 17th-century Great Garden at Kirby Hall, but have a similar rubbly fill,[25] and may have defined a path from an entrance, through the enclosure wall, to the main chamber in the timbered range.

The platform at the east end of the walled enclosure, surrounded by mortared stone walls, may itself be a garden feature. The parterres at Kirby Hall were overlooked by a twenty-metre-wide terrace, revetted with two-metre-high vertical walls.[26] The platform in the bawn at Barryscourt is only eleven metres wide, and would have overlooked a much smaller garden. (Alternatively, the platform may have had a defensive function, perhaps as an artillery platform.)

A mortared stone wall at the foot of the tower-house may be part of the enclosure wall or a low garden feature. The only surviving course of stonework is narrower than the enclosure wall to the east, and separates a soily strip against the tower (a long bed?) from a path (or yard) surface. A few small rectangular foundations set into the path may have supported ornaments.

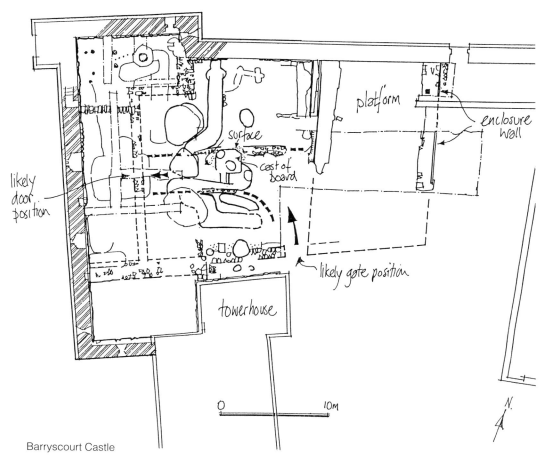

likely door position

surface

cost of board

platform

enclosure wall

likely gate position

towerhouse

0   10m

N.

Barryscourt Castle

21 – Plan of garden beds, etc
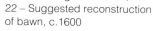
22 – Suggested reconstruction
of bawn, c.1600

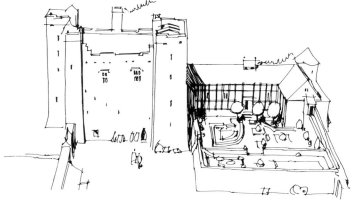

The beds and planting holes are mostly within ten metres of the hall or gallery, and do not present a symmetrical pattern. But they are far from random. Two wide beds follow the outline of the range whilst respecting a pair of earlier beds, already mentioned, defining a path to the middle of the hall or gallery. A row of tree planting holes suggests a line of trees only five metres from the building.

The excavation of the garden beds is not yet over. A few beds still need untangling, and samples need to be taken and processed to get an idea of the plants involved in the arrangement. All of the garden beds are likely to be in this corner of the bawn, overlooked by the timbered range and enclosed from the rest of the bawn [22].

―――――

DATES

There is no date for the start of Barryscourt. Carrigtwohill, the nearby village, was a Barry manor before 1200, but the earliest surviving mention of Barryscourt is from the second half of the 16th century.[27] In 1581 the castle was 'defaced and despoiled', but the tower-house was modernised in the 1580s and 1590s (inscribed dates on new windows and fireplaces). In time, the family seat moved to Castlelyons, and by 1620 the invoices for running repairs to the castle were no longer passing through the accounts. A short occupation, from the mid-16th century to the early 17th century would fit the historical material.

The short lifespan of the moated castle – between thirty and one hundred years – suits the archaeological stratigraphy. There is no indication that the moat was recut or cleaned out, and no obvious realigning of buildings on the site.

No coins have been found during three seasons of excavations in the bawn, and the recovered pottery is interesting but not useful at this stage. (Study of the pottery from the last two seasons may reveal a few contemporary pieces.).

The historical, architectural, and stratigraphic evidence suggests a short and late occupation at Barryscourt. It is hoped that further excavation will recover waterlogged timber from the edge of the moat, and this should provide a dendrochronological date for the early use of the site.

―――――

CONCLUSION

A number of unexpected discoveries were made in the bawn at Barryscourt. The remains of the timber hall or gallery are minimal and would not normally (without one side of the building standing in stone) be interpreted as the base of such a grand structure. A similar but wider hall may have stood at Cahir Castle, county Tipperary. This building was restored in the 19th century with a new thin inner wall, perhaps because only fragmentary thin stone footings were found. An illustration of Cahir Castle in 1599 appears to show the building thatched and with a cowl for a central hearth.[28]

The discovery of garden remains was not surprising. The garden started sometime in the late 16th century, by which time prestigious families in northern Europe were indulging in hard and soft landscaping. By the early 17th century, walled enclosures were being built specifically to house gardens as far north as Angus in Scotland.[29] Early views of Limerick and Askeaton castles show gardens within the bawn. The surprise at Barryscourt is the lack of symmetry.

The moat was quite unexpected, and is not fully understood. The feature would have had a minimal defensive role; the water was shallow and would have been easily drained. The main barrier would have been on the inside – a fence or hedge on a bank – leaving the water as a decoration and a store for live fish.

FURTHER WORK

The tower-house at Barryscourt was the private house of a major family, the main defensible point of the castle, and part of the administrative centre of the Barry estates. The bawn outside was more than an open yard. The later walled enclosure had a number of major buildings in stone and timber, and a garden, enclosed from the remainder of the yard.

That remainder has not been investigated. It probably contains the farm buildings – the granary and stables and barn – which serviced the surrounding land. But this assumption is not very safe in the light of the discoveries made in the area excavated.

A great deal of information is becoming available from the excavation of half of the bawn. That information would more than double with the excavation of the remainder (the accessible area), despite the fact that the archaeological layers will be shallower and the preservation poorer than in the area already open. It is hoped that a further season of excavation will take place inside the bawn, to tie up loose ends in the area already opened and investigate the second half.

The author

Dave Pollock spent sixteen years directing excavations and illustrating guide books and display panels in Scotland before moving to county Tipperary in 1993. He has continued as a freelance field archaeologist, undertaking excavations ahead of developments (mostly in counties Tipperary and Waterford), and carrying out investigations for the National Monuments Service at Dungarvan Castle and Barryscourt. His ambition is to work indoors during bad weather and outdoors only on the best of summer days.

Acknowledgements

I would first like to thank the Barryscourt Trust for inviting me to speak, and especially Noel Jameson and Robert Williams for their encouragement during the excavations. I would like to thank members of the National Monuments Service, particularly Aighleann O'Shaughnessy, Denis Power and Ana Dolan for their help and encouragement. Finally, I would like to thank my assistant Gerry O'Neill and a large number of people who have put up with some unpleasant weather and a good deal of heavy work to move the excavation this far.

Illustrations

All drawings and photographs by the author.

Notes and References

1   D Pollock, *Preliminary report on archaeological investigations at Barryscourt Castle, Carrigtwohill, Co. Cork, in September-October 1997*, excavation report 96E238* (1997), p6

2   C Rynne, *A preliminary report on excavations at Barryscourt Castle, Co. Cork, during 1994*, excavation report 93E76* (1994)

3   K O'Conor, *The Archaeology of Medieval Rural Settlement in Ireland* (Dublin, 1998), p63

4   R Glasscock, 'Kilmagoura', *Medieval Archaeology*, 12 (1968), pp196-7; D Sweetman, 'Excavations of a medieval moated site at Rigsdale, County Cork, 1977-8', *Proceedings of the Royal Irish Academy*, 81C (1981) pp103-205: 195-7; M Hurley, 'Kilferagh, Co. Kilkenny: Corn-drying kiln and settlement site', *Cork Archaeological Studies*, 1 (1987), pp88-100; M Doody, 'Moated site, Ballyveelish 1, Co. Tipperary', *Cork Archaeological Studies*, 1 (1987), pp74-87

5   O'Conor, *The Archaeology of Medieval Rural Settlement in Ireland*, pp58-69

6   TB Barry, *The Archaeology of Medieval Ireland* (London, 1987), p92

7   T O'Keeffe, *Barryscourt Castle and the Irish Tower-House* (Cork, 1997), p16

8   For example, J Monk and R Tobin, *Barryscourt Castle: An Architectural Survey*, report for the Barryscourt Trust (Cork, 1991)

9   P Kerrigan, *Castles and Fortifications in Ireland 1485-1945* (Cork, 1995), p26

10   Rynne, *A preliminary report on excavations at Barryscourt Castle*, p6

11   C McCutcheon, 'A note on the pottery from Barryscourt Castle' in D Pollock, *Archive report on archaeological investigations at Barryscourt Castle, Carrigtwohill, Co. Cork*, excavation report 96E238* (1996)

12   A Vince, 'The Saxon and medieval pottery of London', *Medieval Archaeology*, 29

(1985), p65

[13] M McCarthy and C Brooks, *Medieval Pottery in Britain AD 900-1600* (Leicester, 1988) p346

[14] McCutcheon, 'A note on the pottery from Barryscourt Castle'

[15] McCarthy and Brooks, *Medieval Pottery in Britain*, p89

[16] Hurley, 'Kilferagh, Co. Kilkenny: Corn-drying kiln and settlement site', p97; Doody, 'Moated site, Ballyveelish 1, Co. Tipperary', pp74-87

[17] J Moran and D Pollock, 'Excavations at Craigcaffie Tower, by Stranraer', *Transactions of the Dumfriesshire and Galloway Natural History and Antiquarian Society*, lxxi (1996) pp119-31

[18] J Moran, *Archeaological monitoring and excavation at Clonamicklon Castle, Gurtnahoe, Thurles, Co. Tipperary*, excavation report 96E291* (1996)

[19] TB Barry, *Medieval Moated Sites of South-East Ireland* (Oxford, 1977), p81

[20] *ibid.*, p74

[21] AM Lennon, *Watching brief at Barryscourt Castle, Co. Cork, April-May 1995*, excavation report* (1995), p3

[22] Pollock, *Preliminary report on archaeological investigations at Barryscourt Castle*, p2; C Rynne, *Trenching at Barryscourt Castle, County Cork, May 1993*, excavation report 93E76* (1993), p4

[23] B Dix, I Soden and T Hylton, 'Kirby Hall and its Gardens: Excavations in 1987-1994', *Archaeological Journal*, 152 (1995), pp291-380: 330

[24] For example, at Castle Bromwich Hall; see C Currie and M Locock, 'Excavations at Castle Bromwich Hall Gardens 1989-91', *Post-Medieval Archaeology*, 27 (1993), pp119-99

[25] Dix *et al*, 'Kirby Hall and its Gardens', p328

[26] *ibid.*

[27] Monk and Tobin, *Barryscourt Castle*, p6

[28] T Stafford, *Pacata Hibernia* (London, 1633)

[29] C Tabraham, *Scottish Castles and Fortifications* (Edinburgh, 1986), p71

* copies with the National Monuments Service and the National Museum

———

THE BARRYSCOURT LECTURES

The Barryscourt Trust presents a series of bi-annual lectures on Medieval Ireland
at Barryscourt Castle, Carrigtwohill, Co Cork.
The lectures are being published individually, and a clothbound compilation
will be published at four-yearly intervals.

I – BARRYSCOURT CASTLE AND THE IRISH TOWER-HOUSE
Tadhg O'Keeffe
October 1996 (published, 1997)   ISBN 0946641 82X, 32 pages, illus, £4.95

II – THE IMPACT OF THE ANGLO-NORMANS ON MUNSTER
AF O'Brien
May 1997 (published, 1997)   ISBN 0946641 838, 32 pages, illus, £4.95

III – TECHNOLOGICAL CHANGE IN ANGLO-NORMAN MUNSTER
Colin Rynne
October 1997 (published, 1998)   ISBN 0946641 846, 32 pages, illus, £4.95

IV – IRISH GARDENS AND GARDENING BEFORE CROMWELL
Terence Reeves-Smyth
May 1998 (published, 1999)   ISBN 0946641 96X, 48 pages, illus, £4.95

V – OUTSIDE THE TOWER: RECENT EXCAVATIONS AT BARRYSCOURT
Dave Pollock
October 1998 (published, 1999)   ISBN 0946641 978, 32 pages, illus, £4.95

VI – BARRYSCOURT CASTLE REFURNISHED
Victor Chinnery
May 1999 (for publication: Sept 1999)   ISBN 0946846 197, 32 pages, illus, £4.95

VII – LANDSCAPE AND SETTLEMENT IN EAST CORK, 1100-1700
Kieran O'Conor
October 1999 (for publication: Dec 1999)   ISBN 0946846 200, 32 pages, illus, £4.95

VIII – THE ORIGIN AND DEVELOPMENT OF THE TOWER-HOUSE
David Sweetman
May 2000 (for publication: June 2000)   ISBN 0946846 294, 32 pages, illus, £4.95

THE BARRYSCOURT LECTURES ON MEDIEVAL IRELAND
Volume 1
for publication: September 2000   ISBN 0946846 308, 280 pages, £25 clothbound

For further details on the lecture series, contact:
The Barryscourt Trust, Barryscourt Castle, Carrigtwohill, Co Cork (tel 021-883864).

For further details on the publications, or to order copies, contact: Gandon Editions
Oysterhaven, Kinsale, Co Cork (tel 021-770830 / fax 021-770755).

BARRYSCOURT LECTURES

BARRYSCOURT REFURNISHED
The Reinstatement of a Late Sixteenth Century Irish Domestic Interior
– Usage, Interior Decoration, Furnishings & Accessories
at Barryscourt Castle

AO DIO 1588 IHS D B ET E R MEFIERI FECERUNT

'In the Year of Our Lord 1588 DB and ER caused me to be made'
(Inscription on chimney piece in the Great Chamber at Barryscourt)

———

———

pages 178-179
1 – A general view of the Great Chamber on the second floor of Barryscourt Castle.
The woollen hangings, placed across the 'high end' of the room to indicate its special status, are
formed as alternating panes in the Barry colours of red and white. (photo: Con Brogan, Dúchas)

pages 182-183
2 – A general view of the Hall on the first floor at Barryscourt (photo: Con Brogan, Dúchas)

All photos by the author unless otherwise stated

Barryscourt Refurnished

The reinstatement of a late 16th-century Irish domestic interior

Victor Chinnery

THE BARRYSCOURT TRUST
IN ASSOCIATION WITH CORK COUNTY COUNCIL AND GANDON EDITIONS

FOREWORD

The present essay has grown out of a project to report on the possibilities of refurnishing the tower-house at Barryscourt in the manner in which the Old English household of David and Ellen Barry may have lived there in c.1600. The original report, submitted to Dúchas, The Heritage Service and the Barryscourt Trust in February 1998, briefly reviewed the scant available evidence on the material culture of the landowning classes in Munster during the period 1450 to 1650, taking the Barry family as a member of this group and attempting to place them in the wider context of their class in north-west Europe. The report took into account specialist discussion relating to the physical development of the tower at Barryscourt, since when work has progressed on the repair of the stone and timber fabric of the tower-house, and in 1999 the first phase of furnishing the interiors was achieved.[1]

Given the known biography of David Barry and his family, the extensive survival of the original building, and the nature of the modern restoration, it was suggested that a scheme of replica furnishings could offer a credible representation of the interiors of the tower-house as they might have appeared following the renovations of 1586 to 1596, and that this should be supported by a thorough programme of research.

The heyday of Barryscourt was in the period after the completion of the late 16th-century refit, and preceding David Barry's death in 1617. After David Barry's death, Ellen married Sir John Fitz-Edmond FitzGerald of Ballymaloe. The Cloyne Harp of 1621 bears their arms and initials, and at the time of writing is on view in the National Museum of Ireland at Collins Barracks, Dublin. Soon after this the castle appears to have been largely forsaken (though still maintained) by Barry's grandson (also David), who inherited on the death of his grandfather, married a daughter of the Great Earl of Cork, and moved to a new seat at Castlelyons.

The inherent challenge at Barryscourt has therefore been to construct an appropriate material metaphor to illustrate the life of an Old English family in a typical tower-house in the first decade of the 17th century. To achieve this we have reviewed the wider social and practical conditions in a house of this kind, and researched the range of wooden, metal, ceramic and textile furnishings that it might be expected to contain.

I – THE INITIAL DISCUSSION

THE BARRY FAMILY AND THEIR OLD ENGLISH HERITAGE

A central aspect of the reinterpretation is to determine quite how far the life of the household may have leaned towards or away from 'Irish' and 'English' manners respectively, and at the same time to identify such national stereotypes in terms of the physical furnishings. All cultures are a blend of the influences available to them, and the factions in late 16th-century Irish society sported affectations of 'Irishness' or 'Englishness' which proclaimed clear social, religious and political messages.

David Barry's high social standing in Ireland is not in doubt (in 1611 he was listed as one of the 25 Lords Temporal),[2] but in the absence of a specific biography we must look elsewhere for evidence of the ways in which his social status, ancestry and allegiances may have been expressed. Clues lie in the meagre documentary evidence that does exist, and in the standing architecture and archaeology of the site. This base view can be further expanded with information drawn from the comparative context of Barry's contemporaries in south Munster and more widely in Ireland.

Irish society in 1600 was loosely divided into three socio-political groups. The most traditional of these were the native Irish (the Gaels or 'mere [pure] Irish'), descendants of the original inhabitants and the earliest Celtic invaders, who still formed a substantial and independent faction. This native population had never been dominated by the partial Norman settlement of Ireland, and old military rivalries simmered beneath the surface. English travellers professed to find them a curious and backward race, though their comments are not to be accepted without question. Edmund Campion found a rich and warm personality in the native Irish, recording them as 'religious, frank, amorous, ireful, sufferable of pains infinite, very glorious, many sorcerers, excellent horsemen, delighted with wars, great almsgivers, passing in hospitality ... sharp-witted, lovers of learning, capable of any study whereunto they bend themselves, constant in travail, adventurous, intractable, kindhearted...'[3]

The well-recorded Irish generosity in hospitality is one characteristic that allows itself to be reflected in the physical arrangements for dining and entertaining at Barryscourt. Many early commentators recorded with some sense of personal gratitude the Irish penchant for offering lavish hospitality to friends and strangers alike. Many travellers noted a disdain amongst the native Irish for those material comforts and trappings of household life that were indispensable to the English. Andrew Boorde noted that 'The Irish care not for pot nor pan, Ketil nor mattrys, fetherbed nor such implements of household', and Fynes Moryson also alluded to a lack of civilised furnishings: 'These wild Irish never set any candles upon tables; what do I speak of tables? since indeed they have no tables, but set their meat upon a bundle of grass and use the same grass for napkins to wash their hands. But I mean that they do not set candles upon any high place to give light to the house, but place a great candle of reeds and butter upon the floor in the midst of a great room [and] make fires in the midst of the room, the smoke whereof goeth out at a hole in the top thereof...'[4]

Clearly, Barryscourt, with its four chimneys, was more advanced than the archaic setting thus described by Moryson, but even he cannot have been surprised at the Gaelic taste for central hearths, for only a generation previously the introduction of chimneys was a novelty even amongst the English middle classes, and in 1617 it was not unusual in England still to find an old-fashioned house retaining its central hearth. Thirty years earlier William Harrison had noted that in Essex 'There are old men yet dwelling in the village where I remaine, which have noted ... the multitude of chimnies latelie erected, whereas in their young dayes there were not above two or three...'[5]

The second group, the Old English or 'English-Irish' (some commentators referred to them as the 'Old foreigners'), were largely of Norman-English descent. After settling in medieval Ireland they had, to some extent, rejected their English background and had become gaelicised in their habits, though rarely did they integrate fully with their Gaelic Irish neighbours. Many spoke Irish as their first language, but smugly regarded themselves as the upholders of civilised (by which they meant Anglicised) standards in Ireland. Indeed, contemporary English observers characterised them as the 'Civill Irish', to contrast with their view of the Gaels as the 'Wilde Irish'. A fair amount of intermarriage took place between the two, and on the surface the leading families shared certain similarities, though at the same time perceiving clear cultural differences between themselves. It is by no means clear how far political affiliations might have influenced a differing cultural style and domestic manners between these disparate groups. Certainly, the landowning classes amongst the Gaelic Irish built their towers in much the same manner as did the Old English of the same class. It is generally impossible to distinguish between them in the planning and decorative detail of the stone ruins to be seen today, but, if contemporary observers are to be believed, their manner of living within the towers was significantly different. Encouraged by legal controls, the Old English often wore English dress as opposed to the glib and mantle of the Gaels, and by this device signalled a tacit support for the Elizabethan government. In many ways a hybrid group, the Old English were often thought too Irish for the English and too English for the Irish. Yet their allegiance to the Crown was at best rather shaky, and members of the Old English group occasionally reverted to gaelicised ways, causing them to be regarded by Crown agents with suspicion.

The third group were the New English (or 'New foreigners'), the more recent wave of adventurers, colonists, undertakers and Elizabethan administrators who came to Ireland from the mid-16th century onwards, seeking to strengthen English economic and political dominance, often seeking to serve their own ends and becoming more numerous and more important in the early 17th century. The attempt to establish and broaden the English foothold in Ireland during the period 1560 to 1640 is well chronicled.

After the Norman conquest of England, the Barrys had first established themselves in south Wales, before extending into southern Ireland.[6] As Cambro-Normans by descent, they were firmly part of the Old English faction, and were linked by marriage to other Old English families, notably the Powers, the FitzGeralds and the Roches. David himself married Ellen Roche, daughter of Lord Fermoy, and his son David married Eilish Power. It was reported on one hand that Lord Barry spoke English surprisingly well, but another report of 1585 states that he had become disaffected and had returned to Irish ways. However, reports such as these should generally be treated with caution as, by denigrating his competitors, the writer may have hoped to promote his own ambitions. Many English commentators found it expedient not to promote conditions in Ireland in a positive manner. Around 1629 the historian Geoffrey Keating (himself of Old English descent) criticised the prejudice displayed by English historians, noting that, from the earliest times, '...Cambrensis, Spenser, Stanihurst, Hanmer, Camden, Barckly, Moryson, Davies, Campion and every other new foreigner who has written on Ireland ... have displayed no inclination to treat of the virtues or good qualities of the nobles among the old foreigners and the native Irish who then dwelt in Ireland.'[7]

However, our main task here is to estimate how far the cultural identity of the Barry family might be reflected in the domestic arrangements and style of living at Barryscourt. Unfortunately, little specific analysis has been carried out in this area, and it remains unclear which precise synthesis of Irish and English manners might have been favoured by a 'typical' Old English noble household, though there are clues. Some of the major landed families in Ireland (the Butlers, O'Briens, Burkes and various branches of the FitzGeralds) lived in undoubted sophistication, The remnants of the buildings associated with these families, and such fragmentary inventories as are available, each confirm this hypothesis,[8] but at Barryscourt the style of the building is more befitting that of the gentry than of the nobility. Such is revealed in the modest scale (though large by most standards) and traditional planning of the tower-house, and in the detailing of fireplaces and windows that deviate very little from the conventional vernacular of the period. Where some contemporary buildings (such as Ormond Castle and Myrtle Grove) embody a distinct awareness of urbane European Renaissance styling, Barryscourt offers a more provincial taste in which the architectural detail is both simplified and anachronistically tinged with a sub-medieval character. Yet this was not the only seat of the Lord Barry, and so is not a unique indicator of his wealth and status.

The Barrys apparently upheld the Gaelic tradition for hospitality. In 1575 Sir Henry Sidney wrote to Sir Francis Walsingham that he was 'well entertained at the Viscount Barrie's house called Barriescourt',[9] and thirty years later, in 1606, Sir John Davies (the Attorney-General) wrote that he had dined with Viscount Barry, 'who at his castle at Barrie Court gave us civil and plentiful entertainment'.[10]

The large size of both the Hall and Great Chamber, relative to the more cramped private chambers, may be taken as evidence of a highly developed approach to convivial life [1, 2]. If it is impossible to be sure just how Anglicised Barry's household may have been, we may not be wrong to work with an assumption that he represented an 'average' for his class and time, and that the style of living to which he subscribed would probably have been influenced partly by native Irish custom and partly by the wider Anglo-Flemish lifestyle transmitted through political and trading contacts. Our interpretation, then, should embrace 'typical' manifestations of both cultures.

The term 'Anglo-Flemish' should be understood here in its widest sense, including by implication the wider Netherlandish, German, French, Spanish, Italian and Ottoman influences that were the hallmark of the Anglo-Flemish sphere of material culture. The Irish archaeological and documentary record includes directly and indirectly material from each of these regions, and we may assume that a blend of cultural influences was available to the Old English gentry, whether at first or second hand.

We should have no doubt that southern Ireland was in direct contact with the trading markets of the Mediterranean and north-west Europe. A broad range of imported goods, artifacts and manners were accessible in the region, some acquired direct from source and others re-exported via the English south coast ports and Bristol.[11]

The style of life at Barryscourt must have shared many similarities with other gentry households in north-west Europe. The archaeology and trading history of Cork and Youghal bears witness to a large variety of imported luxuries, especially pewter, brass, pottery, glass, textiles and dyes, wines and spices. Direct evidence of the Barrys' involvement with a supplier in Cork comes from the 1582 inventory of Christopher Galwey, a prominent Cork merchant to whom David Barry owed £20, and a further £4 'on his harness' (more likely his body armour than a horse harness). 'My Lady Dame Ellyne Barry' owed Galwey the huge sum of £60, and had left in pawn with him a silver cup to the value of a mere £3. Other than the 'harness', the nature of the debts is not specified, but no doubt some had accumulated against the supply of provisions for Barryscourt. Galwey's inventory reveals his interests in Gascony wine, leather, wheat, rye, salt, alum and iron.[12] In the inventory, Ellen Barry is referred to in the first instance as 'David Barry's wife', and subsequently as 'My Lady Dame Ellyne Barry'.

Records of travel in Europe by members of the Barry family speak of a broad experience, whilst seats such as Ormond Castle testify that cultivated and expansive living was not unknown in the region. 'Keeping up with the neighbours' is part of the normal process by which cultural and art-historical patterns are transmitted, and Lord Barry would have learned much from the example set by his contemporaries.

A seminal influence on Barry was undoubtedly his developing relationship with the English adventurer, Sir Walter Raleigh. The two started off as sworn enemies, one of their first contacts being in an armed skirmish at Cloyne.[13] In February 1580 Raleigh wrote to Walsingham, noting that 'Davy Barrey had broken all his castles and entred publikly into the action of rebellion', as a result of which Lord de Grey of Wilton (the Lord Deputy) had bestowed on him (Raleigh) 'the kepinge of on of his castles called Barre Court and the iland adjoyninge thereunto; which hows he gave mee in charge to keap to her Majesties use, being a great strenght to the countre and a safty for all passengers between Corke and Youghall'. However, he went on to allege that Thomas Butler (Earl of Ormond, Governor of Munster and General of the Forces) had intervened and grabbed the castle for himself. Raleigh interpreted this as personal acquisitiveness on Butler's part, 'as I think all is to litle for hyme – or els unwillinge any Inglishman should have any think'.

Raleigh long entertained ambitions to acquire the Barryscourt estate, which included Fota Island, for himself. The letter continues: 'I beseich your Honor that I may by your means injoy the keping of this Barrey Court and the iland', and the following year Raleigh wrote to de Grey (who forwarded a copy to Walsingham) offering to repair the defaced castle of Barryscourt at his own cost and seeking ongoing custodianship. The grant was confirmed by Walsingham, but Raleigh was thwarted by Burghley, who felt that Raleigh's applications for Irish lands boded ill for future Anglo-Irish relations.[14]

Despite their inauspicious start, Raleigh and Barry learned to rub along together in mutual respect. From having denounced Barry as a traitor in 1580/81, Raleigh wrote to Burghley in 1593 from Dorchester concerning 'This honorable gentleman, the Lord Barry, one that is well affected to her majesty and her Estate ... I think that his [Lord Barry's] pardon which her Highnes graunted him hath wrought his true affection, and his entire disposicion to honnor and serve her Maiesty with such unfeined obedience as can be required ... This noble gentleman hath, to my knowl-edg, a long time lived civilly and conformablie to all her majesties direc-tions and commandments...'[15]

Whatever the true state of affairs, by 1586 Barry had clearly attained a position whereby he was able to return to Barryscourt and start the programme of repairs which are the focus of the current restoration. It is safe to assume that he was, to some extent, coming under the influence of foreign manners, for he was certainly maintaining contacts with the English camp at this time. The eventual extent of his familiarity is suggest-ed by the occasion when, on the eve of Raleigh's departure for New Guinea in 1617, David Barry (together with other principal gentlemen of Munster, including Lord Roche and Richard Boyle, the Great Earl of Cork) was on the guest list of an intimate party held at Sir Randall Clayton's house in order to bid Raleigh farewell.[16]

The Barry line merged more closely into the New English camp after the marriage in 1621 of David Barry's grandson to Alice Boyle, eldest daughter of the Earl of Cork. Some time later she wrote to her father com-plaining that her husband's family had unjustly accused her of responsibili-ty for his persistent insolvency as a result of her 'living after the English fashion', incidentally suggesting that the English manner of living was more costly than the traditional ways approved by her Barry in-laws. No doubt, household furnishings were but one element of her indulgent ways, even if these were not for Barryscourt. Richard Boyle's own lavish lifestyle is amply recorded in the Lismore papers.[17]

THE FUNCTIONS OF THE IRISH TOWER-HOUSE

Reporting back to Philip II of Spain in 1567, Diego Ortiz noted the dis-tinctive Irish pattern of large and small landed families living in fortified tower-houses, writing that 'every petty gentleman lives in a stone tower'. A map surveying the distribution of tower-houses in Britain and Ireland reveals an exceptional concentration in the south and west of Ireland [3], where the tower-house with its cattle enclosure (the bawn) formed a pre-dominant type of organised settlement. County Cork still has over 300 rural tower-houses surviving to some degree, of which Barryscourt is a par-ticularly large and well-detailed example.

The size of individual towers to some extent reflects the social sta-tus and aspirations of the families who built and lived in them – from tiny three-chamber towers occupied by middling farmers, to the great castles of the MacCarthys at Blarney or the O'Briens at Bunratty. Barryscourt falls towards the upper end of this scale and survives in good state complete with its bawn wall. The tower-house placed security above comfort, and

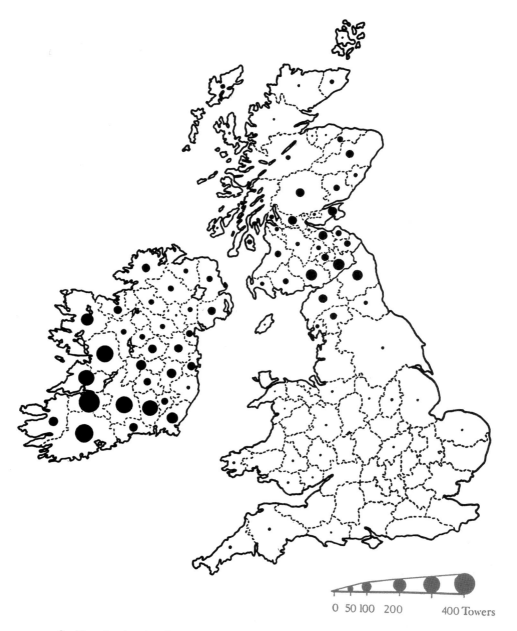

3 – Map showing the distribution by county of tower-houses in Britain and Ireland
This reveals the intense concentration in Cork and neighbouring counties in south-west Ireland,
with densities ranging from 300 to 400 towers per county for the region
(courtesy Peter Smith (after Smith, 1988, 388))

the primary role of a settlement like Barryscourt is defensive, both as protection from marauding enemies and as a secure base from which the inhabitants could launch cattle-raids of their own.

THE BARRYSCOURT TOWER-HOUSE AND ROOM USAGE

The origins and development of the present range of buildings at Barryscourt have been much debated, but there is now a strong presumption that the present tower represents a new build in the middle years of the 16th century.[18] The hypothesis of a mid-16th-century dating is strengthened by the results of a dendrochronology report on the oak lintel removed from the main door of the tower, which proposes a felling date of 1550.[19]

The first main vault appears to have collapsed at an early date (perhaps in the course of Barry's own slighting of his castles, noted by Raleigh in 1580),[20] and the rebuilding of the vault probably formed the first stage of the major works, which culminated in the remodelling of the upper floors, taking place between 1586 and 1596 (on the evidence of dates on a window frame and fireplaces). By 1599 work was sufficiently complete for Barryscourt to be described in a family pedigree as 'the lord Barrys chiefe house',[21] which is also a reminder that the family must have spent only part of its time in residence at Barryscourt. Duty demanded that attention be paid to the administration of other estates, and besides, once the household had used Barryscourt and its basic facilities for a few months in succession, it did no harm to move on to another house for a time, 'that the castle might sweeten'.

It is well to bear in mind that the present buildings offer an incomplete survival of the spaces and accommodation originally offered. The exterior hall which once lay to the north of the tower-house has all but disappeared, and we must look to the archaeology for traces of this and the other structures which might once have occupied the bawn area (kitchen, bakehouse, larders, smithy, stables, etc).[22]

The tower itself offers only minimal physical evidence of the functions fulfilled by the original room spaces, and we cannot be certain how these were intended to be used. Nevertheless, the planning follows late-medieval European conventions in the way that it appears to be divided into the private areas of the upper apartment (devoted to the needs of the family, senior officers of the household, and high-status visitors) and the public areas of the lower hall and associated chambers, where access is permitted to the wider household and to lower-status visitors. In the medieval period, privacy was a rare commodity, even in royal palaces, but specialisation and exclusivity of architectural spaces developed gradually during the 15th and 16th centuries.[23]

The status of visitors governed the access they might be granted to specific areas, and in turn the status of the household would have been consciously proclaimed in the furnishing and decoration of those spaces. The best furniture, tablewares and hangings were reserved for the family apartment, centred on the Great Chamber, serving not only for private comfort, but also as a means of impressing powerful guests by the sophistication of the lord and his house. In the Hall, displays of plate and treasure would be laid out on public occasions such as feasts and courts. The parade of wealth on a shelved court cupboard in the sight of visitors was widely practised in medieval and post-medieval Europe, and the consequent promotion of influence and family alliances must be seen as an important by-product of the hospitality offered by a great house. For the most lavish of Irish examples, we might consider the collection of plate and precious curios known as the Kildare Rental, inherited in 1513 by Garret Óg, 9th Earl of Kildare, from his father, which amounted to 79 pieces of gilt and white plate, including novelties such as a 'salt with a lady holden it' and 'an ewer of an ostrycheis egg'. This magnificent collection would have been displayed prominently at Maynooth Castle when occasion demanded.[24]

THE PHILOSOPHY OF THE REFURNISHING PROJECT

The aim of the project has been to recreate a full impression of the appearance of the tower-house interiors at the beginning of the 17th century. As already argued, it is reasonable to assume that the form and usage of the furnishings would have followed contemporary European precedent to some extent, though with a leavening of acknowledged Irish artifact-types (the *sugán* chair, the mether, the *lamhóg* or piggin, the usquebaugh flask, butter-kegs, Irish ruggs or mantles, distinctive forms of sword and lance, etc). Some of these items survived into 19th-century usage and later, and each deserves to be represented. Indeed, future research may be able to reveal other distinctive Irish preferences and artifacts, and a project of this kind must always be regarded as susceptible to ongoing research and future development.

In 1600 the renovated tower provided the Barrys with sophisticated architectural comforts in the form of wall-fireplaces, garderobes and luxuries such as glazed windows that mirror trends recorded more widely in the British Isles. The subsidiary rooms of the upper apartment must have been somewhat cramped for a large family (Ellen bore two sons and seven daughters) plus household officers and attendants, but the Great Chamber itself is ample, and life was undoubtedly comfortable to a degree. If the architectural decoration is not highly cultured by international standards, this is not to say that the Barrys may not have owned luxury furnishings more sophisticated than the setting in which they were used.

In view of the extreme rarity of original Irish material of the late 16th century, the policy of the refurnishing scheme is necessarily to compose the displays almost entirely of replica material. This carries the twin advantage of allowing us to represent the interiors as close as possible to their likely original appearance, in a fresh state that will not be at variance with the newly restored building, and of including textiles and other transitory materials that were the stuff of everyday experience, but which are now archaeological rarities.

Throughout the refurnishing exercise as a whole, conjecture has been minimised by reference to comparative European and Irish archaeological and documentary sources, and by proper attention to the detailing of design, materials and craftsmanship. On the one hand, the incomplete knowledge of specific conditions at Barryscourt must bring into question the accuracy of any reconstruction, but at the same time it liberates us to illustrate an 'average' view of life in a high-status Old English tower-house. The exercise has offered a unique opportunity to interpret Irish society in relation to the wider European scene, and to reflect clear sociological differences between conditions in the private apartments of the upper tower and the communal life of the Hall.

Since no account or inventory specific to the building has survived to show how Barryscourt was furnished and equipped, we must construct a hypothesis based on broadly similar establishments. Contemporary domestic inventories are extremely rare in Ireland, but four valuable examples have been taken into account – those of Nicholas Faggan, a Cork merchant of 1578,[25] Sir William Herbert, a Welsh undertaker at Castleisland, county Kerry, in 1590;[26] a Cork merchant John Skiddy and his son, living in Waterford city in 1640;[27] and Thomas Roinane, a Cork merchant and Alderman of 1641.[28]

Unfortunately, the relevance of these documents is limited, since none lists their contents on a room-by-room basis, only one lists the contents of a castle, and none was of the Old English landed class. However, the economic and physical scale of each household appears to be broadly similar to Barryscourt, they are broadly contemporary in date, and they record a range of furnishings and artifacts available in Ireland at those dates. A further eighteen Cork inventories compiled between 1547 and 1582 provided a valuable flavour of material conditions in the region.[29]

Five other inventories of noble Irish testators have also been made available, perhaps corresponding more closely to Lord Barry's class, but representing undoubtedly more wealthy testators.[30] With specific exceptions (such as the presence of usquebaugh flasks), these Irish inventories differ little in content and terminology from comparative English documents.

Being a castle, Castleisland remains in some ways the closest model for Barryscourt, though the similarities are at best tenuous. The inventory seems to represent a batch of goods brought in lock, stock and barrel by Sir William Herbert to equip his newly refurbished yet short-lived castle. But this is also partly true of Barryscourt, which had undergone its own process of rehabilitation in the fourteen or so years prior to 1600. It is a matter of some interest for the present project that the demesne at Castleisland was laid out with a garden, including an orchard, recreational walks around the castle, and a hop yard to serve the needs of the brewhouse.[31]

———

II – THE INTERPRETATION OF THE INTERIORS

WALL FINISHES AND INTERIOR DECORATION

Standard practice in late-medieval stone buildings was for all stone surfaces to be washed-over with a paint finish of some description, usually lime, lime casein or distemper. This was applied directly to the finely dressed quoin and ashlar surfaces, whilst the coarser rubblestone walls would usually be first rendered with a base coat of rough-textured lime mortar filled with hair, fine gravel and other material, and sometimes finished with a final skim coat of finer lime plaster bound with hair. Such finishes unified the interior and exterior wall surfaces, were regarded as a sacrificial layer which protected the stone from attrition and weathering, and were easy to renew at intervals. They also incidentally play an important decorative role as the immediate context for the scheme of furnishings.

Wall Render

Unlike the movable furnishings, which have long since disappeared, extensive and incontrovertible physical evidence for the wall-finishes at Barryscourt has survived in situ. It is clear that most if not all of the interior surfaces of the halls, chambers, stairways and passages were finished with a smooth coat of render, which probably obscured every feature of the stone structure, including the quoinwork of fireplace openings, windows and door frames. In the Great Chamber and other high-quality rooms, render survives even on the finely finished stonework of arches and windows. Even where the render does not survive, clear evidence for this practice may be noted where the surface of the quoin-stones has been chopped or pitted to provide a key for the plaster, which was probably carried fully around the arrises or run out to a feather edge. It is often impossible to determine whether this practice is original or secondary, but at Barryscourt the finely textured pitting appears to be an original finish to many of the quoin-stones. Evidence for the extensive use of render at Barryscourt lies in areas where the surfaces are protected from the elements, notably on the roof soffits of the main stair within the east wall (where there is pristine survival).

In places where the render finish has recently fallen away from the stone, a pale limewash can be detected over the underlying rubblestone surfaces. This was probably applied as an intermediate measure to help bind the surface before the application of the render coat. It is doubtful if the washed stone rubble ever formed an intentional decorative finish, even in the short-term.

Wall Finishes

Even when the render was not carried onto the quoinwork and mullions, it was common practice to whitewash the walls and stonework together as a single surface, encouraging the daylight to spill in through the windows and to bounce around the interior, a very necessary device in a room with little artificial light and shuttered windows. Instructions for 'whiting the walls', an operation carried out in the hall at Kilkenny Castle in 1668,[32] are common in English accounts. There is little direct evidence of lime-washing on wall surfaces at Barryscourt, but the lack of such evidence does not prove or imply that the render was not whitewashed (or washed in some other colour), since lime coats are highly fugitive under the weathering conditions that the structure has experienced. It may be assumed that the walls and ceilings of every chamber were limewashed regularly, that thick coats of wash built up in the years when the tower was in use, and that the colours used were not pure whites. There is ample evidence of this practice at other sites. The author has also viewed comparative evidence in small castles in south Wales, though he accepts that this is not a conclusive indicator of Irish practice. An exception to the lack of surviving paint colour at Barryscourt lies in the chapel, where there is evidence of colour (currently under investigation) on the rendered walls, possibly the remains of a decorative or religious scheme. The use of internal renders and limewashes was universal in stone buildings.[33]

The survival of intact limewashed domestic interiors from this early period is unknown in Ireland, and is extremely rare in England. For this reason it is worth turning to an English model as a guide to the internal appearance of Barryscourt. The small group of chambers attached to the Vicars Choral at Wells Cathedral, Somerset, is a remarkable set of simple limewashed rooms which have survived almost untouched from the 16th century [4], retaining an ancient finish which corresponds closely with the

4 – The Exchequer of the Vicars Choral, Wells Cathedral, Somerset
An extremely rare survival of a late-medieval chamber in its 16th-century form. The walls are
rendered flush with the fine-moulded quoin-stones of the chimney, window and doorway, and the
old scheme of plain limewash is carried over the entire wall surface, and even the doors. In its
fresh state, the shapes of the stones would have been quite invisible under the wash, the shadows
accentuating the fine edge-mouldings of the openings. This approach was entirely typical of stone-
built domestic interiors throughout medieval and post-medieval north-west Europe, the hard walls
usually softened by the use of textile hangings.

evidence to be seen in Barryscourt and many similar buildings in Ireland. The walls are plaster-rendered over rough stone, the surface of the render running flush against the finer quoin-stones of the chimney piece, windows and doorcases. The cream-coloured wash runs over stone, plaster and wood alike, unifying the surfaces and emphasising the finely moulded edges of fireplace and doorcase. Owing to the effects of damp, the quoins can now be discerned in the discoloured wash, but this would not have been the case originally.

The Exchequer, the main chamber in the building dating originally from c.1420, remains unchanged since the insertion of the fireplace in c.1500. The windows are still closed by the original iron-hinged shutters made from sawn oak boards. A range of timber fittings survives in the form of oak doors, cupboards and muniment boxes, still pale and dry after 500 years of gentle neglect. The general appearance of the rooms reflects those depicted in late-medieval Flemish paintings such as the Merode Altarpiece (now in the Cloisters Collection in New York), representing the typical appearance of small lime-washed chambers all over northern Europe. We can learn much about the appearance and disposition of furnishings from a study of these Flemish pictures.

The exterior walls of the tower and bawn are beyond the scope of this report, but there is extensive survival of render and rough-cast, especially on north-facing walls. It is also likely that the exterior walls of the tower were whitewashed regularly, following common practice in other parts of the British Isles and Europe. A 16th-century Irish poem refers to 'the fair castle with its shining sward ... white-walled rampart amongst the blue hillocks, it seemed to me if I could reach that house I should lack nothing',[34] and other reports speak of the white towers standing out in the landscape like 'dragon's teeth'.

In 16th-century interiors generally, the standing archaeology and documentary evidence point to a robust use of colour, achieved both through the use of paint on walls and furniture, and by the use of colourful textiles. The Irish inventories contain ample evidence for the use of textile hangings, including tapestry and cloth of various kinds, most commonly linen say. At Barryscourt, we have installed a wall of red and white woollen hangings behind the high table in the Great Chamber, the colours reflecting the Barry livery [1].

Contemporary English inventories also refer to widespread use of painted cloth hangings, and walls were commonly painted with schemes of polychrome decoration, many based on imitative themes of textiles, tapestry or panelling. Unfortunately, no evidence has emerged for the use of painted cloths in Ireland, and the physical evidence for wall paintings has been almost entirely destroyed, though there is no reason to assume that practices among the Old English communities in Ireland differed greatly from those in the rest of north-west Europe.

There is no evidence for the use of wall panelling at Barryscourt, and this may always have been somewhat rare in Ireland. However, an interesting local example is the case of Raleigh's house at Myrtle Grove in Youghal, where a panelled and carved chamber in English West Country style still survives, possibly having been installed by Raleigh. Indeed, we could speculate that Barry may have been familiar with the room as a result of his apparent reconciliation with Raleigh, though we cannot know whether Barry ever aspired to something similar for Barryscourt.

ARCHITECTURAL WOODWORK

In common with the vast majority of early Irish stone buildings, almost no trace survives of original woodwork at Barryscourt. The sole exception is the oak lintel, recently dated to 1550.[35] The replacement of the fitted woodwork therefore has to take full account of such evidence as may be revealed by the rebates, sockets and fixing-points in the stone frames, and from the very rare instances in comparable sites where timber fittings have survived. At Clara Castle, county Kilkenny, the main door is a spud door (in the UK termed a harr door), turning on an extended hanging-stile housed at top and bottom in sockets in the lintel and sill-stones, similar to those once at Barryscourt. The Clara door is an old softwood replacement appearing to date from the late 18th or early 19th century, and we must assume that it conformed closely to the door that it replaced. Similarly, the shape, size and method of hanging the window-shutters at Barryscourt is revealed by the traces in the stone, some turning on spuds, whilst others were mounted on iron hinges for which some of the pintles survive. Many of the doors and shutters were secured by wooden bars running in channels within the thickness of the walls.

Clara and Barryscourt both reveal that the main door was originally protected by an iron yett, the effectiveness of which as a main defence may be judged by the fact that in Scotland in 1606 those below the rank of baron were ordered to dismantle their yetts.[36]

There is very little survival of original flooring at Barryscourt. The Hall was originally floored with oak boards laid on joists, whilst other areas of high status (Great Chamber, chapel, bedchamber) may have been paved with stone flags. All other areas were probably floored with rammed earth, formed as the upper surface of the infill above the vaulting, supplemented in areas of heavy traffic (such as passageways and thresholds) by stone flags. Earth floors usually consisted of various combinations of lime, clay and plaster, with an admixture of grit, gravel, crushed brick, broken pottery and glass, etc, as available. Compacted earth floors of lime, ash and clay are surprisingly hard-wearing. There seems to be no surviving evidence of domestic clay tile floors from this period in Ireland, though they were used in ecclesiastic settings.

ROOM USAGE

In its original form, the ground floor of the tower-house was used mainly for storage and as the first line of defence in time of attack, but the great ground-floor room will in future accommodate a modern interpretational exhibition. The chamber to the right of the main entrance no doubt functioned as a guardroom flanking the entry, which is fitted with the usual defensive mechanisms of musket loops and murder hole.

Hall and Kitchen

At the time of writing, the furnishing scheme is incomplete. The following account must therefore address the situation in terms of the intended displays, as yet only partially realised.

In its present form, the castle offers two main chambers located on the first and second floors of the tower. A large household at Barryscourt could not have been comfortably housed within the tower-house alone, and the archaeology has revealed the sites of subsidiary buildings within the bawn. As with many Irish tower-houses, Barryscourt was originally provided with another single-storey timber-framed hall attached to the tower and lying within the bawn, now disappeared, but recently confirmed by the archaeology.[37] This hall may have provided the main venue for feasting, but is now beyond the scope of physical representation. Therefore, the first-floor Hall in the tower must suffice to represent the semi-public side of life of the court house of the Barrys.

The great vaulted first-floor Hall is laid out with a formalised arrangement of a long table across the 'high' end, flanked by two long tables of slighter construction, providing a ceremonial setting for formal occasions such as manorial court sessions, conferences and feasts, and the practical provision for the day-to-day needs of the wider household. This traditional arrangement was recommended in some advice handed out by Bishop Grosseteste of Lincoln in the 1340s, who counselled the lord to let his 'freemen and guests be seated at tables on either side together, as far as possible, not here four, there three'. The lord himself, as host to the occasion, was to 'be seated at all times in the middle of the high table, that [his] presence as lord ... is made manifest to all, and that [he] may see plainly on either side all the service and all the faults'.[38]

At Barryscourt the high table is provided with a great chair for the lord, flanked by lesser seating for others, according to their status. An unknown traveller in Ireland observed the hierarchical nature of this arrangement, pointing out a more practical purpose: 'The more honourable person sits in the centre; the next in dignity sits at his right, and so on in order until the range of seats is filled. All sit facing towards the entrance door: that thus, they say, they may always be ready to repel the attacks of their enemies '[39] Yet, when necessary, the tables and benches could be easily turned up and set aside to clear the centre of the room for dancing and games (as recorded by Shakespeare in *Romeo & Juliet*).[40]

Around the walls are placed other impressive heirloom pieces of the family, by which the wealth and history of the house (in the form of gilt dishes and ancient curios) would be displayed to impress and awe visitors and minions of the household alike, thus earning the respect of the one and the subservience of the other.

Following common medieval practice, the main kitchen at Barryscourt was probably a semi-permanent structure placed within the bawn at a safe distance from other buildings, where it could burn down accidentally without placing other buildings at risk. There may well have been some provision for cooking within the tower, if only for ministering to the family and important guests, but the bulk of the cooking would have been done in the outside kitchen.

The large heated room lying off the Hall is now furnished in a suitably practical manner as a kitchen. There is no evidence that this room served as such in 1600, but it offers the opportunity to illustrate the form and equipment of a kitchen of the period, with a variety of brass, iron and wooden implements and vessels. At Castleisland, the larder was well stocked with meal, malt, butter, cheeses, bacon, bread, beer, soap, starch and 'spices of all sortes', whilst future needs were covered by 'onyons seades [and] other seades for garde'.

The Great Chamber

Reserved for the use of the family and important guests, the upper floors are furnished in a more fashionable manner than the Hall, with better-quality and more comfortable pieces. Here the family would entertain their more important guests and spend their leisure time. Apart from the traditional pastimes of singing, dancing, storytelling, feasting and fighting, a wide variety of games were played in settled times. Shovelboard was a popular game on which high wagers were often set. Backgammon and chess (playing tables, dice and cards are frequently mentioned in lists of imports from England),[41] troumadam (similar to the modern bagatelle), Nine Men's Morris, Fox and Geese, and many other board games all required their special equipment. The girls would have their dolls and the

5 – The great oak six-leg dining table made for the Great Chamber at Barryscourt

6 – The 'swallowing-box', a removable fitting at the end of the great dining table

7 – Ash and sycamore trestle table for the Hall, mounted on turned trestles

8 – An oak armchair for a man

9 – An oak armchair for a lady

boys their toy weapons and armour, all provided for the serious purpose of learning adult roles.

The Muniment Room

All houses involved with political affairs required an archive equipped for the production and storage of letters, accounts and other necessary documents, usually referred to as 'evidences' (Kilkenny Castle boasted an 'evidence chamber' later in the 17th century).[42] A candidate for this function at Barryscourt would be the south-west turret chamber off the Great Chamber. In such a room the family papers would be kept, and correspondence maintained. Models for the fitted furnishings survive in England, in the form of chests, nests of drawers and cupboards with plank doors.[43]

The Upper Floors

The Dublin chronicler Richard Stanihurst wrote in 1584 that it was the custom of the Irish to sleep within the security of the towers, where night-watchmen were posted on the roof to call aloud, warning off marauders and announcing that the head of the household slept lightly. The upper room in the north-west turret (above the chapel), is the only candidate for a private bed-sitting room for David Barry and his immediate family.

---

previous pages

5 – The great oak six-leg dining table made for the Great Chamber at Barryscourt
This table, together with the set of stools, forms and a court cupboard, emulates the carved and turned decoration of the Kilbrogan table in order to reflect a regional style appropriate to county Cork and to the social status of the Barry household. The frieze is carved with the commemorative initials DB and ER for David Barry and his wife Ellen Roche, as on the fireplace in the same room. All the wooden furnishings are 'as new' replicas and are not artificially aged. Most are simply finished to represent the pale appearance that such pieces would have assumed in David Barry's lifetime, whilst others are painted in simple colours derived from earth pigments.

6 – The 'swallowing-box', a removable fitting at the end of the great dining table
The box is located in slots under the board, and is intended to receive the brass discs used in the popular game of shovelboard, the ancestor of the modern 'shove ha'penny'. This reconstruction is based on two examples surviving in 16th-century English houses.

7 – Ash and sycamore trestle table for the Hall, mounted on turned trestles
This piece is based on a table featured in a late-medieval German wall painting, and is inspired by the recorded prowess of Irish turners in the period.

8 – An oak armchair for a man, the back panel carved with a simple architectural device

9 – An oak armchair for a lady, of wide form to accommodate the ample skirts of the period

Senior officers of the household, such as the Steward and priests, might share the small chambers in the upper towers. During the day, palliasses would have been stored for the general use of visitors and senior household servants. The lower servants, soldiers, and others of little consequence would spend their nights as best they could, huddled before the fireplaces in adjacent tower chambers or in the various service buildings of the bawn.

FURNISHINGS

The functions of particular chambers may be determined to some extent from their sizes and fittings, but, in the absence of an inventory offering lists of contents, we have to infer a furnishing scheme for Barryscourt by comparison with similar establishments and from comparable English material. However, it has firmly been the intention of the project not to impose an English order on Barryscourt, but as far as possible to take account of the rare Irish documentation that is available.

The high points at Castleisland included three field bedsteads of walnut, each supplied with a set of hangings (red and yellow taffeta sarsenet, green say and yellow dornix), with three pairs of 'color' bedsheets amongst the fine linen. Much of the furniture is less specific (long table-boards, square table-boards, bedsteads and cupboards, chests and stools), but some special items are noted, including spruce tables, leather chairs and a close stool with two pewter pans.

The obvious caveats are that Castleisland was a more substantial household than Barryscourt (three tester bedsteads certainly implies more extensive private accommodation, though at least one of these may have stood in the Great Chamber), and that the contents reflect the class and

---

overleaf

10 – The oak bench or settle for the Great Chamber
Many early illustrations show a low-back settle of this type placed across the front of the fireplace, a comforting feature during a long winter. Hence this rear view shows its decorative side to the room.

11 – The joiner-made oak altar table of 1610, from the old Kilbrogan church at Bandon, county Cork
This table is one of the earliest surviving pieces of oak furniture with an Irish provenance, and was probably made in Bandon itself or in Cork city. The feet have been cut short, and the capping rail is missing from the stretchers. The dark colour and generally distressed condition are typical of many examples of ancient oak furniture as they appear today. The brass plate on the top reads: 'ORIGINAL COMMUNION TABLE / used in Christ Church Kilbrogan from the time of the Building of the Church AD 1610 to AD 1862 / Restored & Preserved September 1862 / Honble & Revd C R Bernard Rector / John Berwick Edward Bell Esqrs Churchwardens'. (photo: Con Brogan, Dúchas)

12, 13 – The oak bedstead, set up with a comfortable array of mattresses, pillows and counterpane, and mounted with its linen hangings. With the curtains drawn, the bed is a private and comfortable domain in a world where privacy and comfort were rare commodities.

opposite (extended captions on page 205)
10 – The oak bench or settle for the Great Chamber
11 – The joiner-made oak altar table of 1610, from the old Kilbrogan church at Bandon, county Cork

Anglo-Welsh tastes of Sir William Herbert of Monmouthshire who had acquired the 'Castell of the Ilande' some years previously following the Desmond Survey. We would not, therefore, take Castleisland as a precise guide for Barryscourt, though useful parallels may be observed. The inventory gives a clear idea of the balance of furnishings and equipment thought necessary in a fortress that is also a home, whilst this and other inventories reveal specific articles available in southern Ireland in the period, confirming some parallels with England and providing clues to the range of aspirations and possibilities open to the Old and New English families who could afford them.

Another glimpse of extensive furnishings after the English manner may be found in the 1615 will of the merchant John Roth Fitzpiers of Rothe House, which still stands in Kilkenny city. In the course of a long document he refers to 'all the bedstedds, boordes, chairs, stooles, and of all and evry uther the stuffes, furnitures and utensils of my saide house ... all my diapr, holland, and lynin ... my tapistrie coverlet, the sey greene hangings, or curtyns of both my best bedstedds ... all my drawing tables, bedsteeds, cupboords, livery cupboards, virginalls, wainscott, seelings of my

14 – An early 17th-century American four-post slat-back armchair of a type common in medieval Europe

This example is remarkably similar to the *sugán* chair, seated with straw rope, which survived as a common Irish type from the Middle Ages into the 20th century. Such a chair would be reserved for the use of honoured guests at the high table. (courtesy Boston Museum of Fine Arts)

15 – A replica baby-walker of a type used in training an infant to walk in comparative safety
The child stood inside this contraption, supported under its arms, propelled on wooden castors.

hall and chambers (panelling), benchs, long-stools (forms), scabetts (stools), ioynt-stools chairs (backstools) my great cipresse chest and cipresse countor ... all my pewter, brasse, batry, iron, beddings of feathers and flocks ... (and) all my plate'.[44]

If town merchants could afford furnishings of such kind, then a major landowning family such as the Barrys could certainly do likewise. Taking the example of the Old English Earls of Kildare, there seems little doubt that a Lord Temporal such as David Barry would choose to house himself and his family in at least minimal comfort.

Wooden Furniture for Barryscourt

The needs of a late-medieval household were met by a relatively simple range of furniture-types, though design and construction became increasingly sophisticated towards the end of the 16th century. The range included tables (for dining, food preparation, writing and similar tasks), seating (chairs, backstools, stools, benches), display cupboards, storage (chests, boxes, cupboards), sleeping (bedsteads, truckle-beds), and special pieces for children's use (cradles, high chairs, baby-walkers [15]).

It is interesting to contemplate the conceptual differences between items provided primarily for functional purposes (benches, stools, boxes, work-tables, etc) and those provided for purposes of parade and the promotion of social status (the master's chair, dining-tables, display cupboards, storage chests, bedsteads, etc). The latter were elaborated in conventional ways to raise their status above the mundane, and to reflect the aspirations of their owners (chairs and chests adorned with heraldry, beds with rich hangings, etc).

Furniture was almost exclusively made from oak, ash, elm and sycamore, though occasionally more luxurious native and imported timbers are noted such as walnut, spruce (both found at Castleisland in 1590), cypress, yew tree and juniper. The prime furniture-makers were the joiners (who specialised in framed and panelled pieces, often decorated with carving), whilst cheaper work was supplied by carpenters (who made boarded case-pieces and stools) and turners (who made turned or 'thrown' work, especially chairs and stools). Other methods and materials such as basket-work chairs frequently appear.

At Barryscourt, the public status of the Hall [2] is reflected in its furnishings, which consist of trestle tables (two supported on turned trestles or 'dormants') [7] and a range of simple turned and boarded stools and benches for seating. The chief seat is a great turned armchair (here represented as an heirloom painted in the Barry livery), placed centrally behind the dais table in the manner of the Judge's chair in a modern courthouse, and flanked by armchairs seated with straw rope (*sugán* chairs – see

Glossary) [14] for important guests. In the 14th century, the Priory of the Holy Trinity at Kilmainham had a number of 'rough wooden chairs with straw seats'.[45] Their retainers and other low-status guests would be seated at the lower tables on stools and benches. The proposals for this room include a great chest painted with the arms of Barry and their relations, together with a display cupboard to hold the pewter and plate on view.

The nearby kitchen is furnished with simple boarded storage shelves, cupboards and chests, with coopered tubs and barrels, stake-legged tables for cutting meat and dressing dishes, a grindstone and a basic range of utensils for boiling, spit-roasting, and serving food and drink.

Upstairs, the furniture in the Great Chamber is altogether of better quality, made by joiners and decorated with carving, conducive to a more civilised life. A long joined-frame dining table [5] (marked out for shovel-board and provided with a 'swallowing box' to catch the brass 'men' as they shoot over the end [6]) is placed to take advantage of the light from the large windows, with the lord's chair set at its head [8], and one for his lady at the other end [9]. A panelled settle is ranged for comfort in front of the fire [10], and a fine games table is planned to accompany it. Chests and open cupboards are placed against the walls for the display of valuable accessories such as dishes, boxes and candlesticks, and hanging on the wall near the dining table is a case of shelves to hold the fragile drinking glasses out of harm's way.

The style and finish of the wooden furniture replicated at Barryscourt reflects the current state of knowledge in such matters, and particular concern has been given to following the small clues that do exist as to the regional character of furniture in Munster at the end of the 16th century. Of unique relevance is the altar table of 1610 from Kilbrogan church at Bandon [11]. This is the only surviving piece of con-temporary Irish oak furniture identified thus far, and has provided a signifi-cant stylistic indicator, relevant to both the class and region under consideration. The simple joiner-made table with carved and turned deco-ration is in a style broadly familiar from the plentiful examples of English vernacular oak furniture. In the absence of other Irish models, the Kilbrogan table has provided a simple style for the main joined furniture of the upper apartments. A suite of matching table, stools [17], forms and court cupboard (three-tier serving table) [16] was produced using this model.

Another rare early Irish survival is the ornate and celebrated stone table of 1533 from Maynooth Castle, made for Garret Óg, 9th Earl of Kildare, and this has been proposed as a credible model for a walnut games table for the Great Chamber.

A specialised piece of dining equipment, planned for the Great Chamber, is an oyster table. No demonstrable example has survived, but the sparse descriptions found in inventories indicate that they were usually round, with a brass or stone top in the middle of which was a hole through which the empty shells were dropped into a waiting basket. Ample evidence of the consumption of oysters at Barryscourt is provided by the huge number of discarded shells that still litter the site.

David Barry's bedchamber is approached by a narrow spiral stair and is small by any standards, yet it is supplied with an ample fireplace and its own garderobe. The chief piece of furniture would probably have been a simple wooden tester bedstead, kitted out with an elaborate set of bedding and hangings [12, 13]. Castleisland contained three beds of this kind, though Fynes Moryson warned that the visitor should not expect among the native Irish 'any beds, much less feather beds and sheets'. This experience was supported by Luke Gernon, who warned in 1620 that, as a guest in an Irish tower, 'When you come to your bedchamber do not expect canopy and curtaynes'. However, it is well to remember that both were describing the provisions for an unimportant guest in a secondary chamber in a Gaelic Irish house, and not the private lodging of an Old English lord.

Textiles

Soft furnishings provided the main source of colour and comfort in a great medieval house, the owner being judged by his range of linen, bedding, table carpets, hangings and cushions. Castleisland had tapestry and say hangings, turkeywork table-carpets and cushions, a red taffeta Spanish quilt, and a long list of linen (long and square board cloths, cupboard cloths, towels, napkins, sheets, 'color sheets' and pillowcases). Specific textiles amongst the linens included calico, holland, dowlas and fustian, whilst other textiles included wedmoll, silk, taffeta, taffeta sarsenet, arras, carrell and dornix.

The Native Irish and the Old English both harboured a traditional preference for cloth of yellow (dyed with saffron) and a bluish purple (dyed with orchell). Both dyes were grown locally and imported in the 15th century, and decreasingly in the 16th century. In the later 16th century they were gradually superseded by imported madder and woad, perhaps signifying a new preference for red (dyed with Flemish madder), blue (dyed with woad) and green (achieved by dyeing with woad over saffron or weld).[46] Interestingly, attempts were made c.1585 to grow woad at Inchiquin and other places, but the scheme failed because the local landowners 'seem to be incensed that their cattle will all die, if they should come to feed on ground where woad hath grown'.[47]

A textile frequently mentioned in English inventories was 'Irish stitch' embroidery, referring to the zigzag pattern now known as 'flame stitch', 'Bargello work' or 'Hungarian point'. More research is needed to

demonstrate if the name derives from a wide use or manufacture in Ireland itself.

'Irish ruggs' or 'caddows' were a particular Irish speciality, deriving from the shaggy Irish cloak or mantle, worn universally in Ireland and seen in effigy on the figures of Richard Boyle (1st Earl of Cork) and his wife on her tomb in St Patrick's Cathedral, Dublin. Rugs (the best were said to come from Waterford)[48] were exported to England and all over Europe, where they were in great demand as bed coverlets and were known as 'Hibernes'. John Skiddy of Waterford owned three 'shaggs', listed among his textiles, and a 'caddowe' on his best bedstead. Thomas Roinane had three caddows amongst his seven bedsteads. Little is known about the construction and true appearance of Irish rugs, though there are contemporary descriptions and several early illustrations that seem to show them. The display at Barryscourt has used a modern Greek flokati rug for this purpose, as being superficially most like the early Irish rug.[49] Other than rare archaeological fragments, the famous St Brighid's Mantle, now in Bruges cathedral, is the only known survival of a medieval Irish mantle.[50]

Floor rugs were extremely rare at this period, since knotted textiles (whether imported Eastern rugs or their English-made equivalent known as 'turkeywork') were too expensive to lay on the floor. However, there is a wide precedent for laying plaited rush matting on floors (and even against the lower walls) for padding and warmth.

Ceramics

The archaeological record in Cork indicates that coarse earthenwares were produced locally and imported from England (Wiltshire and Hampshire-Surrey border wares) and Europe. These were mainly functional pieces (jugs, cups, dishes, bowls, porringers, pipkins, chafing dishes, costrels, chamber pots, candlesticks). The earthenware body was finished with a clear lead glaze (redwares, showing red over iron-rich clay) or tinted green, brown and yellow over a paler body ('Tickney' or Border wares). Black glazes were tinted with iron oxides over red clays (the so-called 'Cistercian' wares).

Finely made brown salt-glazed stonewares were imported from the

---

opposite

16 – Oak court cupboard, a typical three-tier serving-table, supplied in conjunction with the dining table in the Great Chamber. Here the simple lunette-carved frieze and turned supports are seen to good effect.

17 – Two oak stools from the set of eight supplied for use with the dining table in the Great Chamber

Rhineland in huge numbers throughout the 16th century, and a notable example of a 16th-century Cologne jug may be seen in Cork City Museum, excavated in the city, where it had been buried containing a coin hoard. More colourful luxury tablewares were imported from several parts of Europe, including slipwares and painted wares from France, Iberia, Italy and the Netherlands.

Sites of 16th-century occupation such as Barryscourt usually provide large numbers of pottery sherds, but in fact the archaeological excavation in the bawn area at Barryscourt has revealed very little by way of ceramic finds on the site.[51] It is suggested that the household unusually relied less on pottery and more on treen (for kitchen use and for the common tables of the Hall) and pewter (for the upper table and the Great Chamber). Evidence of either is not likely to survive on site, since the worn-out treen vessels would have been used for kindling after extensive use, and the pewter recycled as valuable scrap.

Glass

Though still something of a rarity at the end of the 16th century, there is evidence for the use of glass both for windows and tableware in the more affluent Irish house. The presence of window glass in the new Great Chamber at Barryscourt is confirmed by the provision of glazing rebates in the new stone window frames. The Castleisland inventory includes a basket full of drinking glasses, which may have been cheap drinking glasses made from coarse green-tinted metal known as 'waldglas' or 'forest glass'. These were imported from England and Europe, and there is evidence for sporadic production at Youghal and Waterford (1591), and Cork (1606), ancestors of the modern Waterford glass industry.[52]

A high-status house such as Barryscourt would also enjoy access to high-quality imported Venice glasses, or to the imitations ('façon de Venise') made in Germany, France, the Netherlands and England. Fragments of two baluster-stem drinking glasses are in the archaeological collections at the Cork City Museum, and represent a type in use by David Barry's contemporaries. Fragile luxuries such as these would be reserved for use in the upper apartment, stored in a special glass-case that hung on the wall of the Great Chamber. The finest enamelled drinking glasses from Venice or Syria were sometimes treasured as objects of special significance, and passed down as heirlooms.

Metalwork

We know that the Barrys owned at least one piece of silver, since Lady Ellen had pawned a silver cup with the Cork merchant Christopher

Galwey in 1582,[53] but we cannot know how extensive their collection of plate may have been. The range of metal objects in everyday domestic use is likely to have consisted predominantly of base metals, including cast and wrought iron implements of various kinds (domestic and military), together with cooking and dining wares of pewter, brass ('battry' or 'latten') and bronze.

Iron

In sophisticated houses, hearths were equipped in fairly standard manner throughout Europe, with an assembly of iron fittings, sometimes referred to in inventories as the 'iron chimney'. The most important element was the pair of andirons that helped to support the fire of logs or turves. A cast-iron plate called a 'back' protected the wall at the rear of the hearth, and at the same time radiated heat forward into the room. The fire was main-tained with the use of a set of firetools, which might include a poker, tongs, a log fork, a small shovel (or 'slice') and an ash-rake. At Barryscourt, the kitchen hearth will be provided with appropriate cooking utensils, pots and pans.

Reflecting the military functions of the castle, an important ele-ment of the contents would have been a store of weapons and armour, to supplement the personal arms that all men carried with them. Armour was rarely displayed in a decorative manner at this early date. Instead, inven-tories frequently include items of armour and weapons stored in a central armoury, ready for action. Though it is not a likely location for an armoury at Barryscourt, a room in the south-west turret may be set aside for this purpose, showing a representative selection under secure conditions. A list of typical weapons might include polearms (black bills, brown bills, forest bills, halberds, partisans, pikes, glaives), swords, rapiers, daggers, longbows, crossbows, arrows and guns (arquebuses, muskets, pistols, calivers, demi-cannon, powder-flasks). The armour might include complete or part-suits of body armour (almain rivets, corselets, cuirasses, breasts and backs, jacks, hauberks, brigandines) and single helmets (sallets, bascinets, morions, bur-gonets, pot-helmets), besides many other specialised tools for defence and attack. Most of these were represented amongst the list of 'Armor and Munition' at Castleisland, where there was armour sufficient for at least 38 men together with edge-weapons, handguns and breech-loading light artillery.

Pewter

A bright white alloy of tin with copper for durability, and lead for worka-bility, pewter was designed specifically to imitate the gleam of silver in the dining hall, and so were kept in a bright, shining state. Many inventories featured a garnish of pewter dining wares, which, given the lack of pottery at Barryscourt, would be used on the high table in the Hall and the formal dining table in the Great Chamber. Pewter wares were also displayed with other treasures on livery cupboards or shelves when not in use. Castleisland contained a long list of pewter wares (platters, porringers, dishes, basins, saucers, plates, spoons, bottles, salts, candlesticks, chamber pots), some of which were supplied in sixes (half a garnish). Nicholas Faggan had nine pewter trenchers amongst his pewter wares, and Thomas Roinane boasted no less than two dozen pewter dishes. Inventories and customs accounts make clear that the use of pewter utensils from England became more widespread in Ireland towards the end of the 16th century; a curious corollary being the prolific return trade in scrap pewter carried back from Cork to Bristol for recycling.[54]

Copper alloys

Alloys of copper with zinc (brass) or tin (bronze), were used for a variety of display goods (ewers, dishes, candlesticks), essentially of a yellow colour intended to imitate gold. The brightly polished metal gleamed in the light of the fire or candles, adding a commendable richness of effect. It was also used for cooking pots [19] and other kitchen utensils because of its resistance to the effects of fire, and the longevity of copper alloys led to old-fashioned implements surviving in use over many years. The brass items at Castleisland were not specified separately, but are fairly obvious amongst the long list of 'brasse and iron' (a cauldron, a mortar and pestle, a grater, a skimmer, a chafing dish, a basting ladle, a mustard pot, a great pan for charcoal, and a plate candlestick for the Hall).

Treen, leather, cooperage and basketwork

The word 'treen' encompasses a wide range of wooden wares, especially suitable for sturdy everyday use [18] (see Glossary). Most of the spoons, dishes, bowls, goblets, cups and trenchers in common household use would have been made from whittled or turned wood ('Their Platters are of wood, by cunning turners made').[55] Timbers for tablewares were generally selected from those most easily available and with the blandest textures, usually beech, willow, ash, sycamore and maple. At Barryscourt, where we have noted the scarcity of pottery finds, treen dishes and vessels would have been used in the kitchen and by diners at the lower tables in the Hall.

Wooden eating bowls, drinking cups and spoons were soon exhausted by rough use and regular scouring with pewterwort, and the accounts of

18 – A group of replica turned wooden 'treen' items, including bowls, trencher plates and a ladle. These would have formed the standard dining wares for the lower tables in the Hall.

19 – A replica copper alloy (bronze) tripod cauldron or 'flesh pot', used in the kitchen for boiling stews and pottages over an open hearth

many large households show treenwares being purchased regularly and in huge numbers. They were often too cheap to be valued individually in probate inventories, though when they appeared in bulk they could be worth listing. As a result we find that Sir William Herbert owned no less than eighteen dozen wooden trenchers, including two dozen of each for meat and fruit. The latter were sometimes reserved for best use, being finely painted with illustrated verses to be read aloud by sophisticated company at the end of a meal. Two distinctive Irish treen items in ancient use, which are now represented amongst David Barry's belongings, were the drinking vessels called the mether and the *lamhóg*, or piggin (see Glossary).

Perhaps the most serviceable material for the storage and serving of liquids were those constructed from leather, boiled in oil (*cuir bouilli*), stitched into shape and coated with pitch, forming costrels, large water-bags (called 'budgets') or jugs (known as 'bombards' and 'blackjacks') [21]. Examples of each are provided for use in the Hall. At Castleisland 'two blake jacks' held the beer for the table.

Contemporary accounts and illustrations show a wide variety of coopered vessels such as tankards, tubs, barrels and casks for drinking,

20 – A replica coopered tankard with hinged cover, similar to that shown standing on the dining table in a woodcut in John Derricke's *The Image of Irelande* (1581)
This piece is based on one of many recovered from the wreck of the *Mary Rose* of 1545. Such vessels were manufactured in the Baltic area, and traded all over Europe.

21 – A replica great leather blackjack or bombard, for serving beer at table

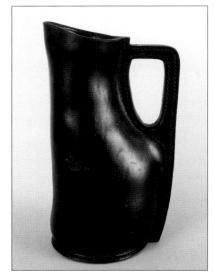

washing and storage of wet and dry goods. Coopered tankards from Scandinavia were exported all over Europe (many were found on the *Mary Rose* and on the *Vasa*), and were used in New England and Ireland. The well-known woodcut in John Derricke's *The Image of Irelande* (1581) shows a long table provided with, amongst other things, a large coopered tankard [20]. Since tower-houses were rarely provided with wells, domestic water was no doubt brought to the kitchen and other rooms in large containers known as 'tankers'.

In addition to casks, a wide variety of baskets were in use for specific tasks such as carrying and storage of dry goods. Several forms of traditional Irish basket are known from archaeology, including the familiar types woven from willow and other cut branches, as well as rush, bents, grasses, splint and other materials. The more formal basket typology mainly followed the Dutch models that are widely illustrated in contemporary paintings, since Dutch basketmakers emigrated and worked very widely in Europe and the New World.

SANITATION

Barryscourt tower is equipped with a number of privies or 'garderobes', with shafts carrying waste materials away from chambers. Castleisland was supplied with a close stool with two pewter pans for the use of Sir William Herbert and his family, but the ample built-in sanitary arrangements at Barryscourt would have made such specialised furniture unnecessary. Further indications at Barryscourt suggest that sanitation and cleanliness were well catered for – for example, in the way that the main window-ledges of the Great Chamber are supplied with slop-chutes that empty to the outside in a runway under the sill. (The original exterior spout survives on the two-light south-east window.)

––––––

The author

Victor Chinnery is the author of *Oak Furniture – The British Tradition*, the standard work on the early oak furniture of the British Isles. In partnership with his wife Janet, their consultancy company advises on the interpretation of historic interiors, their furnishings and interior decoration. At Barryscourt their enquiries into international trade with Ireland and the material culture of Irish tower-houses have informed the experimental scheme to replicate the physical conditions in Irish towers at the end of the 16th century.

Acknowledgements

The reinstatement scheme outlined above has been compiled in response to the original vision of Noel Jameson, Robert (Kim) Williams, Peter Barry and the trustees of the Barryscourt Trust, who have striven tirelessly towards its achievement. The scheme is not necessarily definitive, and is understandably limited by available budgets, but it is the result of an ongoing programme of research and experimental archaeology that is striving to answer a variety of questions in a meaningful way. At the time of writing, the scheme is incomplete, but it is anticipated that many gaps will be filled in the future to provide a more complete picture of the way of life in an Irish tower-house.

The initial version of this essay was prepared as a report for Dúchas, The Heritage Service in 1998, and I warmly acknowledge the involvement of Dermot Burke and Chris O'Grady, successive directors of the National Monuments Service, whose support enabled the production of the present work. I am indebted beyond words to my wife Janet for much of the research, background reading, ideas and discussion that contributed to the paper. The following colleagues and institutions, whose co-operation and good fellowship have made our visits to Ireland such a pleasure, are to be thanked individually for their untiring contributions: Noel Jameson, Robert (Kim) Williams, Peter Barry, John Ludlow, Ken Thompson and all members of the Barryscourt Trust; Aighleann O'Shaughnessy, Senior Conservation Architect, and the staff of Dúchas, The Heritage Service; Mrs Shirley Murray; Joe Murphy, University College Cork; Jane Fenlon; Fionnuala Carragher, Ulster Folk and Transport Museum; Cork City Museum; National Museum of Ireland.

Endnotes

[1] Judith Monk and Redmond Tobin, *Barryscourt Castle – An Architectural Survey* (Barryscourt Trust, Cork, 1991); Tadgh O'Keeffe, *Barryscourt Castle and the Irish Tower-House*, Barryscourt Lectures, no. 1 (Barryscourt Trust, Cork, 1997); Dave Pollock, *Archive Report on the Archaeological Investigation at Barryscourt Castle* (licence no. 96E238) (unpublished, Archaeografix, Fethard, Co Tipperary, 1996); Dave Pollock, *Preliminary Report on the Archaeological Investigation at Barryscourt Castle* (licence no. 96E238 extension) (unpublished, Archaeografix, Fethard, Co Tipperary, 1998)

[2] Cal. Carew MSS, vi, 164-70; Constantia Maxwell, *Irish History from Contemporary Sources* (1509-1610) (George Allen & Unwin, London, 1923) p385

[3] Edmund Campion, *History of Ireland* (1633 ed.) ch. v

[4] Fynes Moryson, Itinerary 1617, 3, iii, p162

[5] Rev William Harrison, *A Description of England* (1587) ch. 12

[6] AF O'Brien, *The Impact of the Anglo-Normans on Munster*, Barryscourt Lectures, no. 2 (Barryscourt Trust, Cork, 1997)

[7] Geoffrey Keating, *History of Ireland*, c.1629, initially circulated in manuscript, published nearly 100 years later; Maxwell, *Irish History from Contemporary Sources*, 321, footnote 1. See also Jane Fenlon, *Barryscourt Research Project (Gardens)*, unpublished report to the Barryscourt Trust (1996) p4

[8] See also Rosemary Ffolliott, 'Household Stuff', *The Irish Ancestor* (Dublin, 1969) p43; Fenlon, *Barryscourt Research Project*, pp16-17

[9] Fenlon, *Barryscourt Research Project*, p4

[10] *ibid.*, p5

[11] Ada Kathleen Longfield, *Anglo-Irish Trade in the Sixteenth Century* (Routledge, London, 1929)

[12] Richard Caulfield, *The Council Book of the Corporation of the City of Cork 1609-43 and 1690-1800* (Guildford, 1876) p1154

[13] Sir John Pope Hennessy, *Ralegh in Ireland* (Kegan Paul, Trench & Co, London, 1883) p22

[14] *ibid.*, p162

[15] *ibid.*, p187

[16] Dorothea Townshend, *Life and Letters of the Great Earl of Cork* (Duckworth, London, 1904) p123

[17] See Rev AB Grosart, *The Lismore Papers* (London, 1886); Townshend, *Life and Letters*

[18] O'Keeffe, *Barryscourt Castle*, p16

[19] Ref. letter to Dave Pollock from David Brown, Queen's University of Belfast, School of Archaeology and Palaeoecology, 9/8/2000

[20] Pope Hennessy, *Ralegh in Ireland*, p187

[21] Fenlon, *Barryscourt Research Project*, pp4-5

[22] Dave Pollock, *The Bawn Exposed: Recent Excavations at Barryscourt*, Barryscourt Lectures, no. 5 (Barryscourt Trust, Cork, 1999)

[23] Mark Girouard, *Life in the English Country House* (Yale University Press, London and New Haven, 1978); Mark Girouard, *Life in the French Country House* (Cassell & Co, London, 2000); O'Keeffe, *Barryscourt Castle*, pp8, 20-3, fig. 10

[24] Peter Somerville Large, *The Irish Country House – A Social History* (Sinclair-Stevenson, Dublin, 1995) pp37-8

[25] Longfield, *Anglo-Irish Trade*, pp187

[26] NLI MS 7861, ff.166-74

[27] Chancery Inquisitions for Co Waterford, Charles I, part 5, no. 9; see Julian C Walton, 'The Household Effects of a Waterford Merchant Family in 1640', *Journal of the Cork Historical and Archaeological Society*, lxxxiii, no. 238 (1978) pp99-105

[28] *JRSAI*, iv (1856-7) pp75-6

[29] Caulfield, *The Council Book*, Appendix A

[30] Thanks are due to Jane Fenlon (Maynooth Castle, Kilkenny Castle and Cork House) and Noel Jameson (Dunluce Castle) for calling these items to our attention. We are also grateful to Joe Murphy of University College Cork library for providing copies from published sources.

[31] Somerville Large, *The Irish Country House*, p49

[32] Mike Salter, *Castles and Stronghouses of Ireland* (Folly Publications, Malvern, 1993) p12; Jane Fenlon, *Irish Inventories: Phase I 1550-1650, relating to Barryscourt*, unpublished report to the National Monuments Service (1997) p4

[33] See AR Powys, *Repair of Ancient Buildings* (JM Dent, London, 1929 (reprinted by the Society for Protection of Ancient Buildings, London, 1995)) pp86-99; Margaret Wood, *The English Mediaeval House* (1965; reprinted Bracken Books, London, 1985) ch. 31

[34] Hospitality of Cú Chonnacht Óg Maguire, before 1589; Maxwell, *Irish History from Contemporary Sources*, p335. The term 'fair', as used here, denotes not only beauty, but also paleness or the colour white.

[35] See endnote 20

[36] Roger Miket and David Roberts, *The Medieval Castles of Skye and Lochalsh* (1990) p87 (ISBN 095160 220)

[37] Pollock, *The Bawn Exposed*

[38] Quoted in Colin Platt, *The Architecture of Medieval Britain – A Social History* (Yale University Press, New Haven and London, 1990) pp244-5

[39] In Cardinal Moran's *History of the Catholic Archbishops of Dublin* (1579) pp91-3; Maxwell, *Irish History from Contemporary Sources*, p320

[40] Act 1, scene 5, line 29

[41] Longfield, *Anglo-Irish Trade*, ch. xii et al

[42] Fenlon, *Irish Inventories*, p5

[43] Penelope Eames, 'Furniture in England, France and the Netherlands from the Twelfth to the Fifteenth Century', *Journal of the Furniture History Society* (London, 1977)

[44] Thanks are due to the Kilkenny Historical Society for providing a transcription of the will of John Roth Fitzpiers. Rothe House has been restored in recent years and is open to the public. The will is also quoted in Ffolliott, 'Household Stuff', p43.

[45] Somerville-Large, *The Irish Country House*, p19

[46] Longfield, *Anglo-Irish Trade*, pp180-1

[47] *ibid.*, p183

[48] Fynes Moryson, *A Description of Ireland* (1600-03) p422

[49] Peter Thornton, *The Italian Renaissance Interior 1400-1600* (Weidenfeld & Nicholson, London, 1991) figs 119, 174

[50] BRS Megaw, 'The Irish Shaggy Mantle', *Journal of the Manx Museum* (1945-6) p175; Mairead Dunlevy, *Dress in Ireland* (Batsford, London, 1989) pp39-42

[51] Dave Pollock, pers. comm., 1999

[52] Longfield, *Anglo-Irish Trade*, pp125-6; Eleanor S Godfrey, *The Development of English Glassmaking 1560-1640* (Clarendon Press, Oxford, 1975) pp52-3

[53] Caulfield, *The Council Book*, p1154

[54] Longfield, *Anglo-Irish Trade*, p187 et al

[55] John Derricke, *The Image of Irelande* (1581)

References and additional bibliography

A small number of Irish inventories and wills have been consulted, including the following:

inv: Earl of Kildare, Maynooth Castle, 1575
inv :   Nicholas Faggan, Cork merchant, 1578
inv :   Christopher Galwey, Cork merchant, 1582
inv :   Sir William Herbert, Castleisland, Co Kerry, 1590
will: John Roth Fitzpiers, Rothe House, Kilkenny, 1615
inv :   Earl of Desmond, Kilkenny Castle, 1628/39
inv :   Earl of Ormond, Kilkenny Castle, 1639
inv :   John Skiddy, Waterford merchant, 1640
inv :   Thomas Roinane, Cork merchant, 1641
inv :   Duchess of Buckingham, Dunluce Castle, 1645
inv :   Earl of Cork, Cork House, Dublin, 1645

Herbert Cescinsky and Ernest R Gribble, *Early English Furniture and Woodwork*, 2 vols (Waverley, London, 1922)

Victor Chinnery, *Oak Furniture – The British Tradition* (Baron Publishing, Woodbridge, 1979)

Peter Davey and Richard Hodges (eds), *Ceramics and Trade* (University of Sheffield, 1983)

Sir John Davies (Attorney General for Ireland under James I), *A Discovery of the True Causes why Ireland was never entirely Subdued nor Brought under Obedience of the Crown of England until the Beginning of His Majesty's Happy Reign*

Mairead Dunlevy, *Ceramics in Ireland* (National Museum of Ireland, Dublin, 1988)

Edward Edwards, *Life of Ralegh* and *Letters of Ralegh*, 2 vols (MacMillan & Co, London, 1868)

Rachel Field, *Irons in the Fire* (Crowood Press, Marlborough, Wiltshire, 1984)

RF Foster (ed.), *The Oxford Illustrated History of Ireland* (Oxford University Press, 1989)

Desmond Fitzgerald, The Knight of Glin, *Irish Furniture*, The Irish Heritage Series (Eason & Son, Dublin, 1978)

John Hurst, David Neal and HJE van Beuningen, *Pottery Produced and Traded in North-West Europe 1350-1650*, Rotterdam Papers VI (Museum Boymans-van Beuningen, Rotterdam, 1986)

Lucy Anne McKail, *Recreating Authenticity: A study examining the increasing use of replicas in Museums and Historic Houses, from a critical and theoretical point of view*, unpublished MA dissertation (Institute of Archaeology, University College London, 1999)

Raghnall Ó Floinn, 'Later Medieval Decorative Arts', *The Illustrated Archaeology of Ireland* (Country House, Dublin, 1991)

Edward H Pinto, *Treen and Other Wooden Bygones* (Bell, London, 1969)

Mark Redknap (ed.), *Artifacts from Wrecks*, Oxbow Monograph 84 (Oxford 1997)

J Seymour Lindsay, *Iron and Brass Implements of the English House* (Medici Society, 1927; revised Alec Tiranti, 1964)

Peter Smith, *Houses of the Welsh Countryside – A Study in Historical Geography* (HMSO, London, 2nd ed., 1988)

Edmund Spenser, *A View of the State of Ireland, written dialogue-wise between Eudoxus and Ireneus* (1595)

———

Glossary of terms

Caddow – An 'Irish rugg' or mantle. This distinctive Irish outer garment or cloak, typically made from a thick shaggy woollen textile with a long curled pile, was indispensable to the Native Irish, who were noted for their ability to sleep happily curled up in their mantles in the open air. As life became more settled, the mantle continued to serve as a bed coverlet, for which purpose they were exported in huge numbers all over Europe.

Lamhóg (Gaelic lit. 'love oak') – probably a toasting vessel, similar to the English wassail bowl. A confusion has arisen amongst English scholars, who now use the term to refer to the turned waisted single-handled drinking cup, which Irish scholars refer to as a 'piggin' (NMI). In England this term is used to refer to a small stave vessel with a single upstanding stave for handle, which is called a noggin or *lamhóg* by NMI; see Pinto 1969.

Mether (*meadar*) – A four-handled wooden drinking cup for communal use, typically square in section at the top, tapering down to a round-section base and raised on four feet; identified with the honeyed ale drink called metheglin (Welsh 'meddeglyn') or mead. The square mouth made it impossible to drink from one side (the trick being to drink from one of the corners) and Irish hosts took great delight in passing the cup to their English guests, who invariably spilled the drink down themselves. This traditional Irish form (an early example is the Dunvegan Cup of 1493; Ó Floinn 1991, 193) survived into the 19th century, when it provided inspiration for Arts and Crafts Revival copies in wood and silver. A yew tree mether found in county Armagh, was inscribed and dated DERMOT TULLY 1590 (engraved illustration in the *Dublin Penny Journal*, 6 February 1834).

Pewterwort – A non-flowering plant of the horsetail family (Equisetaceae, esp. the marsh-growing variety), also known as 'scouring rush' or 'Dutch rush', the bushy fronds of which are covered with a gritty excrescence with abrasive qualities, used to scour pewter and treen utensils; though further diminishing the short useful life of such soft materials.

Porringer – A pewter or ceramic bowl for eating soups, pottage and other liquid food; typically provided with one or two flat projecting handles (therefore also termed an 'ear dish').

Sugán chair – An open-framed chair seated with a woven web of straw rope (*sugán*), the frame typically with square-section posts and round (draw-shaved) rails. Whilst we can find no direct evidence for the use of such chairs at the turn of the 16th century, they are recorded in Irish medieval accounts, and became a standard product in the 19th century. Parallel accounts of similar chairs are found in 16th-century Europe and (rather later) in colonial New England, where a fine armchair has survived from the early or mid-17th century (Boston Museum of Fine Arts). It is therefore assumed that they have a long unbroken history in Ireland, as elsewhere.

Treen, treenware – Wooden tablewares (i.e. literally 'made from trees'), particularly bowls and trenchers, commonly produced by turning on a lathe or by whittling. The author has not encountered the term in Ireland.

Trencher, trencher plate – A flat pewter or treen plate for eating solid or dry foods; may be round or square. The term derives from the slice of bread (Fr. tranche) used for this purpose in earlier times.

Turkeywork – A heavy English woollen knotted-pile textile made in imitation of Turkey carpets. This was very colourful and extremely hardwearing, and so was popular for upholstery covers and bedcovers. Produced in London, Norwich and Yorkshire, turkeywork was widely exported to Europe and the New World.

Yett – An iron grille door overlying the wooden door at the main entrance to a towerhouse, enhancing the defensive character of the wooden door. The yett swung outwards on hinges, and could be pulled firmly into place from inside by means of chains running through holes in the stone door frame. The holes are often confused with musket-loops, but their true purpose is clarified by the heavy wear produced by the running of the chain.

––––––

BARRYSCOURT LECTURES

1 – The circular keep at Nenagh Castle, county Tipperary, which was originally built
*c.*1200 by the Anglo-Norman lord Theobald Walter, an ancestor of the Butler family

THE BARRYSCOURT LECTURES VII

Medieval Rural Settlement in Munster

Kieran O'Conor

THE BARRYSCOURT TRUST
IN ASSOCIATION WITH CORK COUNTY COUNCIL AND GANDON EDITIONS

INTRODUCTION AND BACKGROUND

This paper examines the nature of the surviving archaeological and historical evidence for rural settlement and life in high medieval Munster during the period from the arrival of the Anglo-Normans in the late 12th century until the second half of the 14th century. Unlike today, it is clear that society in Munster during this period was overwhelmingly rural in nature. Like the rest of Europe, the vast majority of people of all social ranks and ethnic origins in Munster during the whole medieval period from the 12th century to c.1600 lived and worked outside towns and cities. Medieval rural settlement in the context of this paper is defined as meaning the house types, fortifications, agricultural buildings, field systems, and sorts of settlements people inhabited and laboured in throughout the countryside of Munster during the high medieval period, be they of colonial or Gaelic-Irish origin. By understanding what settlement forms existed in high medieval Munster, it becomes possible to piece together a picture of what the rural landscape in the province looked like at any given time during this era, and also how it evolved and changed over time.

Very little sustained research has been carried out over the years on the subject of high medieval settlement in Ireland, including Munster. There are a number of reasons for this paucity of

2 – The circular keep on the motte at Shanid, county Limerick.
The ringfort adjacent to it has a later cruciform shape built within it.

work – not all immediately obvious to the casual observer. It is certainly clear that for much of the 20th century there was little sustained academic interest in the archaeology of the whole medieval period from the 12th century to the late 16th century. There seems to have been a tendency amongst Irish archaeologists, seen elsewhere in Europe, to study periods for which there were little or no surviving written sources, where it was felt that the discipline of archaeology would make the most impact.[1] Yet this lack of work on medieval archaeology in general over much of the last century seems to be due to more complex reasons than this, at least to certain commentators. Some archaeologists very definitely believe that the effects of nationalism on Irish society contributed to this dearth of archaeological work on the medieval period, as it was associated in the minds of many with English rule and colonisation from 1169 onwards.[2]

It was really during the 1970s and 1980s that attitudes changed towards the archaeology of medieval Ireland and became more positive.[3] The great majority of excavations of sites of general medieval date carried out in Munster since the 1980s have, however, been concentrated in urban areas. Large-scale excavations have taken place in recent years within the medieval cities of Cork, Limerick and Waterford. These investigations were carried out in response to urban renewal and development, both partly funded by the EU.[4] The most striking feature about the medieval excavations in these old cities of Munster is the fact that so many of the excavations have been published, despite the complexity of these sites.[5] Specifically, the recent 900-page or so publication of the later medieval and Viking Age excavations at Waterford is clearly a major contribution to the study of European urban archaeology.[6]

There have been, in contrast, remarkably few publications of excavations of medieval rural sites in Munster. This seems strange given the fact, as noted above, that the vast majority of people lived outside towns and cities during the whole medieval period, down to quite recently. In all, leaving aside castle excavations, published information exists for a mere fourteen excavations of medieval rural settlement sites in Munster. This is a very small number indeed considering the size of the province, which is similar to Wales in area. Many of these investigations, furthermore, were small in scale and produced little in the way of artifacts and structures.[7] Others were done in advance of development, and were limited to specific areas of these sites that were under threat of destruction. Such sites were excavated purely because they lay in the way of development, and were not chosen for investigation because they had the ability to answer specific questions about rural society in medieval Munster.[8] Excavation has as yet provided little information about life in the countryside of Munster during the period under review.

Archaeological fieldwork can really be defined as the examination and recording of the standing remains of the past without excavation. It is a cheap, unobtrusive and valuable means of gaining information about past societies. Since 1984 a whole series of volumes and books have been published which list and describe archaeological sites of all periods in various Munster counties and districts.[9] The sites listed in these volumes, most but not all of which have been produced by the Archaeological Survey of Ireland (who are part of the National Monuments Service, Dúchas), include many descriptions of high medieval rural sites. Fieldwork is also being carried out by the Archaeological Survey in Clare, Kerry, Limerick and south Tipperary. When this fieldwork is complete within the next two or three years, all this work will constitute a massive record describing literally tens of thousands of standing archaeological monuments in the Munster landscape. The existence of these written descriptions (often accompanied by sketch plans and photographs) and the volumes that spring from them mean that researchers in the future will be able to more efficiently plan and proceed with projects analysing past landscapes, periods and specific monument types. Many hundreds of basic descriptions of medieval monuments in Munster exist or will exist in the Archaeological Survey's files, with annotated versions of these notes in their published county volumes. The consultation of these files will be the obvious starting point for any future archaeological research on medieval rural settlement in Munster. The problem, however, is that there has been very little in-depth analysis as yet of Munster's medieval rural landscape using these resources. Simply, sustained archaeological research using excavation, field survey and other related archaeological techniques has not been carried out to date in what were rural areas of medieval Munster. This means, therefore, that much of what is said in this paper is based on relatively flimsy archaeological evidence.

The first part of this paper will discuss the settlement forms that existed in the landscape of Anglo-Norman-dominated parts of high medieval Munster during the period from the very late 12th century through to the mid-14th century. The second section will examine the nature of settlement in the parts of Munster, such as much of modern Clare, south Kerry and west Cork, that saw little or sustained Anglo-Norman colonisation during this period, and that basically remained under the control of indigenous Gaelic-Irish lords, if only at a local level.

THE MANORIAL LANDSCAPE
OF ANGLO-NORMAN MUNSTER

AF O'Brien, in the second of the Barryscourt Lectures, discussed the major impact that the Anglo-Normans had on many parts of Munster.[10] The con-

3 – Knockgraffon motte, county Tipperary

quered land was divided by the newcomers into landed estates known as manors. A feudal economy, based on the intensive production of cereal crops, particularly wheat and oats, was introduced into these conquered districts during the course of the late 12th century and the 13th century.[11] Each manor was administered and worked from a centre or *caput*, at which was located the residence of the manorial lord or, at least, was the location of one of his homes if he held a number of manors or was a great magnate. These lordly residences on certain Anglo-Norman manors in Munster were often located in castles of different types. The residences could either be large masonry castles such as Adare, county Limerick, or smaller masonry castles such as hall-houses and mottes and ringworks [1, 3-5]. The latter two types of castle had defences made of earth and timber. Recent research, bringing together excavated and historical evidence from Britain and Ireland, would indicate that many of these motte and ringwork castles originally had strong timber defences which may have included mural towers and looped palisades.[12] Basically many of these earth and timber castles had similar defences to masonry castles, but these were built, like the domestic buildings within them, of wood and also probably clay. Figures for the numbers of mottes and ringworks in Munster will not be known until the Archaeological Survey of Ireland has completed its fieldwork in the province in a few years time. Fieldwork in Tipperary by the latter institution, for example, has suggested that anything up to fifty mottes and ringworks are identifiable today within the boundaries of this county.[13]

The Archaeological Survey has also identified seven hall-houses and three possible ones in the same county.[14] Hall-houses are small masonry castles, and usually consist of a defended two-storey rectangular block with a first-floor entrance.[15] These figures, combined with other known masonry castles of Anglo-Norman date in the county, such as Nenagh and Roscrea, surely indicate that Tipperary was very heavily incastellated by the Anglo-Normans during the course of the late 12th and the 13th century [1, 3-5].

The recent recognition of a ringwork at Ballysimon, county Limerick, through excavation, has added to the known number of castles in that county.[16] It is also possible that a number of pre-existing promontory forts along the Cork and Kerry coast were turned into castles by the Anglo-Normans, presumably in most cases by reusing the linear ditches and banks of these old fortifications, but changing them by placing complex timber fortifications on them.[17] Possibly these reused promontory forts should be classified as partial ringworks due to their transformation into timber castles by the Anglo-Normans. Partial ringworks can be defined as ringworks that are located on sites that have strong natural defences, such as ridge ends, cliff tops, spurs and promontories, both coastal and inland. The only side of a site like this that needs to be artificially defended by a bank, ditch and timber fortifications is the exposed one, which is usually the natural line of approach to it. The main defences on the other sides of such a site are steep natural slopes and cliff faces.[18]

Despite the Archaeological Survey's recognition of new castles of late 12th and 13th-century date in the province, it is also abundantly clear that some parts of Anglo-Norman Munster, such as east and north Cork, had few castles.[19] Presumably the lack of castles of Anglo-Norman date in such areas is a testimony to the peacefulness of these districts during the 13th century in particular, and the relative ease with which the Anglo-Normans took over these lands from the late 12th century onwards. Many manorial centres in such areas (and even in more disturbed parts of the province) were marked by undefended manor houses or halls, presumably built of timber and clay. For example, an undefended mud-walled hall or manor house, whose straw thatch and rafters were supported on crucks, is mentioned in an extent of the lands of Thomas FitzMaurice in Kerry in 1298.[20]

Part of the lands on manors in Munster and other parts of southeastern Ireland (certainly in areas of fertile soil) were farmed directly by Anglo-Norman lords during the course of the late 12th, 13th and early 14th century. These demesne lands were not let out to tenants like the rest of the manor. Farm buildings needed to work these demesne lands, as well as domestic buildings servicing the lordly residences, would have occurred around or within these castles, or beside undefended manor houses.[21] It is clear that the overwhelming majority of these agricultural buildings at

4 – Moatquarter motte, county Tipperary

5 – A possible ringwork at Cullahill, county Tipperary (photo: Elizabeth FitzPatrick)

manorial centres were built of wood and clay, and therefore have not survived. What sort of buildings were these? A 1303 extent of the manor of Inch, near Thurles in county Tipperary, gives some idea as to how a manorial centre in a rich part of Anglo-Norman Munster would have looked during the 13th and early 14th century. The remains at Inch today consist of nothing more than a six-metre-high motte standing alone in a field. The 1303 extent, however, suggests that a hall, chamber, kitchen, larder, fish house, stables, granary, malt-kiln, byre, barn and sheep house stood beside this motte in this year.[22] A dovecote also existed beside the motte in this year.[23] It appears on present evidence that the practice of rearing domestic doves for eating came in with the Anglo-Normans. Dovecotes are often mentioned in other surviving Anglo-Norman manorial and monastic records.[24] Manure from these dovecotes may also have been used as fertiliser for gardens and arable fields. An actual masonry dovecote, possibly 13th century in date, still stands beside the Cistercian abbey at Kilcooly, county Tipperary.[25] This is a reminder that great monasteries like Kilcooly were not just places of worship and spiritual life during the medieval period, but were also the centres of landed estates in much the same way castles were during this period. Presumably timber agricultural buildings occurred in the vicinity of these abbeys as well. It is most likely, however, that the vast majority of dovecotes in Anglo-Norman Ireland were constructed of wood or clay and were covered by a thatched or wooden shingle roof, as seems to have been the case at Inch. Peafowl were also commonly kept for the table on Anglo-Norman manors.[26] Pheasants also seem to have been introduced by the Anglo-Normans, probably before 1200.[27] These birds are mentioned as existing on Anglo-Norman manors in Ireland in the first years of the 13th century.[28] Pheasants were regarded as a delicacy during high medieval times, and were associated with the upper echelons of lordly society, being served at important banquets.[29]

An old castle garden is also referred to at Inch in this 1303 extent.[30] This garden was presumably once used for growing herbs, fruit and vegetables, although it had been rented out for pasture in the latter year.[31] Gardens at medieval manorial centres like Inch were bounded by ditches, palisades or thorn hedges.[32] Presumably fairly stout fences were needed around such places to keep out roaming animals.

A mill and fishponds are also mentioned as being located within the bounds of the manor of Inch in 1303, presumably close to the motte.[33] The overwhelming evidence suggests that watermills were by far the most common type of mill used in Anglo-Norman Ireland.[34] Windmills, while they existed, seem to have been relatively rare in medieval Ireland.[35] It is possible that more windmills would have been erected if the Anglo-Normans had properly conquered and settled the mountain and drumlin areas of Ireland, which they did not, as these areas tended to be left to

Gaelic-Irish lords. Such hilly and exposed areas would have had many suitable locations for harnessing wind power. This choice of watermill as the main type of corn mill on Anglo-Norman manors seems be linked to the fact that intensive Anglo-Norman settlement in Ireland tended to be lowland and riverine in nature. Mills were clearly important places in the rural landscape of medieval Ireland. Anglo-Norman lords derived a large amount of their annual manorial income from them, as their tenants were obliged to have their corn ground at these places.[36] Field evidence from Leinster suggests watermills were located close to manorial centres, and this probably was the case in Anglo-Norman Munster as well.[37]

Fishponds, like the ones mentioned at Inch in 1303, are quite regularly mentioned in the surviving manorial records from Anglo-Norman Ireland. For example, a fishpond was under construction in Limerick in 1211-12.[38] Fishponds are referred to on De Burgo lands in Tipperary in 1243.[39] Fish was a cheap form of protein, and played an important part in the medieval diet. Medieval fishponds were usually located close to manorial centres to prevent poachers from taking the fish within them.[40] Probably the best known fishponds in Munster are the ones beside Leamaneh Castle in county Clare, but these seem to be 17th century in date.[41] Interestingly, there appears to be evidence for pre-Norman fishponds in Munster. A late 11th-century reference exists to a fishpond at the O'Brien centre at Kincora in county Clare, apparently stocked with salmon.[42] Medieval fishponds were often quite shallow, and often no more than a metre in depth, as this facilitated the easy harvesting of fish within them.[43] Fishponds of early medieval and Anglo-Norman date have not yet been recognised in the Munster landscape despite these references to them.

What, in theory, then should fieldworkers be looking for when searching for fishponds of general medieval date? The simplest type of fishpond in medieval times was often nothing more than a dam across a stream, with a bypass to divert flood waters.[44] Narrow excavated ponds strung out like a necklace along a stream may also represent the remains of a medieval fishpond.[45] Very often, however, medieval fishponds occur in England and Wales today as relatively narrow, rectangular or sub-rectangular grass-covered depressions near streams or rivers. Such depressions can occur singly or in groups, and, as noted, are relatively shallow in depth. These depressions are often flat-bottomed as well, and can sometimes have raised platform areas within their interiors.[46] Recent work has also uncovered quite an amount of archaeological and historical evidence, largely from Munster, for sophisticated fish traps and fish weirs on various rivers and in sheltered coastal and estuarine areas.[47] Certainly many of the fish caught in these fish traps would have been consumed immediately, but it is highly likely that many were also placed in fishponds and taken out to be eaten at some later date.

It is also clear that other features of the manorial landscape linked to demesne farming by Anglo-Norman lords, particularly the more powerful ones, have not as yet been recognised in the field by modern Irish archaeologists. Rabbits were almost certainly introduced to Ireland by the Anglo-Normans in the years after 1169, as the first reference to them in this country comes in 1185.[48] Rabbits were prized for their meat, fur and skins during the whole medieval period.[49] Unlike now, rabbits were expensive commodities across medieval Europe.[50] Anglo-Norman lords introduced rabbits onto their manors to produce valuable meat and skins from poor, hitherto unprofitable parts of their lands.[51] References to rabbit warrens (the places where they were kept) and rabbit farming occur in various surviving Anglo-Norman records. For example, references exist to rabbit-farming on manors in royal hands in Ireland for the year 1211-12.[52] Again, for example, rabbit warrens are mentioned on the manor of Lisronagh, county Tipperary, in 1333.[53] Presumably ferrets and nets were used to catch rabbits during medieval times.

Nothing is really known about the archaeology of rabbit farming in Ireland simply because no research has been carried out on it.[54] Earthworks known as pillow mounds are associated with medieval and post-medieval rabbit farming in England and Wales. These monuments are usually somewhat narrow cigar-shaped or rectangular mounds, usually about one metre in height and sometimes surrounded by a slight ditch. Sometimes, however, pillow mounds can be circular or cruciform in plan.[55] Pillow mounds were erected to provide safe, easily made, dry burrows for rabbits. There is some evidence for 13th-century pillow mounds in England and Wales, but most excavations have shown them to be late-medieval and post-medieval in date. Pillow mounds have not been recognised in the Irish landscape. This might imply that the reason why pillow mounds do not seem to exist in the Irish countryside, at least in any numbers, is simply because this monument-type was not yet part of the cultural assemblage of the Anglo-Norman and English colonists who came to Ireland in the late 12th and 13th century.[56] Yet references exist to rabbit farming in Ireland almost from the onset of Anglo-Norman settlement in this country. It is possible that some rabbit warrens in medieval Ireland were just located on a suitable, well-drained slope – in effect, a field surrounded by a ditch, bank, palisade, hedge or stone wall to keep out predators such as wolves and foxes.[57]

Many small islands also acted as rabbit warrens in medieval England.[58] This was possibly the case for some rabbit warrens in medieval Ireland. For example, Coney Island is a fairly common placename for many riverine, lake and coastal islands.[59] Perhaps the reason why such things as pillow mounds, however, do not seem to really exist in Ireland may be related to the fact that absolutely thousands of deserted earthworks, in particular ringforts, stood in the Irish landscape during medieval times in a way not seen in Britain.[60] It is entirely possible that rabbits were encouraged to burrow into these earthworks, especially deserted ringforts, as these would have provided good locations for dry, easily dug burrows. An early 15th-century reference, for example, exists to a rabbit warren in a place called Rathsax in county Tipperary.[61] Is it possible that the ringfort implied in this placename was reused as a rabbit warren? A cruciform earthwork occurs within the ringfort beside the circular donjon and motte at Shanid, county Limerick [2]. Is this an early pillow mound-type earthwork located within an earlier ringfort beside an important Anglo-Norman manorial centre? It could alternatively be the base for a rare windmill of Anglo-Norman date. In all, it is possible that many deserted ringforts were reused on Anglo-Norman manors as locations for rabbit warrens.

It is also highly likely that important Anglo-Norman lords in Munster, both secular and ecclesiastical, would have had deer parks within the bounds of their demesne manors. References to deer parks exist in Ireland from the first decade of the 13th century. For example, the archbishop of Dublin was granted permission by the king to build a park and erect a 'deer-leap' at Kicopsentan in 1206.[62] In 1228 Walter de Riddelsford asked permission of the king to divert a roadway around his park of Garnenan.[63] Other references exist to deer parks in Anglo-Norman Ireland. About 3,200 deer parks owned by magnates, bishops, monasteries and even minor lords had been erected in England by c.1300.[64] It is generally held that the occurrence of deer parks in any given area during the medieval period automatically meant the introduction of fallow deer to stock them.[65] Fallow deer were infinitely more amenable to systematic management than red deer, and were much better suited to being enclosed within deer parks in comparison to the latter species.[66] Fallow deer were valued during the medieval period for their venison, and were often given as gifts to favoured subjects and tenants.[67] For example, the king granted John Comyn, archbishop of Dublin, thirty deer from the park of Brewood in 1213.[68] Fallow deer, like rabbits, were also introduced onto a manor to produce quality, high-status meat from poor, marginal, non-arable land.[69] The keeping of fallow deer was yet another means used by the Anglo-Normans of turning a profit from unprofitable land.

It has been argued recently that the first direct evidence for fallow deer in Ireland comes from the 1240s.[70] Yet, as just noted, the occurrence of documentary references from the early 13th century to the building of parks and gifts of deer strongly implies that fallow deer were being managed in Ireland long before c.1240. Early archaeological evidence for fallow deer in Ireland comes from a pre-masonry castle phase at Carlow – in a context argued to date to before c.1210.[71] In all, both the archaeological and historical evidence hints that fallow deer and associated deer parks were to be seen in the manorial landscape of Anglo-Norman dominated parts of Ireland by at least the early 13th century. Presumably their introduction was linked to the efforts of Anglo-Norman lords during the late 12th and the 13th century to develop their new lands.

What did deer parks physically look like in the medieval period? In England, at least, it appears that the average deer park was about two hundred acres in extent.[72] It was generally rectangular in shape but had rounded corners. It was usually demarcated by a wide, high earthen bank with a ditch on either side. The summit of this bank was often capped by a wooden palisade, but sometimes by a wall.[73] The land enclosed within these deer parks mainly, but not always, consisted of woodland and pasture. Some parks, however, were built on heathland or in mountain areas.[74] Future fieldwork should attempt to recognise deer parks of Anglo-Norman date in the Irish landscape.

Woodland was also actively managed and conserved on manors in medieval times to provide material for building, domestic and industrial purposes. Medieval woodland was often bounded and even subdivided by massive banks and ditches or walls to keep out animals that would eat or trample young trees and regrowth.[75] Officially designated medieval forests are not to be confused with deer parks and ordinary manorial woodland, although there were similarities. A medieval 'forest' came to mean a relatively large area or district in which deer were preserved by law for the purpose of hunting by and the provision of venison for whoever held the forest rights, be he the king or a major magnate. The term did not just mean a wooded area, but could also mean bogland, mountain land and even ordinary farmed countryside.[76] It is equally clear, however, that the various royal forests in Ireland had much mature timber within them.[77] For example, in 1253 the king gave two hundred oaks from the forest of Cratloe in modern-day south-east Clare to Robert de Muscegros as a gift.[78] It must be remembered that not all forests in Ireland were royal; major magnates could hold them too. For example, the historically attested forests of Ross and Taghmon in county Wexford were controlled by the Marshal family in the early 13th century.[79]

This discussion all shows that many features associated with the manorialised landscape of the Anglo-Norman-dominated parts of medieval Ireland have yet to be recognised by fieldwork and excavation. What about the archaeology of the tenants who farmed and lived on these Anglo-Norman manors in Munster and elsewhere? It must be remembered that the conquest of certain parts of Ireland by Anglo-Norman knights from 1169 onwards, including large parts of Munster, was not just a removal in these areas of the pre-existing Gaelic-Irish aristocracy and their replacement by new lords from England and south Wales. Indigenous Irish tenants always existed in large numbers on the manors of Anglo-Norman

Ireland, but there still seems to have been a labour shortage in Ireland during the late 12th and early 13th century.[80] Anglo-Norman lords in many regions of Ireland actively encouraged peasant immigration from England, Wales, and sometimes even further afield to help work their new lands for them. The peasant population of Anglo-Norman Ireland, including large parts of Cork, Kerry, Limerick and Tipperary, became divided into two ethnic groups – one Irish and the other essentially English.[81] It is clear that in some districts of Munster this immigration was high. For example, the population of the manor of Moyaliff, county Tipperary, was mostly of English origin in 1305.[82]

It is true to say that unlike England, a minuscule amount of excavation has occurred in Ireland on all types of peasant settlement of general Anglo-Norman date.[83] Much of the discussion that has taken place so far on the specific subject of English peasant settlement in Anglo-Norman Ireland has been carried out by historical geographers and settlement historians.[84] Scholars once presumed without question that these English peasants on Anglo-Norman manors lived in villages or rural boroughs (essentially an agricultural village in physical terms, where some of its inhabitants were burgesses with the same privileges and rights as townsfolk) clustered around a church and the residence of the manorial lord, be it some form of castle or undefended manor house. It was believed that each day the inhabitants of these English villages would travel out from them to cultivate their scattered strips, rented from their manorial lords, which lay in large open fields that surrounded their settlements, or, instead, went out to work on their lord's demesne land either for cash or as part of their labour services.[85] It was felt that the only dispersed settlement on these Anglo-Norman manors was associated with native Irish tenants – usually called *betaghs* in the sources – who seemed to have lived in house clusters in townlands away from manorial centres and their associated villages or rural boroughs populated by English tenants.[86]

This view has been somewhat modified by research over the last two decades or so. Ultimately, two somewhat differing models of rural settlement have been postulated for the areas of Anglo-Norman Ireland that saw dense English peasant immigration, which included large parts of Munster. The first model proposes that the pre-existing Irish townland system went against the formation of large villages throughout Anglo-Norman Ireland. Instead, much smaller villages occurred at manorial centres, and these were mainly populated by the lowermost grades of English tenants who often worked as labourers on the demesne lands of these manors. Where settlements had borough status, presumably burgesses also lived at these places. This view sees English free tenants and their dependents living on compact holdings of their own in townlands away from the manorial centres.[87] Simply, this first model sees a mix of nucleated and dispersed settlement occurring on any given manor right from the beginning of Anglo-Norman settlement in Ireland.[88] It is probably best to suggest that the majority of free tenants on Anglo-Norman manors can be classified as prosperous peasants, who held their land in perpetuity, either by military service or the payment of a money rent.[89] They were perhaps the social equivalents in medieval times of the strong-farmer class of 19th and 20th-century Ireland. The existence of well-to-do peasants in Anglo-Norman Ireland is a reminder that rural society in medieval Europe was not a simple Hollywood-type situation of grasping manorial lords tyrannising impoverished peasants. It was, in reality, a far more complex society where men of lower status to lords could achieve and were allowed a measure of wealth and success.

The second model is slightly different in its conclusions to this first one. This second interpretation of the available evidence for rural settlement in densely settled parts of Anglo-Norman Ireland holds that large English midlands-style villages were a feature of the primary phase of manorial development in Ireland, say up to c.1250. According to this view, the only dispersed settlement within the bounds of Anglo-Norman manors during this period was associated with Gaelic-Irish tenants. There was then a movement out from these large villages by English free tenants during the course of the later 13th and 14th century into the townlands that made up the manors of Anglo-Norman Ireland. It is believed that this secondary movement was linked to the colonisation and development of hitherto marginal land on Anglo-Norman manors, and perhaps was also associated with a trend towards pastoralism seen after 1300.[90] This shows that scholars still believe that villages (some of which had borough status) occurred beside manorial centres in the regions of Munster and elsewhere in Ireland that experienced heavy English peasant immigration from the late 12th century onwards. The debate is ultimately about the size and development of these nucleated settlements over time.[91] Archaeological excavation at selected sites is clearly the way forward to help solve this question.[92]

What has the discipline of archaeology done to help elucidate the nature of villages in Anglo-Norman Ireland? The answer really is very little so far, despite its potential for answering important questions. One important finding, however, has emerged from the few archaeological excavations that have taken place at manorial centres of Anglo-Norman date. It is clear from fieldwork that the earthworks of deserted villages are few in Ireland in comparison to England. Apart from certain places, especially south Tipperary, deserted village earthworks are rare at places that the historical sources suggest were once the centres of Anglo-Norman manors that had substantial English peasant populations on them. Very often, flat fields exist around Anglo-Norman castles and their associated churches in Munster and elsewhere.[93] This does not mean, however, that no villages existed at these places during the Anglo-Norman period. The few small-scale archaeological investigations that have taken place in the fields surrounding known manorial centres of Anglo-Norman date in the parts of Ireland that saw much English immigration have uncovered evidence for peasant houses dating to the latter period. Again, it must be stressed that there was no visible evidence of these buildings above ground prior to these excavations.[94] Simply, the fact that flat fields occur and no earthworks exist today around a known manorial centre of Anglo-Norman date cannot be taken as archaeological evidence that no nucleated settlement existed at the site during the course of the 13th and 14th centuries. Rose Cleary's small excavation at Bourchier's Castle, county Limerick, carried out in advance of a car-park development, illustrates this point perfectly. It provided evidence for two medieval houses of general 13th and 14th-century date [6].[95] There was no sign of these houses prior to excavation, and they lay in a totally flat field.[96] It has been suggested that these houses were part of a village that once existed beside a manorial centre in the 13th and 14th centuries.[97]

It has been argued that the reason why so few deserted village or

6 – Rose Cleary's reconstruction of one of the 13th-century peasant houses found at Lough Gur, county Limerick

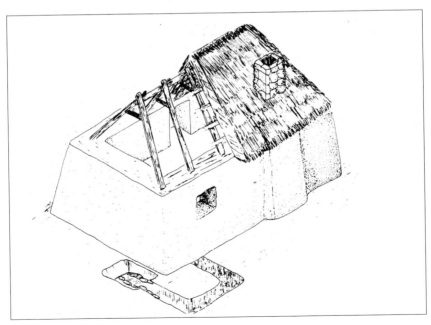

7 – An aerial view of a moated site

borough earthworks of medieval date occur in the Irish countryside today is because so many of these places were deserted prior to c.1400. The combined effects of the Gaelic Resurgence, the Bruce Wars, famine, the Black Death, and, as noted, a trend towards pastoralism seen from 1300 onwards meant that many villages and rural boroughs founded by the Anglo-Normans were deserted during the course of the 14th century.[98] Simply, many nucleated settlements beside Anglo-Norman manorial centres were not inhabited long enough to leave traces above ground after these villages were deserted, or at least largely abandoned.

A major research question, therefore, for any future archaeological study on the manorial landscape of Anglo-Norman Munster is when did English colonists or their descendants settle in the townlands that made up the manors, and live away from the manorial centres? Was dispersed settlement by English free tenants always a feature of manorial life in Anglo-Norman eastern Ireland from the late 12th century onwards, or was it something that only started to happen from the late 13th century onwards?

Certainly, archaeological evidence for dispersed settlement associated with the colonists exists in the landscape of eastern Ireland. Moated sites usually appear today as rectangular banked and ditched enclosures [7]. Originally these earthworks would have had timber defences surmounting their banks, with mostly clay and wooden buildings within their interiors.[99] About a thousand moated sites seem to exist in the Irish countryside today, with large numbers extant in the Munster counties of Cork,

Limerick and Tipperary.[100] Some moated sites in Ireland functioned as monastic granges located on scattered lands belonging to the great monasteries of high medieval Ireland.[101] At least some moated sites in the Roscommon area were built by Gaelic-Irish lords of the first rank in the very early years of the 14th century.[102] The accepted view for many years, however, was that most moated sites in Ireland functioned as the defended manor houses and farmsteads of minor Anglo-Norman lords, despite the fact that few of them occur at known manorial centres.[103]

A more recent view, however, while realising that some may have been the homes of unimportant Anglo-Norman lords, tends to the opinion that many moated sites in Ireland may have been the defended farmsteads of men of the free-tenant class. The majority of free tenants are probably best described as wealthy English peasant farmers who rented relatively large holdings on manors from their lords.[104]

The general consensus amongst scholars as to the dating of moated sites in Ireland is that they belong to the late 13th and early 14th century. It is also widely held that most moated sites are associated with a secondary movement out from established Anglo-Norman centres onto more peripheral lands within the bounds of manors. This movement onto more marginal or underutilised land is seen as taking place from the mid-13th century onwards.[105]

How reliable is the dating evidence for moated sites in Ireland? Certainly, the construction of the moated site at Rigsdale, county Cork, was securely dated on coin and pottery evidence to the late 13th or early 14th century.[106] The moated site at Mylerspark in county Wexford has been dated on historical grounds to the 1280s.[107] Literary and historical evidence would suggest that the moated site at Cloonfree, county Roscommon, was built around the year 1300.[108] At first glance, therefore, if it is accepted that all moated sites in Ireland date to the late 13th and early 14th century, and that at least some of them were the homes of free tenants, this might mean that Graham's view of dispersed settlement on Anglo-Norman manors dating to after 1250 or so is substantially correct. This would in turn suggest that all English tenants on Anglo-Norman manors in Ireland lived in large nucleated settlements beside manorial centres up to the mid-13th century, only moving out away from these places after the latter date.

Yet it must be remembered that the dating of moated sites in Ireland exclusively to the late 13th and early 14th century is not really based on strong foundations at present. Only about four excavations of moated sites have been fully published to date – a paltry amount considering there are up to a thousand moated sites in Ireland.[109] For example, the moated site at Ballyveelish, county Tipperary, was partially excavated in 1982. The excavator indicated that the artefactual evidence suggested that the earthwork was constructed and occupied at some stage in the 13th or 14th century. He tended, however, towards a late 13th or early 14th-century date for the site simply because this was and is the accepted view for the dating of moated sites in Ireland.[110] This date for Ballyveelish could be correct, but it has also been argued that there is nothing particularly diagnostic in the finds to be absolutely certain that this moated site was constructed in the late 13th century or slightly later. It could, in fact, be earlier in date.[111] Really more moated sites need to be excavated in Ireland and their reports published to conclusively ascertain when this settlement form first appeared in the landscape of Anglo-Norman Ireland. Future excavation may indicate that some moated sites in Ireland date to the first years of the 13th century, or possibly even a bit earlier. If this was the case, this would strongly hint that dispersed settlement occurred on Anglo-Norman manors right from the beginning of the colonisation process, with English free tenants living away from manorial centres from the start. The main point here is that future excavation at moated sites may well be the key to understanding exactly when dispersed settlement associated with English tenants on Anglo-Norman manors first appeared.

GAELIC-IRISH SETTLEMENT
IN 13th AND 14th-CENTURY MUNSTER

It was already noted that many tenants on Anglo-Norman manors in Munster were of Gaelic-Irish stock. This section, however, examines the areas of Munster, such as west Cork, south Kerry and Clare (along with certain other parts of the province), that saw the large-scale survival of Gaelic-Irish lords. It was noted above that little archaeological work has been undertaken to date on rural settlement in the areas of Ireland that were heavily settled and occupied by the Anglo-Normans during the course of the late 12th, 13th and early 14th century. It is equally clear that even less work has been carried out over the years on the parts of the country controlled (at least at a local level) by Gaelic-Irish lords during this same period.[112]

What differences existed between the landscape of Gaelic-Irish-dominated parts of Munster on one hand, and the countryside of areas of the province heavily settled by the Anglo-Normans and their English tenants on the other? One major difference lies in the fact that there is very little evidence in Munster, and, indeed, all Ireland, for Gaelic-Irish castles of general high medieval date.[113] The field evidence and the surviving historical sources suggest that Gaelic-Irish lords in Munster rarely built fortifications that can be classified in a physical sense as castles before they began to erect tower-houses from the late 14th and early 15th century onwards, in much the same way that lords of Anglo-Norman descent were doing at the same time. One possible example of a Gaelic-Irish-built masonry castle of 13th-century date is Carrigogunnell, county Limerick, which was occupied by the O'Briens during this period.[114] There may well be other examples of Gaelic-Irish castles of high medieval date in the province, but it cannot be ignored that the overall picture suggests that the overwhelming majority of timber castles and masonry castles of pre-late 14th-century date in Munster were built by the Anglo-Normans.

Certainly, Gaelic-Irish lords had the military and economic resources to capture Anglo-Norman castles right from the late 12th century. The erection and endowment of mainly Augustinian and Cistercian monasteries on their lands, such as Corcomroe, county Clare, show that the technical skills needed to build large castles existed within the territories under their control. In this respect, various valid social, economic and military reasons have been given by various scholars as to why Gaelic-Irish lords did not regularly build castles during the high medieval period.[115] Royal and aristocratic wealth and power in Gaelic Ireland during the late 12th, 13th and 14th century did not need to find expression in the building of such things as complex masonry and timber castles. There were other ways of doing this, and it has been suggested that high status in Gaelic Ireland, certainly before c.1400, and to a certain extent right up to the late 16th and early 17th century, was shown through feasting, the ability to keep armed men, the ownership of large herds of cattle and horses, the patronage of the Church and the learned classes, and, lastly, ceremonies at inauguration sites.[116] In all, the lack of castles in Gaelic Ireland during the high medieval period should not be taken as a sign of Gaelic-Irish poverty or backwardness in comparison to the Anglo-Normans. Instead, it was a reflection of the different way in which Gaelic society was organised during this period.

Where, then, and in what did Gaelic-Irish lords live in Munster during the period under discussion? The *Caithreim Thoirdhealbaigh*, or *The Battle Triumphs of Turlough*, is a Gaelic-Irish prose narrative, interspersed with long poems, written before the mid-14th century, possibly as early as c.1330. It deals with an internecine struggle between different branches of the O'Briens for control of the lordship of Thomond (at this stage mainly modern Clare) during the course of the second half of the 13th and early 14th century. It is highly partisan towards the Clann Toirdelbaig, one of the two opposing O'Brien factions, and is also hostile towards Anglo-Norman settlers in Thomond.[117] At first glance, it is clear that this source tells us much about the politics of north-west Munster during the late 13th and early 14th century. There is also much information in the text of the *Caithreim Thoirdhealbaigh*, however, about the nature of Gaelic-Irish settlement and society in Munster during the latter period. The term 'longport' is used regularly in this text to describe the Gaelic-Irish strongholds that seem to have been dotted throughout the landscape of 13th and early 14th-century Clare. For example, Conor O'Brien is described as having built a 'longport comnaide' or a 'stronghold with earthworks' at Clonroad, Ennis, county Clare, around 1260.[118] The site is mentioned again in 1276 or 1277, 1284 and 1317.[119] The 'morlongport' or 'great stronghold' of Cumea MacConmara of Clanncullen is mentioned in 1278.[120] The longport of O'Brien is mentioned in 1308.[121] The longport or stronghold of Murtough O'Brien was attacked in 1311.[122] The longport of Dermot O'Brien is referred to in 1317.[123] Other references to these strongholds exist in the *Caithreim Thoirdhealbaigh*. Certainly some of these longporta were only temporary fortifications, but it has been argued that the majority of them mentioned in the latter source, and indeed the various annals from throughout Ireland, functioned as permanent defended sites.[124]

What was a longport? One longport in what is now Clare may well have been a crannóg or crannóg-like natural island fortress located out on Inchiquin Lough near Corofin in county Clare.[125] It was suggested by the antiquarian George MacNamara at the beginning of the last century that a 13th-century masonry castle lay out on this island, but a review of his description of this structure and its cut stones suggests it to be a much later tower-house.[126] The island, however, seems to have been encircled by a drystone cashel-type wall originally.[127] The evidence, therefore, suggests that the 13th and early 14th-century longport on Inchiquin Lough may well have been a crannóg or natural island whose edges were defended by a drystone wall. It is now firmly established that some crannógs and natural island fortresses were occupied and used as habitations and fortresses by Gaelic-Irish lords right up to the 17th century.[128] It is possible that some of the crannógs on other Clare lakes may well have been fortified and used as the high medieval residences of Gaelic-Irish lords in this particular region of Munster. Yet crannógs are rare in general throughout Munster simply because there are few lakes in the province. Most longporta mentioned in the sources throughout Ireland seem to have been dry-land sites.[129] For example, the longport mentioned at Cloonfree, county Roscommon, in 1306 seems to have been a moated site.[130]

Were the Munster longporta moated sites? Certainly the areas of the province that saw widespread Gaelic lordly survival (i.e. Clare, south Kerry and west Cork) have almost no moated sites within their bounds today, just as there are few masonry or timber castles of general high medieval date [8].

Yet the evidence from the *Caithreim Thoirdhealbaigh* suggests that the landscape of Irish-dominated parts of Munster during the 13th and 14th century was dotted with defended residences belonging to Gaelic lords. Thousands of ringforts, whether drystone-walled cashels or earthen

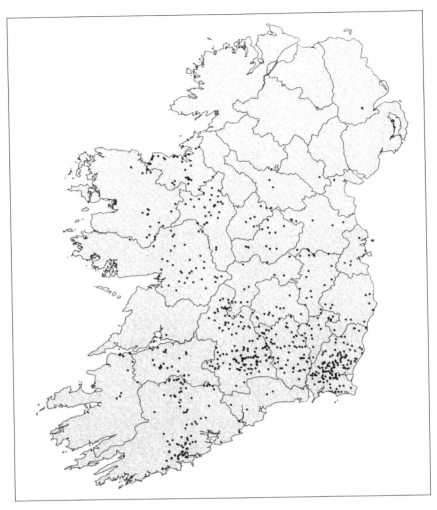

8 – Distribution map of moated sites in Ireland (Discovery Programme)

banked and ditched enclosures, survive in the Munster countryside today, including many in west Cork, Kerry and Clare. The view held by most Irish archaeologists is that ringforts were rarely if ever occupied after 1000AD.[131] Increasing, archaeological evidence is beginning to challenge this assumption, suggesting that while the majority of ringforts were abandoned by the latter year, at least some were occupied and built after this date.[132] Much of this evidence comes from west Munster. Erin Gibbon's excavation at Ballynaveenoragh on the Dingle Peninsula has shown that this cashel had a 13th-century phase to it.[133] The results of the excavation at Mooghaun hill fort in county Clare by Eoin Grogan has indicated that at least one of the two, clearly later, cashels built within this prehistoric enclosure seems to have been occupied and possibly even constructed at some stage during the 13th and 14th century.[134] A whole series of cashels in the Burren area of county Clare were clearly occupied in the late-medieval period, right up to the 17th century, and provides evidence for the long-term use of this monument type in this particular area.[135] This all shows that at least some cashels in Munster were occupied and even constructed in Munster right throughout the whole later medieval period from after 1000AD up to the 17th century. This perhaps suggests that some of the longporta referred to in the *Caithreim Thoirdhealbaigh* were cashels. This evidence also hints that possibly many of the relict field systems associated with cashels in the Burren area today actually belong to the high and late-medieval periods, and are not earlier in date [9].

What about earthen ringforts? Again some evidence is suggesting that some ringforts were occupied and even constructed long after the year 1000.[136] The well-defended ringfort at Beal Boru, county Clare, was apparently built in the early 11th century and remained in use until the first years of the 12th century.[137] Yet there is not a lot of evidence from Munster for the high medieval usage of earthen ringforts. An analysis of the excavation report of the ringfort at the Bowling Green, Thurles, county Tipperary, possibly suggests it was inhabited into the 13th century.[138] Sometime before 1242 Donnchad O'Brien built 'a circular hold and princely residence of earth' at Clonroad, Ennis, county Clare.[139] This has been taken by various writers to refer to the construction of a ringfort.[140] John Hunt's excavation at Clonroad in 1941, while rich in finds of general later medieval date, failed to confirm that a ringfort once existed here.[141] Etienne Rynne's excavation of two ringforts at Shannon Airport in the 1960s, however, produced evidence to suggest that these sites were occupied and constructed during the late 16th century and early 17th century.[142] This, then, is at least some evidence to suggest that certain ringforts in Munster continued to be built throughout the whole medieval period. It could also be argued that because there is quite good evidence for the medieval usage of cashels in Munster, this must also be taken as a strong hint that some earthen ringforts topped by wooden palisades continued to be occupied and built in the province after the 12th century. Why continue to use cashels and not their earthen equivalents? It is possible, therefore, that many of the longporta mentioned in the *Caithreim Thoirdhealbaigh* were, in fact, earthen ringforts.

One small question needs to be answered. It is argued here that at least some earthen ringforts and cashels continued to be inhabited and even built by Gaelic lords in Munster after the 12th century. Clearly these sites were defended lordly residences and had many of the functions of cas-

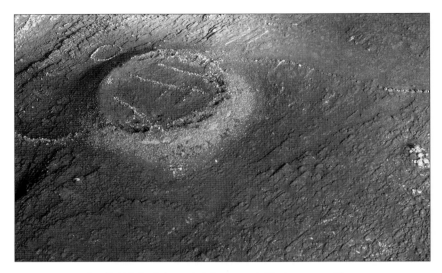

9 – Caithir Scríbín cashel, Leamaneh North, county Clare

tles. Should they not be called castles? As noted above, it has been argued
recently that mottes and ringwork castles, usually built by Anglo-Norman
lords, carried quite serious timber defences such as towers and palisades,
looped for archery. The evidence would suggest that the ordinary wooden
or post-and-wattle palisades or thick drystone walls seen around different
types of ringfort were not regarded by Anglo-Norman commentators as
castles in the way mottes and ringworks were during the high medieval
period.[143] Far more resources seem to have been put into the construction
of motte and ringwork castles in terms of their timber defences and buildings, and this made them militarily stronger and structurally complex to
look at in comparison to ringforts. Mottes and ringworks would have dominated their surrounding landscapes in a way ringforts never could. This all
hints that Gaelic lords were not interested in constructing visually impressive residences, unlike the Anglo-Normans.

CONCLUSION

This review of archaeological work carried out on the subject of medieval
rural settlement in Munster indicates how little research has been done on
this topic over the years. A large-scale research excavation has not yet
taken place in the province, or elsewhere in Ireland, at an Anglo-Norman
manorial centre, so little is known about the actual physical layout of
these places apart from what the surviving historical sources tell us. The

same historical sources suggest that such things as deer parks, fishponds, rabbit warrens, watermills, bounded forests and managed woodland all existed in the manorial landscape of Anglo-Norman Ireland, which included large parts of Munster. Yet these features have not been physically recognised in the field to date simply because nobody has really looked for them as yet. The question of when dispersed settlement associated with English tenants first existed on Anglo-Norman manors in Munster is another priority for future research. Clearly more excavation of manorial villages and rural boroughs is required to give much-needed information about the growth and decline of these settlements in the 13th and 14th century. Arguably, all these questions could be answered under the auspices of a major project concentrating on the archaeology of a well-defined Anglo-Norman manor.

The whole subject of Gaelic-Irish settlement in high medieval Munster is also a major priority for future research. There are strong hints from the available evidence to suggest that earthen ringforts, and particularly cashels, continued to be used and even built in Munster in this period and later. More excavation at selected ringforts in Munster is needed to clarify this further. One point clearly emerging from recent research is that the archaeology of high medieval Gaelic Ireland is far less visible in the landscape today when compared to the remains left by the Anglo-Normans. This seems to be due to the way Gaelic-Irish society was organised in this period. Lordly status in Gaelic Ireland was demonstrated in different ways to Anglo-Norman Ireland during the 13th and 14th century, and this difference has left its mark on the archaeology of the period.

The author

Kieran O'Conor is a lecturer in the Department of Archaeology, NUI, Galway. He is author of the 1998 book *The Archaeology of Medieval Rural Settlement in Ireland* and many articles on the subject of castles and medieval settlement. He has just finished co-editing a book on castles in Ireland and Wales, which will be published early in 2003.

Acknowledgements

I would like to thank the Barryscourt Trust and Noel Jameson in particular for inviting me to offer this contribution to the understanding of the medieval period in Munster. Thanks are due also to Prof Terry Barry, Dr Niall Brady and Mary Dillon for their comments on drafts of the text. I would also like to thank my wife Karena Morton for her help.

Endnotes

[1] KD O'Conor, *The Archaeology of Medieval Rural Settlement in Ireland* (Dublin, 1998) p10

[2] TB Barry, *The Archaeology of Medieval Ireland* (London and New York, 1987) p10; TE McNeill, *Castles in Ireland, Feudal Power in a Gaelic World* (London and New York, 1997) p2; O'Conor, *The Archaeology*, p10

[3] Barry, *The Archaeology*, pp1-2; O'Conor, *The Archaeology*, p12

[4] O'Conor, *The Archaeology*, pp14-15

[5] A Lynch, 'Excavations of the medieval town defences at Charlotte's Quay, Limerick', *Proceedings of the Royal Irish Academy*, 84c (1984), pp281-331; MF Hurley, 'Excavations in medieval Cork: St Peter's Market', *Journal of the Cork Historical and Archaeological Society*, 91 (1986) pp1-25; RM Cleary, MF Hurley and E Shee-Twohig, *Excavations by D.C. Twohig at Skiddy's Castle and Christ Church, Cork, 1974-77* (Cork, 1997); MF Hurley, *Excavations at the North Gate, Cork* (Cork, 1997). These are just some examples of published urban excavations in Munster.

[6] MF Hurley, OMB Scully and SWJ McCutcheon, *Late Viking Age and Medieval Waterford. Excavations 1986-1992* (Waterford)

[7] J Hunt, 'Clonroad More, Ennis', *JRSAI*, 76 (1946) pp195-209; SP O'Riordáin, 'Excavations at Lissard, County Limerick, and other sites in the vicinity', *JRSAI*, 66 (1936) pp173-85. These are examples of small excavations of medieval rural sites in Munster.

[8] MG Doody, 'Moated site, Ballyveelish I, Co. Tipperary', in RM Cleary, MF Hurley and EA Twohig (eds), *Archaeological excavations on the Cork-Dublin gas pipeline 1981-1982*, (Cork, 1987) pp74-87; RM Cleary, 'Excavations at Lough Gur, Co. Limerick: Part II', *Journal of the Cork Historical and Archaeological Society*, 87 (1982) pp77-106; Cleary, Excavations at Lough Gur, Co. Limerick: Part III', *Journal of the Cork Historical and Archaeological Society*, 88 (1983) pp51-80; D Sweetman, 'Excavations of a medieval moated site at Rigsdale, County Cork, 1977-8', *Proceedings of the Royal Irish Academy*, 81c (1981) pp103-205

[9] G Stout, *Archaeological Survey of the Barony of Ikerrin* (Roscrea, 1984); D Power, E Byrne, U Egan, S Lane and M Sleeman, *Archaeological Inventory of County Cork: Volume 1 – West Cork* (Dublin, 1992); Power et al, *Archaeological Inventory of County Cork: Volume 2 – East and South Cork* (Dublin, 1994); A O'Sullivan and J Sheahan, *The Iveragh Peninsula: an Archaeological Survey of South Kerry* (Cork, 1996); Power et al, *Archaeological Inventory of County Cork: Volume 3 – Mid-Cork* (Dublin, 1997); M Moore, *Archaeological Inventory of Co. Waterford* (Dublin, 1999).

[10] AF O'Brien, *The Impact of the Anglo-Normans on Munster*, Barryscourt Lectures, no. 2, (Cork, 1997)

[11] K Down, 'Colonial society and economy in the Middle Ages', in A Cosgrove (ed.), *A New History of Ireland II: Medieval Ireland, 1169-1534* (Oxford, 1987) pp439-91; M Hennessy, 'Manorial organization in early thirteenth-century Tipperary', *Irish Geography*, 29 (1996) pp116-25

[12] KD O'Conor, 'Motte castles in Ireland; permanent fortresses, residences and manorial centres', *Chateau Gaillard*, 20 (2002) pp175-80

[13] C O'Brien and J Farrelly, *Archaeological Inventory of County Tipperary: volume 1 – North Tipperary* (Dublin, forthcoming)

[14] D Sweetman, 'The hall house in Ireland', in J Kenyon and K O'Conor (eds), *The Castle in Ireland and Wales* (Dublin, 2003) pp121-32

[15] D Sweetman, *The Medieval Castles of Ireland* (Cork, 1999) pp89-104

[16] T Collins and A Cummins, *Excavations of a Medieval Ringwork at Ballysimon, county*

Limerick (Limerick, 2001)

[17] BJ Graham, 'Timber and earthen fortifications in Western Ireland', *Medieval Archaeology*, 32 (1988) p120

[18] DC King, *The Castle in England and Wales* (London and Sydney, 1988) p57

[19] McNeill, *Castles in Ireland*, pp70, 76

[20] A Gailey, 'Changes in Irish rural housing', in P O'Flanagan, P Ferguson and K Whelan (eds), *Rural Ireland – modernisation and change, 1600-1900* (Cork, 1987) p89

[21] O' Conor, *The Archaeology*, pp26-33

[22] *The Red Book of Ormond*, NB White (ed.), (Dublin, 1932) pp52-3

[23] *ibid.*

[24] F Kelly, *Early Irish Farming* (Dublin, 1997) p107

[25] R Stalley, *The Cisterian Monasteries of Ireland* (London and New Haven, 1987) p175

[26] Down, 'Colonial Society', p478

[27] Kelly, *Early Irish Farming*, p300

[28] O Davies and DB Quinn (eds), 'The Irish pipe roll of 14 John', *Ulster Journal of Archaeology*, 4 (1941) pp32-3

[29] O Rackham, *The History of the Countryside* (London, 1986) p60

[30] *Red Book of Ormond*, pp52-3

[31] *ibid.*

[32] T Reeves-Smyth, *Irish Gardens and Gardening before Cromwell*, Barryscourt Lectures, no. 4 (Cork, 1999) pp115, 137

[33] *Red Book of Ormond*, pp52-3

[34] C Rynne, Technological Change in Anglo-Norman Munster, Barryscourt Lectures, no. 3 (Cork, 1998) p71

[35] O'Conor, *The Archaeology*, pp33-4

[36] *ibid.*, p33

[37] *ibid.*, pp33-4

[38] Davies and Quinn (eds), 'The Irish pipe roll of 14 John', pp70-1

[39] Hennessy, 'Manorial organization', p121

[40] Rackham, *The History of the Countryside*, p366

[41] O'Conor, *The Archaeology*, p34

[42] The Annals of Clonmacnoise, D Murphy (ed.), (Dublin, 1896)

[43] Rackham, *The History of the Countryside*, p366

[44] *ibid.*

[45] A Brown, *Fieldwork for Archaeologists and Local Historians* (London, 1987) p91

[46] Rackham, *The History of the Countryside*, p366

[47] A O'Sullivan, 'Harvesting the waters', *Archaeology Ireland*, vol. 8, no. 1 (1994) pp10-12; A O'Sullivan, 'Medieval fishweirs on the Deel Estuary, Co. Limerick', *Archaeology Ireland*, vol. 9, no. 2 (1995) pp15-17; A O'Sullivan, 'Medieval fishweirs and coastal settlement in north Munster', *Group for the Study of Irish Historic Settlement*, 4 (1995) pp3-5; A O'Sullivan, 'Medieval fish traps at Bunratty, Co. Clare', *The Other Clare*, 21 (1997) pp40-2

[48] Kelly, *Early Irish Farming*, p131

[49] *ibid.*, p133

[50] Rackham, *The History of the Countryside*, pp47-9

[51] *ibid.*, pp.49-50

[52] Davies and Quinn (eds), 'The Irish pipe roll of 14 John', pp33, 59

[53] E Curtis, *The History of Medieval Ireland from 1110 to 1513* (London, 1938) p219

[54] O'Conor, *The Archaeology*, pp33-4

[55] M Aston, *Interpreting the Landscape – Landscape Archaeology and Local History* (London, 1985) p115

56 O'Conor, *The Archaeology*, p34

57 *ibid.*, pp34-5

58 Rackham, *The History of the Countryside*, p46

59 PW Joyce, *Irish Names of Places*, 3 (Dublin, 1913) p281

60 *Topographia Hibernica: The History and Topography of Ireland by Gerald of Wales*, JJ O'Meara (ed.), (Harmondsworth, 1982) p119

61 *Calendar of Ormond Deeds*, 1172-1603, 3, (Dublin, 1932-43) p14

62 *Calendar of Documents Relating to Ireland, 1171-[1307]*, HS Sweetman and GF Handcock (eds), 5 vols (PRO, London, 1875-86) 1171-1251, no. 316

63 *Calendar of Documents Relating to Ireland*, 1171-1251, no. 1641

64 Rackham, *The History of the Countryside*, p123

65 *ibid.*, pp122-5

66 *ibid.*, p122

67 Kelly, *Early Irish Farming*, p272; Rackham, *The History of the Countryside*, p123

68 *Calendar of Documents Relating to Ireland, 1171-1251*, no. 477

69 O Rackham, *Ancient Woodland: its History, Vegetation and Uses in England* (London, 1980) pp49-50

70 F McCormick, 'Early evidence for wild animals in Ireland', in N Benecke (ed.), *The Holocene History of the European Vertebrate Fauna* (Berlin, 1999) p360

71 KD O'Conor, 'The origins of Carlow Castle', *Archaeology Ireland*, vol. 11, no. 3, pp13-16

72 Rackham, *The History of the Countryside*, p123

73 *ibid.*, p125

74 *ibid.*, pp125-6

75 O Rackham, 'Woodland', in P Crabtree (ed.), *Medieval Archaeology, An Encyclopedia* (New York and London, 2001) pp381-2; A O Sullivan, 'Woodmanship and the supply of underwood and timber to Anglo-Norman Dublin', in C Manning (ed.), *Dublin and Beyond the Pale* (Dublin, 1998) pp59-70

76 Rackham, *The History of the Countryside*, p133; O Rackham, 'Forests', in Crabtree (ed.), *Medieval Archaeology*, p111; O'Sullivan, 'Woodmanship', p67

77 O'Sullivan, 'Woodmanship', p67

78 *Calendar of Documents Relating to Ireland, 1252-1284*, no. 51

79 GH Orpen, 'Charters of the Earl Richard Marshal of the forests of Ross and Taghmon', *JRSAI*, 64 (1934) pp54-63

80 AJ Otway-Ruthven, *A History of Medieval Ireland* (London, 1968) p115

81 O'Conor, *The Archaeology*, pp41-3

82 *Red Book of Ormond*, pp64-7

83 O'Conor, *The Archaeology*, pp48-69

84 KJ Edwards, FW Hamond and A Simms, 'The medieval settlement of Newcastle Lyons, Co. Dublin: an interdisciplinary approach', *Proceedings of the Royal Irish Academy*, 83c (1983) pp351-76; BJ Graham, 'Anglo-Norman manorial settlement in Ireland: an assessment', *Irish Geography*, 18 (1985) pp6-10; BJ Graham, *Anglo-Norman Settlement in Ireland* (Athlone, 1985) pp16-17; AJ Otway-Ruthven, 'The organization of Anglo-Irish agriculture in the Middle Ages', *JRSAI*, 81 (1951) pp1-13; AJ Otway-Ruthven, 'The character of Norman settlement in Ireland', *Historical Studies*, 5 (1965) pp75-84; Otway-Ruthven, *A History*, pp107-18; A Simms, 'Settlement patterns of medieval colonisation in Ireland: the example of Duleek in Co. Meath', in P Flatres (ed.) *Paysages Ruraux Européens* (Rennes, 1979), 159-77; A Simms, 'Rural settlement in medieval Ireland: the example of the royal manors of Newcastle Lyons and Esker in south Co. Dublin', in BK Roberts and RE Glasscock (eds), *Villages, Fields and Frontiers* (Oxford, 1983); pp133-52; A Simms, 'The geography of Irish manors: the example of

the Llanthony cells of Duleek and Colp in County Meath', in J Bradley (ed), *Settlement and Society in Medieval Ireland*, (Kilkenny, 1988) pp291-326

[85] Otway-Ruthven, 'The organization of Anglo-Irish agriculture', pp1-13; Otway-Ruthven, 'The character of Norman settlement', pp75-84; Otway-Ruthven, *A History*, pp107-18

[86] O'Conor, *The Archaeology*, p44

[87] Edwards et al, 'The medieval settlement of Newcastle Lyons', pp351-76; Simms, 'Settlement patterns', pp159-77; Simms, 'Rural settlement in medieval Ireland', pp133-52; Simms, 'The geography of Irish manors', pp291-326

[88] O'Conor, *The Archaeology*, 70-1

[89] T O'Keeffe, *Medieval Ireland – An Archaeology* (Stroud, 2000) p59

[90] Graham, 'Anglo-Norman manorial settlement', pp6-10; Graham, *Anglo-Norman Settlement in Ireland*, pp16-17; BJ Graham, 'The High Middle Ages: c.1100-c.1350', in BJ Graham and LJ Proudfoot (eds), *A Historical Geography of Ireland* (London, 1993) p74

[91] O'Conor, *The Archaeology*, p70

[92] *ibid.*, pp70-1, 138-40

[93] O' Conor, The Archaeology, pp 46-7.

[94] O'Conor, The Archaeology, pp 46-57.

[95] Cleary, 'Excavations at Lough Gur, Co. Limerick: Part II', pp77-106; Cleary, 'Excavations at Lough Gur, Co. Limerick: Part III, pp51-80

[96] O'Conor, *The Archaeology*, p51

[97] Barry, *The Archaeology*, p81

[98] O'Conor, *The Archaeology*, pp47-8

[99] *ibid.*, p58

[100] TB Barry, 'The shifting frontier: medieval moated sites in counties Cork and Limerick', in FA Aberg and AE Brown (eds), *Medieval Moated Sites in North-West Europe* (Oxford, 1981) pp71-85; TB Barry, 'The chronology and development of medieval rural settlement in Munster', *Journal of the Cork Historical and Archaeological Society*, 105 (2000) pp195-6; O'Conor, *The Archaeology*, pp58, 63

[101] Graham, *Anglo-Norman Settlement in Ireland*, p22

[102] O'Conor, *The Archaeology*, 87-9; KD O'Conor, 'The morphology of Gaelic lordly sites in north Connacht', in PJ Duffy, D Edwards and E FitzPatrick (eds), *Gaelic Ireland, c.1250-c.1650* (Dublin, 2001), 338-41; T Finan and KD O'Conor, 'The moated site at Cloonfree, Co. Roscommon', *Journal of the Galway Archaeological and Historical Society*, 54 (2002) pp72-87

[103] TB Barry, *The Moated Sites of South-East Ireland* (Oxford, 1977) pp101-2; TB Barry, 'Rural settlement in Ireland in the Middle Ages', *Ruralia*, 1 (1996) p137; Barry, 'The chronology', p195

[104] McNeill, *Castles in Ireland*, pp148-9; O'Conor, *The Archaeology*, pp61-9; O'Keeffe, *Medieval Ireland*, p12

[105] Barry, 'The chronology', pp195-6; CA Empey, 'Medieval Knocktopher – a study in manorial settlement: part 1', *Old Kilkenny Review*, vol. 2, no. 4 (1982) p235; McNeill, *Castles in Ireland*, pp148-9; O'Keeffe, *Medieval Ireland*, pp77-80

[106] Sweetman, 'Excavations of a medieval moated site at Rigsdale', pp200-13

[107] W Colfer, 'In search of the barricade and ditch of Ballyconnor, Co. Wexford', *Archaeology Ireland*, vol. 10, no. 2 (1996) pp16-19

[108] Finan and O'Conor, 'The moated site at Cloonfree', pp72-87

[109] O'Conor, *The Archaeology*, pp63-8

[110] Doody, 'Moated site, Ballyveelish', p83

[111] O'Conor, *The Archaeology*, pp67-8

[112] Barry, *The Archaeology*, pp51, 100; O'Conor, *The Archaeology*, pp73-4; O'Conor, 'Gaelic lordly sites', pp329-31

[113] McNeill, *Castles in Ireland*, pp157-64, 167-8, 234; O'Conor, The Archaeology, pp75-7

[114] McNeill, *Castles in Ireland*, pp160, 194-6

[115] *ibid.*, pp167-8; KW Nicholls, 'Gaelic society and economy in the High Middle Ages', in Cosgrove (ed.), *A New History of Ireland II*, p403; O'Conor, *The Archaeology*, pp97-101

[116] Finan and O'Conor, 'The moated site at Cloonfree', p86

[117] TJ Westropp, 'On the external evidence bearing on the historic character of the "Wars of Turlough" by John, son of Rory MacGrath', *Transactions of the Royal Irish Academy*, 12 (1903) pp133-98; LF McNamara, 'An examination of the medieval Irish text "Caithreim Thoirdhealbaigh"', *North Munster Antiquity Journal*, 8 (1961) pp189-92

[118] *Caithreim Thoirdhealbaigh*, 2 vols, SH O'Grady (ed.), (London, 1929) i, p4; ii, p5

[119] *ibid.*, i, pp5-8, 24, 132; ii, pp6-7, 26, 116

[120] *ibid.*, i, p11; ii, p12

[121] *ibid.*, i, p37; ii, p37

[122] *ibid.*, i, p50; ii, p48

[123] *ibid.*, i, p132; ii, p116

[124] O'Conor, *The Archaeology*, pp84-7

[125] *Caithreim Thoirdhealbaigh*, i, pp70, 92, 134, 136; ii, pp63, 85, 118, 120

[126] GV MacNamara, 'Inchiquin, county Clare', JRSAI, 31 (1901) pp224-5

[127] MacNamara, 'Inchiquin', p226

[128] O'Conor, *The Archaeology*, pp70-84; A O'Sullivan, *The Archaeology of Lake Settlement in Ireland* (Dublin, 1998) pp150-177.

[129] O'Conor, *The Archaeology*, p84

[130] O'Conor, *The Archaeology*, p87; Finan and O'Conor, 'The moated site at Cloonfree', pp72-87

[131] N Edwards, *The Archaeology of Early Medieval Ireland* (London, 1990)

[132] O'Conor, *The Archaeology*, pp89-94

[133] *ibid.*, p86

[134] E Grogan, *The North Munster Project* (Dublin, forthcoming)

[135] TJ Westropp, 'Prehistoric stone forts of northern Clare', JRSAI, 27 (1897) p121; TJ Westropp, 'The ancient forts of Ireland: being a contribution towards our knowledge of their types, affinities and structural feature', *Transactions of the Royal Irish Academy*, 31 (1902) p640; O'Conor, *The Archaeology*, p86

[136] O'Conor, *The Archaeology*, pp89-94

[137] MJ O'Kelly, 'Beal Boru', *Journal of the Cork Historical and Archaeological Society*, 67 (1962) pp1-27

[138] T Fanning, 'Excavation of a ringfort at Bowling Green, Thurles, Co. Tipperary', *North Munster Antiquity Journal*, 13 (1970) pp6-21

[139] *Caithreim Thoirdhealbaigh*, i, p2; ii, p2

[140] Westropp, 'The ancient forts of Ireland', p625; C Cairns, *Irish Tower Houses – A Co. Tipperary Case Study* (Athlone, 1987) p6; JA Watt, 'Gaelic polity and cultural identity', in Cosgrove, *A New History of Ireland II*, p333

[141] Hunt, 'Clonroad More', pp195-209

[142] E Rynne, 'Some destroyed sites at Shannon Airport, Co. Clare', *Proceedings of the Royal Irish Academy*, 63c (1963) pp245-77

[143] O'Conor, 'Motte castles in Ireland', pp175-80

BARRYSCOURT LECTURES

Barryscourt Lectures VIII
THE ORIGIN AND DEVELOPMENT
OF THE TOWER-HOUSE IN
IRELAND
David Sweetman

Published by the Barryscourt Trust
in association with Cork County Council
and Gandon Editions, Kinsale.

ISBN 0946846 294

Series Editor   Noel Jameson
Design   John O'Regan
                 (© Gandon, 2000)
Production   Nicola Dearey, Gandon
Printing   Betaprint, Dublin
Distribution   Gandon, Kinsale

Publication of this lecture was sponsored
by Dúchas, The Heritage Service

Dúchas The Heritage Service

BARRYSCOURT LECTURE SERIES

Barryscourt Castle is a fine 16th-century
tower-house at Carrigtwohill, Co Cork.
The Barryscourt Trust was established in
1987 with the aim of conserving,
enhancing and developing the heritage
potential of the castle.

In 1996, the Barryscourt Trust instituted
a bi-annual series of lectures on Medieval
Ireland. They deal with aspects of
medieval history, archaeology, art and
architecture, and will be delivered by
scholars specialising in the period.

The lectures are being published
individually, and a clothbound
compilation will be published at four-
yearly intervals.

For further details on the lecture series,
contact:

THE BARRYSCOURT TRUST
Barryscourt Castle
Carrigtwohill, Co Cork
tel: 021-4883864

For further details on the publications,
or to order copies, contact:

GANDON EDITIONS
Oysterhaven, Kinsale, Co Cork
tel: 021-4770830 / fax: 021-4770755
e-mail: gandon@eircom.net

THE ORIGIN AND DEVELOPMENT
OF THE TOWER-HOUSE IN IRELAND

1 – Artramon, county Wexford
a simple eastern tower-house

THE BARRYSCOURT LECTURES VIII

The Origin and Development of the Tower-House in Ireland

David Sweetman

THE BARRYSCOURT TRUST
IN ASSOCIATION WITH CORK COUNTY COUNCIL AND GANDON EDITIONS

Tower-houses are the most numerous but probably the least understood type of castle in Ireland. They have been described as simple, poorly defended towers, all more or less of the same design, and as really being fortified houses, the ordinary and typical residences of the Irish and Anglo-Irish gentry.[1] Leask suggested that the impetus for the building of tower-houses came from the £10 grant offered by Henry VI in 1429 for the building of towers within the Pale (Dublin, Kildare, Louth and Meath).[2] However, this proposition has frequently been argued against by Barry and his postgraduate students, who see the origin of the tower-house in the 14th-century fortalice.[3] Barry has also put forward the suggestion that the tower-house might be a compromise between the early stone castles and the manor houses of the 16th and 17th centuries.[4] O'Keeffe follows much the same line, and sees the origin of the tower-house in the great towers of the early stone fortresses.[5] It is interesting to note that Barry argues that some of the tower-houses of the Pale were built, from the middle of the 14th century onwards, in strategic locations for protection against the lawless Irish.[6] In other words, they were built for defensive purposes and not merely as residences with fortification taking a secondary role, as suggested by Leask.[7] Barry again argues for a mid-14th-century date

2 – Rockfleet, county Mayo
a simple western tower-house

for the origin of the tower-houses,[8] and states that one of the reasons why there might be few standing remains of this period still to be found is that, since these are the earliest examples, they will be in a more dilapidated state. This argument hardly holds water when one considers the good condition of such prehistoric sites as the tombs of the Boyne Valley, not to mention the remains of the large early stone fortresses of the Anglo-Normans like Trim, county Meath, and Carrickfergus, county Antrim. Barry also states that it is often difficult to date these structures because of the lack of architectural details of windows and doorways.[9] A note of warning should be sounded here: even if such architectural details survive, one must be careful to establish that the windows or doorways are original features of the building. Windows were easy to replace, and often were, as fashion changed. Even when we get dates carved in fireplaces along with their owners' initials we cannot be sure whether these initials belong to the original owner or whether the fireplace itself might not be a later insertion.

Barry states that the general lawless conditions in Ireland meant that, unlike England, people could not afford to construct undefended hall-type manor houses, suggesting that the tower-house was a cheaper compromise between the hall-house and the large stone fortresses.[10] He also says that Johnson and Craig both suggested that the small rectangular keeps at such castles as Athenry, county Galway [3], could have been the precursors or examples for the tower-houses,[11] and argues that if we accept that these earlier small seigniorial castles were exemplars for the tower-house, then we need look no further for their origins.

Over the last decade or more, the Archaeological Survey of Ireland has recorded most of the known archaeological sites in the country, and almost half of the twenty-six counties have been published in inventory form. From this work it has now been established that there are a number of small seigniorial castles which are hall-houses.[12] They appear mainly to be isolated, poorly defended buildings, dating mostly from the 13th century, but some examples can also be assigned to the 14th century and later. They basically consist of a two-storey structure with a defended ground floor and a first-floor hall with the entrance at that level. Their distribution appears to be mainly west of a central central north-south divide, but they also occur in parts of Tipperary and Offaly, with later examples in Meath, Westmeath, Wexford and Wicklow. At Athenry Castle, the keep is in effect a hall with first-floor entrance. Similar structures can be seen at Askeaton, county Limerick, Rindown, county Roscommon, and Dunamase, county Laois, though the ruined remains at the latter may only represent a single-storey hall. As stated above, the early hall-houses appear to be a western phenomenon, whereas the later ones, such as Kindlestown, county Wicklow, and Dunmoe, county Meath [6], appear to have an east-

3 – Athenry Castle, county Galway
an early 13th-century hall-keep

4 – Castlekirk, Lough Corrib, county Galway
ground and first-floor plans of a typical hall-house
(after MacNeill, 1997)

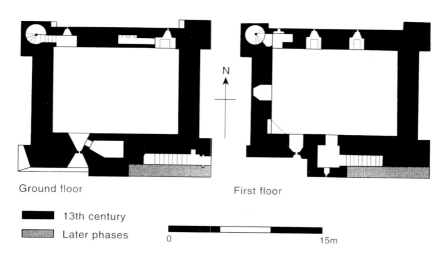

Ground floor   First floor

N

■ 13th century

▨ Later phases

0   15m

5 – Dunmore, county Galway, an early hall-house which dates to *c*.1225

left: 6 – Dunmoe, county Meath; *right:* 7 – Clonshire, county Limerick

ern distribution. This is not, of course, an absolute rule, and a very fine example of a late hall-house can be seen at Ballycarbery, county Kerry,[13] but I have yet to encounter the simple early 13th-century examples in the eastern portion of the country.

In Wexford especially, but also in Wicklow, there are examples of late medieval halls with attached towers [8]. In one instance, at Oldcourt in Wicklow, the hall is no longer extant and the remaining tower has been mistakenly identified as a tower-house.[14] These structures are service towers, and contain the stairs and the solar, as well as bedchambers. They are so like tower-houses that they have obvious links with them. The combination of hall and service tower is also very similar to the association of hall and solar that one finds in large stone fortresses such as Trim and Askeaton.[15] Other late hall-houses, such as Delvin, county Westmeath, Dunmoe, Kindlestown and Ballycarbery (already mentioned), are very like tower-houses but with one important difference: the hall is always at first-floor level in the hall-house. Ballycarbery has a square projecting angle tower similar to the simple early tower-houses of the Pale. The hall-house at Dunmoe [6] had a circular tower at each angle, as did Delvin, and these have obvious parallels with tower-houses in Louth, such as Milltown [16] and Haynestown [17].[16] It should also be noted that many of the early hall-houses originally had wooden floors, and at a later stage these were replaced with vaulting, a feature of the early tower-house. Some hall-houses had a third storey added to them, and good examples of this can be seen at Shrule, county Mayo, and Dunmore, county Galway [5].[17] At Shrule, the added storey also carries bartizans – a feature of later tower-houses in the western half of the country. Despite the still-unclear picture of the distribution and exact nature of the hall-house in Ireland, I would strongly contend that the Irish tower-house owes its origin to the hall-house, especially those of the 14th century.

————

8 – Slade, county Wexford
a late-medieval hall-house with service tower

9 – Roodstown, county Louth, a simple tower-house of the Pale
opposite: 10 – Killincoole, county Louth,
the two projecting angle towers are typical of the county

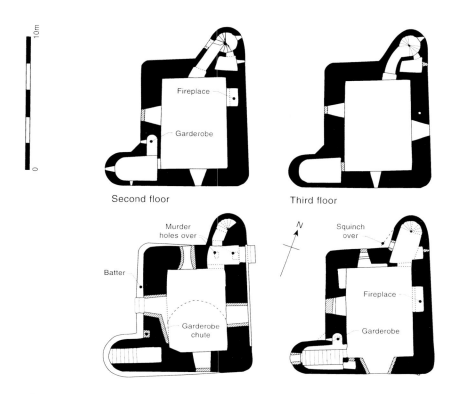

Second floor

Third floor

The earliest tower-houses in Ireland are the simple rectangular examples to be seen mainly in the eastern half of the country, especially within the Pale where the £10 grant of Henry VI in 1429 applied. The distribution of the tower-house can be roughly divided in three. The earliest and simplest types, as exemplified by Roodstown [9] and Kilincoole [10], both in county Louth, are to be found in the eastern part of the country, while the later, more sophisticated ones such as Aughnanure, county Galway [26], and Blarney, county Cork, are found in the west. The third area falls between the other two, with a mixture of simple and later, more complex structures sited in the midland counties. A typical simple type of tower-house in the midlands is Clara, county Kilkenny, while that at Ballagharahin, county Laois [11, 12, 13], is a late example with more defensive features, as well as being more commodious.[18] This is by no means a hard and fast rule; simple rectangular tower-houses can be found in the western half of the country, while relatively large examples, such as Dunsoghly, county Dublin [14, 15], are to be found in the east. However, there are several differences between the simple tower-houses of the east and those found in the west. Most of the simple tower-houses of the east can be dated to the 15th century and differ in certain details from those of the west. The examples from the Pale

Ballagharahin (Ballagh) Castle, county Laois, a late 16th-century tower-house

11 – view of castle; 12 – cross-loop covering doorway; 13 – 16th-century doorway

Dunsoghly, county Dublin, a late tower-house similar to Bunratty, county Clare

14 – view of castle with church on left; 15 – plan of castle and church

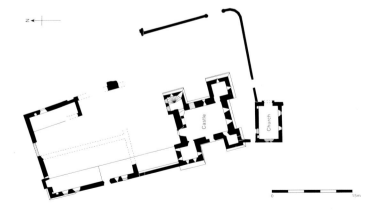

usually have vaults over the ground floor, have one or more projecting angle towers, and do not have bartizans or running machicolations. Where simple tower-houses are found in the west they usually carry bartizans and running machicolations, but do not have projecting angle towers.

The method of stone-dressing on the windows and doorways of the tower-houses has been looked at in some detail in recent years in some of the counties recorded by the Archaeological Survey of Ireland, in particular in Laois, Louth, Offaly, Tipperary and Galway, and can now be fairly accurately dated,[19] especially in relation to later examples. Unfortunately, few, if any, 15th-century tower-houses have date stones, and the fashion of putting owners, initials with their dates on fireplaces and over doorways seems to belong purely to the 16th and 17th centuries.

Various authors in the last fifteen years have attempted to quantify the total number of tower-houses that were built in Ireland. Terry Barry states that up to 7,000 examples are known,[20] while Cairns suggests a total of at least 3,500.[21] It is difficult to know what these authors are basing their figures on, but Barry appears to be using a combination of O'Danachair's distribution map of tower-houses[22] and his postgraduate students' theses on county surveys of the subject, while Cairns bases his figure on his own research for his PhD thesis. McNeill is almost dismissive in his treatment of tower-houses.[23] Of these authors, only McNeill had the opportunity to use the most up-to-date work by the Archaeological Survey of Ireland to verify their figures, since it was not until quite recently that the survey had progressed far enough to make an accurate count. Based on recent field-work, the Archaeological Survey now has a record of about 1,057 tower-houses, and the addition of sixty-one for the north of Ireland gives a total of c.1,118 examples. This figure only includes sites which have definite remains on the ground. Present data in the Archaeological Survey of Ireland show that there are 1,057 definite tower-houses, 2,834 castles (all types, excluding tower-houses) and 1,303 sites of castles. Many of these castles and sites of castles were undoubtedly tower-houses, but others were hall-houses, fortified houses and strong houses. Castle sites marked on various maps such as the first edition of the Ordnance Survey and the Downe Survey are also included, and need to be treated with some caution. However, if we assume that two-thirds of all the other castles and sites of castles, other than the definite examples, were tower-houses, then we would have had a maximum of c.3,800 in Ireland.

The figure of 3,000 tower-houses is quoted by Barry[24] and is taken from O'Danachair's distribution map, which in turn is based on the OS markings. These sites include medieval stone fortresses, hall-houses and strong houses, and cannot be considered as a true count or distribution of extant tower-houses in Ireland. Based on the most up-to-date Archaeological Survey figures for the whole of the country, the most likely total count of tower-houses is about 2,000. However, included in the total figure of 2,834 for all standing remains of castles, excluding tower-houses, there must be a number of tower-houses which have been classified as other types of castles. Even if two-thirds of these should be classified as tower-houses, we are still only going to reach a maximum figure of c. 3,000 possible tower-houses. If every type of castle, site of castle and possible castle site are added together, we get a grand total of 6,364. This figure, however, includes all the Downe Survey map markings, strong houses, fortified houses, etc, so there is no way that Barry's suggested total of 7,000 tower-houses can be realised.[25]

———

As stated above, I believe that the main impetus for tower-house-building within the Pale was the 1429 £10 grant of Henry VI. Most of the tower-houses within the Pale take a very simple form and can be dated to the 15th century. Typical examples are to be found in county Louth, and have been looked at in some detail.[26] Virtually all the Louth examples have projecting towers on their angles, and frequently are diagonally opposite each other. These angle towers contained the stairs and the garderobes, and good examples are to be found at Killincoole [10] and Milltown [16].[27] At Glaspistol there is only one projecting tower, which contains the spiral stair, while the garderobe is within the wall of another angle and is accessed via a mural passage. In these early towers, barrel vaults are invariably found over the ground floor and access to the upper floors is by spiral stairs, whereas in the later simple towers the floors are all of wood. The stair is nearly always situated immediately to the right or left just inside the doorway, and is protected with a murder hole and wooden door. There are variations in the plans of the towers of the early period: for instance, at Balregan, county Louth, the entrance is in the south-east angle and leads into a lobby and then into the barrel-vaulted ground floor. The entrance to the mural stairs is in the centre of the south wall. There is a spiral stair from first to second floor in the north-west angle. Dunmahon has projecting towers on the north-east and north-west angles, one projecting northwards, the other eastwards. Haynestown [17] has a circular tower on each angle, albeit of different sizes and slightly different shapes. The courthouse in Ardee has towers on the south-west and south-east angles, both projecting westwards. From the limited number of examples given above it can be seen that there are considerable variations in the basic plan of the early simple tower-houses of county Louth, and this is reflected in the other counties of the Pale and the eastern counties of Ulster.

In Castletown, Dundalk, there is a large tower-house which was built c. 1472 by Richard Bellew. It has a square or rectangular projecting

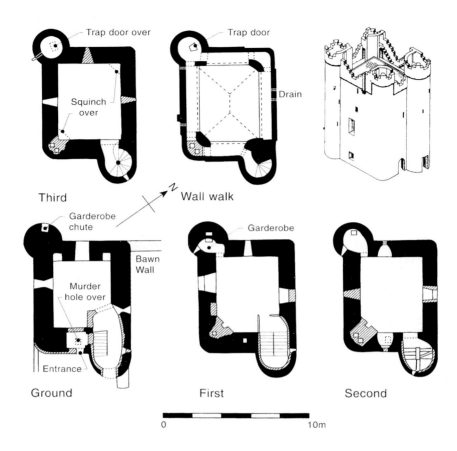

Third

Wall walk

Ground

First

Second

16 – Milltown, county Louth

17 – Haynestown, county Louth

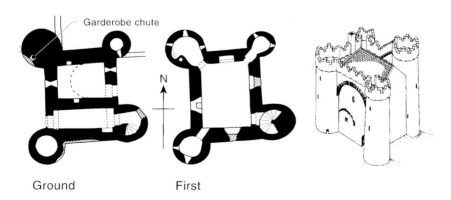

Ground

First

18 – Bunratty Castle, county Clare,
a late 15th-century tower-house

tower at each angle and is very similar in design and date to Dunsoghly, county Dublin [14, 15]. Bunratty, county Clare [18], is also of the same design, and is probably the finest of these late 15th-century tower-houses. There are also a number of small, simple towers in the eastern part of the country which are not early in the series. For instance, at Clara, county Kilkenny, there is a simple rectangular tower of five storeys and small bawn at the north, where it protects the doorway. Although it is used by Leask as a typesite,[28] it is quite different from the early tower-houses of the Pale in that it does not have projecting towers on the angles and lacks the barrel vault over the ground floor. It has, however, a vault over the fourth level, as well as subsidiary chambers up to this level. These are features of the later tower-houses of the midlands and the western half of the country. Where a vault exists in a tower-house, then invariably the main hall and private chambers are immediately above.[29] It should, however, be pointed out that a number of late tower-houses in Waterford have vaults over the ground floor, which in most instances in Ireland is an indicator of an early date. County Waterford has the remains of thirty tower-houses, less than half that of Wexford, which is only slightly larger. Many of the Waterford towers had vaults over one of the upper storeys as well as over the ground floor, usually an indication of lateness. Many of these tower-houses are ruinous, which may be the result of the upper vault pressing out the side walls, causing collapse. Towers in Waterford with upper-level vaults are of 16th-century date, as is indicated by the presence of musket loops and other late features, such as ogee-headed windows with hood-mouldings. These tower-houses also lack projecting angle towers, a common feature of the early Pale examples. Clonea, one of the larger tower-houses in this county, has vaults over the ground and first floors, and is six storeys high. Many of the Waterford examples have bartizans, a feature of later tower-houses.

There are only the remains of eight tower-houses in Wicklow, and most of these are in poor condition, but as far as can be ascertained they are of the simple early Pale type. Wexford, its southern neighbour, on the other hand, has over sixty examples, many in good condition. The tower-houses of this county vary considerably in ground size, but are never more than three or four storeys high. Like most of the tower-houses outside the Pale, the Wexford examples lack projecting angle towers, and the stairs and garderobes are therefore contained within the walls at the angles. Kilcloggan is one of the few that has two projecting towers, one each at the north and west angles, containing the stairs and garderobes respectively. In keeping with this example of a Pale-type tower-house, it has a barrel-vaulted ground floor. The presence of a vault only over the ground floor, with wooden floors at the other levels, is a good indicator of an early date in the development of the tower-house. Where there is more than one vault, the building invariably dates from a later phase in the development of the tower-house. The vaults were, for the most part, built to carry the hall, and in later examples those in the upper floors were designed to carry the private chambers and upper hall. An example of a late tower-house in Wexford is to be found at Mountgarrett. It has five storeys and no vault over the ground floor. An unusual feature of this castle is that it has four garderobes, all in different locations so that the same chute could not be used for any of them. Another unusual feature of some of the Wexford tower-houses (also to be found in Cork and Galway) is the presence of a portcullis, which was operated from a chamber above the doorway. Examples of this are to be found at Butlerstown, Ballyconor Big, Clougheast and Sigginstown. Another feature of some of the bigger tower-houses, and also to be found in Wexford at Ballyteige, Ballycogly, Ballyhack and Clougheast, is an oubliette (secret chamber). Virtually all the Wexford tower-houses are well equipped with fireplaces, garderobes and gun loops, as well as yetts (iron grilles) to protect the doorways.

In the midland counties of Laois and Offaly there is quite a variation of tower-house type, but with most of them belonging to the 16th

19 – Rathmacknee, county Wexford,
late simple eastern tower-house with substantial bawn wall

rather than the 15th century. In Laois there are the standing remains of twenty-nine tower-houses, fifteen of which can be fairly securely dated through historical references to the date of their erection, the type of stone-dressing or by date stones. Eleven can be dated to the 16th century, and only four appear to be early. The early examples all have barrel vaults over the ground floor, whereas the later ones seldom have vaults, and if they do, they are over an upper floor, as at Gortnaclea. Details on the later examples include finely dressed stonework in the windows, which often have ogee heads and well-finished doorways with yett-holes. The later tower-houses are usually larger and taller and contain fireplaces, something lacking in the earlier examples. Some of the Laois tower-houses appear to have been built as late as the first quarter of the 17th century, as at Ballinakill, said to have been erected by Sir Thomas Ridgeway between 1606 and 1612. Shrule has a date stone of 1640, and at Tintore there is a date stone in the fireplace of 1635. Two castles can be dated on historical grounds to the earlier period, Galesquarter to 1425 and Castlebrack to 1427. Bawns were found at six of the Laois tower-houses, and three of these had gun loops in their walls.

Offaly, which lies to the north and west of county Laois, has forty-three standing remains of tower-houses. The majority of these, like the Laois examples, can be dated to the later 16th and early 17th centuries. Many of the tower-houses in both counties can be attributed to the Laois/Offaly plantations of between 1556 and 1626. These counties form an almost square area in the midlands, within which the tower-houses are fairly evenly distributed, except for a central portion in the north-west of Laois. North-east Offaly, from Tullamore eastwards, has the remains of eight tower-houses, most, if not all, of which can be dated to the 15th century and are plainly influenced by the development of those found within the Pale, the one exception being Ballydrohid. A striking feature about the Laois/Offaly tower-houses, which is also true of most examples west of a north-to-south imaginary divide, is that they lack projecting angle towers and barrel vaults over the ground floor, which are features of the Pale, the south-east and north-east sites. Like most of the western and southern examples, they invariably have bartizans and are internally divided into large and small chambers at the upper levels. This can be clearly seen at Burnchurch, county Kilkenny, and Ballynahow, county Tipperary.

There are the remains of about 125 tower-houses in county Cork, thirty-one of which have bawns. With few exceptions, they are rectangular, four or five storeys high, and have barrel vaults over two floor levels. Their size and layout are typical of late 16th and 17th-century tower-houses of the western half of Ireland. The county Cork tower-houses are nearly always sited close to water with a solid coastal distribution, and are frequently located on promontories, some of which are on lakes or inlets.

20 – Carrigaphooca Castle, county Cork

left: 21 – Ballycowan, county Offaly; *right:* 22 – Clodah, county Cork

23 – Cloghleagh, county Cork

Cork has no simple towers like those of the Pale, and in common with the rest of the western examples, with a few exceptions they lack projecting angle towers. There are, however, examples of tower-houses with subsidiary towers that were added to give extra accommodation, as at Barryscourt, Kilcoe and Dunmanus West. These subsidiary towers are usually one storey higher than the main block.

As stated above, most of the Cork tower-houses have two vaults. Where the lower vault is over the ground floor, then the upper one is over the second floor, and when the lower one is over the first floor, the upper one is over the third. In some instances, such as at Dundeady and Dunlough, the vaults are corbelled like that found over the upper level at Termonfeckin, county Louth. The principal rooms and hall are invariably found directly over the vaulting, and the upper chamber will have contained the principal domestic quarters equipped with a large fireplace. Some have small side chambers, sometimes with small fireplaces, which were used as sleeping quarters. These upper levels are always well lit with large mullioned and transomed windows, often with seats in the embrasures and having decorated and carved stonework. These windows will frequently be ogee-headed with hood-mouldings.

A defensive feature in four of the Cork tower-houses is a gable-shaped oversailing found in the side walls, as seen at Raheen. The oversailing is pierced with musket holes so that fire can be directed at the base of the walls as well as providing flanking fire.[30] Another defensive feature found in county Cork that is not usual in tower-houses is a portcullis slot. The portcullis was placed just in front of the doorway or in the passage behind, and took the place of the more common yett (iron grille). The tower-houses with extant bawns are late in date, and this can also be seen in other counties such as Limerick, Clare and Galway. These bawns were defended by projecting mural towers with gun loops to provide flanking fire. At Ballincollig the tower is relatively insignificant, while the mural towers assumed a more important role and contained chambers with garderobes. Another variant is to be found at Mashanglass, where the rectangular tower-house has triangular bastions or spurs at its south-east and north-west angles to provide flanking fire. These bastions or spurs are only two storeys high with entrance at first-floor level, the ground floor being solid. Similar features are found at Ireton's Castle, Lehinch, county Tipperary, which is a Z-plan fortified house built *c*.1650.

Tower-houses were built mainly by large, wealthy landowners, both Gaelic and Old English, and they represent places of power and control in most of Munster. For instance, Barryscourt Castle [24] near Midleton, which is a large tower-house of the 15th century with later additions, was the chief seat of the Barrys in the cantred of Olethen. It is built on a slight rise in flat, low-lying land, and consists of a 15th-century rectangular block with tower added in the 16th century at the north-east and south-west angles. A projecting tower at the south-east angle is part of the original tower. The second-floor level, directly over the barrel vault, contains the principal rooms, and the hall is lit by large windows that have three lights and are transomed and mullioned, set in wide embrasures with seats. In the west wall is a fireplace with carved surround, which has a date stone of 1588. Unusually for tower-houses, Barryscourt has its own chapel contained within the building. A spiral stair gives access to the upper chambers, which are commodious, well lit, and supplied with fireplaces and garderobes.

Blarney, probably Ireland's most famous castle, was the principal residence of the MacCarthys, lords of Muskerry. It is spectacularly sited on

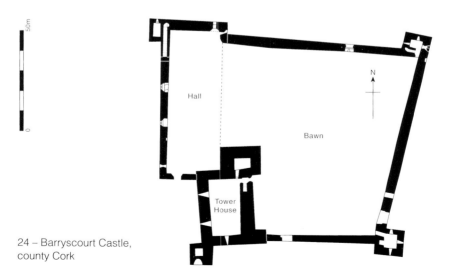

24 – Barryscourt Castle, county Cork

top of a limestone outcrop, overlooking the junction of two rivers. It was built in two phases, a primary tower (c.1480) of four storeys and a slightly later addition of five storeys. The addition of a second tower within a short period of time is a common feature of the later and larger tower-houses in the south-west. The opes for the most part are small and simple, and this, combined with its naturally defensive position and its extensive run of wall-top machicolations, makes it a formidable castle. Large oriel windows, as well as some other large windows, were inserted in the 16th century to let in more light. The third floor, which is one of the principal chambers, had two large fireplaces. The two towers work independently of each other. The earlier tower has small slit windows, while the later one has mullioned ones that appear to be part of the original structure. However, many of the windows have been widened and fireplaces have been inserted to make it more commodious.

There are over 200 standing remains of tower-houses in county Galway. They are similar in plan to the county Cork examples, and have much in common with those found in Clare, Limerick and Tipperary. The internal arrangements are the same as Cork in relation to the position of the vaults and the private chambers. Stairs are frequently intramural up to first-floor level, and spiral the rest of the way to the uppermost storey. Many of the late tower-houses of Galway are very well preserved, and often have large well-defended bawns with gatehouses and flanking towers. They have defensive features such as gun loops, machicolations, bartizans and portcullises. Some of the late tower-houses in Galway and elsewhere had no garderobes because the use of the chamber pot had become fashionable. In the late tower-house at Loughohery in south Tipperary there is a small chute in one of the angles at first-floor level, directly below an ope and gun loops. This chute exits at ground level like a garderobe but has no seating arrangement, and its position in the wall below the opes shows that it was designed merely to take away waste matter. Very fine examples of tower-houses in Galway with bawns are to be found at Fiddaun [29], Pallas and Aughnanure [26]. All three of these sites have inner and outer bawns, but Aughnanure is probably the best preserved. It was the stronghold of the O'Flahertys, and is sited near the shores of Lough Corrib on the Drimneen River. The outer bawn wall, which encloses a large irregular-shaped area, has four mural towers to provide flanking fire. In the south-west angle is the remains of a large hall. The tower-house is protected by an inner bawn wall, and is itself defended by bartizans. It has a gatehouse and drawbridge at the north-west. The plan of this tower-house and many of these late examples are reminiscent of the early large Anglo-Norman fortresses in that they are heavily defended and the tower acts as an isolated keep.

Like Blarney, county Cork, a number of the Galway tower-houses

25 – Derryhivenny, county Galway,
a late tower-house, almost house-like, with substantial bawn wall

26 – Aughnanure, county Galway

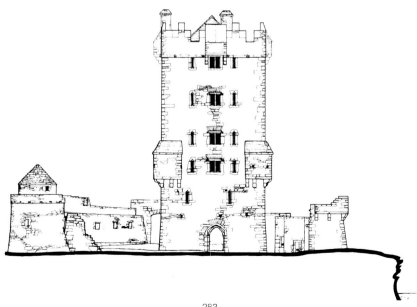

were constructed in two phases. The earlier one contains the stairs and small chambers, while the later tower has the main chambers. Ardamullivan, which is a late 16th-century structure, was built in two phases and is six storeys high. It has the remains of late medieval mural paintings at first- and fourth-floor level.

In the northern part of Ireland most of the tower-houses are similar to those found in the Pale, and are therefore mainly early simple types. Many of them, especially in county Down, have projecting towers breaking forward from the same wall, and sometimes, as at Ardglass, the entrance is situated between these angle towers. This type of tower-house is also to be found in Ardee, county Louth. These projecting towers, like those built on diagonally opposite angles, carry the stairs and garderobes. A feature of some of these northern tower-houses is that they have an arch at high level spanning the gap between the projecting towers which carries a chamber sited directly over the doorway. This feature is not solely confined to northern tower-houses, and can be seen at Ballyadams, county Laois, Bunratty, county Clare [18], and at Haynestown, county Louth [17]. Some of the northern tower-houses have bawns, such as Audley's Castle and Kirkistown, both in county Down. At Audley's Castle there are the remains of a hall-like building in the south-east angle of its bawn and a tower with gateway in the north-east. Kirkistown was built in 1622 and is a simple late tower-house type with no projecting towers. Narrowwater, county Down, is also similar, and is like some of the late western tower-houses such as Fiddaun, county Galway [27, 28], with their simple towers and substantial bawns. At Nendrum, county Down, the ground floor is divided into two separate chambers with no communication between them. One chamber contains the stair which gives access to the upper floors. This is the same type of plan to be seen at Haynestown, county Louth, and highlights the closeness of the tower-house types between those two counties.

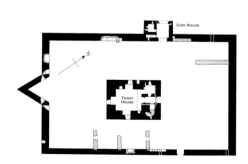

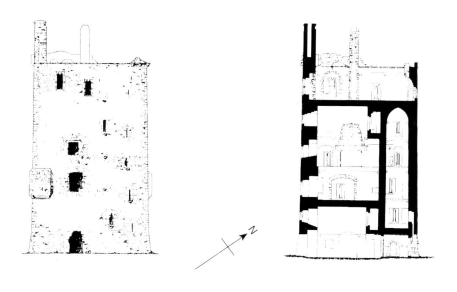

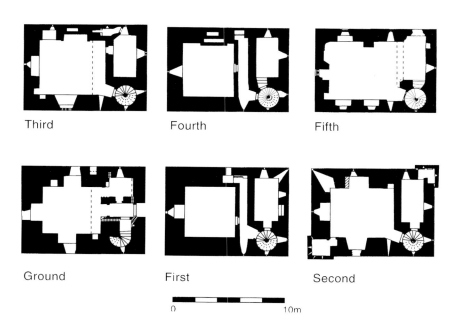

Third   Fourth   Fifth

Ground   First   Second

0   10m

Fiddaun Castle, county Galway, a late western tower-house
27 – plans, section and elevation; *opposite:* 28 – plan of tower-house and bawn

In summary, it can be stated that the tower-houses of the eastern half of the country, whether north or south, tend to be simple and date from the early part of the development of this type of castle. They also generally have projecting towers on some angles, and lack defensive features such as bartizans. The later tower-houses of the east are generally also simple, but they lack angle towers and often have well-defended bawns. The tower-houses of the midlands and the west can nearly all be assigned to the later part of the development, and are larger, more sophisticated and more commodious, having fireplaces and large windows. Some of the tower-houses of the western half of the country have relatively simple towers, but have substantial, well-defended bawns and gatehouses. Finally, I would argue that the origin of the tower-house lies in the later hall-houses of the east, such as Dunmoe, county Meath [6], and Kindlestown, county Wicklow, and this fits well with the early dating of the tower-houses of the Pale.

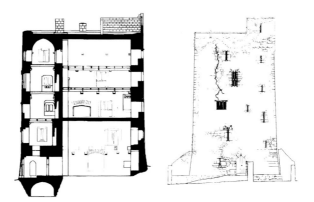

29 – Bourchier's Castle, Lough Gur, county Limerick

The author

David Sweetman MA, FSA, MRIAI is chief archaeologist in Dúchas (formerly the Office of Public Works). He is general editor of the county *Archaeological Survey* series, and has been widely published, with many archaeological excavation reports to his credit. He is a member of many academic bodies and learned societies both in Ireland and abroad. His most recent book is *Medieval Castles of Ireland* (Collins Press, Cork, 1999).

Acknowledgements

The author would like to thank Emer Condit for editing the paper, Antoinette Robinson for typing it, and Noel Jameson for inviting me to give the lecture. We would like to thank Dúchas for the illustrations.

Notes and References

[1] H Leask, *Irish castles and castellated houses* (Dundalk 1941), 75-7

[2] *ibid.*, 76-7

[3] T Barry, 'The archaeology of the tower-house in late medieval Ireland' in H Anderson and T Wienberg (eds), *The study of medieval archaeology*, 211-17 (Stockholm 1993) 211-15

[4] *ibid.*, 214

[5] T O'Keeffe, *Barryscourt Castle and the Irish tower-house* (Kinsale 1997) 8-13

[6] T Barry 'The last frontier: defence and settlement in late medieval Ireland' in T Barry, R Frame and K Simms (eds), *Colony and frontier in medieval Ireland*, 212-28 (London 1995) 217

[7] Leask, op. cit., 76

[8] Barry (1995), 222

[9] *ibid.*

[10] *ibid.*, 222

[11] *ibid.*, 223

[12] D Sweetman, *The medieval castles of Ireland* (Dublin 1999) 89-104

[13] A O'Sullivan and J Sheehan, *The Iveragh Peninsula: an archaeological survey of south Kerry* (Cork 1996) 365-9

[14] E Grogan and A Kilfeather, *Archaeological Inventory of county Wicklow* (Dublin 1997) 190

[15] Sweetman, op. cit., 64-5, 118-20

[16] *ibid.*, 143

[17] *ibid.*, pl. 12, fig. 73

[18] *ibid.*,137-62

[19] PD Sweetman, O Alcock and B Moran, *Archaeological Inventory of county Laois* (Dublin 1995) 110-16; V Buckley and PD Sweetman, *Archaeological Survey of county Louth* (Dublin 1991) 302-51; C O'Brien and PD Sweetman, *Archaeological Inventory of county Offaly* (Dublin 1997) 139-53; O Alcock, K de hÓra, and P Gosling, *Archaeological Inventory of county Galway, vol. II* (Dublin 1999) 393-418; C O'Brien and J Farrelly, *Archaeological Inventory of Tipperary North Riding* (forthcoming)

[20] Barry (1995), 220-1

[21] CT Cairns, *Irish tower-houses* (Athlone 1987) 5

[22] T Barry, *The archaeology of medieval Ireland* (London 1987)187-8; Barry (1993), 211

[23] T McNeill, *Castles in Ireland: feudal power in a Gaelic world* (London 1997), 211-29

[24] Barry (1993) 211

[25] Barry (1995) 220

[26] Buckley and Sweetman, op. cit., 301-60

[27] *ibid.*, 318-19, 329-31

[28] Leask, op. cit., 82-6

[29] Sweetman (1999), 158

[30] D Power, E Byrne, U Egan, S Lane and M Sleeman, *Archaeological Inventory of county Cork: West Cork, vol. I* (Dublin 1992) 329

THE BARRYSCOURT LECTURES

I – BARRYSCOURT CASTLE AND THE IRISH TOWER-HOUSE
Tadhg O'Keeffe
ISBN 0946641 82X, 1997, 32 pages, illus, £4.95

II – THE IMPACT OF THE ANGLO-NORMANS ON MUNSTER
AF O'Brien
ISBN 0946641 838, 1997, 32 pages, illus, £4.95

III – TECHNOLOGICAL CHANGE IN ANGLO-NORMAN MUNSTER
Colin Rynne
ISBN 0946641 846, 1998, 32 pages, illus, £4.95

IV – IRISH GARDENS AND GARDENING BEFORE CROMWELL
Terence Reeves-Smyth
ISBN 0946641 96X, 1999, 48 pages, illus, £4.95

V – OUTSIDE THE TOWER: RECENT EXCAVATIONS AT BARRYSCOURT
Dave Pollock
ISBN 0946641 978, 1999, 32 pages, illus, £4.95

VI – BARRYSCOURT CASTLE REFURNISHED
Victor Chinnery
(for publication: Nov 2000) ISBN 0946846 197, 32 pages, illus, £4.95

VII – ARCHAEOLOGY OF MEDIEVAL RURAL SETTLEMENT IN MUNSTER
Kieran O'Conor
(for publication: Dec 2000) ISBN 0946846 200, 32 pages, illus, £4.95

VIII – THE ORIGIN AND DEVELOPMENT OF THE TOWER-HOUSE IN IRELAND
David Sweetman
ISBN 0946846 294, 2000, 32 pages, illus, £4.95

IX – TOWNS IN MEDIEVAL IRELAND
Brian Graham
(lecture 20 Oct, for pub. Dec 2000) ISBN 0946846 60X, 32 pages, illus, £4.95

X – THE MEDIEVAL BARRY LORDSHIPS
Kenneth Nicholls
(lecture 21 May, for pub. July 2001) ISBN 0946846 618, 32 pages, illus, £4.95

XI – IRISH MEDIEVAL WALL-PAINTING
Karena Morton
(lecture Oct, for pub. Dec 2001) ISBN 0946846 626, 32 pages, illus, £4.95

THE BARRYSCOURT LECTURES ON MEDIEVAL IRELAND – vol. 1
(for publication: Spring 2001) ISBN 0946846 308, 280 pages, £25 clothbound

available from: Gandon Editions, Oysterhaven, Kinsale, Co Cork (tel 021-4770830)

BARRYSCOURT LECTURES

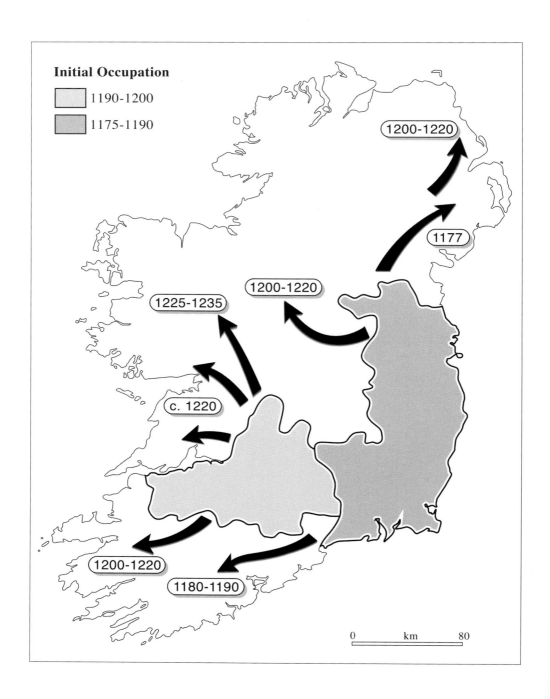

Initial Occupation

1190-1200

1175-1190

1200-1220

1177

1200-1220

1225-1235

c. 1220

1200-1220

1180-1190

0   km   80

1 – The Anglo-Morman colonisation of Ireland

Towns in Medieval Ireland

Brian Graham

THE BARRYSCOURT TRUST
IN ASSOCIATION WITH CORK COUNTY COUNCIL AND GANDON EDITIONS

INTRODUCTION

It was long held that the defining processes in the history of Irish economy and society between 1100 and 1500 resulted from the invasion of the Anglo-Normans in 1169 and their subsequent colonisation of much of the island. For GH Orpen, for example, the colonisation transformed an anarchic pre-Norman Gaelic Ireland into a 13th-century *Pax Normanica*, only for it to be shattered by the Gaelic Revival of the14th century.[1] Although Orpen's narrative was driven by his belief in the civilising qualities of the Anglo-Normans, its discussion of political, economic and social issues largely sets medieval Ireland apart from any broader consideration of contemporary events and processes in Britain and Europe. Conversely, the rapidly expanding historiography of medieval Ireland in recent years depicts a dynamic era of social and economic transformation, in which the Anglo-Norman colonisation played an important role, but cannot be regarded as the overriding causative process in these changes.[2]

It is the shift in ways of thinking about medieval Ireland that provides the basis for this discussion of urbanisation, in which towns are regarded as a product of society and in which it is assumed that certain processes of social change are required before towns can evolve. In particular, these include the emergence of a hierarchical social structure with an identifiable elite, flows of goods to dominant central places, and the emergence of politically organised territories. In Ireland these changes were probably well under way by the 9th century, while the 11th and 12th centuries saw the development of lordships very similar to feudal kingdoms in Europe. This chapter first considers three themes that underpin the discussion of towns in medieval Ireland and the relevance of urbanisation to the continuing debate on the nature of medieval Irish society. These are: continuity and change, regionalism and social diversity, and the interconnections between places and processes of social change. The themes are used to explore the processes of urbanisation and commercialisation that so clearly define medieval Ireland.

———

THE THEMES

Continuity and Change

Continuity and change refers here to the surprisingly complex interrelationships between the Gaelic and Anglo-Norman worlds, and the ways in which both societies were transformed though their mutual interaction.

Continuity can mean no more than the relatively simple idea of permanence of settlement and site within the limitations of the physical environment, or the constraints placed upon Anglo-Norman activities in Ireland by existing political and social institutions and geographical boundaries. Continuity, however, is also a politically sensitive concept in that it can imply connotations of assimilation rather than change, whereby Irish society absorbed the Anglo-Normans, as it had the Vikings before them. Again, because assumptions of continuity can minimise the changes wrought within the indigenous medieval Irish world by invasion and colonisation, they possess obvious ideological resonances for Irish nationalist historiography. Viewed in this way, a theory of continuity can create a misleading impression of stasis, as did the unchanging order of things assumed in some traditional histories of Celtic Ireland.

When the Anglo-Normans' invasion began in 1169, the geography of Ireland and the nature of its economy and society were scarcely unknown to them. Long-established trading linkages existed between England, Wales and port towns such as Dublin, Waterford and Wexford, which had been founded by the Vikings in the 10th century. By the 12th century these entrepôts had fallen under the hegemony of Irish kings, who controlled a settled, bounded, if politically very fragmented society. The reform of the Irish church in the first half of the 12th century established the beginnings of a diocesan system and introduced continental religious orders, both processes that reflected the indigenous geography of local and regional secular power. Thus it is unsurprising that the Anglo-Normans used or modified existing Celtic and Norse land divisions and settlements, and adopted the geography of the reformed Roman church. Orpen's revolutionary interpretation of the Anglo-Norman invasion has now been modified to a distinctly more evolutionary model in which the Anglo-Normans are seen to have simultaneously built upon, but were also constrained by, existing political, social and settlement structures. Consequently, it is now generally accepted that the idea of a clear divide before and after 1169 is a product of scholarship, which concentrated upon either the documentary and archaeological sources for early medieval Irish history or those for the Anglo-Norman colony.

Nevertheless, revising the impact of the Anglo-Norman colonisation should not detract from its role as one of the most significant forces for social change in medieval Ireland. The political transformation of the Gaelic-Irish ruling classes, albeit connected to wider developments then taking place in Europe, owed much to the Anglo-Norman presence in Ireland. In turn, although never overwhelmed by the Gaelic-Irish world, Anglo-Norman society in Ireland was altered irrevocably by dealing with it, leading to the 'degeneracy' of the colony much bemoaned of in 14th-century government sources. This more complex interaction is summed up in the semantic transition from 'Anglo-Norman' to 'Anglo-Irish', the dating of which, it can be argued, varies according to the individual, institution, or part of the country being described.[3] As a generalisation, 'Anglo-Irish' seems a more accurate descriptor after c.1220, although it is highly debatable if the people so described would themselves have regarded their political identity as such, given that the term itself does not occur until the 14th century. Thus traditional explanations of Anglo-Irish decline, which stressed a Gaelic-Irish resurgence during the late 14th century and the 15th century, can no longer be sustained. Instead, contemporary explanations tend to be couched in terms of a fragmentation of power from an early date, one which produced complex and constantly shifting patterns of cultural and political interaction between Anglo-Irish and Gaelic lordships.

Regionalism and Diversity

The regionalisation of medieval Ireland has indeed long been recognised. Pre-Anglo-Norman Ireland was heavily fragmented into approximately 150 *tuatha* – tribal kingdoms – which formed the basis of the kinship system. In that system, every free man belonged to the kindred group or joint-family – the *fine* – each of which owed loyalty to the small rural community of the *tuath*. As FJ Byrne contends, this was geographically too limited an area to evolve into a state or lordship, while its king lacked military resources.[4] Gradually, however, during the 10th and 11th centuries, power became concentrated in the hands of over-kings who welded *tuatha* together and were able to mobilise armies, a process which must have been related to the growth of trade and to the Viking incursions and settlement that began in the 9th century. Bradley, for example, maintains that the extent of Viking settlement in Ireland has been seriously underestimated, and compares their transformation of the Irish economy to that of the Scandinavians in Normandy during the 10th century.[5] By the 12th century, the *tuatha* were giving way to much larger, embryonic feudal kingdoms administered by kings, on the Continental model.[6]

The basic geographical principles of the Anglo-Norman colonisation established by Orpen still largely hold. As Frame has long contended, Anglo-Norman Ireland has to be seen less as a single polity than as a patchwork of lordships, the boundaries of which were often identical to those of the pre-existing Gaelic-Irish kingdoms.[7] The irony, he argues, is that although this fragmented geography is widely recognised, the history of medieval Ireland has often been written from the perspective of the royal archives, which record the attempts to impose centralised government across the island.[8] The regionalisation of Anglo-Norman Ireland was also a function of the island's complicated distribution of mountains, hills and boglands. The colonisers sought the good agricultural soils and avoided the wet, continuity being more than merely a matter of expediency or politics, but evidence that the Anglo-Normans understood the interconnections between the distribution of arable cultivation and the monastic and secular centres of early medieval Ireland. But the rich all-purpose grassland soils which they coveted were also fragmented and located in different parts of the lowlands, thereby emphasising the importance of these various nuclear zones for regional sub-cultures.[9]

Indeed, the modern idea in which a bipolar Gaelic and Anglo-Norman medieval Ireland is replaced by a hybrid society, one that became markedly more diverse as the centralising influence of the English crown progressively waned in the 14th and 15th centuries, depends on this regionalisation of the island, forged through a combination of politics, processes of continuity, and its physical geography. Cosgrove sees Ireland at the end of the Middle Ages as a synthesis of *Saxain*, *Gaill* and *Gáedhil* – respectively the English, the English-by-blood but born and usually resident in Ireland, and the Gaelic-Irish.[10] Descent did not define allegiance, nor did ethnicity define territory. Away from the nominal English suzerainty of the region around Dublin, power was heavily fragmented, so much so, in fact, that it has been argued that any history of Ireland in this period can only comprise a series of local histories.

Interconnected Places and Processes

In one sense, this final theme clearly overlaps with the idea of regional diversity in that, as Robin Frame argues, a multiplicity of interactions allowed apparently irreconcilable societies to coexist within Ireland, meanwhile permitting the Crown to negotiate complex accommodations that allowed it to exercise influence far beyond the contracting regions under its direct control. More powerfully, however, the theme of interconnectedness is also defined by Ireland's role in the wider medieval world. As Davies contends, the Anglo-Normans did not consciously set out to conquer Ireland, nor did national ambitions or national animus inform their actions.[11] Instead, medieval Ireland and its urbanisation can be seen as part of a story of ever-shifting patterns of culture, economy, language, religion and rule across these islands and beyond.[12] In the earlier medieval period, for example, the Vikings had already drawn Ireland into extensive trading networks, later exploited by the Irish kings who took over control of the Viking (by then Hiberno-Norse) ports. Again the ecclesiastical reforms of the first half of the 12th century had drawn Ireland within the ambit of the Roman church, but not entirely at the expense of its own distinctive

Christian traditions. Interconnectedness thus created a diversity of influences, which intermeshed with Ireland's own particularities in a web of spatially variable outcomes. Hence, medieval Ireland can be interpreted as part of several overlapping worlds – the Gaelic, the British Isles, northwest European feudalism.

While this reading is anathema to nationalist historians of Ireland, the argument that the relationships that defined the archipelago were feudal rather than colonial remains a persuasive one. Frame envisages a medieval political development of the British Isles within which a feudal aristocracy helped foster institutional and cultural uniformity.[13] His emphasis on a commonality of social structures is an important corrective too in the sense that pre-Anglo-Norman society had already evolved distinctly feudal traits, which cannot therefore be attributed simply to the Anglo-Norman invasion and colonisation. Moreover, medieval Ireland's geographical interconnectivity extended beyond the archipelago. The Anglo-Norman colonisation was part of a much more extensive movement of peoples throughout Europe during the 12th and 13th centuries, while the island was increasingly drawn into a north-west European, Anglo-Norman cultural ambit. Thus, medieval Ireland shared in the many means – lordship, incastellation, manorial system, chartered borough, and the market patent – which had evolved in France, Germany and Britain to put into practice, or articulate, feudal economic and social obligations.

———

THE GEOGRAPHY OF ECONOMY AND SOCIETY IN MEDIEVAL IRELAND

These three themes combine to inform the current understanding of the medieval economy and society of Ireland in which urbanisation was a key process. Although once regarded as having had a devastating effect, the impact of the Viking incursions and subsequent settlement in the 9th and 10th centuries has now been qualified and revised into a more assimilative model in which the Hiberno-Norse contributed to, but did not cause, the profound changes already occurring in Irish society. While pre-Viking trade appears to have been primarily with Britain and north-west Europe, it does seem that Ireland became part of a northern trading network during the 9th and 10th centuries. But all the evidence of the extensive archaeological excavations of Viking Dublin points to a rapid restoration of the routes to south-west England and France, as the Vikings became assimilated into Irish society during the 11th century. The material artefacts found in Viking Dublin were neither Viking nor Celtic nor Anglo-

Saxon, but related rather to a common north-west European milieu. Thus, Ireland was being integrated into that world long before the Anglo-Norman colonisation of the late 12th century.[14]

The key processes of change in Irish society between the 9th and 11th centuries concerned the emergence of a redistributive, hierarchical, rank society, which subsumed the previous system, defined by reciprocity and kinship. A redistributive structure, which is based on clientship and defined by flows of goods towards dominant central places, is a prerequisite for urbanisation in that it reflects the evolution of a social hierarchy based upon the power to control production. A class of peasant rent-payers probably emerged in Ireland as early as the 9th century, together with the concept of dynastic overlordship. The 11th and 12th centuries saw the development of lordships very similar to feudal kingdoms in Europe – essentially bounded embryonic states governed by kings who were sufficiently powerful to launch military campaigns and fortify their territories. The earliest indications of systematic incastellation in Ireland date to the very late 10th century, when Brian Boruma constructed a succession of fortresses in Munster. By the 12th century, the Ua Briain kings of Thomond and the Ua Conchobair kings of Connacht are recorded as constructing networks of castles to consolidate their control over their respective kingdoms.[15]

In concert with this transformation of secular society, the remarkably diverse and very secular Irish Church was also being changed by 12th-century reform, a process which began before the Anglo-Norman invasion but markedly accelerated after it. The creation of a parochial system was heavily influenced by the delimitation of the Anglo-Norman manorial structure, the boundaries of which it generally shared. Patronage by feudal lords lay at the heart of the acquisition of Church lands, and by the later 13th century there was little to distinguish the abbeys from the other great landowners of the age. As was the norm elsewhere in the feudal societies of north-west Europe, magnates of the Church, such as archbishops of Dublin, who held a whole succession of manors around the fringes of the city, were also great secular lords.

The Anglo-Norman soldiers who came to Ireland in 1169 were not embarked on a systematic conquest, but rather were mercenaries enlisted by the deposed king of Leinster, Diarmait Mac Murchada, in an attempt to regain his territories. They were led by ambitious Welsh marcher lords such as Robert fitz Stephen and Richard fitz Gilbert de Clare, far better known as Strongbow. Giraldus Cambrensis sums up their motivations when he remarks of Strongbow that his name was greater than his prospects, name, and not possessions, being his principal inheritance. To these freebooters, Ireland, situated beyond the immediate control of the English crown, offered opportunities of power, wealth, land and prestige likely to be denied to them in their homelands by the feudal laws of primogeniture. They took their chances, and thus the initial Anglo-Norman colonisation of Ireland was very much a question of individual enterprise and initiative. As Ó Corráin argues, Diarmait's invitation inevitably become an invasion, while the initial Anglo-Norman colonisation of Ireland, like most great changes in history, was its unforeseen and unplanned consequence.[16]

The crown did become involved more systematically following Henry II's visit to Ireland in 1171-72, although the king's intentions have been the subject of some debate. What is not is dispute, however, is that Henry had received the homage of the hierarchy of the Irish church as well as that of the Gaelic-Irish kings and Anglo-Norman barons by the time of his departure from Ireland in 1172. Nonetheless, the tensions that ultimately were to ensure the intense territorial fragmentation of later medieval Ireland were already apparent from the outset of the Anglo-Norman colonisation. By granting major lordships, while lacking the resources or inclination to conquer Ireland, the crown abrogated substantial powers, which often made individual barons remote from the mechanisms of government established in Dublin. However, these magnates also required the rewards and social prestige which the Crown could confer, and, to some extent, most were 'royalist'. Consequently, Flanagan sees 'improvisation' as having been the defining characteristic of Anglo-Norman Ireland, Henry and his successors lacking the time, men, resources and control over the adventurer-settlers of Ireland to adopt any other strategy.[17]

Empey regards the concept of lordship as simultaneously embracing the personal ties which mutually bound lord and vassal, with the idea of a bounded territory in which the lord exercised his prerogatives.[18] In a parallel fashion, the manor – the essential subdivision of the lordship and the focal point of the new social and economic order – was a military, economic, social and juridical institution, and a geographical unit. The boundaries of lordships and their internal subinfeudation were often identical to those of the pre-existing Gaelic-Irish kingdoms. One of the best examples is Henry II's charter of 1172 granting Meath to Hugh de Lacy to hold, as the Ua Mael Sechlainn kings of Midhe had before him. By the mid-13th century the Anglo-Normans had colonised some two-thirds of the island [1]. In those areas beyond their direct imprint, including most of Ulster, much of the west coast, part of the central lowlands, and almost all the uplands, a degree of Gaelic-Irish political autonomy was preserved, as was a social and economic system which, as we will see, was somewhat different to that of the colony. As Nicholls states, however, the extant documentation of this society is so deficient and late that only a few deductions can be hazarded for the 150 years following the Anglo-Norman invasion.[19]

The spatial relationships between the two broad medieval cultures were complex, ambiguous and dynamic, and never fully resolved, although the Church and the economy provided powerful unifying bonds.

The initial Anglo-Norman settlements were often but not necessarily located at existing centres of power. This continuity could be no more than simple expediency, reflecting the extant distribution of resources and population and the need to redistribute land rapidly, or even an attempt to capture and replace the structures of Gaelic-Irish political power. Everywhere the Anglo-Normans embarked on a conscious process of incastellation throughout their lordships. Many early fortifications were earthwork mottes or ringworks, but from the beginning major castles were built in stone, arguably symbolic of a commitment to the new lands and evidence of an intention to stay and transform them. Stone fortresses such as Trim and Carrickfergus were designed for defence, but also to reflect the prestige of their lords and to act as the centres of administration in their respective fiefdoms.[20]

The establishment of military hegemony over lordship and manor underpinned the subsequent development of the Anglo-Norman colonisation. We know little about the demography of the Anglo-Norman colony or of the origins and numbers of migrants who settled on the Irish manors. Estimates of the medieval population of Ireland, c.1300, range from 400,000 to 800,000, although it is impossible to calculate the ratio of Anglo-Norman to Gaelic Irish. Although the immigration of large numbers of peasants into 13th-century Ireland is an important factor demarcating its experience from that of England after the Norman conquest of 1066, there is no evidence of the nobility using middlemen – the *locatores* of eastern Europe – to organise this movement. Hence, Empey regards Wales as being the best exemplar for Ireland, its Anglo-Norman colonisation also being shaped by the requirements of a military aristocracy rather than the broad-based peasant movement characteristic of central and eastern Europe.[21]

The agricultural economy formed the basis of all production in Anglo-Norman Ireland. The essential problem for feudal landholders was how to develop and maintain the rural economy. It is likely that the Anglo-Normans expanded and extended existing systems of agricultural production, not least because these were subject to the constraints of the physical environment. They colonised the fertile but fragmented grassland soils and controlled the two richest grain-growing areas in the island, which were located in the south-east along the rivers Barrow and Nore, and around the Boyne in the lordship of Meath. Arable production seems to have been particularly significant up to 1300, although grazing was always important.

Cereal growing began to contract in the 14th century, partly because of changing patterns of agricultural output in Ireland, these being heavily influenced by the demands of the English market. During the 13th century, grain production had been bolstered by the system of purveyance for the royal armies. Growing resistance by merchants, resentful of the long delays that occurred in payment, combined with declining production in Irish agriculture to end purveyance in the 1320s.[22] The decline in cereal production is also indicative of a succession of internal crises which marked the first half of the 14th century in Ireland. Lyons' account of the relationship between population, famine and plague concludes that the demographic base of the Anglo-Norman colony was probably substantially eroded in the late 13th and early 14th centuries.[23] Famine occurred with increasing frequency after c.1270, and later the great north European famine coincided with the very considerable political instability and warfare within Ireland, brought about by the Bruce invasion of 1315-18. Moreover, the early part of the 14th century seems to have been exceptionally wet. Thus Lyons emphasises that the economic downturn in medieval Ireland occurred long before the first visitation of the Black Death in 1348-50. It is possible that the Anglo-Irish population could have been almost halved by the end of the 14th century because of plague, although Lyons believes that its impacts varied regionally, being most profound in Leinster and close to the ports.

In traditional medieval historiography, this half-century of crisis was regarded as having precipitated the final decline of the Anglo-Norman colony, and thus provided one key element in the explanation of economic and social change after c.1300. The other was the notion of a Gaelic revival or resurgence, a concept that embraces both cultural and territorial dimensions in that it implied a return to Gaelic values and physical reconquest. Recent historiography, however, points to a more complex set of interactions, and also to the conclusion that decline has been exaggerated. There is, however, minimal research into the type of structural transformation that occurred in later 14th-century England, and we know little of the ways in which feudal social and property relationships were being dissolved in Ireland or of the consequences for landholding and settlement. Rather, the debate on the later 14th century is dominated by the revision of the Gaelic Resurgence. The idea of a static Gaelic-Irish society acting as a repository for age-old traditions is now widely regarded as the conscious creation of 14th-century scholars who provided the intellectual justification for the late-medieval Gaelic-Irish lords. Moreover, although the reasons are not adequately researched, there was an economic revival in the later 14th century, a recovery best symbolised by the first appearance of rural and urban tower-houses. These tall, rectilinear keep buildings were probably largely built by a new class of freeholding lesser lords, both Gaelic and Anglo-Irish. Although possessing some limited defensive merit, they are now seen as essentially domestic structures, while the availability of the financial resources sufficient to construct an estimated 7,000 tower-houses in the late 14th century and the 15th century fits ill with the concept of an economic crisis or a Gaelic Revival.[24]

Contemporary explanations portray a more complex interaction between Gaelic-Irish and Anglo-Irish Ireland at this time, and also a very marked geographical variation in those relationships. Frame maintains that the dichotomy was real enough, but sees it as representing two poles or limits rather than defining the reality of life for much of the population.[25] Large swathes of Ireland remained in the hands of the Anglo-Irish aristocracy although not necessarily within the remit of the Dublin government. The area under its control contracted during the first half of the 15th century to the Pale – the fortified, but still relatively permeable frontier that extended around the four counties of Louth, Meath, Dublin and Kildare. Elsewhere political fragmentation and a loss of central government control produced a mosaic of autonomous and semi-autonomous Gaelic-Irish and Anglo-Irish lordships. Smyth cogently sums up the 15th century as the fusion of a number of relatively powerful port-centred economic regions with the administrative-political superstructures of the great lordships.[26] Beyond these core territories lay rural-based, less stratified and generally (though not invariably) smaller political lordships. The hybridisation of this society is recorded in the finely differentiated cultural geography that can be reclaimed from the patterns of naming of places and people. Given the lack of central government records, documentation is very deficient, but it is probable that a semblance of the manorial economy continued, while economic differences between Gael and Gall became less marked. Certainly, as the evidence of urbanisation also attests, there is little to suggest that the political decline of the English crown in Ireland in the 15th century was necessarily matched by any real transformation in the socioeconomic structure.

MEDIEVAL IRISH URBANISATION

The few Viking ports excepted, it was once assumed that the Anglo-Normans were responsible for the initial urbanisation of Ireland. In marked contrast, a well-established case can now be sustained that not only were the Hiberno-Norse towns much more substantial than was previously imagined, but also that indigenous urbanisation developed in the earlier medieval period around monastic and secular cores. The extent of Hiberno-Norse urbanisation in the 11th and 12th centuries, particularly at

Dublin, Waterford, Wexford and Limerick, has been corroborated by archaeological investigation. Hiberno-Norse Dublin was an organised, planned town with property plots, houses and defences, very much part of the wider Anglo-Norman world prior to the invasion. Moreover, excavation has demonstrated the striking continuity of house plots and property boundaries from the 10th to the 13th century, the Anglo-Normans not making any major effort to develop, improve or enlarge the city for at least thirty years after it fell under their control.

The dating and meaning of indigenous urbanisation is, however, much more obscure. There is a significant danger of 'urbanisation by assertion', while claims that substantial towns existed around Irish monasteries as early as the 7th century should be treated with circumspection.[27] Nevertheless, as early as c.1000, several centuries before the Anglo-Norman invasion, the economic and political benefits of defended urban settlements were already apparent, while the Viking towns all fell under the suzerainty of Irish kings during the 11th century. As the defended town accompanied the growth of centralised authority throughout medieval Europe, it is difficult to conceive that those self-same Irish leaders were not engaged in efforts to stimulate urban development around their principal seats of power. Often these were located next to monasteries, or at sites where the monastery now appears as the more readily identifiable artefact. Because of its cause-effect implications, the term 'monastic town', which occurs widely in the literature, is ambiguous and probably best avoided. Many extant ecclesiastical monuments of this period actually reflect the exercise of royal patronage rather than the centrality within early medieval Irish society of religious ceremonial centres, nor is there anything unusual in European medieval towns developing around monastic cores. In ways not yet fully understood, it seems probable that, following the example of the Hiberno-Norse towns, which were themselves influenced by the Anglo-Saxon burhs of England, Irish kings were increasingly involved in the development of an indigenous urbanisation during the 11th and 12th centuries, a process that occurred around both castle and monastic cores.

Despite the many difficulties of the evidence, it is apparent that the actual number of early medieval towns must have been very small. Further, there is nothing to suggest that the elaboration of a hierarchical urban network was anything other than an achievement of the Anglo-Normans, who, in addition to the Hiberno-Norse towns, adapted some settlements, including Kells, Kildare and Athlone, which were most probably examples of early medieval indigenous urbanisation. But continuity was not inevitable as other important early medieval sites attest. Glendalough, Clonmacnoise and Clonard, for example, largely disappear from the documentary record, apparently because they sank into decline soon after the invasion. It could be that they were poorly located with regard to the colonists' scheme of settlement, or, conversely, that they were the victims of deliberate neglect as the Anglo-Normans consciously consolidated their political control by undermining existing mechanisms and centres of power. It might also be inferred that these settlements possessed only the most limited urban economic and morphological structures if they could be so readily abandoned.

The medieval urbanisation of Ireland was simply part of a much more extensive development of European towns during the 12th and 13th centuries. The chartered borough was one of the 'standard' methods of economic development employed throughout medieval Europe.[28] For example, many such settlements were established in Normandy, England and Wales by feudal lords from the 11th century onwards, the pace of foundation accelerating rapidly after 1100. The lord granted a charter which gave tenants, or burgesses, the rights to a plot of land – the burgage – within a borough on which to build a house, and usually a small acreage outside the settlement with access, for example, to woodland (for building timber and firewood), peat bog and grazing. Theoretically, at least, burgesses were also granted a range of economic privileges and monopolies. The most common package of borough rights in Anglo-Norman Ireland was that modelled on the charter of the small Normandy town of Breteuil-sur-Iton.

While the borough charter held the promise of urban life, much of this potential was never translated into reality. Those boroughs that did evolve into towns generally possessed salient political and economic advantages. Inevitably, the capital manors of the most important and powerful lords were the first Anglo-Norman settlements to be granted charters in the various Irish lordships. Dominated by motte or stone castles, their sites were chosen with regard to strategic factors such as control of territories and communications, and are thus often one of the most obvious explanations of continuity. That these settlements were likely to become the largest towns replicated the experience of medieval England, where an early arrival was the most significant contribution to eventual urban prosperity.[29]

Such towns, however, were relatively few in number – as were great lords. Colonisation of the lordships, and even the manors retained by the major magnates, was largely the responsibility of those whom Empey calls immediate lords of the soil.[30] Thus the majority of medieval Irish boroughs were founded by Anglo-Norman fiefholders of comparatively minor significance, and functioned as the market places necessary to the mutual dependence of peasantry and aristocracy. Their market tolls, fines, rents and taxes were a source of profit for feudal lords, while the peasantry could convert surplus production into cash – an increasingly important process as labour services were commuted in favour of money rents.[31] The custom of Breteuil was granted freely, however, and despite their legal status, most boroughs were never more than agricultural settlements.

Approximately 330 medieval Irish boroughs have been identified [2]. There may well have been more as only a very few possess extant charters, the remainder being identified from stray references to burgages and burgesses. These settlements can best be classified by their roles in the feudal economy. No more than twenty-five can be categorised as major towns, but a further eighty settlements possessed sufficient evidence of urban criteria to be classified as small towns, operating as the principal market centres within which peasant exchange occurred. Almost 70% of these developed around a castle core, a proportion very similar to that found in Normandy. The remaining chartered settlements can be classified as agricultural rural boroughs. Although manorial extents record some specialisation of labour – millers, bakers, brewers and the like – their burgess populations were largely agriculturalists. It seems likely that this wholesale creation of speculative boroughs provided one means of attracting tenants to the Irish manors, burgess status and the expectation of freedom from all but the most minimal of labour services acting as a lure to prospective peasant migrants.

In terms of morphology, most towns seem to have had a predominantly linear layout.[32] The houses often had their gable ends to the street with burgages behind. As elsewhere in Europe, these long thin plots, generally held at a rent of 12d per annum, were perhaps the diagnostic morphological features of the Irish medieval town. The market place, occasionally marked by a market cross, was either the main street of a linear town or sometimes a triangular extension at one end. A few town plans were more elaborate, the most common such form, as at Clonmel, Carrick-on-Suir or Drogheda, being an irregular chequer. Uniquely, Kells developed on a concentric plan, presumably dictated by its pre-Anglo-Norman morphology.[33] Around fifty medieval Irish towns were walled, the most intensive period of construction occurring between 1250 and 1320. Not all walls were of stone, a number being of suitably reinforced earth, while the larger towns had between four and six gates. The most extensive enclosed areas were at Drogheda and Kilkenny, which were both twin boroughs, while New Ross was the largest unitary walled town.[34]

Little is known about the relationships between urbanisation and the economic organisation of the lordships. Within any one territory, the network of towns and boroughs presumably acted as the framework for marketing circuits of the type identified in medieval England. Here, markets were granted on different days in the various boroughs so that middlemen, who collected the tolls, and itinerant traders could travel around from place to place. Very limited evidence points to similar arrangements

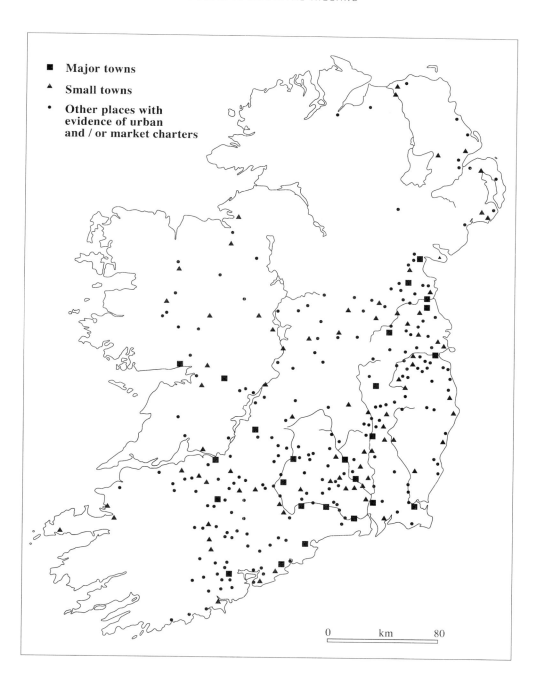

■ Major towns

▲ Small towns

• Other places with
evidence of urban
and / or market charters

0   km   80

2 – Towns and chartered boroughs in medieval Ireland, *c.*1130

within individual lordships in Anglo-Norman Ireland. But nowhere can the precise hierarchical relationships of settlements be worked out. Again, there is very little information on the urban division of labour. From the evidence of manorial extents, it can be assumed that the populations of rural boroughs were essentially agriculturalists, but even in the small market towns and larger mercantile centres, the degree of non-agricultural employment is unclear. Presumably, most industry took the form of food processing. There must also have been craftsmen of various sorts in the towns, but rarely is any evidence found of them.

Medieval Ireland's external trade was largely conducted through the twenty-five major towns, a process which is unusually well recorded because of the survival of customs returns for the period between 1276 and 1333.[35] The south-eastern ports of New Ross and Waterford, which served the fertile and densely colonised valleys of the Nore, Barrow and Suir, dominated Ireland's overseas trade with Britain and continental Europe, accounting for almost 50% of the customs receipts paid during this period. Cork, Dublin and Drogheda were also significant ports, while the most important inland town was Kilkenny, centre of one of the greatest of the private lordships. The major towns were either directly in the hands of the Crown or, conversely, held by the most powerful baronial families for whom the settlements were vital economic assets. Youghal, for example, provided over 60% of the income of the estates of the lords of Inchiquin in the late 13th century.

Urban populations – and those of the rural boroughs too – seem to have been primarily colonial. The major towns were dominated socially and economically by a burgess class of artisans, traders and merchants, most probably organised into guilds. But that is not to say that the Gaelic-Irish were excluded, for people with Gaelic names were always present in towns. There must have been some form of segregation, however, because 'Irishtowns', presumably inhabited by people of Gaelic-Irish ancestry, survive in a number of medieval towns, including Ardee, Athlone, Clonmel, Drogheda, Dublin, Enniscorthy and New Ross, while those at Kilkenny and Limerick were both separately walled. Indeed, Irishtown at Kilkenny possessed its own borough constitution. Again, there may have been separate suburbs in Dublin, Waterford, Wexford, Cork and Limerick for the descendants of the Hiberno-Norse – the Ostmen.

Direct demographic evidence is rare and we are largely dependent on urban population estimates, which have been calculated from data on burgage rent. These assume the standard rent of 12d per burgage and a household multiplier of five, a calculation that excludes the non-burgess household in a town and overlooks the evidence that 'burgages', particularly in smaller settlements, may have included agricultural land. Total burgage rents must therefore often have included the latter, and thus cannot always be used to calculate burgess populations. Given these vagaries, estimates suggest that very few towns had populations in excess of 2,000, while most had fewer than 1,000 inhabitants. Although projections for Dublin range from 10,000 to 25,000, the next largest town seems to have been New Ross, which, based on evidence from burgage rents, may have had a population of between 2,500 and 3,000. There is, however, no demographic data at all for a number of important towns, including Limerick, Cork, Drogheda and Waterford. Again, we know little of the impact of the Black Death of 1348-50 on urban populations, although one contemporary account talks about the cities of Dublin and Drogheda being almost destroyed and 'wasted of men'.

A further enigma in relation to medieval urbanisation in Ireland concerns those parts of the island, especially in the north and west, but also in the midlands, which lay beyond the area of Anglo-Norman colonisation. It is difficult to conceive that the Gaelic leaders in these regions lacked contacts with the colonists, if only through war. There is, moreover, evidence of intermarriage, while many Anglo-Norman lords were assimilated to some extent into Gaelic society. Why, then, did Gaelic lords not adopt the concept of towns as a means of developing a territory when in eastern Europe, for example, Slavic princes followed the model of German settlers and became enthusiastic sponsors of towns? The problem is exacerbated by the absence of documentary evidence that might compare to the fiscal and legal records of Crown administration in medieval Ireland, which provide much of the evidence of Anglo-Norman urbanisation. The pastoral nature of the economy may have militated against urbanisation, restricting its occurrence to a handful of ecclesiastical centres such as Armagh, Clogher and Clonfert. Another example, Rosscarbery, was described as a walled town with two gates and almost two hundred houses in 1519. One interesting possibility concerns Killaloe, where the borough may have been incorporated prior to the Anglo-Norman settlement of the lower Shannon region. But the only other evidence of Gaelic lords founding chartered settlements, either immediately before or after the invasion, concerns a solitary and probably abortive attempt to establish a market. Nor (Sligo excepted) does there appear to be any record of an Anglo-Norman borough continuing to exist under a Gaelic secular lord during the 15th and 16th centuries.

In contrast, ample evidence survives to show that Gaelic lords were enthusiastic builders of castles, and these may have acted as nuclei for settlement agglomerations and exchange. Nevertheless, virtually nothing is known of the organisation of marketing in Gaelic Ireland, any evidence being very late. Towards the end of the 15th century, for example, English merchants in the ancient market towns of Meath were complaining about Irish markets at Cavan, Longford and Granard, which suggests that these may have been a recent development. But in terms of the evidence, it is not until the 16th century that a 'real town' of Gaelic provenance grew up under the protection of the O'Reillys at Cavan.

Meanwhile, there seems to have been a substantial continuity of urbanisation in the Anglo-Irish lordships. The fate of the several hundred rural boroughs is obscure, not least because of gaping lacunae in the documentary record. Deserted medieval settlements can be identified in the landscape, but it is exceptionally difficult to date their abandonment. Some evidence suggests, however, that the principal period of desertion of medieval settlements did not occur until the 17th century. Few larger towns disappeared, and indeed there is ample evidence of urban wealth in the 15th century. Trade continued to flourish with England and Europe and between the various Irish lordships. Town walls were maintained, or even expanded, while urban tower-houses and substantial church building attest to the existence of wealthy urban elites. Thus, the evidence of urbanisation and commercialisation again supports the conclusion that the political decline of the English in late medieval Ireland was not matched by a parallel downturn in the economy.

―――――

CONCLUSION

The transformation of Irish economy and society in the later Middle Ages, which shared many similarities with that of Britain and north-west Europe, provided the context for the evolution and subsequent development of urbanisation. The Anglo-Normans adapted to, but also irrevocably altered extant political and economic structures. In turn, they borrowed much from Gaelic-Irish culture and exploited its political fragmentation to create the system of lordships that, through time, further accentuated the intense regionalism of Ireland so readily apparent in early medieval society. By the end of the Middle Ages, the complex threads of continuity and change had combined to create an Ireland that was highly decentralised in political terms, culturally diverse, yet possessing some salient economic unity through the continuing importance of the mercantile economy which integrated it into the wider European realm. The inability of the crown to establish centralised English political control over Ireland was essentially predestined by the abrogation of power to individual barons in the early years of the Anglo-Norman colonisation. Yet this political failure cannot conceal the enduring strength of the urban and commercial economy, particularly after the upturn of the later 14th century – the factor which above all others demonstrates the oversimplification inherent in the concept of a Gaelic Revival. Fourteenth and 15th-century Ireland maintained its trading links with Britain and Europe, some of the more distant ports, such as Galway, with its rich Iberian trade, effectively functioning as 'city states'. Changes did take place and there was some attenuation of Anglo-Irish settlement in the more exposed marches. But the well-established communities of the more intensely settled arable regions survived, and indeed prospered, despite the more militant and effective system of Gaelic-Irish opposition already apparent in the 14th century. In sum, while fragmentation defines the condition of Ireland throughout the Middle Ages, it had become a remarkably more diverse society by 1500, testimony to the myriad interactions between Anglo-Irish and Gaelic-Irish, and the innumerable permutations thereof.

The author

Brian Graham is Professor of Human Geography and Director of the Academy for Irish Cultural Heritages at the University of Ulster.

Endnotes

[1] GH Orpen, *Ireland under the Normans* (Oxford, 1911-20; reprinted 1968)

[2] See, for example, BJ Graham and LJ Proudfoot (eds), *An Historical Geography of Ireland* (London, 1993); TB Barry (ed.), *A History of Settlement in Ireland* (London, 2000)

[3] FX Martin, 'Introduction: Medieval Ireland', in A Cosgrove (ed.), *A New History of Ireland II: Medieval Ireland, 1169-1534* (Oxford, 1987) pl. iii

[4] FJ Byrne, *Irish Kings and High Kings* (London, 1973)

[5] J Bradley, 'The interpretation of Scandinavian settlement in Ireland', in J Bradley (ed.), *Settlement and Society in Medieval Ireland* (Kilkenny, 1988) pp49-78

[6] BJ Graham, 'Early medieval Ireland: settlement as an indicator of economic and social transformation, c.500-1100', in Graham and Proudfoot (eds), *An Historical Geography of Ireland*, pp19-57

[7] See, for example, R Frame, *The Political Development of the British Isles, 1100-1400* (Oxford, 1990)

[8] R Frame, *Ireland and Britain, 1170-1450* (London, 1998)

[9] WJ Smyth, 'The meaning of Ireland: agendas and perspectives in cultural geography', in Graham and Proudfoot (eds), *An Historical Geography of Ireland*, pp339-438

[10] See the chapters by Cosgrove in Cosgrove (ed.), *A New History of Ireland I*, pp525-90

[11] RR Davies, *Domination and Conquest: The Experience of Ireland, Scotland and Wales, 1100-1300* (Cambridge, 1990)

[12] See, for example, S Howe, *Ireland and Empire: Colonial Legacies in Irish History and Culture* (Oxford, 2000)

[13] Frame, *Political Development of the British Isles*

[14] See, for example, P Wallace, *The Viking Age Buildings of Dublin* (Dublin, 1992)

[15] BJ Graham, 'Medieval timber and earthwork fortifications in medieval Ireland',

Medieval Archaeology, xxxii (1988) pp110-29; 'Medieval settlement in County Roscommon', *Proceedings of the Royal Irish Academy*, 88c (1988) pp19-38

[16] D Ó Corráin, *Ireland before the Normans* (Dublin, 1972)

[17] MT Flanagan, *Irish Society, Anglo-Norman Settlers, Angevin Kingship* (Oxford, 1989)

[18] CA Empey, 'Conquest and settlement patterns of Anglo-Norman settlement in North Minster and South Leinster', *Irish Economic and Social History*, 13 (1986) pp5-31

[19] K Nicholls, 'Gaelic society and economy in the High Middle Ages', in Cosgrove (ed.), *New History of Ireland II*, pp397-448

[20] T McNeill, *Castles in Ireland: Feudal Power in a Gaelic World* (London, 1997); D Sweetman, *The Medieval Castles of Ireland* (Cork, 1999)

[21] Empey, 'Conquest and settlement patterns'

[22] K Down, 'Colonial economy and society in the High Middle Ages', in Cosgrove (ed.), *New History of Ireland II*, pp439-91

[23] M Lyons, 'Weather, famine, pestilence and plague in Ireland, 900-1500', in EM Crawford (ed.), *Famine: The Irish Experience* (Edinburgh, 1989) pp31-74

[24] T O'Keefe, *Barryscourt Castle and the Irish Tower-House*, Barryscourt Lectures, no. 1 (Cork, 1997); T O'Keefe, *Medieval Ireland: An Archaeology* (Stroud, 2000)

[25] Frame, *Political Development of the British Isles*

[26] Smyth, 'The making of Ireland'

[27] BJ Graham, 'Urban genesis in early medieval Ireland', *Journal of Historical Geography*, 13 (1987) pp3-16; M Volante, 'Reassessing the Irish "monastic town"', *Irish Historical Studies*, xxxi, no. 121 (1998) pp1-18

[28] See, for example, A Simms, 'Core and periphery in medieval Europe: the Irish experience in a wider context', in WJ Smyth and K Whelan (eds), *The Common Ground: Essays on the Historical Geography of Ireland* (Cork, 1988) pp22-40

[29] M Beresford, *New Towns of the Middle Ages* (London, 1967)

[30] Empey, 'Conquest and settlement patterns'

[31] BJ Graham, 'The definition and classification of medieval Irish towns, *Irish Geography*, 21 (1988) pp20-32; 'The high middle ages: *c.*1100 to *c.*1350', in Graham and Proudfoot (eds), *An Historical Geography of Ireland*, pp58-98

[32] Detailed studies of individual medieval towns are to be found in the separate fascicles of A Simms and HB Clarke (eds), *Irish Historic Towns Atlas* (Dublin, various dates)

[33] A Simms and K Simms, *Irish Historic Towns Atlas: Kells* (Dublin, 1990)

[34] A Thomas, *The Walled Towns of Ireland* (Dublin, 1992)

[35] A particularly noteworthy regional account of urbanisation is provided by AF O'Brien, 'Politics, economy and society: the development of Cork and the Irish south-coast region *c.*1170 to *c.*1583', in P O'Flanagan and CG Buttimer (eds), *Cork: History and Society* (Dublin, 1994) pp83-156

———

BARRYSCOURT LECTURES

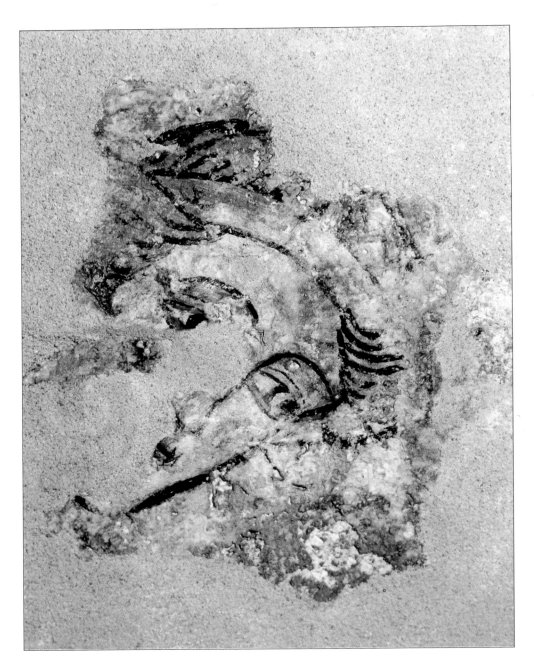

1 – Ardamullivan Castle, county Galway: detail showing the face of St Michael
The red colour in this photograph was analysed, and is red ochre with 1-4% cinnabar (vermilion).
(photo: Con Brogan, Dúchas, The Heritage Service)

THE BARRYSCOURT LECTURES X

Irish Medieval Wall Painting

Karena Morton

THE BARRYSCOURT TRUST
IN ASSOCIATION WITH CORK COUNTY COUNCIL AND GANDON EDITIONS

INTRODUCTION

Medieval wall paintings survive or are recorded in far greater numbers from Ireland than might be appreciated. Up to now, wall paintings collectively have not been the focus of study as reflected in the published literature. One reason for their apparent scarcity is that those that survive tend to be in a very deteriorated and fragmentary state, and are found in ruinous monuments. Many of the scholars who have commented on the known wall paintings felt that they were beyond repair. However, the rediscovery of wall paintings through recent conservation programmes has not only proved some of these predictions as being premature, but has significantly added to the wall-painting corpus.[1] This is further supplemented by new finds made through fieldwork investigation.

Wall paintings embellish the walls, vaults and carved architectural elements of buildings. All wall surfaces, whether flat or curved, whether plain, lime-washed or plastered, could be painted. Paint was used to accentuate details of carved architectural elements. Red can be made out on several capitals, as well as the window arches, in the chancel at Corcomroe Abbey, county Clare, and on the capitals of the piscina on the south wall at Kilfane Church, county Kilkenny [4]. Traces of blue and orange can be seen on the east window in Clonfert Cathedral and on the tomb canopy at Abbeyknockmoy, county Galway. Blue colour can be seen externally on a carved head at the apex of a window opening at Lorrha, county Tipperary.[2]

Occasionally, more elaborate motifs can be seen on carved elements. The underside of the carved head of John the Baptist at the apex of the tomb canopy at Abbeyknockmoy is decorated with zigzag design in black and white [3]. Traces of red and white are found on the tomb in Clare Island Abbey, county Mayo [5]. The carved heads in the chancel at Cormac's Chapel in Cashel, county Tipperary, are an integral part of the paint decoration on the vault, and some of the excavated carved stone fragments from Kells Priory in county Kilkenny retain traces of painted plaster.

Equally, incised decoration forms a considerable part of the wall-painting remains in Ireland today. Scoring the still-wet plaster was a technique employed to map out the intended design of a wall painting, and it afforded a practice run when applying complicated or perhaps intricate designs or inscriptions. Changes could be made to the design as necessary – either when the plaster was still wet or, indeed, at a later stage when the paint was being applied to the now-dry plaster. It appears that these incised drawings were not intended to be visible, but rather that they served as a kind of 'cartoon' or preliminary sketch. Incised drawings are particularly resilient to weathering as they were fixed when the plaster set.

Aside from being decorative, wall paintings also served devotional and instructional purposes. They helped convey messages, often with a religious moral, to a mainly illiterate congregation, explaining themselves by their pictorial content. Wall paintings are often referred to as the *Biblia Pauperum* or Poor Man's Bible.[3]

Wall paintings contain a wealth of information for study, giving insights into the lives of the people that produced them. Information on craftsmen and patrons, religious beliefs, costume, weapons, materials and technology, dating or building sequences, are all inherent aspects of medieval wall paintings. In this way, the choices of materials and technologies, or subject matter and style, etc, used in making wall paintings are reflections of social, religious and historical factors current at that time. Wall paintings are therefore of interest to scholars in many related fields, such as art historians, architectural historians, archaeologists, material scientists, as well as wall-painting and architectural conservators. Their study relies on the close and careful examination, often only afforded through conservation. In many ways conservation is an information-gathering process.

SURVIVAL AND CONDITION

Wall paintings are found in both ecclesiastical and secular contexts in buildings, which have often been in a ruinous condition for long periods of their history. They generally survive in areas that have afforded them some measure of protection from the elements, such as under vaults or arches, and in window and tomb surrounds [3, 5-7]. Incised decoration is more durable than paint alone by virtue of the technique of scribing the design into the still-wet plaster. In exposed locations, therefore, frequently only the incised component of a wall painting survives today; the paint layers have become detached and lost in the intervening period. Wall paintings are often concealed by later building alterations or additions, as well as by limewash or plaster layers, by ivy growth, and by products of deterioration such as microbiology and calcite layers. In this way, wall-painting evidence at a given site is not always easily identifiable [8].

The extent of the surviving wall painting varies enormously from site to site. Sometimes only a small fragment of painted plaster testifies the one-time existence of a wall painting, while at other sites relatively complete painting schemes are found. In religious foundations, wall paintings are located in various parts of both the church itself and associated buildings – chancel, transepts, chapels, cloisters, refectory, dormitory, etc. Secular wall paintings are less common at this time but have been identified or recorded in a number of castles, including four tower-houses. All four wall paintings from tower-houses adorned second-storey rooms. The

2 – Clare Island Abbey, county Mayo
Horseman, a figure of a Gaelic lord on horseback to be seen on the earlier phase of paintings at this site.

3 – Abbeyknockmoy, county Galway
North wall of the chancel
At the apex of the O'Kelly tomb, just above the carved head of St John the Baptist, painted decoration of white and black chevrons survive where protected from the elements.

opposite

4 – Kilfane church, county Kilkenny
In the piscina, the capitals have been accentuated with red paint.

5 – Clare Island, county Mayo
The earliest phase of paintings: red is used to paint a stag on lime white plaster of the wall, and also used to embellish the carved element of the tomb canopy.

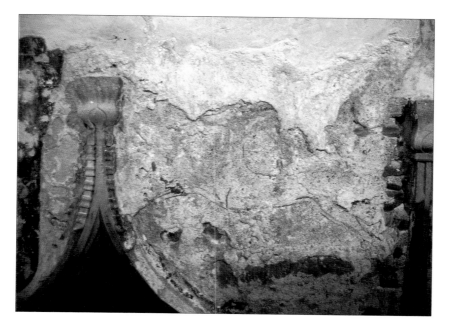

paintings in Barryscourt Castle are to be found in the chapel, situated in the adjoining tower to the north of the Great Hall. Whether the painted rooms in the other three tower-houses functioned as a chapel – exclusively as a chapel or had several functions, perhaps including that of a chapel – is yet to be established. These latter three tower-houses are of two-part construction and occur in a 'cluster' in the south Galway / north Clare area. Tower-house castles with two separate but interlocking sections are commonly seen in this area, and also in county Limerick.[4] The larger chambers at Ardamullivan and Ballyportry castles were decorated with a scheme of wall paintings, while the paintings at Urlanmore Castle, county Clare, adorned the smaller chamber at second-storey level.

Most of the evidence for wall paintings comes from in-situ remains, but some painted plaster fragments have been recovered through archaeological excavation. These include early fragments of painted plaster recovered from a 7th-century context during the excavations of Clonmacnoise.[5] The wall-painting evidence from Kells Priory, county Kilkenny, is particularly significant in that it comes from both in-situ remains and excavated fragments which, when examined, together indicate certain building sequences and help to suggest the site's history.[6]

Wall paintings are often trapped behind or concealed by other materials. Painted windows, doors and tomb-openings were frequently blocked up or concealed in later building phases [9]. These paintings remain undetected until such time as the later materials are removed or fall away. In addition to masking wall paintings with its foliage, ivy can penetrate and dislocate plaster layers. Although ivy causes plaster detachment, it is often the only thing that holds the plaster fragments in their correct relative position, and hence its treatment and removal should be left to the wall-painting conservator.

Several wall paintings are known only from past records, both descriptive and illustrative. Roe remarked that the Trinity at Abbeyknockmoy and St Audeon's were now destroyed, and that she had to rely on earlier records in describing the treatment of the Trinity of these two wall paintings.[7] In fact, slight traces of the Trinity at Abbeyknockmoy were recovered during conservation of these wall paintings in 1989. Gleeson recorded a hunting scene at Urlanmore Castle.[8] Here the scene was incised into the plaster, and traces of red-brown and slate-grey to black colours were discernible. His published note included an annotated photograph; a stag being attacked by two hounds is indicated. In the same year, 1936, Wallace, in addition to the hunting scene, recorded a Madonna and Child on the south wall.[9] During an inspection of the site in 1997 the hunting scene could still be made out, but only small traces of paint survived in the position where the Madonna was recorded. The larger side of this two-part tower collapsed some time ago. As far back as 1936,

Wallace stated that access to the small first-floor room was only possible by ladder. However, during a storm in February 1999, the remainder of the castle, and with it the wall paintings, collapsed. Large lumps of the rubble wall with adhering wall painting lie scattered on the site today. This material merits archaeological and conservation recording and assessment.

These records of wall paintings are especially valuable where they include illustrations or photographs, as with Westropp's drawing of St Michael Weighing the Souls, amongst other images, at Clare Island, and the illustrations of the Abbeyknockmoy paintings, including Ledwich's.[10] This illustration shows the area of the O'Kelly tomb on the north wall of the chancel. Virtually nothing of this part of the painting survives today.[11] Gleeson's illustration of the hunting scene at Urlanmore Castle, and that published in *The Irish Builder* of the wall painting at St Audeon's, make valuable contributions to the wall-painting record. Many of these wall paintings, or at least parts of these paintings, have since perished, making the records of them particularly important.

CONSERVATION OF WALL PAINTINGS

The significance of a wall painting is rooted in its association with its host building. Wall paintings that survive in situ still occupy the position and architectural context for which they were originally intended. Their conservation, therefore, is inextricably linked with the conservation of the host building. Their significance can only be realised if wall paintings are conserved and studied in this context. The removal of wall paintings from their support wall, although technically possible, should only be undertaken as a last resort – where for example the host building is absolutely beyond repair.

The non-specialist might often consider that wall paintings are too far deteriorated to be recoverable. However, the condition and conservation potential of wall paintings can only be assessed by a wall-painting conservator. In recent years a number of medieval wall paintings have been or are currently the subject of conservation programmes, and the results are far-reaching.

Wall-painting conservation, by its nature, can be a slow process, phased out over a number of years. In broad terms many of the conservation problems and, indeed, treatment procedures are common to a number of sites in Ireland. Apart from neglect and vandalism, water in its various forms is the main cause of deterioration. Water ingress, such as from rising damp, failing roofs and condensation, cause wall paintings to undergo physical, chemical and biological attack, and ultimately to decay. Water can transport soluble salts throughout the fabric of the wall painting.

6 – Muckross Friary,
county Kerry
The underside of the arch
has provided shelter for the
floral designs. Two or more
stencils were used in this
area of repeating patterns.

7 – Adare Friary, county
Limerick
A rosette of red petals
survives on the chamfered
edge of the piscina, where
there is some overhead
protection from the elements.

opposite, bottom
10 – Clare Island, county
Mayo
View of the chancel prior to
conservation: the whole is
heavily disguised by
microbial growth.

8 – Kells Priory, county Kilkenny
In the centre of this image, a 13th-century window with roll moulding still retains traces of red and black paint. The opening was blocked in the 15th century during the construction of the Prior's Tower to the south.

9 – Moylough Abbey, county Tipperary
Building alterations involving the blocking of an opening and plastering the walls, as well as ivy growth, concealed, until recently, false ashlar masonry pattern painted on the window splays.

Under drying conditions, salts will crystallise, with an increase in volume on or just below the surface, physically disrupting the paint layer. In addition, the increase in volume of water under freezing conditions will cause further physical disruption.

Water is essential for microbiology and higher forms of plant life, and the ruinous conditions of many sites housing wall paintings means that microbiology is a major problem [10]. In addition to being visually disturbing, the microbiology can etch, erode and weaken underlying plaster layers. It is not sufficient to treat and remove the microbiology that is visually manifested on the surface of the wall paintings. The source of water, which sustains microbiological growth, has to be identified and removed. The primary objective, therefore, is to identify the faults in the host building; the routes by which water can enter and penetrate a building's fabric are not always clear. Weatherproofing the building can be achieved in many ways – grouting, pointing, rendering, fenestration, ventilation, heating, etc. Several measures can be put in place in a sequential manner to address building faults or environmental requirements systematically. Although the cause of deterioration – water – may be common to a number of sites, frequently the solution has to be site-specific since individual factors and the interplay between these factors will dictate the remedies undertaken and even the order in which they are undertaken.

Great care is needed in the treatment of microbiological growth on wall paintings. In order not to introduce impurities into the walls by using a biocide, the directors of the Abbeyknockmoy conservation programme, Madeleine Katkov and Christoph Oldenbourg, pioneered the use of germicidal ultraviolet light for the irradiation of microbiological growth. Germicidal ultraviolet light acts by interfering with the genetic material and damaging the cell walls. This kills the growth and allows it to be removed more judiciously. The same method has been used at a number of Irish sites since then [11]. If water ingress is left unchecked, microbiology will re-establish itself on the wall paintings.

Under bad conditions, plaster layers become delaminated and can also detach from their support wall. A liquid adhesive plaster (lime-based) can be injected into the voids of the detaching plaster layers to secure them to their support wall. Depending on the size of the void, inert fillers are added to the grouting mixture to reduce shrinkage. Lime sets by reacting with carbon dioxide in the air, so frequently materials such as brick dust need to be added that will allow it to set in conditions where air is excluded. 'Fresco' presses are used to support and cushion the wet and heavy area under repair and to help ease it back onto the support wall [12].

Wall paintings are often trapped behind layers of overlying materials. These overlying layers can be efflorescence, calcite deposits, or intentionally applied later limewashes or plaster. Microscopic cross-section examination to establish the stratigraphy of the layers, and whether or not more than one painting phase existed, precedes any uncovering process. A variety of hand tools and mini-electric tools are used for uncovering, many of which are adapted dental and medical tools.

The effects of cement on wall paintings can be very damaging, with the formation of a veil of efflorescence, gypsum and calcite deposits, as can readily be appreciated in the case of Clare Island. Effluents originating from a concrete floor which was laid above the vault in the early 1900s now heavily disguise the figure of St Michael, which was clearly visible during the Praeger survey of the island in 1909-11.[12] The removal of these products is necessary not only for aesthetic reasons but also on technical grounds. The effluent layers can be very opaque and extremely hard, and they exert physical stresses on the wall painting. To date, uncovering has proved very painstaking, time-consuming, and not entirely successful. Following successful trials, the conservation directors at this site, Madeleine Katkov and Christoph Oldenbourg, are exploring the option of using lasers in the uncovering of this area of painting.

Effecting plaster repairs is another important task in the conservation of wall paintings. Plaster repairs reduce the visual impact of the damages in the original, and help to pull together the design of the paintings. The technical function of these repairs is to improve the stability of the original plaster and reduce the likelihood of condensation and reinfestation by microbiological organisms. They are designed to be open-porous in order to draw damaging salts out of the original plaster, as with a poultice, and can therefore be considered sacrificial if necessary. It is important that the plaster repairs match the original materials closely and yet remain discernible. In this way, plaster repairs will need to employ sand that provides a good, but not an exact match in colour and texture to the wall-painting layers [13-15].

The success of any conservation programme depends heavily on achieving the right climatic conditions within the host building. Ideally, environmental conditions – in particular, relative humidity and temperature – are monitored before, during and after any interventions, so that changes that may be effected by a new roof, glazing, pointing and rendering can be evaluated. In many instances, the building in which wall paintings occur may never have provided the ideal environment to ensure their long-term survival. This may not have been a concern, the dictates of taste, fashion and beliefs necessitating change of the interior embellishment at regular intervals. This said, it is clear that wall paintings do survive where protected from the environment. It is also clear from an examination of the exterior fabric of medieval buildings that the practice of applying an external render or harling [16] was commonplace. This practice makes complete sense, providing as it does an extra layer of

Barryscourt Castle, county Cork

opposite

11 – Ultraviolet germicidal lights arranged for irradiation of microbiology on the chapel wall paintings

12– A 'forest' of fresco presses are employed to support the vault plaster

as the grouting materials set

13 – Sample plaster mixes using a variety of sand colours and grain sizes are applied to the wall and assessed for the most suitable match

above

14 – South wall prior to plaster repairs

15 – South wall after plaster repairs have been applied and cut back, but are not yet fully dry

16 – Newtown Castle, Ballyvaughan, county Clare (now the Burren College of Art)
Substantive amounts of external render survive in place.

17 – Ballyportry Castle, county Clare
The exterior of this castle was partially rendered in spring 2001, and the dramatic improvement in the internal climate was almost instantly apparent.

weatherproofing and insulation to the building, thereby improving living conditions within. When adopting an integrated approach to the conservation of wall paintings and their host buildings, the application of an external render is often advocated. Certainly, in the few instances where it has been applied, the dramatic improvement in the internal climate and, consequently, in the conditions and preservation of the wall paintings is immediately apparent.

The thin external shelter or render, which was first applied a couple of years ago on the exterior of Clare Island Abbey, is considered by the conservation directors to have been the single most effective measure in the control of the internal climate. The effect has been so marked that there are plans to apply a more substantial render in the near future. The same positive modification of the internal climate has been achieved in Ballyportry Castle, where only partial rendering was carried out [17].

MATERIALS AND TECHNOLOGY OF MEDIEVAL WALL PAINTINGS

The walls of abbeys, priories and castles were generally constructed from rubble masonry, with finely dressed or carved details in sandstone or limestone being reserved for architectural features such as door, windows and tomb surrounds. The walls were intended for plastering, and the decoration of these plaster surfaces is a likely consequence. Certainly the paint evidence, albeit fragmentary, supports the idea that building interiors were extensively decorated. Wall plaster was commonly decorated with lines at right angles to each other in imitation of ashlar blocks, called masonry pattern [18]. On occasion, the background or blocks were variously toned with yellow, pink or cream to create the effect of the tonal differences to be found in natural stone [19]. The visual effects of a fine stone wall were obviously desirable, but not always practicable or affordable.

The current evidence from Ireland shows that medieval wall paintings employed lime rather than gypsum plasters. In some cases paint decoration could be applied onto a thin limewash layer, but more often it was applied on a build up of plaster layers. The plaster was generally, but not always, composed of two layers using a traditional mix of two or three parts sand to one part lime. The first application is coarser and thicker in consistency, with larger inclusions, sometimes with recognisable bits of shell or, as is the case at Barryscourt Castle, charcoal [20]. This first layer was applied to even out any undulations in the support wall. In theory, the second plaster layer, which is finer, with less and smaller inclusions, provided a flat, smooth surface on which to paint. However, there are a number of Irish wall paintings where the paint scheme is applied to extremely

Kells Priory, county Kilkenny

18 – North-east corner of the choir: a red horizontal line of false ashlar masonry pattern is visible on the right side of this image.

19 – Many of the excavated archaeological fragments of plaster were painted with false ashlar masonry pattern.

20 – Barryscourt Castle, county Cork
Lumps of charcoal are conspicuous in the under-plaster of the chapel's wall paintings.

21 – Ballyportry Castle, county Clare
Elaborate wall paintings were sometimes applied to very uneven plaster surfaces.
In this image, the head and arrow-pierced shoulder of St Sebastian can be made out.

uneven plaster finishes [21]. In these incidences it would appear that the significance of the painting was in the imagery portrayed and the message conveyed, rather than in the perfection of its technical execution.

The production of a wall painting required thought and planning. The scheme had to be devised and approved, and then made fit to the allocated space. Scaffolding would generally have been required to complete the work. On Irish wall paintings, frequently the intended design was mapped out on the wall with incised lines into the still-damp plaster. This method allowed the artist to visualise the space required for each component of the painted scheme. It acted much like a preliminary sketch. It is interesting to observe that the subsequent paint does not always follow the lines exactly. Corrections could be made when applying the paint where the artist saw that, for example, more space was required here or less there [22]. There is clear evidence for the use of a compass in the design of many of the incised consecration crosses [23] and 'architectural drawings', and for the use of a rule when setting out guidelines for a band of inscription, or indeed when ashlar blocks are being suggested.

When painting, some repeating patterns could be achieved by using stencils – for example, the floral motifs at Muckross Friary, county Kerry [6]. As yet, the actual stencils used have not been recovered from archaeological excavation in Ireland, but their use is surmised from observations of the consistency in detail of certain decorative motifs.

The majority of Irish examples are lime paintings rather than frescoes. The pigments were painted on to a limewash layer immediately overlying the finer plaster layer [24, 25], whereas in true fresco painting the pigments are applied to wet (fresh) plaster. As the plaster sets the colours are chemically bonded and are consequently more durable. Pigments, which are not compatible with lime, could be applied onto dry plaster (a secco) using an organic binding medium. The paintings at Cormac's Chapel are fresco with secco additions.[13]

In her study on the materials and technologies of Irish medieval wall paintings, McGrath obtained pigment samples for analysis from six Irish wall paintings, of which five produced results.[14] The extant plaster at this time in St Audeon's proved to be too friable to sample. A complete selection of the range of colours at each site was not achieved due to restricted access in the absence of scaffolding. It also appears that overlying limewash layers prohibited the visual pinpointing of the full range of colours for analysis. Cormac's Chapel was found to be by far the richest site of the six from which samples for analysis were obtained.[15]

Since then, in the course of conservation programmes at a number of sites, further colours have been specifically targeted for pigment analysis. The colours found on medieval wall paintings in Ireland include pigments most commonly obtained from mineral earths such as red, yellow

22 – Clare Island, county Mayo

Incised lines were extensively used in mapping out the intended location of the painted 'stone' ribs which divide the vault paintings into sections. In many cases, when the artist came to paint, he shifted the rib a little to one side or other of the position designated by the incised line. Soluble salts have crystallised on the surface, causing paint disruption.

23 – Court Abbey, county Sligo

A compass was generally employed when marking out onsecration crosses.

24 – Jerpoint Abbey, county Kilkenny
Detail of a boar from one of the coats of arms: the incised lines used to map out the design, the brush stokes in the limewash layer, and the details of the boar's bristles are all clear.

25 – Ballyportry Castle, county Clare
Detail of the foot of St Sebastian showing clear indications of the brush strokes in the limewash layer.

26 – Fore Abbey, county Westmeath
Detail of masonry pattern in the piscina. A decorative embellishment, possibly a flower, can be seen in one of the blocks.

27 – Court Abbey, county Sligo
Bands of yellow outlined in black, as well as cross-hatching in red, can be made out, albeit disguised by microbiology.

and brown ochres. Together with lime white and charcoal or bone black, this apparently limited range of pigments could be mixed to provide a broader palette.

Occasionally more unusual colours are found. Analysis carried out as part of the conservation programme at Abbeyknockmoy suggested that malachite was most probably present in the robes of one of the living kings.[16] Malachite is a natural green pigment.[17] Azurite and malachite were mined in the Tipperary area, and azurite is still to be found today in the Tynagh mines, county Galway.[18] Vermilion or cinnabar is mercuric sulphide (HgS), and was identified by analysis at Cormac's Chapel and at Ardamullivan Castle [1].[19]

To date, the paintings at Cormac's Chapel exhibit the greatest range of pigments found on an Irish medieval wall painting. Minium or red lead, lead-white, green earth (terra verte), ultramarine blue and gold leaf have been identified by analysis.[20] Ultramarine is derived from the semi-precious stone lapis lazuli, and being costly and a symbol of luxury, was considered in a class with gold.[21] It was generally paid for separately in addition to the cost of the wall painting. Lapis lazuli is an example of one of the pigments which is not compatible with lime, and when used on a painting it was applied as a later secco addition. Clearly many of the pigments used at Cormac's Chapel were luxury and costly imports, underlining the importance of these paintings and the patron.

SUBJECT MATTER

One common motif is ashlar masonry pattern. Here the semblance of an ashlar wall was created by painting a series of lines at right angles to each other. Generally red, orange and sometimes black colours are used to mark out the 'joint' lines on a plain white or toned background [18, 19]. White joint lines on a red background are recorded from Cashel Cathedral, county Tipperary, and Molana (or Ballyintray) Abbey, county Waterford.[22] The 'blocks' created in this masonry design could be coloured in the tones available in natural stones, as at Kells Priory, or to suggest quoins-stones, as at Moylough Abbey [9], and possibly in one of the recesses on the south wall of the choir at Adare Friary, county Limerick. Although masonry pattern is found at a number of religious sites, it has not yet been recorded from a secular building in Ireland. Leask recorded masonry pattern within and over the twin-arched piscina and ambry at Fore Abbey, county Westmeath, and Stalley recorded this motif at the Cistercian sites of Grey Abbey, county Down, and Graiguenamanagh Abbey, county Kilkenny.[23]

Masonry pattern can be found in situ on the east wall of the choir and from excavated fragments from Kells Priory, county Kilkenny. In

England the stone blocks were sometimes further adorned with other coloured motifs, including stars, roses, crosses and fleurs-de-lys.[24] At Fore Abbey, an additional, although not recognisable motif, perhaps a rosette, can be made out within the blockwork of double masonry lines [26]. Vermilion fleurs-de-lys were recorded in the piscina in the Lady chapel at Kells Priory,[25] but it is not clear whether or not they were associated with the masonry pattern at that site. Floral motifs, scroll-work and geometric designs of chevrons, zigzags and diaper-work are still to be found at Adare Friary, Muckross Friary [6], Court Abbey, county Sligo [27], and Kilfane Church, county Kilkenny [29, 30].

Consecration crosses are commonly found on medieval plasterwork. These crosses can be incised and/or painted [28]. An incised consecration cross can be seen on the west wall of the dormitory at Askeaton Friary, county Limerick, and two consecration crosses occur in the nave and a further two in the croft at Cormac's Chapel. Two crosses are clearly visible on the south wall (west of sedilia) in the chancel at Corcomroe Abbey, county Clare, and the remains of four crosses, incised and partly painted in red, can be made out in Kilfane Church. The Askeaton Friary and Court Abbey examples exist today as incised lines without colour. Originally, elements of many of these crosses would have been painted, as suggested by the slight tonal differences that are still perceptible in the limewash layer.

Another decoration commonly found are incised and, indeed, painted boats or ships. Boats are found at the Franciscan sites of Ennis Friary, county Clare [31], Court Abbey, county Sligo, Ross Friary, county Galway, and Moyne Friary, county Mayo.[26] They occur at the Augustinian sites of Molana, county Waterford, and possibly at Kells Priory and at the Cistercian site of Corcomroe Abbey.[27] A large ship painted in black, as well as a small, incised boat, can be seen at Cashel Cathedral [32, 33]. Boats are also known from two tower-houses – Urlanmore Castle, county Clare, and at Barryscourt Castle [34] – and a further example from Reginald's Tower in Waterford. Stalley stated that ships were much used in medieval times to symbolise 'the voyage through life, or the Christian church protecting the faithful from the torments of the deep'.[28] This concern with the salvation of one's soul is a recurring theme in medieval art.

The representations of boats seen at many Irish sites could possibly be a symbol of pilgrimage. It is clear that large number of pilgrims travelled by sea to Santiago de Compostela.[29] Many Irish ports were associated with religious traffic – Drogheda, Dublin, Wexford, New Ross, Waterford, Youghal, Cork, Kinsale, Dingle, Limerick and Galway. Stalley discussed the evolution in ship design, and noted the improvements made in the 15th century. With these improvements, increasing numbers of people made the pilgrimage by sea to avoid the lengthy and difficult journey over land.

The decoration of the chapel at Barryscourt Castle is unusual in that it included an Ogham inscription [35].[30] In addition, it appears that this ogham script predates the application of colour to the plaster layers.

Substantial traces of incised 'architectural' designs – now, at least, without colour – can be seen at the three Cistercian abbeys of Corcomroe Abbey, county Clare, Hore Abbey, county Tipperary, and Jerpoint Abbey, county Kilkenny. Stalley suggested that the incised lines at Corcomroe were preparatory constructional drawings for the building itself rather than being part of the wall decoration.[31] Certainly, the drawings on the north wall of the south transept chapel include architectural 'doodles'. The position of the drawing on the north wall of the north transept however required scaffolding for its execution. Alternatively these incised designs may have been preliminary drawings of architectural elements intended for painting. It is of note that the wall paintings at Corcomroe include an incised boat on the north wall of the chancel and other incised decoration elsewhere in the south transept chapels. On the north wall of the chancel at Hore Abbey, a series of incised lines suggests a repeating pattern of two or three pointed arches, reminiscent of the design of a triple sedilia [36]. Fragmentary remains of incised lines – perhaps an architectural detail – can be made out in one of the recesses in the north transept at Jerpoint Abbey.

At least four heraldic coats of arms are still to be seen on the north wall of the chancel at Jerpoint Abbey [37]. The current wall-painting conservation programme in the chapel at Barryscourt Castle has failed as yet to uncover the coats of arms referred to by Macalister.[32]

The extent of the evidence for figurative representations can vary enormously from site to site. A single fragment of painted plaster, representing a face, found during excavations at Kells Priory, county Kilkenny [38], testifies that figurative representation, in conjunction with simple masonry and geometric patterns, once embellished the interior of this church. Together, the in-situ and excavated paint fragments suggest the combination of subjects that might originally have adorned the walls of Kells Priory. Large wall surfaces, perhaps marked out with ashlar masonry pattern and punctuated at strategic points by figures of saints or angels, and framed by borders of geometric design, quoins, and perhaps further

Kilfane Church, county Kilkenny

28 – One of four incised consecration crosses, painted red, surviving today

29 – The decorated surround of a niche in the east wall

30 – East wall niche at northern end: a band of yellow ochre and a band of geometric patterns with red triangles outlined in black can be seen against the lime white background

31– Ennis Friary, county Clare
An incised boat located on a pier to the
south transept chapel

Cashel Cathedral, county Tipperary

32 – Large ship painted in black on the
pier between the two north transept
chapels

33 – Incised boat on the north wall of the
chancel

Barryscourt Castle, county Cork

34 – South wall of the chapel: detail with incised boat

35 – North wall of the chapel: ogham inscription

36 – Hore Abbey, county Tipperary: architectural 'doodle'?

37 – Jerpoint Abbey, county Kilkenny North wall of the chancel: detail of the coats of arms

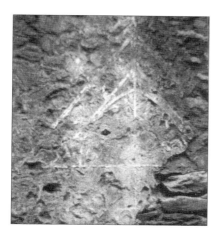

38 – Kells Priory, county Kilkenny
A selection of the painted plaster fragments found during the excavations at this site. The fragment in the top left of this image represents a face – an eye, eyebrow and a curl of hair are clearly seen, and this survival demonstrates that figurative subject matter was included amongst ashlar masonry pattern and other ornamental motifs at this site.

adorned by fleurs-de-lys [33] and other motifs, can be envisaged.

A range of both real and imaginary beasts, so common on architectural carvings of this period, are to be found in the second phase of wall paintings on the vault of Clare Island Abbey.[34] Hunting scenes, and particularly stag hunts, are commonly represented in medieval art, and occur on wall paintings at three Irish sites, and in the case of Clare Island the same subject occurs on several occasions. These stag hunts can take various forms. The stag is shown pursued by a hound in the first phase of wall paintings at Clare Island Abbey, while in the second phase of paintings at Clare Island, and those at Urlanmore Castle [39], the stag is being bitten by two or more hounds. A third type, also found on the vault at Clare Island, and at Holycross Abbey,[35] shows a man with a hound straining on a slip-lease, and separated from the stag by a bush or tree. These latter two examples differ in that the Clare Island figure kneels, while the Holycross figure is standing, blowing a horn, and accompanied by two archers standing behind him.

Given the context of these hunting scenes occurring in church sites, and, perhaps, a chapel in a secular building, and given the combination of scenes with which they occur, it seems likely that they had a religious significance. The stag, an emblem of solitude and purity [36] became in

Urlanmore Castle, county Clare

39 – Remains of a hunting scene, photographed in 1997,
two years before the tower-house and, with it, the wall paintings collapsed.
It is just possible, with the aid of illustration 40 (see also Gleeson's illustration – endnote 8), to make
out a hound at the front quarters of a stag, and the mouth and front legs of a second hound (albeit
heavily disguised by microbiology and plaster losses) at the stag's hind quarters.

40 – Drawing of the remains of a stag-hunt, made from a projected slide [39].
Two hounds – one with a neck collar, the other without – attack, respectively, the front and
hindquarters of a stag. Although the head of the stag was too deteriorated to make out, the details
of his ribcage, as well as aspects of the hounds, were quite visible. (drawing by the author, 2003)

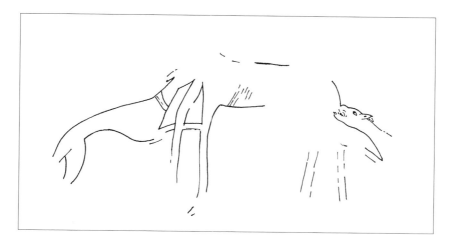

the Middle Ages a symbol of the Christian soul. The stag hunt could therefore be interpreted as in pursuit of a Christian soul. Park considered the stag in the Gorleston Psalter stag hunt as symbolising the Christian soul being attacked by the 'ungodly'.[37] Elsewhere on the vault paintings at Clare Island are images of hounds pursuing hares, and a hunting cat whose prey is no longer visible, and there are partial traces of what appears to be a falconry scene.

Scenes from the New Testament include the baptism of Christ and the three Maji in the chancel at Cormac's Chapel,[38] the Crucifixion at Abbeyknockmoy and Clare Island, and the Passion cycle at Ardamullivan Castle.[39] Single figures of saints, generally identified by their symbols or attributes, occur in a number of paintings. In 1780 Lucombe described figures, which he took to represent St Patrick, St Bridget and St Columba, in Adare Friary. Westropp confirmed that there were indeed figures visible at this site when he was a young boy.[40] The paintings have suffered losses from long-term exposure, and none of the figures is discernible amongst the extant paint traces at the site today. Also at Adare, this time in the Augustinian priory, in addition to consecration crosses and diaper work, a 'crowned female figure' is recorded.[41]

At Abbeyknockmoy, the most substantive area of wall painting surviving today is to be seen on the eastern end of the north wall of the chancel. On the upper register, the popular morality warning on the transitory nature of earthly riches, known as *Le trois rois vifs et les trois rois morts*, is painted [41]. The kings, lavishly dressed, while out hunting encounter three grisly crowned skeletons who warn them to prepare for their own deaths rather than focus on the material goods and pleasures of this world. Crawford traced the inscription under the feet of the three dead kings and sent it to Professor Macalister who recognised that it was the actual warning that the spectres addressed to the kings. Macalister translated it as 'We have been as you are, you shall be as we are'.[42]

In the lower register at Abbeyknockmoy are the very fragmentary remains of the Trinity,[43] a common theme in Irish medieval art. This subject was also represented at St Audeon's Church, Dublin,[44] as well as the martyrdom of St Sebastian [42]. The same subject – the martyrdom of St Sebastian – occurs at Ballyportry Castle, county Clare [21, 25]. The paintings here are, to a large extent, covered by later limewash layers. However, in areas where the limewash has come away the shape of the penetrating arrows is similar to those at Abbeyknockmoy.

The Abbeyknockmoy paintings originally extended further to the west to the area in and around the O'Kelly tomb,[45] as well as on other walls throughout the church buildings. In the area above the O'Kelly tomb, two individuals are thought to be portraits of Malachie and Fionola O'Kelly. On the back wall, within the tomb recess, was the Crucifixion,

Abbeyknockmoy,
county Galway

41 – The three living
kings, wearing fine
clothing, are shown,
each carrying his own
bird and enjoying
hunting.

42 – Martyrdom of
St Sebastian

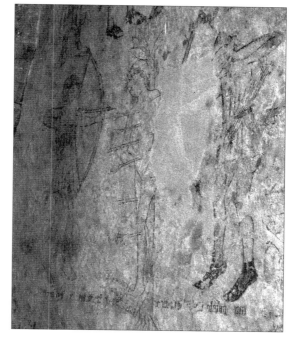

45 – Lismore Cathedral, county Waterford
One of two fragments of plaster discovered as loose in-fill in the chancel wall during recent building works. A column and capital dominate the centre part of this fragment.

46 – Enniscorthy Castle, county Wexford
An incised figure with 16th-century dress can be seen in the oubliette in the south-west tower of the castle.

opposite

Ardamullivan Castle, county Galway

43 – St Michael Weighing the Souls: outline sketch of the paint remains visible

44 – View of the north-west corner showing a number of religious figures, including a bishop in the act of blessing

now perished. The same subject is similarly positioned in the tomb recess at Clare Island Abbey.[46] Crawford described the figure seen to the right in Ledwich's illustration as holding scales, and postulated that it was St Michael in judgement.[47] St Michael Weighing the Souls is also to be found at Clare Island, on this occasion surrounded by musicians playing an organ and lyres, serpents and dragons, a cattle-raid scene, a double-headed eagle, an array of fishermen, wrestlers, and hunting scenes, as well as a pelican feeding her young.[48] A further representation of St Michael Weighing the Souls is currently being uncovered in the secular context of a tower-house at Ardamullivan Castle, county Galway. St Michael with scales conveys the idea that one's sins and good deeds are weighed against each other on the Day of Judgement. St Michael was a popular figure throughout the medieval period.[49]

The archangel at Ardamullivan [43] is shown in the conventional manner as young, tall and noble, with wavy hair, and probably surmounted by a small cross above his forehead. He wears a long, voluminous pleated robe. Details of his dress have yet to be uncovered. It is not clear whether wings are represented, and if so, how many, or whether St Michael holds a sword or whether the Virgin is represented interceding on the part of good. Again, at Ardamullivan St Michael is represented with a different range of subjects. The other scenes include fragmentary traces of a St Christopher scene, as well as a bishop in the act of blessing [44], and a series of scenes believed to show the Passion of Christ,[50] including the Last Supper and the Pietà.[51]

The wall paintings at Ardamullivan are still under conservation, but already there are traces of some twenty figures being uncovered. This evidence dramatically increases the number of known figurative representation on Irish medieval wall paintings, and is a very important discovery.

CONCLUSION

Irish medieval wall painting survives from or is recorded from some sixty-five sites, or more. This number, a marked increase on that generally thought to exist, hints that wall paintings were a common feature in medieval buildings.

Most wall paintings in Ireland range in date from the early 12th century to the 15th century, with some being a little later. The fragments of painted plaster from Clonmacnoise hint that wall paintings also adorned buildings of a much earlier date. Those of Cormac's Chapel, and possibly the two fragments recovered during building work at Lismore Cathedral, Co Waterford [45],[52] are of 12th-century date, while sites like Kells Priory retain painted plaster on the 13th-century window's roll moulding, and also in the 15th-century prior's tower. The dearth of wall paintings of a definite 14th-century date reflects, not surprisingly, the lack of building activity in that century. An incised drawing of a man in the 'dress of a halberdier of the sixteenth century' in the oubliette of the south-west tower at Enniscorthy Castle [46] illustrates the continuing tradition of wall decoration.[53]

Wall paintings are an important, but as yet understudied source on medieval Ireland. They provide a huge amount of information about many aspects of medieval life, such as dress, weaponry, boat design, trade connections and the economy, and religious beliefs. Fortunately, through conservation, much of this inherent information has been brought to light and made available for future study.

———

The author

Karena Morton is a freelance conservator of archaeological finds and wall paintings. She graduated in Archaeology and History of Art, and Urban and Building Conservation, from University College Dublin, and in Archaeological Conservation from the University of Wales, College of Cardiff. She is currently working on a PhD on Irish medieval wall painting at the School of Architecture, UCD.

Acknowledgements

I would like to thank Noel Jameson of the Barryscourt Trust for inviting me to give this paper. I am grateful to Dúchas, The Heritage Service, as the vast majority of the plates in this paper are of wall paintings in their care. I am also grateful to Con Brogan (Dúchas) for kind permission to reproduce plate 1. I would like to thank Siobhán Cuffe and Patrick Wallace for permission to include the Ballyportry photographs, and to Mrs Mary Hawes-Greene for inclusion of Newtown Castle, Ballyvaughan. I am also indebted to the church-wardens at Lismore Cathedral who kindly gave so much of their time and information during the inspection and photography of the painted plaster fragments, and for permission to publish these images. I would particularly like to thank my conservation colleague, Christoph Oldenbourg, who may well be responsible for some of the photographs, but also for reading an early draft of this paper. I would also like to thank Prof Loughlin Kealy, School of Architecture, UCD, and my husband Dr Kieran O'Conor, Dept of Archaeology, NUI Galway, for reading and commenting on drafts of this paper.

Endnotes

All photos by the author unless otherwise stated.

[1] Wall paintings at Abbeyknockmoy and Ardamullivan Castle, county Galway; Clare Island, county Mayo; Askeaton, county Limerick; Cormac's Chapel, Cashel, county

Tipperary; as well as Barryscourt Castle, county Cork, have all been the subject of conservation programmes in recent years.

2 David Sweetman, pers. comm.

3 CE Rouse, *Medieval Wall Paintings* (Shire Publications, Risborough, 1980) p5

4 CJ Donnelly, 'Sectionally constructed tower-houses: a review of the evidence from Co. Limerick', *JRSAI*, 128 (1998) pp26-34

5 Heather King, Dúchas, pers. comm.

6 K Morton, 'Wall painting Report', in Miriam Clynne (ed.), *Kells Priory, Co. Kilkenny, Excavations* (Dúchas, forthcoming)

7 H Roe, 'Illustrations of the Holy Trinity in Ireland, 13th to 17th centuries', *JRSAI*, 109 (1979) pp143-5

8 DF Gleeson, 'Drawing of a Hunting Scene, Urlan Castle, Co. Clare', *JRSAI*, 66 (1936) p193

9 JNA Wallace, 'Frescoes at Urlanmore Castle, Co. Clare', *North Munster Antiquity Journal*, 1-2 (1936-41) pp38-9

10 E Ledwich, *Antiquities of Ireland* (2nd ed., Dublin, 1804) p520

11 *The Irish Builder*, vol. 79, no. 672 (Dublin, 1887) p357; illustration of the *Throne of Grace* at St Audeon's, Cornmarket

12 See illustrations by TJ Westropp made between 1909 and 1911 in vol. 7 of his sketchbooks, held in the Royal Irish Academy: RIA 3A.52

13 H Howard, *Cormac's Chapel, Cashel: analysis of paint samples* (unpublished typescript report for the OPW, 1991)

14 M McGrath, 'The Materials and Techniques of Irish wall-paintings', *JRSAI*, 117 (1987) pp96-124

15 *ibid.*, p99

16 M Katkov and C Oldenbourg, pers. comm.

17 Malachite is a basic carbonate of copper – $CuCo_3.Cu(OH)_2$. RJ Gettens and GL Stout, *Painting Materials* (New York, 1966) pp127-8.

18 M McGrath, 'The wall paintings in Cormac's Cathedral Chapel', *Studies*, 64 (1975) p330

19 K Morton, 'Medieval Wall Paintings at Ardamullivan', *Irish Arts Review Yearbook 2002*, 18 (Dublin, 2001) p107

20 Howard, *Cormac's Chapel, Cashel*

21 Gettens and Stout, *Painting Materials*, pp166-7

22 JC, 'Ancient Irish Painting at the Rock of Cashel and Molana Abbey', *Journal of the Waterford and South East of Ireland Archaeology Society* (1908) pp108-9

23 HG Leask, *Irish Churches and Monastic Buildings*, ii (Dundalk, 1966) p47; R Stalley, *The Cistercian Monasteries of Ireland* (London and New Haven, 1987) p214

24 Rouse, *Medieval Wall Paintings*, p14

25 Rev W Carrigan, *The History and Antiquities of the Diocese of Ossory*, 4 (Dublin, 1905) p68

26 RAS Macalister, 'On Graffitti Representing Ships on the Wall of Moyne Priory, Co. Mayo', *JRSAI*, 73 (1943) pp107-17

27 E Rynne, 'Boat graffito in Corcomroe Abbey', *North Munster Antiquity Journal*, 11 (1968) p76

28 R Stalley, 'Sailing to Santiago de Compostela and its artistic influence in Ireland', in J Bradley (ed.), *Settlement and Society in Medieval Ireland* (Kilkenny, 1988) p409

29 *ibid.*, pp397-8

30 RAS Macalister, 'Miscellanea – Excursion of the Society to Cork', *JRSAI*, 62 (1932) p223. I am grateful to Prof Damien McManus, Department of Old Irish at Trinity College Dublin, for his more recent examination of the extant section of ogham, which

unfortunately is too fragmentary and eroded to decipher.

[31] Stalley, *Cistercian Monasteries of Ireland*, pp49-50

[32] Macalister, 'Miscellanea – Excursion of the Society to Cork', p223

[33] Although no longer clear, Rev Carrigan recorded vermilion fleurs-de-lys, *The History and Antiquities of the Diocese of Ossory*, p68

[34] K Morton and C Oldenbourg, Catalogue of the wall paintings in Clare Island Abbey, in P Gosling, C Manning, and J Waddell (eds), *New Survey of Clare Island: The Abbey*, (Royal Irish Academy, Dublin, forthcoming)

[35] Illustrated in HS Crawford, 'Mural decoration at Holy Cross Abbey', *JRSAI*, 45 (1915) p151

[36] E Hulme, *Symbolism in Christian Art* (2nd ed., Biddles of Guildford, 1975) p167

[37] D Park, 'Cistercian wall painting and panel painting', in D Park and C Norton (eds), *Cistercian art and architecture in the British Isles* (Cambridge, 1986) p204

[38] R Stalley, 'Solving a mystery at Cashel', *Irish Arts Review Yearbook 2002*, 18 (Dublin, 2001) pp25-9

[39] Morton, 'Medieval Wall Paintings at Ardamullivan', pp104-13

[40] P Lucombe, *A Tour through Ireland* (Dublin, 1780) p361; TJ Westropp, 'Paintings at Adare 'Abbey', Co. Limerick', *JRSAI*, 45 (1915-16) pp151-2

[41] RF Hewson, 'The Augustinian priory, Adare', *North Munster Antiquity Journal*, 1-2 (1936-41) pp108-12

[42] HS Crawford, 'Mural paintings and inscriptions at Knockmoy Abbey', *JRSAI*, 49 (1919) p28

[43] Many scholars have illustrated the wall painting at Abbeyknockmoy. Probably the most reliable guide to how the Trinity once looked is provided by the illustration of the paintings at the eastern end of the north wall, seen in the sketch made by GV Du Noyer, *c.*1858 (now in the Royal Society of Antiquaries library). This drawing is reproduced by JA Glynn, 'Knockmoy Abbey, County Galway', *JRSAI*, 34 (1904) p243.

[44] *The Irish Builder*, vol. 79, no. 672 (Dublin, 1887) p357. Illustration of the *Throne of Grace* at St Audeon's, Cornmarket. Sadly, no trace of this painting survives today.

[45] As illustrated in Ledwich, *Antiquities of Ireland*, p520

[46] TJ Westropp, 'Cliara Abbey', *Proceedings of the Royal Irish Academy*, 31c (1911-15) pp29-37; K Morton and C Oldenbourg, 'Catalogue of the wall paintings in Clare Island Abbey'

[47] Crawford, 'Mural Paintings and Inscriptions at Knockmoy Abbey', p25

[48] Morton and Oldenbourg, 'Catalogue of the wall paintings in Clare Island Abbey'

[49] H Roe, 'The Cult of St. Michael in Ireland', Caoimhín Ó Danachair (ed.) *Folk and Farm: essays in honour of A.T. Lucas* (Royal Society of Antiquaries, 1975) pp251-64

[50] The present writer believes that a fragmentary scene painted on the north wall of the dormitory at Askeaton Friary, county Limerick, is from the Passion. The scene is framed with a border of yellow and red design. A figure with a halo is placed on the right within its own border. His profiled head faces into the scene and towards, perhaps, another figure and a number of objects, believed to be the instruments of the Passion, most notably a lance, and perhaps a rod with sponge, and a ladder. The exposed location of the painting has faded the colours and details of this painting, making it somewhat difficult to read.

[51] Morton, 'Medieval Wall Paintings at Ardamullivan', pp104-13

[52] T O'Keeffe, 'Lismore and Cashel: reflections on the beginnings of Romanesque architecture in Munster', *JRSAI*, 124 (1994) pp135-8

[53] PH Hore, *History of the town and county of Wexford*, 6 (London, 1900-11) pp339-40